CONSTITUTIONAL SEMIOTICS

This book offers an outline of the foundations of a theory of constitutional semiotics. It provides a systematic account of the concept of constitutional semiotics and its role in the representation and signification of meaning in constitution, constitutional law, and constitutionalism. The book explores the constitutional signification of meaning that is stretched between rational entrenchment and constitutional imagination. It provides a critical assessment of the rationalist entrapment of constitutional modernity and justifies the need to turn to 'shadow constitutionalisms': textual, symbolic-imaginary and visual constitutionalism.

The book puts forward innovative incentives for constitutional analysis based on constitutional semiotics as a paradigm for representation of meaning in rational, textual, symbolic-imaginary and visual constitutionalism. The book focuses on the textual, imaginative and visual discourse of constitutionalism, which is built upon collective constitutional imaginaries and on the peculiar normativity of constitutional geometry and constitutional mythology as borderline phenomena entrenched in rational, textual, symbolic-imaginary and visual constitutionalism.

The book analyses concepts such as: constitutional text and texture, authoritative constitutional narratives and authoritative constitutional narrators, constitutional semiotic community, constitutional utopia, constitutional taboo, normative ideology and normative ideas, constitutional myth and mythology, constitutional symbolism, constitutional code and constitutional geometric form. It explores the textual entrenchment of constitutionalism and its repercussions for representation and signification of meaning.

Constitutional Semiotics

The Conceptual Foundations of a Constitutional Theory and Meta-Theory

Martin Belov

•HART•
OXFORD • LONDON • NEW YORK • NEW DELHI • SYDNEY

HART PUBLISHING

Bloomsbury Publishing Plc

Kemp House, Chawley Park, Cumnor Hill, Oxford, OX2 9PH, UK

1385 Broadway, New York, NY 10018, USA

29 Earlsfort Terrace, Dublin 2, Ireland

HART PUBLISHING, the Hart/Stag logo, BLOOMSBURY and the Diana logo are trademarks of Bloomsbury Publishing Plc

First published in Great Britain 2022

A catalogue record for this book is available from the British Library.

A catalogue record for this book is available from the Library of Congress.

Library of Congress Control Number: 2022932620

ISBN: HB: 978-1-50993-140-8
ePDF: 978-1-50993-142-2
ePub: 978-1-50993-141-5

Typeset by Compuscript Ltd, Shannon

I devote this book to my family: my wife Teodora, my children Albena and Boyan, my mother Nina and my father Kiril

The writing of this book has been funded with a research grant by the Bulgarian Ministry of Education and Science and the Centre for Advanced Studies (CAS-Sofia)

CONTENTS

PART V
CONSTITUTIONAL GEOMETRY AND CONSTITUTIONAL ALGEBRA AS SEMIOTIC PARADIGMS FOR ORDERING AND EXPLAINING THE CONSTITUTION, CONSTITUTIONALISM AND CONSTITUTIONAL LAW

Introduction

Constitutional semiotics is a relatively poorly researched field of scientific knowledge which constitutes a novel branch of scientific exploration. The literature on constitutional semiotics is rather scarce. There is an insufficiency of literature devoted especially and precisely to constitutional semiotics as a holistic analytical paradigm, while literature on general and legal semiotics is rather abundant. Constitutional semiotics is also not included in the curricula of most academic institutions and universities either as a separate course or as part of the courses on constitutional and comparative constitutional law.

This reduces the chance for a better understanding of the symbolic-imaginary dimension of the constitution, constitutionalism and constitutional law. There is a scarcity of knowledge regarding the signification systems used by the constitution and constitutional law. Hence, constitutional law is perceived as formal-procedural and institutional construct with entirely rational ontology and teleology, the signification of which is limited to textual forms of representation of meaning. The predominance of rational, normative-institutional and textual constitutionalism discriminates against the symbolic-imaginary, visual, performative, emotional and transcendental characteristics of constitutional law. It hinders the exposure of the role of what I shall call in this book 'shadow constitutionalisms', and this reduces the epistemic potential of constitutional theory.

Indeed, semiotics is a well-established field of knowledge with deep roots in the intellectual traditions of contemporary science and higher education. The debates of the patriarchs of general semiotics – Ferdinand de Saussure[1] and Charles Peirce[2] – have been widely expanded and further developed by a range of important authors.[3] Nowadays, semiotics constitutes a solid scientific approach with

[1] See F de Saussure, *Course in General Linguistics* (London, Forgotten Books, 2018) 1–260.

[2] See C Peirce, *Collected Papers of Charles Sanders Peirce, Volumes I and II: Principles of Philosophy and Elements of Logic* (edited by Charles Hartshorne Paul Weiss) (Cambridge, MA, Belknap Press, 1932) 1–962; C Peirce, *Peirce on Signs: Writings on Semiotic* (edited by J Hoopes) (Chapel Hill, University of North Carolina Press, 1991) 1–294; N Howser and C Kloesel (eds), *The Essential Peirce, Volume 1: Selected Philosophical Writings (1867–1893)* (Bloomington, Indiana University Press, 1992) 1–448; and Peirce Edition Project (ed), *The Essential Peirce, Volume 2: Selected Philosophical Writings, 1893–1913* (Bloomington, Indiana University Press, 1998) 1–624.

[3] J Broekman and L Cata Backer, *Lawyers Making Meaning: The Semiotics of Law in Legal Education II* (Dordrecht, Springer, 2013) 35–57; D Holdcroft, *Saussure: Signs, System and Arbitrariness* (Cambridge, Cambridge University Press, 1991); E Koerner, *Ferdinand de Saussure* (Berlin, Vieweg+Teubner Verlag, 1973); 1–468; JJ Liszka, *A General Introduction to the Semiotic of Charles Sanders Peirce* (Bloomington, Indiana University Press, 1996) 1–168; M Bergman, *Peirce's Philosophy of Communication: The Rhetorical Underpinnings of the Theory of Signs* (London, Bloomsbury, 2011) 1–206; R Kevelson, *Peirce, Science, Signs* (New York, Peter Lang, 1996); R Barthes, *Elements of Semiology* (New York, Hill & Wang,

many followers and academic institutions working on it, and extensive scientific discourse resulting in numerous publications, journals and conferences. Semiotics is also sufficiently institutionalised, having its scientific associations while also being part of the curricula of many academic institutions.

Nevertheless, all this counts for semiotics as a general approach to the signification of meaning and the systems for the signification of meaning in the social sciences and humanities. Semiotics is a well-developed approach in the spheres of literature and the visual arts. However, it is not that widely used in legal sciences. This is the case notwithstanding the fact that law is textually expressed and is demonstrated to the people via range of signifiers. These signifiers are not limited to written textual form, but go beyond it and include art, architecture, performance and behaviour. But even if the semiotic approach is limited to the textual signification of legal concepts, it is much more rarely used than is the case in social sciences and humanities and in the arts.

In recent years there has been a visible increase in the interest of legal scholars in the semiotic approach to law. This interest has produced a mushrooming of literature on legal semiotics.[4] However, this process has been asymmetrical and to an extent intuitive, and has not been based on a single or predominant discourse framing legal semiotics as a coherent sphere of scientific knowledge. There is no overwhelming consensus as to what legal semiotics is, how it relates to general semiotics, which its specific characteristics are or its distinct analytical target, methodology and expected outcomes.

In a sense, the recent expansion of the legal semiotic discourse has been democratic due to the lack of an overarching scheme and a clear predominant narrative. It is still very much open for definition, exploration and construction. It is asymmetrical, polycentric and emerging discourse which is loosely unified

1977) 35–54; D Chandler, *Semiotics: The Basics* (Abingdon, Routledge, 2017) 1–352; T Sebeok, *Signs: An Introduction to Semiotics* (Toronto, University of Toronto Press, 2001) 1–216; T Sebeok, *A Sign is Just a Sign* (Bloomington, Indiana University Press, 1991); U Eco, *A Theory of Semiotics* (Bloomington, Indiana University Press, 1978) 1–368; W Noth, *Handbook of Semiotics* (Bloomington, Indiana University Press, 1995) 1–576; T Sebeok, *Global Semiotics* (Bloomington, Indiana University Press, 2001).

[4] See, eg, A Wagner, J Broekman (eds), *Prospects of Legal Semiotics* (Dordrecht, Springer, 2010) 1–244; B Jackson, *Semiotics and Legal Theory* (London, Kegan Paul, 1985); B Jackson, *Making Sense in Law: Linguistic, Psychological, and Semiotic Perspectives* (Liverpool, Deborah Charles Publications, 1995) 1–516; B Jackson, 'Legal Semiotics and Semiotic Aspects of Jurisprudence' in A Wagner and J Broekman (eds), *Prospects of Legal Semiotics* (Dordrecht, Springer, 2010) 3–36; A Wagner, T Summerfield and F Wanegas (eds), *Contemporary Issues of the Semiotics of Law* (Oxford, Hart Publishing, 2005) 1–286, S Tiefenbrun, *Decoding International Law: Semiotics and the Humanities* (Oxford, Oxford University Press, 2010) 1–559; JM Balkin, 'The Hohfeldian Approach to Law and Semiotics' (1990) 44 *University of Miami Law Review* 5; JM Balkin, 'The Promise of Legal Semiotics' (1990–91) 69 *University of Texas Law Review* 1831; R Kevelson (ed), *Law and Semiotics*, vols 1 and 2 (New York, Plenum Press,1988); R Kevelson, *The Law as a System of Signs* (New York, Plenum Press, 1988); J Paul, 'The Politics of Legal Semiotics' (1990–91) 69 *Texas Law Review* 1779; J Murray, 'Nome Law: Deleuze & Guattari on the Emergence of Law' (2006) 2 *International Journal for the Semiotics of Law* 127; J Murray, 'Deleuze & Guattari's Intensive & Pragmatic Semiotic of Emergent Law' (2007) 1 *International Journal for the Semiotics of Law* 7.

on the basis of the following reasons. The first reason which allows us to speak of a common legal semiotic project is the unifying interest in signification of legal and legally relevant meaning. The authors writing in the field of legal semiotics explore how legal content and legal signifieds are demonstrated to their addressees in the process of legal semiosis and the (mostly textual) signification of meaning. In that regard, most of the authors use Peirce's or Saussure's explanatory schemes of semiosis, applying them to law and transforming them into models for exploring the particularities of the legal discourse and thus of legal semiosis.[5]

It should be noted that it is not uncommon for legal scholars to go beyond the initial schemes, dogmatic imperatives, conceptual framework and constraints of general semiotics. In other words, the semiotic approach is used as an occasion for reflection on the signification of meaning in law not necessarily following the original concepts launched in general semiotics. In that regard, legal semiotics differs from the debates on general semiotics and goes beyond their frameworks, conceptual paradigms and methodological imperatives.

The two main factors outlined above – the interest in the signification of legal content and the broad use of semiotic methodology – allows the conceptualisation of legal semiotics as a common scientific approach, discourse and scientific field of knowledge. However, they are rather broad, flexible and fuzzy. This fact enables the inclusion of a multitude of narratives that are generally interested in the way in which law is perceived, demonstrated, signified, communicated and felt by the people within the scope of legal semiotic studies. Thus, they are framed in terms of legal semiotics. In that regard, legal semiotics borrows considerably from political anthropology, legal epistemology, social psychology and the theory of arts.

Hence, at present, legal semiotics seems to be rather bulky, all-encompassing and thus incoherent concept. It includes wide range of topics, discourses and scientific contributions united by the increasing interest in the systems for signification of legal and legally relevant meaning, broadly or narrowly using the methodology and conceptual apparatus developed in general semiotics and striving at expanding legal science beyond the constraints of more traditional approaches such as legal positivism, legal realism and legal institutionalism.

This general impetus of legal semiotics to broaden the horizons of legal science has to be welcomed. It is a timely attempt – or more precisely a multitude of loosely related attempts – at addressing the challenges of the ongoing communication, communicative and visual revolution compared by some authors to 'digital baroque'.[6] Together, they multiply the signification plains, realities and discourses and have a deep impact on the role, functions, structure, performance

[5] For an interesting Peirceian approach to legal style, see B Bor and M Könczöl, 'Towards a Semiotic Theory of Style in Law: A Peircean Approach' (2019) 15(3) *International Journal of Law in Context* 263, doi:10.1017/S1744552319000272.

[6] On the concept of 'digital baroque', see R Sherwin, *Visualizing Law in the Age of the Digital Baroque. Arabesques and Entanglements* (New York, Routledge, 2011) 1–256.

and perceptions of law.[7] In fact, legal semiotics can hardly be a holistic and unitary project due to the diversity of signifieds allocated in a range of divergent branches of law and the pluralism of signifiers generated in the textual, visual, imaginary and performative discourses of law. In other words, legal semiotics cannot be an entirely homogeneous project based on underlying logic which frames it as a single and unitary whole. In order to be compelling, legal semiotics has to address a multitude of signification issues, which makes a holistic approach inadequate and inefficient. Hence, the patchwork character of legal semiotics has to be welcomed as adequate to the post-modern context.

Legal science needs explanatory devices for legal discourses beyond written law. It must address the way in which law is not only practised by what I shall call later 'authoritative speakers or narrators of the community', but also the modalities in which it is signified, imagined and performed by all members of this community. However, traditional sociological and socio-legal approaches have difficulties in exploring the visual, symbolic-performative, emotional and symbolic-imaginary dimensions of law. They are mostly limited to 'law-in-context' research grounded in the sociology of law and eventually in legal anthropology. Nevertheless, they do not explain and explore how law is visualised, how it is durably imagined and shaped in collective imaginaries signifying legal and legally relevant meaning, how signification systems of law are created, updated and maintained, and how signification of law is generated, spread and preserved.

These are issues of marginal importance for both legal (positivist, institutionalist and realist) and socio-legal (sociological, psychological, socio-cultural and anthropological) approaches to law. They require the development of legal semiotics as a separate sphere of scientific research; in other words, 'law-as-text' and 'law-in-context' must be expanded and complemented with 'law-as-imagination' and 'law-as-signification' approaches. This is what a sound and well-elaborated theory of legal semiotics in general and constitutional semiotics in particular can achieve. Such a theory of legal and constitutional semiotics can have great epistemological, methodological and pragmatic value.

In recent years, in parallel with the increasing number of publications in the sphere of legal semiotics, there has also been a visible rise in interest in socio-legal studies of constitutionalism and constitutional law rooted in psychology and critical, deconstructivist and post-modern approaches such as 'law and literature',[8] 'law and arts' and 'law and culture'.[9] The main topics under consideration are the

[7] See also B de Sousa Santos, 'Three Metaphors for a New Conception of Law: The Frontier, the Baroque, and the South' (1995) 29(4) *Law and Society Review* 569.

[8] On the role of fiction and fictitious thinking and reasoning in law, see H Lind (ed), *Fictional Discourse and the Law* (Abingdon, Routledge, 2006) 1–284. On deriving inspiration from literature and mathematics for the accomplishment of constitutional analysis, see L Tribe and M Dorf, *On Reading the Constitution* (Cambridge, MA, Harvard University Press, 1993) 1–164.

[9] See, eg, L Rosen, *Law as Culture: An Invitation* (Princeton, Princeton University Press, 2008) 1–232; J Feibleman, *Justice, Law and Culture* (Dordrecht, Martinus Nijhoff, 1985); M Asimow and J Silbey, *Law and Popular Culture: A Course Book* (Lake Mary, Vandeplas Publishing, 2020) 1–22; and S Mader and M Asimow, *Law and Popular Culture: A Course Book* (New York, Peter Lang, 2013) 3–23.

importance of emotions, feelings and psychological affiliations[10] for understanding the ontology, teleology, legitimacy and efficiency of law, the reconceptualisation of law as based on constitutional imagination[11] and constitutional imaginaries,[12] the understanding of law as cultural fact and artefact, the role of social interaction for the demonstration of law's properties etc. There are also more pragmatic approaches addressing concrete issues such as the role of emotions and imaginaries for the rise of populism and populist constitutionalism,[13] the emotional foundations of democracy and authoritarianism, the role of images,[14] imaginaries[15] and utopias for concrete political projects or specific political regimes and

[10] See J Lachs, 'Law and the Importance of Feelings' in R Kevelson (ed), *Law and Semiotics*, vol 2 (New York, Plenum Press, 1988) 221–29.

[11] On the concept of constitutional imagination, see O Angeli, 'Global Constitutionalism and Constitutional Imagination' (2017) 6(3) *Global Constitutionalism* 359. Oklopcic distinguishes between different forms of constitutional imagination: constituent imagination, purposeful imagination, quasi-narrative imagination, affective imagination, ambiental imagination, visual imagination and conceptual imagination. See Z Oklopcic, *Beyond the People: Social Imaginary and Constituent Imagination* (Oxford, Oxford University Press, 2018) 1–37. Visual imagination is also explored by E Brann, *The World of the Imagination. Sum and Substance* (Lanham, MD, Rowman & Littlefield, 2017) 15–17. According to Loughlin, constitutional imagination is 'the manner in which constitutions can harness the power of narrative, symbol, ritual and myth to project an account of political existence in ways that shape – and re-shape – political reality'. See M Loughlin, 'The Constitutional Imagination' (2015) 78(1) *Modern Law Review* 3.

[12] See A Amaya and M Del Mar (eds), *Virtue, Emotion and Imagination in Law and Legal Reasoning* (Oxford, Hart Publishing, 2020) 1–275.

[13] See J Přibáň, 'The Promise of Authenticity: On Imaginaries of Constitutional Populism and European Communitas' in '*The End of Globalization? Resurging Nationalism, Authoritarian Constitutionalism and Uncertain Futures of Democracy*', Transnational Law Institute Research Paper Series, TLI Think!, 2020 (22), 38–67; P Blokker, *Imagining Europe: Transnational Contestation and Civic Populism* (London, Palgrave Macmillan, 2021) 1–364; P Blokker, 'Political and Constitutional Imaginaries' in S Adams and J Smith (eds), *Social Imaginaries: Critical Interventions in a Paradigm-in-the-Making* (Lanham, MD, Rowman and Littlefield, 2021), available at: https://ssrn.com/abstract=3784225; P Blokker, 'Populist Constitutionalism' in C de la Torre (ed), *Routledge Handbook of Global Populism* (New York, Routledge, 2018) 113–28; and TT Koncewicz and L Strother, 'The Role of Citizen Emotions in Constitutional Backsliding – Mapping out Frontiers of New Research', *Verfassungsblog*, 21 March 2019, https://verfassungsblog.de/the-role-of-citizen-emotions-in-constitutional-backsliding-mapping-out-frontiers-of-new-research.

[14] For a broader analysis of the role of images in law, see L Mulcahy, 'Sociology of Legal Images' in J Přibáň (ed), *Research Handbook on the Sociology of Law* (Cheltenham, Edward Elgar, 2020); C Douzinas, 'The Legality of the Image' (2000) 63(6) *Modern Law Review* 813; A Wagner and W Pencak, *Images in Law* (Abingdon, Routledge, 2006) 1–328, A Wagner and W Pencak (eds), *Images in Law* (Farnham, Ashgate, 2006) 1–318; and C Spiesel, R Sherwin and N Feigenson, 'Law in the Age of Images: The Challenge of Visual Literacy' in A Wagner, T Summerfield and F Benavides Vanegas (eds), *Contemporary Issues of Semiotics of Law* (Oxford, Hart Publishing, 2005) 231–57; A Young, *Judging the Image: Art, Value, Law* (London, Psychology Press, 2005); C Vismann, 'Image and Law: A Troubled Relationship' (2008) 14(4) *Parallax* 1; and Broekman and Cata Backer (n 3) 141–43.

[15] For the concepts of social imaginaries, see C Taylor, *Modern Social Imaginaries* (Durham, NC, Duke University Press, 2003) 1–232; C Bottici, *Imaginal Politics: Images Beyond Imagination and the Imaginary* (New York, Columbia University Press, 2014) 1–253; J Přibáň, 'Constitutional Imaginaries and Legitimation: On Potentia, Potestas, and Auctoritas in Societal Constitutionalism' (2018) 45 *Journal of Law and Society* 30; S Adams (ed), *Ricoeur and Castoriadis in Discussion: On Human Creation, Historical Novelty, and the Social Imaginary* (Lanham, MD, Rowman & Littlefield, 2017) 1–236; and W Schinkel, *Imagined Societies: A Critique of Immigrant Integration in Western Europe* (Cambridge, Cambridge University Press, 2017) 1–260.

constitutional orders etc.[16] According to J Přibáň, the 'recent popularity of the concepts of imagination and imaginary in legal and constitutional theory is subsequently a mixture of the typically academic ambition of imaginative research, classic notions of theoretical imagination and more recent explorations of modern social imaginaries'.[17]

Many of these scientific attempts are not properly, entirely and genuinely semiotic. This is due to the fact that frequently they do not focus on the process of legal semiosis with its typical structure based on signifiers, signifieds and signification of meaning. Nevertheless, they contribute to the overall semiotic paradigm demonstrating how and why collective symbols, visuals and imaginaries matter for the understanding of law beyond the 'law-in-books' and the traditional 'law-in action' approaches.

To sum up, semiotics has until recently been something of an exotic approach to law with limited epistemic capacity and methodological appeal. It is still to a great extent overshadowed by the predominant legal positivist and legal institutionalist approaches to law, and more traditional 'law in context' sociologically oriented socio-legal studies.[18] In parallel, rationalism and the rational approach to law have are employed more frequently than the emotional, imaginary and symbolic approaches and predominate the legal discourse. In recent years there has been an increase in interest in using alternative analytical paradigms in legal science. Semiotics transformed into legal semiotics and combined with elements of psychology and anthropology is an appealing innovative approach. Nevertheless, it is still a rather novel, relatively poorly researched sphere of knowledge with a lack of clear coherence and visible consensus regarding its object, scope of application and methodology.

Thus, it seems that there is an increasing need for a theory of legal semiotics. We need both a theory of constitutional semiotics focused on the transcendental-symbolic-metaphorical features of law produced by the interplay between the symbolic-imaginary, the ideal and the real,[19] and a meta-theory capable of offering fundamental conceptual and methodological insights, thus providing a sound basis for scientific analysis based on constitutional semiotics.[20]

[16] See S Herman, 'Constitutional Utopianism' (2016) 12 *UTOPIA500* 93, https://scholarlycommons.pacific.edu/utopia500/2016/events/12.

[17] See J Přibáň, *Constitutional Imaginaries: A Theory of European Societal Constitutionalism* (Abingdon, Routledge, 2020) 6.

[18] For a semiotic approach to law in context, see A Wagner, T Summerfield and F Benavides Vanegas (eds), *Contemporary Issues of Semiotics of Law* (Oxford, Hart Publishing, 2005) 125–257.

[19] For the interplay between the imaginary, the ideal and the real, see J Lacan, *Écrits* (New York, WW Norton & Company, 2007) 1–896; J Lacan, *The Language of the Self* (Baltimore, Johns Hopkins University Press, 1956) 29–53; C Castoriadis, *The Imaginary Institution of Society* (Cambridge, Polity Press, 1987) 160–65; and B Olivier, 'Lacan's Subject: The Imaginary, Language, the Real and Philosophy' (2005) 23(1) *South African Journal of Philosophy* 1.

[20] The fundamental role of the symbolic, the imaginary and the fictitious for constituting and understanding the legal orders is demonstrated in O Tans, 'The Imaginary Foundation of Legal Systems: A Mimetic Perspective' (2014) 26(2) *Law & Literature* 127, doi:10.1080/1535685X.2014.888204.

However, it is not completely clear whether such a holistic approach offering unified solutions for all branches of law is possible or efficient. There is a huge variation in the applicability of the semiotic approach in the various branches of law. For example, public law seems much more suitable for semiotic analysis than private or criminal law.

This is why there is an increasing necessity to offer a socio-legal account of constitutionalism and constitutional law focused on the role of the symbolic-imaginary representation of constitutional meaning in the various areas of its semiotic signification. Such a necessity is not visible in more pragmatic, technical and in a sense more legal branches of law, such as tax law, trade law, and civil, criminal and administrative procedure. The substantial divergence of the branches of law, the intrinsic interconnectedness of constitutional law with philosophy, social psychology, sociology, anthropology and political science, and the epistemic necessity to understand the way in which people imagine the state and society with its constitutional framework, institutional architecture and axiological design make a general theory of legal semiotic less feasible while requiring the elaboration of a coherent theory of constitutional semiotics.

Hence, the above issues related to signification, collective imagination and the sharing of legal meaning are particularly important for constitutionalism and constitutional law. Constitutional law is the branch of law which is most prone to semiotic signification. This is due to the fact that it forms the legal foundation of politics, while politics is deeply embedded in signification of meaning and largely dependent on the communicative transmission of symbolic messages, codes and insights.[21] Constitutional law as the legal background of politics has to be emotionally appealing. It needs to be transferrable into the realm of collective imagination through various forms for signification of meaning. Institutions, forms and procedures must be made intelligible for the people. The people (office holders included) should be able not only to follow rules, but also to obey them, believe in them and share their legal experience in symbolically and emotional-imaginarily appealing ways. In that regard, constitutional semiosis is an epistemological approach that transforms constitutional law from a 'game of rules and institutions' into a 'game of codes and imaginaries', at least to a certain extent.

Thus, constitutional rules have to be transmitted in a symbolically appealing way. They have to be able to be grasped not just by the mind, but also by the heart and the soul of the members of the constitutionally framed socio-political community. The signification of values, rules, institutions and durable patterns of behaviour cannot be done only through constitutional text; it also requires recourse to other signification systems, both visual and performative. Thus, the signification potential of art and architecture is usually mobilised to convey constitutional and constitutionally relevant ideas, messages and ranges of signified objects.

[21] For more on political communication, see K Kenski and K Hall Jamieson (eds), *The Oxford Handbook of Political Communication* (Oxford, Oxford University Press, 2019) 1–976.

Hence, constitutions, constitutional law and constitutionalism are prone to textual, visual and performative signification.[22] They contain range of important signifieds that require signification through constitutional text and texture. This is necessary because constitutions and constitutional law are not sterile products of rational deliberation shaped in forms and procedures detached from imagination, beliefs, emotions and other factors of the socio-cultural context. Constitution is not an artefact of pure rationality deprived of emotional and imaginary appeal; it is deeply embedded in collective imaginaries. Its perception, legitimacy and efficiency are to a great extent dependent not only on the rational cognition of its rules, but also on the emotional perception of its imaginary content.[23]

In a sense, the constitution is entrenched in the underground waters of collective imaginaries. It is stuck in the subterrain of the collective subconscious and unconscious. Constitutional 'law-as-imagination' is contained not so much in textual constitutionalism, but in the dispersed constitutional attitudes of the people – a phenomenon which I shall describe and define later on in this book as cloud constitutionalism.[24] In that regard, the constitution and its core messages need to be signified and demonstrated through a range of signifiers produced by what I shall call symbolic-imaginary, visual and performative constitutionalism.[25]

This book addresses the need outlined above to provide a theory of constitutional semiotics. It contains both theories and meta-theories which together form the theoretical foundations of a semiotic approach to constitutions, constitutionalism and constitutional law.

The book is based on the following logic that underlies its separate parts. Part I discusses some conceptual and methodological issues of paradigmatic importance for the whole book. Nevertheless, it does not exhaust the conceptual foundations of constitutional semiotics which also unfold in the subsequent parts.

The next three parts explore the different plains for signification of constitutional and constitutionally relevant meaning. Constitutional and constitutionally relevant meaning can be signified through text and texture, via linguistic forms, but also through art and architecture and via performance.[26] On the basis of the difference of the signifiers and the particularities of the process of constitutional

[22] For more on the role of performative art forms in the expression of legal ideas, see, eg, L Friedman, 'Lexitainment: Legal Process as Theatre' (2000) 50 *De Paul Law Review* 539; F-W Korsten, *Art as an Interface of Law and Justice: Affirmation, Disturbance, Disruption* (Oxford, Hart Publishing, 2021) 1–212; and J Denvir (ed), *Legal Reelism: Movies as Legal Texts* (Chicago, University of Illinois Press, 1996) 1–336.

[23] This is actually the underlying concept behind the famous triple classification of the types of legitimacy outlined by Weber – see M Weber, *Soziologie. Weltgeschichtliche Analysen. Politik* (Stuttgart, Kröner Verlag, 1968) 151 et seq. For the role of constitutional imaginaries for accumulation of legitimacy, see also Přibáň (n 15); and Přibáň (n 17) 1–251.

[24] This is to an extent in line with Castoriadis' idea of the 'labyrinths of the symbolic elaboration of the imaginary in the unconscious'. See Castoriadis (n 19) 142.

[25] For constitutionalism as performance see O Tans, 'Imagined Constitutionality: Rethinking Democratic Citizenship with the Aid of Fiction Theory' (2015) 15(2) *Law, Culture and the Humanities* 9.

[26] See, eg, L Friedman (n 22); and Korsten (n 22) 1–212.

semiosis and the semiotic signification of meaning, I will outline several types of constitutionalism. These are textual, symbolic-imaginary, visual and performative constitutionalism. In addition, I will also explore other forms of constitutionalism which contribute to a proper understanding of the current standing of the research of the systems for signification of constitutional and constitutionally relevant meaning – these are rational, normative-institutional, emotional, quantum and cloud constitutionalism.

Finally, the book devotes special attention to a specific semiotic meta-theory applicable to structured constitutional imaginaries.[27] This is the theory of constitutional geometry also supplemented with a short outline of a theory of constitutional algebra.

The book opens with Part I, which is devoted to some fundamental conceptual and methodological issues. It provides a conceptual overview of the process of constitutional semiosis, explains the general structure of this process, and engages with the paradigmatic issues of signification, signifiers and signifieds in constitutionalism and constitutional law. It explains the peculiarities of constitutional semiotics from a constitutionalist viewpoint without being preoccupied with methodological restraints entrenched in general semiotics. It explores the intellectual stretching of the constitution, constitutionalism and constitutional law between the imperatives of rationality, the need of emotional enchantment and the determinants of constitutional imaginaries and the constitutional imagination.[28] In that regard, constitutional semiotics is defined as an intellectual power field allocated on the border between textuality, normativity, visuality[29] and performance. It is conceived as an intellectual paradigm with conceptual, methodological and pragmatic implications bridging the ideal, normative, factual, emotional and imaginary plains for the unfolding of constitutionalism.

Constitutional semiotics is defined as both a theory and meta-theory of constitutionalism and constitutional law. This is a necessary conceptual delimitation enabling the provision of a coherent and consistent theory of constitutional semiotics. On the basis of a conceptual distinction between theory and meta-theory, I will demonstrate which theories and meta-theories are a necessary part of my general theory of constitutional semiotics. Such preliminary conceptual clarification is also required due to the fact that I propose several novel theories relating to constitutionalism and constitutional law, some of which also play a role as meta-theories. The most important of them are the theories of quantum constitutionalism, cloud constitutionalism, textual, visual, symbolic-imaginary, emotional, performative and normative-institutional constitutionalism. They are components

[27] For more on constitutional imaginaries, see J Komárek, 'Political Economy in the European Constitutional Imaginary: Moving beyond Fiesole', *Verfassungsblog*, 4 September 2020, https://verfassungsblog.de/political-economy-in-the-european-constitutional-imaginary-moving-beyond-fiesole.

[28] See Amaya and Del Mar (n 12) 1–275.

[29] For the concept of visuality, see R Khorakiwala, *From the Colonial to the Contemporary: Images, Iconography, Memories, and Performances of Law in India's High Courts* (Oxford, Hart Publishing, 2020) 1–296.

of my general theory of constitutional semiotics, but have also their own validity and autonomous role, substance and epistemic importance. Constitutional geometry is the most important meta-theory that I will put forward in this book. Part V is devoted to this meta-theory, although I have outlined some of its features in previous publications.[30]

One of the intellectual epicentres of Part I is the rationalist entrapment of modernity and its repercussions for constitutionalism and constitutional law. While admitting the pivotal role of textual, rational and normative-institutional constitutionalism, the book advocates a reassessment of the importance and the role of what I call 'shadow constitutionalisms'. In fact, the whole book is an appeal for a shift in the academic debate and the scientific interest to symbolic-imaginary, emotional, visual and performative constitutionalism[31] in order to achieve a better understanding of the symbolic and transcendental characteristics of constitutions and constitutional law.[32] Hence, the book is an invitation for a reconceptualisation of constitutionalism as a multidiscursive phenomenon through the analytical lenses of semiotics.

Part II explores textual constitutionalism and its role in constitutional semiotics. It defines the concept of textual constitutionalism and offers an account of constitutional communication perceived through the semiotic perspective of textual constitutionalism. The constitution is defined as a discursive semiotic project that is structured around constitutional narratives, constitutional narrators and a constitutional semiotic community. In that regard, this part explores constitutional text and constitutional texture from a semiotic perspective with special emphasis on the concept of authoritative constitutional text and the role of open texture in constitutional semiotics.

Part III is of pivotal importance for understanding constitutional semiotics as a 'game of constitutional imaginaries'. It offers the theory and general typology of the symbolic-imaginary constitutionalism and explores its most important forms. After defining the concept of symbolic-imaginary constitutionalism, I focus on constitutional semiosis via symbolic-imaginary constitutionalism on the border between the collective conscious, subconscious and unconscious. Furthermore, a general comparative typology of symbolic-imaginary constitutionalism is provided and systematised on the basis of what I shall call constitutional semiotic landscapes. Here the teleology and functionality of symbolic-imaginary constitutionalism as a 'game of constitutional semiotic imaginaries' is thoroughly researched. Part III then goes on to explore the semiotic characteristics of constitutional codes,[33] the

[30] See M Belov, 'The Challenges to Westphalian Constitutional Geometry in the Age of Supranational Constitutionalism, Global Governance and Information Revolution' in M Belov (ed), *Global Constitutionalism and its Challenges to Westphalian Constitutional Law* (Oxford, Hart Publishing, 2018) 13–55.

[31] See, eg, C Douzinas, S McVeigh and R Warrington, 'The Alta(e)rs of Law: The Judgement of Legal Aesthetics' (1992) 9(4) *Theory, Culture & Society* 93, doi:10.1177/026327692009004004.

[32] For the transcendental characteristics of constitutional values, see Přibáň (n 17) 40–63.

[33] For the concept of code, see also D Chandler, *Semiotics: The Basics* (Abingdon, Routledge, 2017) 177–222.

normative ideologies and normative ideas and their role in symbolic-imaginary constitutionalism and constitutional semiotics, and the semiotic role of constitutional myths and mythology.

Part IV is devoted to visual constitutionalism. It defines this as a post-modern semiotic concept and pays particular attention to official visual semiotics relating to the constitutional embeddedness and constitutional relevance of official public visuals. Visual constitutionalism is explained as a proper form of constitutionalism embedded in semiotic and socio-legal approaches. Special emphasis is placed on visual constitutionalism and digital constitutional semiotics. More precisely, the 'iconisation',[34] 'emojification' and 'memefication'[35] as forms of signification of constitutionally relevant meaning are explored. Specific chapters are devoted to visual constitutionalism in pop culture, pop art[36] and architecture.

Part V contains the outline of a novel but important epistemic approach to constitutionalism and constitutional law. It offers a detailed account of my theory of constitutional geometry while also paying attention to constitutional algebra as a semiotic phenomenon. Constitutional geometry also performs the role of a meta-theory of constitutional law in its capacity as a semiotic paradigm. In that regard, constitutional geometry and constitutional algebra are presented as semiotic paradigms for ordering and explaining the constitution, constitutionalism and constitutional law. This part of the book focuses on the possibility of ordering and explaining constitutional order through mathematic metaphors. It explores the semiotic role of structured constitutional imaginaries and delimits different aspects and forms of constitutional geometry.

A full, detailed and exhaustive exploration of constitutional semiotics is beyond the scope of any one book, not only due to space constraints but also due to reasons relating to logic and the coherence of argumentation. Hence, extensive research of the constitution, constitutionalism and constitutional law from the viewpoint of semiotics requires analysis accomplished in four main steps or stages that have been employed in a range of subsequent publications. These steps are interconnected, but also autonomous.

The first research step consists in the provision of a theory of constitutional semiotics as a new paradigm and novel approach to the constitution, constitutional law and constitutionalism. The current book is devoted to this first step or stage of scientific analysis. This step should be the initial step from a logical, conceptual and methodological perspective. A coherent theory of constitutional semiotics is a necessary prerequisite for the proper detailed exploring of different elements, aspects or issues of constitutional semiotics. Such a theory has to provide the conceptual and methodological background for the construction of national,

[34] For the iconography of law in a non-digital context, see Khorakiwala (n 29) 1–296.

[35] See B Wiggins, *The Discursive Power of Memes in Digital Culture: Ideology, Semiotics, and Intertextuality* (Abingdon, Routledge, 2019) 1–175; and L Shifman, *Memes in Digital Culture* (Cambridge, MA, MIT Press, 2013) 1–166.

[36] See S Redhead, *Unpopular Cultures: The Birth of Law and Popular Culture* (Manchester, Manchester University Press, 1995).

regional and comparative typologies of constitutional semiotic phenomena and for research into case studies. It provides the paradigmatic core, the thematic framework and the methodological guidance on the basis of which one can compare constitutional semiotics with other closely or remotely, explicitly or implicitly related approaches, theories and paradigms, such as legal and general semiotics, constitutional psychology, the sociology of constitutionalism and constitutional law, constitutional anthropology, constitutionalism and the arts, constitutionalism and literature, and the philosophy and theory of the state and constitutional law.

The second step or stage of research that will lead to an extensive and detailed theory of constitutional semiotics concerns the outlining of the proximities and differences with the above-mentioned related fields of knowledge. It includes an analysis of the theoretical achievements in general semiotics, legal semiotics and the related spheres of knowledge, such as law and the arts, law and literature, constitutional anthropology and the study of collective imaginaries and collective emotions addressing constitutional phenomena. This next stage of research aims at allocating constitutional semiotics on the coordinate axis of the scientific approaches and paradigms which strive to explore the signification of constitutional codes, figures[37] and phenomena through a range of signifiers (textual, visual, performative etc), and the role of imagination, reason, emotions and the collective subconscious and unconscious for the structuring and functioning of the constitutional order. These theories aim at exploring not only the socio-legal context and the socio-legal determinants of the outlook and performance of constitutions, but also the ways in which constitutional orders are represented in the collective reason, imaginaries and emotions, and the shapes through which they get their durable imprints in the realms of the ideal and the imaginary.[38]

This second stage of research presents multiple challenges. One of them is the mushrooming of literature and scientific discourses which loosely belong to the semiotic approach to law.[39] Another is the impossibility of the full detachment of constitutional semiotics from related fields of knowledge and the subsequent improbability for its entire emancipation as a separate and entirely autonomous scientific discipline. Constitutional semiotics will always be embedded in general and legal semiotics, and will be dependent on the scientific achievements of legal epistemology, constitutional and political anthropology, and the sociological and psychological studies of law in general and the constitution and constitutional law in particular.

This intellectual dependence and partial autonomy of constitutional semiotics must not be conceived as a weakness, but rather as a strength. It allows the permanent enrichment of constitutional semiotics with novel theories, analytical

[37] On the role of figures for the signification of legal and legally relevant meaning, see Broekman and Cata Backer (n 3) 141.

[38] The concept, structure and role of social imaginaries are examined by Castoriadis, who also distinguishes between radical and actual imaginary and differentiates between central and secondary (peripheral) imaginary. See Castoriadis (n 19) 127 et seq.

[39] See the *Cambridge Journal of Law, Politics, and Art*, available at: https://www.cjlpa.org/issues.

approaches, discourses and methods. It gives a role to constitutional semiotics in the joint scientific endeavour for the cognition of the signification systems in law and the sources, structure and modalities of the collective legal imagination[40] and imaginaries.

In the current context of the post-modern fragmentation of the social sciences and the humanities, such an interdisciplinary approach and the renouncing of striving to achieve solipsistic (self-contained, self-sufficient and self-enclosed) and holistic scientific approaches is actually a necessity. Hence, constitutional semiotics is bound to be an open, incomplete, partially autonomous branch of scientific knowledge dependent on intellectual, conceptual and methodological borrowings from other scientific disciplines and theories.

The relationship between constitutional semiotics and other approaches, its distinctiveness, specific characteristics and commonality to related concepts are too important to be compressed into a single chapter in a book devoted to a general theory. Initially, I was planning to include such a chapter. Nevertheless, due to space constraints, due to concerns relating to the coherency of argumentation and the admitting of the great importance of more thorough and detailed research of the conceptual embeddedness of constitutional semiotics in related subjects in the social sciences and humanities fields, I will refrain from offering a detailed analysis here. Naturally, reference to such related spheres of research will be made at various points in this book, but this will be done in context and in line with the particular argumentations I will offer rather than as a separate object of argumentation and assessment.

The third step consists in the accomplishment of a comparative semiotic analysis of constitutionalism and constitutional law. Such an analysis will result in the establishment of comparative constitutional semiotic typologies. Constitutional semiotics may be very useful not only when applied to national constitutionalism and in a distinct constitutional order, but also if it is used for comparative research that usually produces comparative typologies.[41] In fact, the comparative research of the systems for signification of meaning and for demonstrating, visualising and performing constitutional imaginaries is almost non-existent. Thus, comparative

[40] Legal imagination is a rather broad concept which is increasingly used and also applied to branches of law which are not necessarily prone to meta-legal normative orders and exposed to socio-legal and semiotic analysis. A good example is N Perrone, *Investment Treaties and the Legal Imagination: How Foreign Investors Play by Their Own Rules* (Oxford, Oxford University Press, 2021) 1–272. An interesting outline of the history of legal imagination is offered in S Stern, 'The Legal Imagination in Historical Perspective' in Amaya and Del Mar (n 12) 217–34. One of the most interesting and exciting analyses of legal imagination in international relations is given in M Koskenniemi, *To the Uttermost Parts of the Earth: Legal Imagination and International Power 1300–1870* (Cambridge, Cambridge University Press, 2021) 1–12. An excellent exploration of legal imagination, its different levels and its importance for legal reasoning is given in M Del Mar, 'The Legal Imagination: Individual, Interactive and Communal' in Amaya and Del Mar (n 12) 235–61.

[41] See, eg, See T Eriksen and R Jenkins, *Flag, Nation and Symbolism in Europe and America* (Abingdon, Routledge, 2007) 1–208; K Cerulo, 'Symbols and the World System: National Anthems and Flags' (1993) 8(2) *Sociological Forum* 243, https://doi.org/10.1007/BF01115492.

constitutional semiotics may allow us to understand how different constitutional systems signify constitutional and constitutionally relevant meaning, which are the typical signifieds and which are the main signifiers, how they are arranged and used, whether there are systems which are more prone to the signification of constitutional phenomena and whether there are rules on the basis of which 'games of constitutional imaginaries' and 'games of constitutional codes' are played.

Comparative constitutional semiotics promises to be an important analytical tool, especially for the structured constitutional imaginaries, but can also be used for a comparative assessment of the elements of symbolic-imaginary constitutionalism – constitutional codes, normative ideologies and ideas, constitutional myths and mythologies, and constitutional utopias. It can also be applied to visual and performative constitutional semiotics. Comparative constitutional semiotics is applicable to all signification systems, but is naturally focused on the signifiers provided by textual constitutionalism as a traditionally predominant signification discourse of constitutional law.

Again, like the previous analytical step, a coherent and detailed analysis of both constitutional semiotics and comparative constitutional semiotics is almost impossible within the space constraints of a single book. Naturally, the ideas, concepts, theories, meta-theories and analytical conclusions which will be given here are also applicable to comparative constitutional semiotic research. In that regard, the theory of constitutional semiotics I propose here is also applicable from a comparative perspective. Hence, my theory of constitutional semiotics is also a theory of comparative constitutional semiotics.

Nevertheless, the book will not offer extensive comparative research apart from examples which are necessary in order to illustrate the thesis they relate to. In parallel to space constraints, an important reason for avoiding a comparative bias of the analysis provided here is the fact that comparative research focuses on more or less concrete issues. The inclusion of this would expand the scope of the book and obscure its theoretical core content, limit the consistency of argumentation, and diminish the analytical appeal of the general theory of constitutional semiotics provided here.

The fourth analytical step devoted to constitutional semiotics is optional. It consists in providing of interesting and important case studies. This is an effort that can be understood as a form or continuation of comparative research based on semiotic analysis. Such analysis will focus on the specific manifestations and instantiations of important semiotic phenomena available in one or more systems for the signification of meaning through signifiers belonging to textual, symbolic-imaginary, visual or performative constitutionalism. Naturally, such analysis has to be done as part of separate forms of scientific research (papers, studies, monographs etc). In this book I will focus only on a limited number of case studies and will limit my analysis to several concrete phenomena in order to avoid the blurring of my general theoretical argumentation.

Hence, this book offers a holistic theory of constitutional semiotics. This theory can also be used in comparative constitutional law and with a view to its application to concrete case studies. It also allows the semiotic research of concrete constitutional and constitutionally relevant phenomena signified in a range of constitutional discourses. It is applicable to textual, normative-institutional, symbolic-imaginary, visual and performative constitutionalism.

Every reader when opening a book wants to know what he or she can learn from it: what are the new ideas it proposes, how does it engage with the existing debate, does it open up novel intellectual horizons and, if so, what are they? Hence, at the end of this brief introduction and before starting the substantial analysis I believe that I have to briefly summarize and outline the novel ideas, theories and concepts that this book claims to launch in the academic debate.

The book offers an original, insightful and complex analysis of the systems for the signification of constitutional and constitutionally relevant meaning. It applies a complex and combined methodological approach. The conceptual apparatus, methodology and analytical suggestions of general and legal semiotics are at the core of the analysis. However, I also use insights from critical legal studies,[42] post-modern deconstructivist approaches[43] to socio-political and constitutional phenomena, and elements of legal epistemology, political anthropology and psychology. The analysis is conceptually influenced mainly by Jacques Derrida,[44] Michel Foucault,[45] Carl Gustav Jung,[46] Jacques Lacan,[47] Cornelius Castoriadis,[48] Ferdinand de Saussure[49] and Charles Peirce.[50] I directly or indirectly engage in debates paradigmatically allocated in the spheres of theory of language,[51] critical and deconstructivist studies, general semiotics, psychology, theory of knowledge, anthropology, epistemology etc.

Thus, I do not limit my research to a single conceptual paradigm or methodology, but instead I use a multitude of theoretical approaches, narratives and

[42] For a concrete example of the impact of critical legal studies on the semiotics of law, see M Ellis, *Critical Global Semiotics: Understanding Sustainable Transformational Citizenship* (Abingdon, Routledge, 2021) 1–268; A Wagner and V Bhatia (eds), *Diversity and Tolerance in Socio-legal Contexts* (Farnham, Ashgate, 2009) 1–250; and A Wagner, 'Images of Racial Discrimination in France' in A Wagner and W Pencak (eds), *Images in Law* (Farnham, Ashgate, 2006) 255–67.

[43] See P Salmon, 'How to Deconstruct the World', *Psyche*, https://psyche.co/guides/how-to-deconstruct-the-world-by-thinking-like-jacques-derrida?fbclid=IwAR1nVvSqfBr8VYxsDbQJdYct2k7B8QTgOwKmpB_zX2DhY-9rAvmNmRxgRA4.

[44] J Derrida, *Of Grammatology* (Baltimore, Johns Hopkins University Press, 2016) 1–560; and J Derrida, 'Force of Law: The Mystical Foundation of Authority' in D Cornell, M Rosenfield and D Carlson (eds), *Deconstruction and the Possibility of Justice* (London, Routledge, 1992).

[45] M Foucault, *The Order of Things: An Archaeology of the Human Sciences* (New York, Vintage, 1994) 1–416; M Foucault, *The Archaeology of Knowledge: And the Discourse on Language* (New York, Vintage, 1982) 1–256; M Foucault, *Power* (New York, The New Press, 2001) 1–528; M Foucault, *Ethics: Subjectivity and Truth* (New York, The New Press, 1998) 1–384.

[46] CG Jung, *Psychology of the Unconscious* (Eastford, Martino Fine Books, 2016) 1–390; CG Jung, *Man and His Symbols* (New York, Dell Publishing, 1968) 1–415.

[47] Lacan (n 19) 1–896.

[48] Castoriadis (n 19) 1–418.

[49] See de Saussure (n 1) 1–260.

[50] See the literature cited in n 2 above.

[51] See, eg, C Belsey, *Poststructuralism: A Very Short Introduction* (Oxford, Oxford University Press, 2002) 1–128.

methodologies in order to establish a novel theory of constitutional semiotics. Naturally, the core ideas and methodological approaches are derived from general and legal semiotics. The above-mentioned fields of knowledge, theoretical approaches and authors, although inspirational for my work, are not followed blindly. In fact, I use the arguments they provide and the overall intellectual spirit and insights they offer in a creative way as building blocks, clues, foundations or framing and paradigmatic constructions in order to allow the establishment of an autonomous theory of constitutional semiotics.

In that regard, I have to admit that my theory is neither monolithic nor fully and entirely semiotic. It is to an extent eclectic and multidiscursive due to the use of a multitude of narratives. It is based on a range of discourses and scientific narratives which are used to create an explanatory framework and toolkit that may allow for a better understanding of the way in which constitutions 'dream', 'remember', 'hope', 'fear',[52] 'love', 'hate' and 'imagine' through recourse to systems of grasping and engaging with the collective imagination of the constitutionally framed socio-legal community.

The ultimate aim of this scientific endeavour is to expose the symbolic-imaginary aspect of the constitution, constitutional law and constitutionalism, to explain the different signification plains and tools available in textual, visual and performative constitutionalism, and to raise awareness of the need to understand the permutations of the symbolic, the imaginary and the real in relation to constitutionalism and constitutional law. Since the main focus is devoted to signification of constitutional meaning via a range of constitutional signifiers representing constitutional signifieds, the book is genuinely semiotic. The predominance of the semiotic approach and its application to the constitution, constitutional law and constitutionalism makes this book a research tool devoted to a theory of constitutional semiotics.

This volume offers a range of theories that are framed by the general theory of constitutional semiotics. I explore several forms of constitutionalism with regard to the level for the signification of constitutional meaning, the signifiers, the signifieds and the peculiarities of the overall process of constitutional semiosis. These types of constitutionalism explored through the prism of constitutional semiotics are textual, symbolic-imaginary, visual and performative constitutionalism. Hence, I propose a new typology of constitutionalism based on semiotic criteria and following the structure of the semiotic process. Thus, in conjunction and in parallel with my general theory of constitutional semiotics, I also provide focused

[52] For the exploitation of fear in public law, see M Belov, 'The Role of Fear Politics in Global Constitutional "Ernstfall": Images of Fear under COVID-19 Health Paternalism' in M Belov (ed), *Populist Constitutionalism and Illiberal Democracies: Between Constitutional Imagination, Normative Entrenchment and Political Reality* (Cambridge, Intersentia, 2021) 187–221; and A Bianchi and A Saab, 'Fear and International Law-Making: An Exploratory Inquiry' (2019) 32 *Leiden Journal of International Law* 351, doi:10.1017/S0922156519000177.

analysis on the semiotic problems relating to signifiers, signifieds and signification in text and texture, arts and architecture, containers of collective emotions and imaginaries, and constitutionally relevant performance.

The theory of constitutional semiotics that I propose is grounded in several conceptual assumptions which are also a new feature in the academic debate. Some of them are structured as new forms of constitutionalism – these are quantum constitutionalism and cloud constitutionalism. Both of these are used as theories explaining the symbolic potential and the multidirectional capacity of constitutional phenomena (in the former case) and the way in which constitutional imaginaries are organised, preserved and gain stability and continuity (in the latter case). At the same time, they are also used as methodological foundations for understanding the structure and teleology of the constitutional order. They are theoretical explanatory paradigms that aim to organise and be used for the explanation of theories relating to constitutional semiosis. In that regard, quantum constitutionalism and cloud constitutionalism are also meta-theories of constitutional law that are also applicable in the sphere of constitutional semiotics.

This book devotes special attention to semiotic metaphors derived from the natural sciences. It explores the semiotic potential of concepts such as constitutional sedimentation,[53] constitutional architecture, constitutional archaeology, constitutional geometry and constitutional algebra to serve as epistemic tools in the process of constitutional semiosis. It also contains extensive analysis of the interconnectedness of constitutional law with the arts and architecture. This is done in the context of the elaboration of my theory of visual constitutionalism. It has already been mentioned that special emphasis is placed on constitutional geometry as both a theory and meta-theory of constitutional semiotics.

One of the main claims of the book is that contemporary constitutionalism as a product of Enlightenment and modernity is overburdened with rationalism, institutionalism and textualism. Indeed, rationalism is one of the key normative ideologies of modern and Western constitutionalism.[54] It is intellectual pillar that, together with humanism, predetermines the outlook of modern Western constitutional civilisation.[55] Constitutional law and the constitution are and must remain rational.

[53] On the concept of constitutional sedimentation, see D Curtin, 'The Sedimentary European Constitution: The Future of "Constitutionalisation" without a Constitution' in I Pernice and E Tanchev (eds), *Ceci n'est pas une Constitution: Constitutionalisation without a Constitution?* (Baden-Baden, Nomos, 2009) 76–86.

[54] For the role of rationalism in modern policy-making, see M Oakeshott, *Rationalism in Politics and Other Essays* (Carmel, Liberty Fund, 1991) 1–582; and W Lecky, *History of the Rise and Influence of the Spirit of Rationalism in Europe* (LEEAF.com Classics, 2013) 1–442.

[55] For humanism as a normative ideology of modern constitutionalism, see M Belov (ed), *The IT Revolution and its Impact on State, Constitutionalism and Public Law* (Oxford, Hart Publishing, 2021) 15–41.

Moreover, constitutional rationality is possible to a great extent due to the textual character of modern constitutions. The written and codified constitution is both a great ideal and an important achievement of Western modernity, which has subsequently been transferred to most states in the world.[56] Hence, the constitution and constitutional law have to retain their rational core and textual character.[57]

Last but not least, the institutional structure of constitutional law is also a precondition for its rationality. Systematic and well-ordered constitutional law is inevitably established through the institutional architecture. This is the reason why I develop an extensive analysis of three separate but also interrelated constitutional discourses which deserve to be defined as distinct forms of constitutionalism: rational, textual and normative-institutional constitutionalism.

However, written text is not the only instrument for the signification of constitutional meaning. Constitutional phenomena are signified also via art, architecture, official symbols, ceremonies and performance. These are represented in the individual and collective conscious, subconscious and unconscious via a range of codes and signifiers belonging to the realm of symbolic-imaginary constitutionalism. Hence, the emotional, symbolic and imaginary aspect of the constitution, constitutionalism and constitutional law must not be neglected. The role of what I shall call 'shadow constitutionalisms' – the emotional, symbolic-imaginary, visual and performative constitutionalism – for the representation of the rational, normative-institutional and 'official' formal-procedural part of constitutional law and thus for the signification of constitutional meaning via instruments not just of textual but also of visual and performative constitutionalism needs to be thoroughly researched. These 'shadow constitutionalisms' deserve to be highlighted and explored, and this can be done most successfully through the instruments and methods and the analytical prism of constitutional semiotics.

In that regard, this book has to be understood as an invitation. It is invitation to reconsider our formalist normative-institutional approach to constitutional law. It is an appeal to retain rationalism while getting rid of the excesses of rationalism that are themselves irrational. It is a claim that what matters in not just how law is or ought to be, but also how law is imagined, represented, felt and experienced in all plains for signification of constitutional and constitutionally relevant meaning. Last but not least, it is a demand to start exploring and explaining constitution and constitutional law as a 'game of codes' and a 'game of imaginaries' contained in text and texture, demonstrated through art, architecture and behaviour, but also preserved in cloud constitutionalism in the shared beliefs of the members

[56] For the huge importance of the constitutional form, both written and printed, see G Frankenberg, *Comparative Constitutional Studies: Between Magic and Deceit* (Cheltenham, Edward Elgar, 2018), 63–66; and T Vesting, *Legal Theory and the Media of Law* (Cheltenham, Edward Elgar, 2018) 1–656. According to Frankenberg, 'writtenness' also testifies to the symbolic dimension of constitutions.'

[57] For the relationship between rationality, the language of law and legal aesthetics in the context of transition from modernity to post-modernity, see Douzinas, McVeigh and Warrington (n 31).

of the constitutionally framed socio-political community. I firmly believe that going beyond the excesses of rationality and textuality, looking at the constitution and constitutional law in a more emotionally, imaginary and symbolic way, and searching for constitutional signification of meaning in signification systems that are not limited to text may have huge epistemic value. Constitutional law is rational, textual and pragmatic, but also emotional, imaginary, symbolic, allegorical and transcendental. That is the reason why I dare to offer this book to your distinguished attention.

PART I

The Constitutional Signification of Meaning: Between Rational Entrenchment, Signification Potential and Constitutional Imagination

1

Constitutional Semiotics as a System of Theories and Meta-theories

This book contains and proposes theories and meta-theories. It is structured on the basis of theories for explaining the imaginary, legal and socio-legal discourses of constitutionalism through the prism of semiotics.[1] Simultaneously, it offers meta-theories for exploring the constitutional theories. Examples include the theories of constitutional geometry, quantum constitutionalism, cloud constitutionalism, constitutional texture and the discursive character of constitutionalism as a range of narratives with normative-institutional but also symbolic-imaginary, emotional, visual and performative dimensions, which are at the same time meta-theories of constitutionalism. They are meta-theories because they contain novel methodological and conceptual approaches to the constitution, constitutionalism and constitutional law. They help us to develop new methods for understanding and organising the theory of the constitution, constitutionalism and constitutional law. Hence, meta-theories have epistemic and pragmatic functions.

It seems fair to provide a brief clarification of what is meant by 'theory' and 'meta-theory', how they relate to each other, how we should differentiate between them and in what sense they are mutually supportive and reinforcing concepts. It is even proper to ask the following question: do we need a separate strand of meta-theories in order to explain constitutional semiotics, its main elements and key problems? Here I am not going to explore and problematically assess the broader concepts of theory and meta-theory used in science in general. This is not necessary because it will divert my explanation from the main topic of this book, which is to offer a theory (including a meta-theory) of constitutional semiotics, and will also be impossible due to space constraints. Moreover, a lot of scientific research has been carried out on the topic of meta-theory in different scientific fields.[2]

[1] On the peculiarities of the legal discourse in comparison to other discourses from a semiotic perspective, see E Menezes de Carvalho, *Semiotics of International Law: Trade and Translation* (Dordrecht, Springer, 2011) 23–37. On the different levels of the discourse, see J Broekman and L Cata Backer, *Lawyers Making Meaning: The Semiotics of Law in Legal Education II* (Dordrecht, Springer, 2013) 95.

[2] See, eg, S Hamilton, 'A Genealogy of Metatheory in IR: How "Ontology" Emerged from the Inter-paradigm Debate' (2017) 9(1) *International Theory* 136, doi:10.1017/S1752971916000257; M Bates, 'An Introduction to Metatheories, Theories, and Models' in KE Fisher, S Erdelez and L McKechnie (eds), *Theories of Information Behavior* (Medford, NJ, Information Today, 2005) 1–431; G Ritzer, Metatheory, *The Blackwell Encyclopedia of Sociology* (Oxford, Blackwell, 2006) 1–24;

That is why I will briefly explain the concepts of constitutional theory and constitutional meta-theory and the relationship between them in constitutional law, focusing exclusively on constitutional semiotics. This means that I will define these concepts and give a short overview of the constitutional theories and meta-theories which I develop in this book.

Naturally, I will not provide an exclusive list of the theories and meta-theories that I am proposing; I will just provide an outline of the most important of them – those which are complex, play a key role in the understanding of constitutional semiotics or demonstrate my particular approach to constitutionalism and constitutional law from a semiotic perspective. This is necessary because, as seen above, there is no singular, consolidated, established or systematised and structured approach to constitutional semiotics. There is no theoretical consensus as to what constitutes the semiotic approach to constitutionalism, what are the main features and elements of constitutional semiotics, and what are the typical theories (or eventually meta-theories) of which it is composed.

Moreover, the question of whether constitutional semiotics itself is a theory, a meta-theory or a combination of the two is also largely neglected. To be more precise, it falls outside of the scope of the non-structured discourse on legal semiotics in general and constitutional semiotics in particular. Hence, after a brief reflection on the concept of constitutional theories and meta-theories, I shall focus on constitutional semiotics and the theories and meta-theories which express my approach to it.

It should be emphasised that I am launching a rather non-traditional approach to constitutional semiotics. This is due to the fact that I am not focusing exclusively on the traditional semiotic issues concerning the representation and signification of meaning and based on the 'holly semiotic Trinity' of signified, signifier and signification. I do use this fundamental semiotic scheme and some of the key semiotic concepts on various occasions, and I devote a special section of the book to it.[3] However, the book offers a much broader account on symbolisation and signification of meaning in the different 'plains of representation' – the constitutional text and texture, the realms of the imaginary, the ideal and the real, the theoretical narratives based on conceptual imaginaries,[4] and the socio-legal plain with its visual,[5] performative and emotional aspects.

Constitutional theory is usually conceived as a system of intellectual reflections focused on constitutionally relevant issues, explained through coherent narrative

M Neufeld, 'Who's Afraid of Meta-theory?' (1994) 23(2) *Millennium* 387, doi:10.1177/03058298940230020401; B Paterson, L Thorne, C Canam and C Jillings, 'Meta-theory' in *Meta-Study of Qualitative Health Research* (New York, SAGE Publications, 2001) 91–108.

[3] See pt I, ch 5 of this book.

[4] See Z Oklopcic, *Beyond the People: Social Imaginary and Constituent Imagination* (Oxford, Oxford University Press, 2018) 1–37.

[5] See R Sherwin, *Visualizing Law in the Age of the Digital Baroque. Arabesques and Entanglements* (New York, Routledge, 2011) 13–56.

and resulting in a form of constitutionally relevant text and texture. Constitutional theory may vary in terms of its scope and object depending on how one defines the range of issues related to constitutionalism. In that regard, constitutional theory may be focused on the normative or institutional dimension exploring positive constitutional law. If constitutionalism is perceived in a broader meaning going beyond positive law – as it is understood by many scholars – then constitutional theory may also include the assessment of facts and empirical data, of behaviour and human performance (socio-legal constitutional theory) or of the behaviour and acts of a specific category of constitutional actor and narrators such as the courts (legal realist constitutional theory), or also may include the theoretical assessment of ideas, imaginaries and ideals, most of which may themselves be part of theories (the philosophical approach).[6]

To sum up, constitutional theory consists in critical and systematic intellectual reflection on constitutionally relevant phenomena. These may belong to the normative reality of positive law. However, they may also be part of the socio-political reality of empirical facts, acts, behaviour and patterns of behaviour with constitutional relevance, of the hybrid reality of authoritative legal and constitutional discourses allocated on the border of the cross-cutting between norms and fact (eg, the judicial decisions of the apex courts)[7] or of the field of ideas, concepts, imaginaries, myths, dreams and other forms of the constitutional imagination.[8]

The last approach – the constitutional philosophy strand focusing on constitutional imaginaries,[9] constitutional imagination and theorising about theories – is of special concern here because it includes or may include both theories and meta-theories. Here it should be clarified that constitutional meta-theory can be briefly defined as theory about theory. It consists in theorising about concepts, issues and phenomena which typically have projections in normative, institutional or socio-legal reality, but with special regard to their implications in constitutional theory. Thus, constitutional meta-theory also explores and explains facts, norms and institutions, both directly and indirectly. It engages with pre-theoretical issues and with deeds, acts, behaviour and their legal institutionalisation and modelling.

[6] On the approaches to legal knowledge, see D Valchev, *General Theory of Law*, vol 1 (Sofia, Ciela, 2016) 35–45 (in Bulgarian).

[7] On the concept of the apex court, see S Schlegel, 'Activism as Defence: The Role of Courts in Shaping the Relationship between Constitutions and International Law. A Comparison of the Apex Courts of Switzerland, Germany, and Austria' in M Belov (ed), *Courts and Judicial Activism under Crisis Conditions: Policy Making in a Time of Illiberalism and Emergency Constitutionalism* (Abingdon, Routledge, 2022) 43–61.

[8] On the concept of constitutional imagination, see M Loughlin, 'The Constitutional Imagination' (2015) 78(1) *Modern Law Review* 1; and O Angeli, 'Global Constitutionalism and Constitutional Imagination' (2017) 6(3) *Global Constitutionalism* 359.

[9] Some of the most important theoretical approaches to constitutional imaginaries are offered by Přibáň and Komárek. See J Přibáň, *Constitutional Imaginaries: A Theory of European Societal Constitutionalism* (Abingdon, Routledge, 2020) 1–251; and J Komárek, 'Political Economy in the European Constitutional Imaginary: Moving beyond Fiesole', *Verfassungsblog*, 4 September 2020, https://verfassungsblog.de/political-economy-in-the-european-constitutional-imaginary-moving-beyond-fiesole.

However, the constitutional meta-theory explores 'raw material' (eg, facts and norms), mainly through the ways in which they have already been reflected in constitutional theory.[10]

In that regard, constitutional meta-theory is also linked to constitutional methodology. Usually constitutional meta-theory is a theory about the methods and methodology that are or should be used in constitutional theory. Thus, constitutional meta-theory is both theory about theory and theory about theories' methodology. It is a conceptual paradigm that frames or, conversely, traces the patterns of constitutional theory. Constitutional meta-theory orders, structures and systematises constitutional theory, and offers conceptual insights relating to the scientific organisation and application of the theoretical methodology.

Several paradigms may seem to stand on the border between theory and meta-theory, thus possibly qualifying both of them. These are semiotics, epistemology, anthropology and ontology. This applies for both their general versions and for their particular manifestations in the fields of law or particularly in constitutional law. Again, I will concentrate on the application of these analytical paradigms in the field of constitutionalism and constitutional law.

Constitutional semiotics, constitutional epistemology and constitutional anthropology possess some of the features of constitutional meta-theory. This is due to the fact that they include in the range of their research targets the theoretical approaches to signs, symbols and other forms of representation of meaning in constitutionalism and constitutional law (constitutional semiotics), the origins and patterns of knowledge and meaning in constitutionalism and constitutional law (constitutional epistemology), and the ways in which constitutionalism and constitutional law are understood, perceived, practised and performed by the members of the constitutional community in a durable way, through inheritance of behavioural patterns and their entrenchment in constitutional culture and collective constitutional consciousness (constitutional anthropology).

Moreover, it is a common feature of constitutional semiotics, constitutional epistemology and constitutional anthropology that they have a strong methodological predisposition and bias. They all suggest different methodological approaches to explaining constitution, constitutional law and constitutionalism. In that regard, they lean towards meta-theoretical methodologies of constitutional law.

Nevertheless, these three analytical scientific paradigms are also theories. This is due to the fact that their aim is not limited to explaining and offering methodological insights and knowledge for the improvement of constitutional theory. Constitutional semiotics, constitutional epistemology and constitutional

[10] According to Přibáň, 'legal theory and internal imaginative and fictional constructions of the system of positive law are subsequently challenged by philosophy of imagination, theories of emotions and rhetoric to disclose elements and contexts typically hidden and covered by legal texts'. See Přibáň (n 9) 17.

anthropology have much more broader range of tasks. They are conceptual approaches that explore the reflection of constitutionalism and constitutional law in the spheres of the imaginary, the symbolic and the ideal. But they also analyse the legal and socio-legal manifestations of constitutional institutions and other constitutionally relevant phenomena. Moreover, they strive at explaining the performative, visual and textual dimensions of constitutionalism. Hence, constitutional semiotics, constitutional epistemology and constitutional anthropology have projections and address issues which relate not only to the theoretical but also to the legal and socio-legal aspects of constitutionalism.

This means that constitutional semiotics, constitutional epistemology and constitutional anthropology are broader analytical paradigms. They contain both theories and meta-theories. They have important methodological implications and offer insightful views on constitutional theory, which qualify them as meta-theories. Simultaneously, they explain and explore the different dimensions of constitutional law, and thus also have a direct approach to it that is not mediated by constitutional theories.

Hence, constitutional semiotics, constitutional epistemology and constitutional anthropology are also theories. They are theories that explain the different dimensions and projections of the constitution and constitutional law in the various constitutional discourses (ideal, symbolic-imaginary, visual, emotional, empirical, normative, institutional etc).

To sum up, constitutional semiotics, constitutional epistemology and constitutional anthropology are mixed phenomena. They possess the characteristics of both meta-theories and theories. This is due to the fact that they are bulky paradigms that actually include a range of theories, some of which gain the status of theories about theories or, in other words, of meta-theories. That is why in the remainder of this chapter I will focus on constitutional semiotics. I will briefly define it and will provide an outline of the main theories and meta-theories which are framed by it and included in it.

This book explores constitutional semiotics both as constitutional theory and constitutional meta-theory. Constitutional semiotics is analysed both as a holistic concept based on an overall logic, a unified methodological approach and a common viewpoint on the constitution, constitutionalism and constitutional law, and as a composite phenomenon and a bulky paradigm.

However, the analysis focuses more on the theoretical than on the meta-theoretical approach. This is due to the fact that this book offers theoretical insights on how to understand the constitution as a container of ideals, symbols[11] and other forms of semiotic representation of meaning rooted in text and texture, in visuality and performance and in forms of structured imaginaries and shared imagination, thus forming imaginary, visual, performative and emotional aspects

[11] On the constitution as a symbol and the general symbolic function of the constitution, see M Lerner, 'Constitution and Court as Symbols' (1937) 46(8) *Yale Law Journal* 1290.

of constitutionalism.[12] Hence, this volume contains the basics of a theory of constitutional semiotics aiming to explain how to grasp and theoretically assess and conceptualise the constitutional imaginaries and all other instruments for the signification and representation of constitutionally relevant meaning.[13]

Hence, this book should be understood as an attempt at providing a relatively coherent theory with elements of meta-theory. It proposes a general theory of constitutional semiotics while at the same time exploring it in a discursive way. In that regard, it contains a range of theories and some meta-theories which can be outlined and systematised in the following way.

The meta-theoretical parts of the book are largely dispersed throughout this volume. In other words it is spread in many parts of the research and is integrated into my theory of constitutional semiotics. Theories and meta-theories are presented as elements of an overall theory of constitutional semiotics. The meta-theoretical discussion in the book is more visible and to an extent autonomous from the theoretical discussion with regard to constitutional geometry. This is so because constitutional geometry is presented in Part V of the book as an analytical and ordering paradigm for both constitutional theory and constitutionalism (the latter also including the constitution and constitutional law).

Hence, constitutional geometry is theory and meta-theory. It is a theory explaining the existence and application of the semiotic shapes and forms in their capacity as ordering schemes used by the constitution to represent meaning in a formalised way via geometric metaphors. It is also a theory analysing and presenting the way in which these semiotic devices are addressed and reflected by constitutional theory. In the latter case, constitutional geometry turns out to be a meta-theory – a theory about the theoretical reproduction of semiotic meaning.

However, most parts of this book contain the outline of a range of theories that contribute to the construction of a general theory of constitutional semiotics. The most important of these are the theories of textual, symbolic-imaginary and visual constitutionalism. The theory of rational constitutionalism is briefly outlined. The idea is to demonstrate the need to focus on 'shadow constitutionalisms', namely constitutional discourses which have been overshadowed by the rationalist tradition in constitutional law. In contrast to textual, symbolic-imaginary and visual constitutionalism, which are themselves objects of theories developed in this book as parts of the general theory of constitutional semiotics, emotional and performative constitutionalism are merely briefly mentioned and outlined. The reason for

[12] In fact, we are witnessing an emotional turn in legal studies in general and in constitutional studies in particular. There is a clear trend for exploring the role of emotions in law. See K Abrams and H Keren, 'Who's Afraid of Law and the Emotions?' (2010) 94(6) *Minnesota Law Review* 1997, available at: https://ssrn.com/abstract=2434251; A Sajo, 'Emotions in Constitutional Institutions' (2016) 8(1) *Emotion Review* 44; A Sajo, 'Emotions in Constitutional Design' (2010) 8(3) *ICON* 354; S Bandes, J Madeira, K Temple and E Kidd White (eds) *Research Handbook on Law and Emotion* (Cheltenham, Edward Elgar, 2021) 1–640; and A Amaya and M Del Mar (eds), *Virtue, Emotion and Imagination in Law and Legal Reasoning* (Oxford, Hart Publishing, 2020) 1–275.

[13] For an insightful analysis of constitutional imaginaries, see Přibáň (n 9) 1–251; and Komárek (n 9).

this is due to space constraints. My plan is to offer a more extensive theoretical research of these phenomena at a later stage. I also propose a theory of quantum constitutionalism[14] and cloud constitutionalism[15] as part of my general theory of constitutional semiotics.

It should be taken into account that while the theory of constitutional semiotics I offer is grounded in the theories of rational, textual, symbolic-imaginary and visual constitutionalism, these theories themselves include a range of other more concrete composite theories. Thus, the book is structured on the basis of the concept of a 'theory within theory' where more concrete theories further develop the general theory of constitutional semiotics, despite having also an autonomous status. This means that the theories of rational, textual, symbolic-imaginary and visual constitutionalism contribute to the clarification of the overall constitutional semiotic paradigm, but are sufficiently coherent and autonomously structured theories themselves, which can also be the object of independent research.

This conclusion is also valid for the range of further theoretical concepts that are constructive elements and thus form part of the theories of rational, textual, symbolic-imaginary and visual constitutionalism. With regard to the theory of textual constitutionalism, these are the theory of constitutional texture, the theory of authoritative speakers of the community, the theory of the constitution as a system of interrelated but also partially independent narratives, and the theory of constitutional semiotic community. The theory of symbolic-imaginary and visual constitutionalism is also structured on the basis of several key theories: the theory of constitutional codes and of constitutionalism as 'game of codes', the theory of constitutional memories,[16] the theory of constitutional myths and mythologies, the theory of normative ideologies and ideas, the theory of constitutional imagination,[17] the theory of constitutional imaginaries in general and structured constitutional imaginaries in particular, and the theory of constitutional semiotic landscapes. It has already been mentioned that constitutional geometry is both a theory and a meta-theory.

This book is not a simple, direct and mechanical application of semiotic concepts, theories and paradigms in the sphere of constitutional law and theory. That is why the research is not organised in a precisely semiotic manner. In other words, I am not following the logic of exploring the signification and representation of meaning through the classical semiotic organisation scheme of semiosis structured on signification of the signified via signifiers. Hence, the structure is not typically semiotic. The analysis I propose here does not begin with a definition of constitutional semiotics, before subsequently explaining the range of elements of

[14] See pt I, ch 2 of this book.
[15] See pt V, ch 7 of this book.
[16] See M Belov, 'Constitutional Memories: How Do Constitutions Cope with Constitutional Past' in M Belov and A Abat i Ninet (eds) *Revolution, Transition, Memory, and Oblivion: Reflections on Constitutional Change* (Cheltenham, Edward Elgar, 2020) 107–26.
[17] On the concept of constitutional imagination see Loughlin (n 8).

the constitutional semiosis: the constitutional signifieds, the constitutional signifiers and the process of constitutional signification.

Instead, the semiotic paradigm is used throughout the whole book as a strategic analytical paradigm allowing for a novel conceptualisation and reconceptualisation of the constitution, constitutionalism and constitutional law. This approach makes it possible to highlight phenomena related to representation and signification of meaning that is implied in the constitutional text and texture by virtue of semiotic devices such as codes, myths, taboos, symbols and geometric forms. The semiotic approach is combined with concepts and methods that are also borrowed from epistemology, anthropology, critical linguistic studies etc. Still, the semiotic approach prevails, which enables the overall definition of the intellectual experiment offered in this book as part of constitutional semiotics.

2

Quantum Constitutionalism as a Trigger of Paradigmatic Turn and the Role of Constitutional Semiotics for its Proper Understanding

Quantum constitutionalism is a novel and original paradigm of constitutional epistemology which also has particular relevance for constitutional semiotics. It is an epistemic paradigm because it aims at explaining specific features of constitutionalism that are largely under-researched in constitutional theory and overshadowed by the traditional structural, institutional and positivist approaches to constitutional law. These features are the mutability and variability of constitutional law, the emancipation of the constitutional practice and constitutional imagination from the initial will of the constitutional legislator imprinted and stuck in the constitutional text, and the potential existence of a range of possible variants for the unfolding of 'law in books' in 'law in action', and in 'law in the collective imagination' or, more precisely, 'law as collective imagination'.

It should be noted that quantum constitutionalism is not constructed for or aiming to be a device of constitutional transitology.[1] In other words, its main focus is not on the constitutional transitions.[2] It does not strive to explain the transition from totalitarianism and authoritarianism to democracy or, conversely, the 'democratic backsliding' or constitutional mimicries and permutations such as 'tendential constitutionalism'[3] that aim at hiding the mimicry of authoritarian or oligarchic elites beneath a democratic façade. Such transitions may be explained within

[1] Constitutional transitology is a branch of constitutional theory (including comparative constitutional theory) which explores the transitions between different regimes. It traditionally focusses on transitions from authoritarian and totalitarian regimes to democracy. See, eg, P Schmitter and T Karl, 'The Conceptual Travels of Transitologists and Consolidologists: How Far to the East Should They Attempt to Go?' (1994) 53(1) *Slavic Review* 173; and M-M Mohamedou and T Sisk (eds), *Democratisation in the 21st Century: Reviving Transitology* (Abingdon, Routledge, 2016) 1–236.

[2] For constitutional transitions, see Z Elkins, 'Constitutional Transition' in R Congleton, B Grofman, and S Voigt (eds), *The Oxford Handbook of Public Choice*, vol 2 (Oxford, Oxford University Press, 2019); and J Colón-Ríos, 'What is a Constitutional Transition', *Victoria University of Wellington Legal Research Papers*, No. 98 (2018).

[3] See M Gutan, 'Romanian Tendential Constitutionalism and the Limits of European Constitutional Culture' in M Belov (ed), *Global Constitutionalism and its Challenges to Westphalian Constitutional Law* (Oxford, Hart Publishing, 2018) 103–33.

quantum constitutionalism as an overarching analytical paradigm, but quantum constitutionalism is not limited to them or focused on transitology. Rather, it is a phenomenon that symbolises and signifies the very idea of permanent constitutional change, transition and shifts in constitutional shapes and meaning due to two main determinants: constitutional context[4] and constitutional imaginaries. Hence, quantum constitutionalism designates the inevitable fuzziness and variableness of constitution, constitutionalism and constitutional law going beyond distinctions of political regimes, constitutional forms of governance and concrete historical periods.

Quantum constitutionalism is a conceptual and methodological approach that looks at constitutional law through the prism of epistemic indeterminacy of legal text, texture and meaning.[5] It is much more of a socio-legal than a legal realist approach. This is due to the fact that it is not limited to textual constitutionalism and the open texture of the constitution and constitutional law. Moreover, it is not focused only or even mainly on the role of courts as both transmitters and producers of legal meaning.

In that regard, quantum constitutionalism is an overarching paradigm that stresses the conceptual mutability of constitutional law, the intrinsic, inevitable and even necessary mismatch between the initial (structural) constitutional model and its subsequent projections in social and political life, and in the constitutional anthropology and constitutional imagination of the constitutionally framed socio-political community. It exposes the reversed proportional relationship between 'constitutional energy' (the potential that the constitution possesses in principle at the moment of its adoption) and the 'constitutional matter and substance' (the imprints of the initial normative model on the constitutional practice with its emotional, performative, visual and imaginary areas). Naturally, the mutability of constitutionalism that is symbolised and grasped by quantum constitutionalism also includes the fuzziness and the potential for the semantic evolution of textual constitutionalism and the constitutional text and texture. The projections of textual constitutionalism in the field of collective imaginaries explored, shaped and influenced by symbolic-imaginary constitutionalism also necessitate the engagement of quantum constitutionalism with the forms of visual and performative representation of the constitution as text in the fields of visual and performative constitutionalism. Thus, quantum constitutionalism becomes a tool of constitutional semiotics.

Hence, quantum constitutionalism goes beyond constitutional epistemology and looks at the signification tools that construct the fine-tuning and internal communication between rational, textual, symbolic-imaginary, visual and performative constitutionalism. These are the instruments by virtue of which the constitutional system communicates and signifies the constitutional change,

[4] See D Law, *Constitutionalism in Context* (Cambridge, Cambridge University Press, 2021).

[5] For the interplay between the relative indeterminacy of meaning and the overdetermination of symbols, see C Castoriadis, *The Imaginary Institution of Society* (Cambridge, Polity Press, 1987) 138.

ascribes and describes the evolving constitutional and constitutionally relevant meaning, and tries to grasp, last but not least in a symbolic-imaginary way, the constant epistemic permutations of the constitution and the constitutional order.

In that regard, quantum constitutionalism performs the role of a meta-theory of constitutionalism and constitutional law. It is a meta-theory with an epistemological core and semiotic functions and teleology. It is especially important in the context of legal post-modernity and post-modern constitutionalism. This is due to the fact that post-modern constitutionalism is prone to deconstruction and multi-discursive analysis, and is based on a sceptical and critical attitude towards the beliefs of full objectivity and eternal truths in law and its socio-legal projections.

Although the quantum aspects of the constitution and constitutional law have always existed notwithstanding the era in which they have been functioning, quantum constitutionalism is more understandable and feasible in the socio-legal and intellectual context of the post-modern age. There are several reasons for this. The most important of them are the prominence of quantum physics and the possibility to use it as a source of constructive analogies, the achievements of critical legal studies at the end of the twentieth and the beginning of the twenty-first centuries, and the increasing readiness of constitutional theory to admit the open texture[6] of constitutional law, the high degree of indeterminacy of constitutional concepts and institutions, and the overall dependency of the constitution on constitutional practice and constitutional imagination.

Mutability and variability of the constitution and the constitutional law are eminent and intrinsically built into the nature of constitutionalism. They are produced by factors both within and beyond positive law. Thus, they expand beyond the restraints of the legal order in the sphere of constitutional politics,[7] but also in the field of the collective constitutional imaginaries. At first glance, this finding goes against one of the main claims of modern constitutional law that is entrenched in rational constitutionalism. Constitutional modernity aims to establish a rational, stable and systematic constitutional order[8] based on predictability and durability. However, this contradiction between quantum constitutionalism and modern rational constitutionalism is rather superficial. Instead, it is rational to assume that constitutional law changes and should change with the shifts and changes in the socio-legal context. Again, it is rational to suppose that the shared beliefs and the structural imaginaries of the people form the shapes of the constitutional order on a daily basis in the same way as the waves slowly break down the rocks in the sea.

[6] On the open texture of law, see HLA Hart, *The Concept of Law* (Oxford, Oxford University Press, 1997) 124–36.

[7] See B Ackerman, 'Constitutional Politics/Constitutional (1999) 99(3) *The Yale Law Journal* 453 et seq.

[8] See D Lee, *Popular Sovereignty in Early Modern Constitutional Thought* (Oxford, Oxford University Press, 2016) 16. Castoriadis even believes that 'the modern world is in the throes of a systematic delirium'; see Castoriadis (n 5) 156.

Hence, quantum constitutionalism is grounded in the rational suggestion that in the ocean of life, it is the sea of collective imaginaries that has a great formative impact on the sea of meaning resulting from the constitution, constitutional law and the constitutional order. Thus, quantum constitutionalism is a theory and a meta-theory of constitutional law that has huge importance for constitutional semiotics. This is due to the fact that it indicates the role of the socio-legal, conceptual, epistemic and functional mutability and changeability of constitutional law for generating constitutional meaning and for signifying constitutional phenomena and processes in an evolutionary and dynamic way. The mismatch between 'constitutional energy' (the intrinsic potential of constitutional institutions) and 'constitutional matter' (the realisation of this potential in the legal and socio-legal relations) generates a range of imaginaries and triggers powerful processes of semiotic signification of constitutional and constitutionally relevant meaning.

The mismatch between 'law in books', 'law in action' and 'law as imagination' or 'law in imagination'[9] require instruments that bind these three discourses and bridge the gaps between them through the representation of meaning and the signification of phenomena which have common importance for all of them, expressed in different ways through text, images,[10] performance etc. Thus, the mutability and variability of the constitution and constitutional law, and the in-built mismatch between constitution-as-potentiality, constitution-as-practice, constitution-as-imagination and constitution-as-emotion[11] defined here through the epistemic lenses of quantum constitutionalism necessitates the use of semiotic methods and a semiotic toolkit. Hence, quantum constitutionalism is a phenomenon found in both constitutional epistemology and constitutional semiotics.

The internal reasons or factors for the mutability and variability of the constitution and constitutional law consist in the openness of the constitutional texture, the indeterminacy of constitutional values, the principles and some of the constitutional norms with a principal character (eg, those relating to human rights).[12] Hence, textual constitutionalism is implicitly entrenched in the indeterminacy and openness of meaning, and the discursive means of its production, reproduction and signification.[13] Another reason is the huge normative potential of the activist interpretation by the courts (especially the constitutional courts) in terms of their ability to expand the meaning initially entrenched in textual constitutionalism. Hence, textual constitutionalism itself is a phenomenon that facilitates the

[9] On the diverse and complex relationship between law and imagination, see R Mullender, M Nicolini, T Bennett and E Mickiewicz (eds), *Law and Imagination in Troubled Times: A Legal and Literary Discourse*, (Abingdon, Routledge, 2020) 1–282.

[10] See C Spiesel, R Sherwin and N Feigenson, 'Law in the Age of Images: The Challenge of Visual Literacy' in A Wagner, T Summerfield and F Benavides Vanegas (eds), *Contemporary Issues of Semiotics of Law* (Oxford, Hart Publishing, 2005) 231–57.

[11] On the relationship between emotions and imagination in law, see A Amaya and M Del Mar (eds), *Virtue, Emotion and Imagination in Law and Legal Reasoning* (Oxford, Hart Publishing, 2020) 1–275.

[12] See R Alexy, *Theorie der Grundrechte* (Frankfurt am Main, Suhrkamp, 1994) 117 et seq.

[13] On the interplay between relative indeterminacy of meaning and the overdetermination of symbols, see Castoriadis (n 5) 138.

development of quantum constitutionalism. Textual constitutionalism, despite the suggestion of stability of meaning imported by modern rational constitutionalism, is among the main producers of conceptual indeterminacy, which is a key determinant of quantum constitutionalism. The indeterminacy of constitutional texture both triggers a range of authoritative and non-authoritative narratives,[14] and results from these.[15]

Thus, the signification of constitutional and constitutionally relevant meaning requires dynamic semiosis, resulting in quantum constitutional semiotics. This is a form of constitutional semiotics which is preconditioned upon and takes into account the dynamic, discursive and indeterminate nature of the process of signification of constitutional and constitutionally relevant meaning. 'Quantum constitutional semiotics' corresponds to the infinite character of the process of constitutional narration, performance, visualisation and imagination. It indicates the infinity and openness of constitutional semiosis.

The external factors that influence the variability and mutability of constitutional meaning mainly relate to the shifts in the socio-legal context and variations in the way in which constitutional law is perceived, imagined, constructed, deconstructed, reconstructed and signified in collective constitutional imaginaries. These imaginaries may be part of constitutional anthropology (thus having an ideal dimension, being part of the realm of ideas), but may also have projections in the physical world through visual arts,[16] the performing arts,[17] architecture, performance and behavioural attitudes. Thus, they are part of symbolic-imaginary, visual and performative constitutionalism.[18]

The relevance of quantum constitutionalism for constitutional semiotics is predetermined by its dependence on symbolic-imaginary, visual, emotional and performative constitutionalism. Another reason is its inevitable initial entrenchment in constitutional text that may subsequently also spread to constitutional texture. In other words, the variability of meaning is closely related to and also dependent on the instruments for signification of these epistemic variations and mutations. Actually they are a core object of the semiotic approach to constitutional change and instruments for conceptualising the predictability of shifts in the constitutional representation of meaning. Thus, they are an analytical target of constitutional semiotics.

[14] On the narratives provided in the course of the application of law by the judiciary, see S Stern, 'Narrative in the Legal Text: Judicial Opinions and Their Narratives' in M Hanne and R Weisberg (eds), *Narrative and Metaphor in the Law* (Cambridge, Cambridge University Press, 2018).

[15] See also D Cornell, 'The Problem of Normative Authority in Legal Interpretation' in R Kevelson (ed), *Law and Semiotics*, vol 1 (New York Plenum Press, 1987) 149–59.

[16] On the role of films in the representation of legal ideas, see J Denvir (ed), *Legal Reelism: Movies as Legal Texts* (Chicago, University of Illinois Press, 1996) 1–336.

[17] On the performative nature of law, see L McDonagh, *Performing Copyright: Law, Theatre and Authorship* (Oxford, Hart Publishing, 2021) 1–256.

[18] On constitutionalism as performance, see O Tans, 'Imagined Constitutionality: Rethinking Democratic Citizenship with the Aid of Fiction Theory' (2019) 15(2) *Law, Culture and the Humanities* 382.

Hence, the shifting and drifting of constitutional meaning relating to institutions, rights and especially constitutional principles, aims and values are triggered by a multitude of factors. These stem from the context in which the institutional system of the valid law and particularly the constitution are necessarily embedded. They can be properly explored only if the symbolic-imaginary, emotional, visual and performative discourses of constitutionalism are taken into account. Thus, constitutional epistemology should broaden its scope. It has to go beyond normative-institutional and textual constitutionalism in terms of their predominantly rationalist outlook and explore other constitutional dimensions and discourses through the prism of the semiotic signification of meaning. Such a combined epistemic-semiotic approach can be offered by quantum constitutionalism as a novel paradigm for constitutional conceptualisation and research. Again, this is a paradigm that has a mixed (epistemic and semiotic) character.

The determinants of the indeterminacy of the constitution, constitutionalism and constitutional law are the factors for the existence of quantum constitutionalism as an overall paradigm framing the phenomenon of inconclusiveness of the constitution and constitutional law and its openness to constitutional change. It has already been explained above that these have divergent natures and origins. Some of them have a socio-legal character. These are the social and political constellations of interests, values, preferences and strategic and tactical goals of the constitutional players on the ground. A special role here is played by political and constitutional anthropology, the range and character of constitutional imaginaries, the predominating normative ideas and ideologies, constitutional myths and mythologies, and the ways in which constitutional content is communicated between stakeholders and within the community of people.

Hence, the elements and forms of symbolic-imaginary, emotional and – to a lesser extent – visual and performative constitutionalism are the most important socio-legal and socio-psychological triggers of the indeterminacy of constitutional law. Thus, they are among the main determinants of quantum constitutionalism.

There are also several important legal reasons for the existence of quantum constitutionalism. Most of these relate to textual constitutionalism and to a lesser extent appertain to and stem from rational and normative-institutional constitutionalism. The open character of the constitutional jurisprudence of the apex courts[19] (the constitutional and supreme courts that have competence to interpret the constitution) in conjunction with their judicial activism[20] are the main factors for the sustaining of quantum constitutionalism that stems from textual constitutionalism. The activist interpretation of constitutional provisions by the constitutional jurisdictions causes the constitutional model to evolve and produces

[19] S Schlegel, 'Activism as Defence: The Role of Courts in Shaping the Relationship between Constitutions and International Law. A Comparison of the Apex Courts of Switzerland, Germany, and Austria' in M Belov (ed), *Courts and Judicial Activism under Crisis Conditions: Policy Making in a Time of Illiberalism and Emergency Constitutionalism* (Abingdon, Routledge, 2021) 43–61.

[20] On the phenomenon and concept of judicial activism, see S Grover, *Judicial Activism and the Democratic Rule of Law: Selected Case Studies* (Dordrecht, Springer, 2020) 1–288.

the so-called 'virtual amendment of the constitution'. Moreover, textual constitutionalism – the textual entrenchment of the constitution and constitutional law – allows for different narrators whose interpretation of the constitutional provisions has legal or intellectual normativity to perform as authoritative speakers of the community.

Thus, quantum constitutionalism results from the conceptual fact of the existence of multidiscursive constitutional narratives produced by a range of authoritative narrators – the authoritative speakers of the constitutionally framed socio-legal community. Some of them (eg, the apex courts, the courts and the Parliament) produce valid law that is binding to the addressees of the constitutional order, while others (eg, constitutional theorists) create narratives and interpretations which may possess factual normativity and psychological binding force that are dependent on their capacity to convince.

In any case, the constitutional narratives shaped by the authoritative speakers of the community produce important signifiers of constitutional meaning of signifieds allocated in factual, normative or intellectual reality. In that regard, the creation of quantum constitutionalism by the authoritative speakers and narrators results in a process of constitutional semiosis. This makes quantum constitutionalism not necessarily a semiotic phenomenon per se, but a phenomenon that is connected to constitutional semiotics and possesses semiotic importance.

Important legal factors for the production of quantum constitutionalism are also the state institutions that can create sources of constitutional law. Parliaments, governments and ministers shape and further develop the constitutional model so extensively that in the moment of the adoption of the constitutional text, it is usually rather difficult to predict in advance what its real content and character will be. This degree of normative dependence of the initial constitutional model from its subsequent further development and 'filling with content' is based on the overall phenomenon of constitutional indeterminacy and openness. This leads to a 'virtual amendment of the constitution' by the constitutional courts and its 'normative filling' by the parliament and the government. Moreover, this allows for the 'epistemic and semiotic discovery and intellectual adjustment' of the constitution by the authoritative speakers and by the constitutional community. This results in the psychological adaptation of the normative-institutional design to the political and constitutional anthropology and to the Zeitgeist.

An important part of this accommodation is the approximation of the 'raw' model of the valid constitution and constitutional law to the collective psychology and semiotic predispositions of the constitutionally framed socio-political community. It is actually an adjustment of the concepts, structures, shapes and bearers of meaning of rational and normative-institutional to symbolic-imaginary and emotional constitutionalism through the means and instruments of textual, visual and performative constitutionalism. In other words, the initial model of a valid constitution and constitutional law is internalised as part of the social psychology and anthropology of the community via the interpretation of the constitutional text and texture and through its performance, demonstration and visualisation. Ultimately, this is not only an epistemic but also a semiotic exercise. The reason is that the intellectual approximation between the constitutional model and the constitutional anthropology is based to a significant extent not only on rational acts of epistemic cognition, but also on symbolic acts of semiotic signification and representation of meaning.[21] Hence, quantum constitutionalism is partially the result of constitutional semiotics in action.

Quantum constitutionalism is a paradigm that is based on a metaphorical comparison with quantum physics. It rests upon the understanding that conceptually it is rarely possible and also difficult in practice to create a well-ordered, rational and theoretically compelling constitutional model which is at the same time fully adjusted to the requirements of the socio-political context, the constitutional and political anthropology and the constitutional imaginaries shared within the constitutionally framed community.

In order to be prescriptive and not purely descriptive, the constitution is necessarily partially detached from this context. If it is fully detached from it, then the constitution is purely fictitious. Conversely, if it is totally context-adequate and precisely describes the power relations at a certain point of history and in a particular jurisdiction, then it is purely descriptive. In such a case, it is incapable of serving as a reformist paradigm framed in legal terms and of providing models for social progress and political reform.

That is why constitutions are models which are partially detached from reality. They are imaginary constructions shaped through norms and institutions that are initially expressed via text and texture. More precisely, they are attached to certain parts of reality and pay attention to the most important elements of reality according to the discretionary view of the constitutional legislator. Thus, there is a certain degree of detachment and at the same time points of intersection and approximation between the constitution as a norm, the constitution as a fact, the constitution as an ideal and the constitution as a preserve or trigger of collective imaginaries of the constitutionally framed socio-political community.[22]

Together, these constitutional discourses produce a field of intellectual pressure and tension that creates degrees of uncertainty, fuzziness, unpredictability, openness and changeability. It is the creative tension between these constitutional dimensions – or, to put it in the terminology and conceptual apparatus of this book, between textual, normative-institutional, emotional, visual, performative and symbolic-imaginary constitutionalism – that produces two phenomena that look different, but are actually closely interrelated. These are the quantum characteristics of the constitution resulting in the mismatch between the initial structure and the subsequent functionality and projection in socio-legal reality, and the need for the signification of meaning. This need is triggered by the above-mentioned mismatch between the different plains for the unfolding, creation and representation of constitutional meaning.

[21] See Castoriadis (n 5) 115–65.
[22] E Black, *Our Constitution: The Myth That Binds Us* (Boulder, Westview Press, 1988).

In other words, the discrepancies, incongruities and asymmetries between the above-mentioned constitutional discourses create pressures for the production and signification of meaning. This pressure is genuinely epistemic, but also has rational-constructive and symbolic-imaginary aspects. It is exactly these symbolic-imaginary aspects that are the proper focus of constitutional semiotics. In any case, they create the need for a theoretical conceptualisation of the mismatch between the initial model of the constitution containing a range of potentialities, probabilities and capabilities, and the subsequent variations of its meaning, organisation, reorganisation, deconstruction, reconstruction and, last but not least, semiotic signification.

Hence, the very concept of quantum constitutionalism is a semiotic one that is based on a metaphoric revealing of meaning.[23] The generation of constitutional meaning in a dynamic way exposes the features of the constitution as a process and not as a stable container of eternal truths. The dynamic and changeable features of the constitution and the meaning that stems from them can remain hidden for rational and normative-institutional constitutionalism. Thus, they have to be traced, 'excavated' and also represented in a semiotic way by virtue of the means available to constitutional semiotics framed through the analytical paradigm of quantum constitutionalism.

The mainstream understanding is that constitutionalism is rational and predicable. Its meaning is supposed to be immediately understandable or at least accessible through recourse to reason and logic. The meaning is accessed as if it is static, stable, unchangeable and almost eternal. A large part of constitutional design – eg, eternal and entrenched clauses in constitutions, procedures for constitutional amendment (especially those of rigid constitutions), restrictions for constitutional interpretation and the organisation of the rule of law around constitutional supremacy – is conceptually grounded in this static, structural and originalist understanding of the constitution and constitutional law.[24] In fact, these are rational and logical safeguards against the excesses of quantum constitutionalism which are perceived as dangers to the stability, consistency and authority of the constitutional order. They provide stability to the constitution against political misuse and challenges from the constitutional players on the ground. Nevertheless, these institutional safeguards of static constitutionalism are not able to prevent the overall process of constitutional mutability and its tendency towards dynamic and thus quantum constitutionalism.

This originalist version of constitutional meaning is focused on the presumed predictability of the constitutional process and its ultimate predetermination by

[23] On the role of metaphors for political and indirectly for constitutional epistemology, see E Miller, 'Metaphor and Political Knowledge' (1979) 73 *American Political Science Review* 155.

[24] For more on constitutional originalism and the originalist approach to the constitution and constitutional law, see E Segall, *Originalism as Faith* (Cambridge, Cambridge University Press, 2018) 254; R Bennett, *Constitutional Originalism: A Debate* (Ithaca, Cornell University Press, 2011) 1–224; and I Wurman, *A Debt against the Living: An Introduction to Originalism* (Cambridge, Cambridge University Press, 2017) 1–172.

the constitutional legislator. The constitutional legislator perceived from that perspective is capable of fixing the constructive and constituent parts of the constitutional order. He or she is supposed to be able to channel the energy of the constitutional order and to predict its creative potential generated throughout the life of the constitution. Thus, the will of the constitutional legislator is presumed to be not only a framing factor of socio-political life, but also a key formant[25] of the collective symbolic-imaginary world of the community.

However, as this book will show, constitutionalism may or actually should also be understood in a different way. It has to be conceptualised as a cultural and not just as a normative phenomenon that is much fuzzier, obscure, context-dependent and, even more importantly, contingent on the collective constitutional imagination and the ways in which constitutional meaning is revealed, expressed, represented and signified than is usually thought to be the case. Constitutionalism is an evolving story told by a range of authoritative narrators, visualisers and performers who give shape to the initial energy of the constitutional design created by the constitutional legislator rather than the monolithic, static and originalist eternal project.

Thus, quantum constitutionalism denominates this conceptual certainty about the intrinsic and in-built uncertainty of constitutional law. Uncertainty stands behind the 'hidden project of constitutionalism' overshadowed by the 'overt and explicit project' of the constitution and constitutional law. The 'overt and explicit project' of the constitution and constitutional law is to create order out of disorder, to rationalise the socio-political world, exposing and framing socio-political relations in a coherent and logical project. The 'hidden project of constitutionalism' is to expose the energy of the constitution and constitutionalism and not only its matter, structure and formal characteristics, to facilitate constitutional law in action, to promote constitutional law as imagination and to encompass, conceptually frame and explore constitutional dynamics and the functional trajectories of the constitutional order. Constitutionalism is an imaginative enterprise that must engage with collective emotions, enchant the public, provide normative and structured imaginaries, and demonstrate them though a range of semiotic signifiers. Thus, a feasible, efficient and legitimate constitution has to promote its normative myths and mythologies, normative ideas and ideologies, constitutional codes and even constitutional utopias through visual and performative representations.

Such a multifaceted signification of constitutional imaginaries in a dynamic and proactive way can be understood properly mostly through the prism of constitutional semiotics and quantum constitutionalism. In this analytical binary couple, constitutional semiotics serves as an instrument for the exploration of the projections of constitutional phenomena in symbolic-imaginary, visual, performative and textual constitutionalism, while quantum constitutionalism defines the temporal and dynamic dimension of the constitutional unfolding and the temporal

[25] See R Sacco, *Einfuhrung in die Rechtsvergleichung* (Baden-Baden, Nomos, 2001) 59–79.

stretching of constitutional meaning. In other words, while constitutional semiotics encompasses the imaginary dimension of the constitution and the constitutional order, quantum constitutionalism grasps its temporal and dynamic dimension. It is exactly this tension between the rational, structural and logical approach of constitutional 'law in books' (and, more precisely, in the texture of valid law) and the imaginary, emotional, visual and performative potential of constitutional law as a variable and changeable category that produces both the need for a quantum constitutionalist approach and the justification of its semiotic bias.

Quantum constitutionalism is shifting the epistemic viewpoint of constitutional analysis. It is based on a system of ideas starting with the belief that the constitution is much more focal point of constitutional conversations expressed in a textual, visual and performative way and a melting pot of reason, emotions and imagination rather than a purely rational, systematic and eternally structured holistic project. Quantum constitutionalism introduces a combination of existential uncertainty and temporal dynamics that allow for the deliberative negotiation of constitutional meaning.[26]

Quantum constitutionalism perceives the constitution as the starting point of discursive and semiotically productive bargaining for content. Constitutionalism as a social construct and as a form of social imagination is understood by quantum constitutionalism as the practice of negotiation of the ways in which the achieved meaning should be expressed and communicated, and the constitutional information should be preserved and contained in structured constitutional imaginaries. Hence, constitutional semiotics is the analytical toolkit that enables the exploration of the unfolding of semiotic constitutional landscapes.[27] This is the process of augmentation of meaning ascribed in the course of constitutional interactions by the authoritative narrators, visualisers and performers of the constitutionally framed socio-legal community. The constitutional codes, myths, mythologies, normative ideologies and ideas gain their concrete shapes and content in the course of constitutional development. Initially, they are just potentialities and nucleuses that can eventually spread their capabilities.

Quantum constitutionalism expresses the existential mutability of constitutional law and the uncertainty of constitutionally explicated meaning resulting in textual constitutionalism. Textual constitutionalism enables the expression of constitutional meaning, but also conceals its intrinsic variability by focusing on constitutional text as a form of assertion of a system of stable signifiers originally ascribed to the social, socio-cultural and social imaginary life by the sovereign. The mixed application of quantum constitutionalism and constitutional semiotic approach destabilises this fragile appearance of stability and eternal truth expressed in textual form. It provokes reflections on alternative systems for the

[26] On the negotiation of meaning in the interpretation and translation of texts, see U Eco, *Mouse or Rat: Translation as Negotiation* (London, Orion, 2004) 1–208.

[27] The concept of constitutional semiotic landscapes is explained in pt III, ch 3 of this book.

signification of constitutionally relevant meaning through the forms of symbolic-imaginary, visual and performative constitutionalism.

Quantum constitutionalism as an analytical paradigm aims to remedy exactly this rigidity and unsubstantiated trust in radical forms of pure rationality and extreme stability of the constitutional order. It is an expression of the variability of meaning of the constitution and constitutional law, and of the dependence of constitutionalism on the socio-legal usage of raw models provided by constitutional law. It is paradigm that aims to change the epistemic and cognitive perspective from the perception of constitutional 'law as text' to its understanding as multidiscursive container of collective constitutional imaginaries and the other signifiers of constitutionally relevant meaning.

In that regard, quantum constitutionalism as a holistic concept has a semiotic function per se. It is a semiotic phenomenon that signifies the indeterminacy of constitutional law, its openness for change and its aptitude for the evolution of initially implied meaning. All these features of the constitution and constitutional law are neglected, underestimated or even rejected by traditional rational and normative-institutional approaches to constitutionalism. They are partially visible only in textual approaches to constitutionalism and constitutional law, and especially in the debates on the role of courts in contemporary legal orders,[28] judicial activism and constitutional courts acting as constitutional legislators.[29] Nevertheless, even in the context of these thematic fields, the problem is not addressed from the viewpoint of the mechanisms for the creation, signification and expression of meaning. This diminishes the epistemic potential of these traditional approaches focused on constitutional text and texture and on constitutional interpretation and thus limited to textual constitutionalism.

Indeed, the indeterminacy of constitutional law, its openness for change and its aptitude for the evolution of the initially implied meaning are produced by a mixture of factors, most of which are beyond the discretion of the constitutional legislator. They are not always predictable and predicted, and usually cannot be controlled, by the constitutional legislator. Constitutional meaning, once expressed in textual form, is prone to emancipation, evolution and change. In other words, the meaning that is originally implied in the constitutional text is fragile and volatile, and is deconstructed, constructed and reconstructed in multiple ways.

Hence, the overall indeterminacy of constitutional meaning is systemically predetermined by the non-existence of objective truth and eternal meaning of things conceptualised as semiotic and epistemic objects.[30] It should be noted that the indeterminacy of constitutional meaning is only partial – in other words, part of the meaning is stable and part of it evolves. However, which part of the meaning

[28] See M Belov, *The Role of Courts in Contemporary Legal Orders* (The Hague, Eleven, 2019) 1–576.

[29] See M Florczak-Wator (ed), *Judicial Law-Making in European Constitutional Courts* (Abingdon, Routledge, 2020) 1–278.

[30] On the claims for the objectivity and determinacy of social meaning, and objectivist rationalism and determinism in social and political life, see Castoriadis (n 5) 41–56.

will remain stable and permanent and which will drift and change along the socio-political application and socio-psychological internalisation of the phenomena (values, principles, institutions and rights) where it is contained and legally framed is not entirely clear at the beginning.

Indeed, the parts of the constitution which are contained in self-executable and strictly and narrowly written provisions seem to have a better chance of remaining intact during the course of the unfolding of the process of their adjustment to empirical reality and collective imaginaries. On the contrary, the values, principles and non-self-executable norms appear prone to indeterminacy and evolution of meaning.

Thus, in an abstract sense, one can speculate that constitutional axiology is the typical object of conceptual and epistemic instability and subsequently of quantum constitutionalism. This is not always the case, since path dependency[31] impacts a lot exactly the theoretically 'stable' part of constitutional design, namely institutional design and architecture.

Good examples of the importance and applicability of quantum constitutionalism on institutional architecture and design can be found in mixed regimes with huge institutional dynamics and potential for shifts in power centres. Who will be the leading institution in the constitutional system – the monarch or the prime minister in the constitutional monarchy, or the president or the prime minister in the semi-presidential republic – cannot always be determined in advance. It is the history, the dynamics of political interdependencies and sometimes even events that are external for the constitutional order (eg, wars, emergencies or disasters) that determine the outlook of the constitutional model. In line with the concept of quantum constitutionalism, this usually happens subsequently and in a way which is not predetermined by the initial constitutional model. A comparison between the French and the remaining European models of semi-presidentialism or between the variations and mutations of constitutional monarchy during the 'long nineteenth century'[32] demonstrate this point.[33]

However, it seems proper to say that it is the evolution and shifts in constitutional axiology and in the symbolic part of the constitution which are extremely relevant for quantum constitutionalism when viewed as a semiotic phenomenon. In other words, from the viewpoint of constitutional semiotics, it is not all

[31] See A Bergek and K Onufrey, 'Is One Path Enough? Multiple Paths and Path Interaction as an Extension of Path Dependency Theory' (2014) 23(5) *Industrial and Corporate Change* 1261, https://doi.org/10.1093/icc/dtt040; H Trouvé et al, 'The Path Dependency Theory: Analytical Framework to Study Institutional Integration. The Case of France' (2010) 10 *International Journal of Integrated Care*, doi:10.5334/ijic.544.

[32] E Hobsbawm, *The Age of Revolution: 1789–1848* (New York, Vintage, 1996) 1–368.

[33] The quantum features of the semi-presidential form of government can be demonstrated by the shift of this system from its initial model defined and described by Maurice Duverger. Actually, most of the semi-presidential models nowadays largely differ in many and even in controversial and contrasting respects from the theoretical model created by Duverger in his book *Échec au roi* (Paris, A Michel, 1977) 1–249.

manifestations of quantum constitutionalism that matter; rather, semiotic relevance is attached mostly to those examples of quantum constitutionalism which are capable of symbolic-imaginary representation in the realm of constitutional ideas and shared constitutional imaginaries and are prone to visual and performative signification. Usually, these forms are related to constitutional axiology and to some parts of institutional design with huge symbolic-imaginary and thus semiotic potential.

The shifts, turns and evolution of constitutional meaning are not limited to textual constitutionalism. There might be 'visual' and 'performative' revolutions which may have a significant impact on the social perception of the constitution and constitutional law. These are representations of constitutional ideas, ideals, myths, mythologies, codes, image, imaginaries or elements of axiological or institutional design that are represented visually and experienced emotionally in social practice in a way that has a huge degree of 'de facto or factual normativity'. Such normativity stems from the inspirational potential of constitutions and their capacity to trigger collective constitutional imaginaries and emotional perceptions of constitutional phenomena, and to promote semiotic insights of constitutional meaning.

The 'visual' and 'performative' revolutions are key moments in the imaginary history of the constitutionally framed socio-political community. They launch strategic changes of constitutionally relevant meaning, forming constitutional semiotic landscapes. They also arrange the constitutional memories and constitutional heritage of the constitutionally framed socio-political community through the use of and recourse to semiotic figures. Hence, the 'visual' and 'performative' revolutions in constitutionalism are hallmarks of constitutional semiotics.

'Lord Elgin's marbles' are good example of such a visual revolution that occurred in the early but formative phase of British constitutionalism. They gave a decisive push towards the inclusion of the humanist values of the antiquity (more precisely, Greek and, by analogy, also Greco-Roman antiquity) in the axiological core of British constitutionalism. In fact, 'Lord Elgin's marbles' served as an instrument for the promotion of the novel values of political and, later on, also constitutional modernity presented as a result of quasi-natural continuity with the humanist Greco-Roman civilisation of antiquity. They were the visual signifier of the 'invented tradition'[34] of humanist values that were entrenched in the constitutional axiology of the emergent modern constitutionalism. Thus, they contributed to an intellectual revolution which was implicitly also a semiotic one.

Such visual revolutions related to Greco-Roman antiquity also occurred elsewhere in the Western world (eg, in the US, France, Italy and Germany). They contributed significantly to the encoding of elements of symbolic-imaginary constitutionalism and especially of constitutional myths and mythologies,

[34] On the concept of 'invented tradition' see E Hobsbawm and T Ranger (eds) *The Invention of Tradition* (Cambridge, Cambridge University Press, 2012) 1–324.

normative ideologies and ideas in both the constitutional texture and the visual codes and allegories of modern Western constitutionalism.

It is important to stress that quantum constitutionalism is not a new form or particular type of constitutionalism, but is a new approach to constitutionalism in general as a holistic concept or to its particular dimensions. It is not a constitutional prototype, but a constitutional theory and meta-theory, as mentioned above.

There are different forms of constitutionalism. According to the historical phase of their emergence, we can differentiate between modern and post-modern (and eventually pre-modern) constitutionalism, constitutionalism of the eighteenth, nineteenth, twentieth and twenty-first centuries, anticipated or belated constitutionalism. One can distinguish libertarian, neoliberal, liberal, liberal-democratic, radical democratic, republican, revolutionary,[35] populist,[36] illiberal,[37] monarchical, authoritarian, technocratic or communitarian constitutionalism depending on its underlying ideology. Monarchical and republican constitutionalism and their different subtypes can also be classified based on the form of government, while Unitarian, federalist and confederal constitutionalism are distinctions based on the territorial model of the state. If we take the content of constitutionalism into account, then there can be other forms of constitutionalism that can be outlined as part of the typology – these are political constitutionalism, financial constitutionalism, digital and algorithmic constitutionalism[38] etc. The difference between national, subnational, supranational and global constitutionalism relates to its scope and its connection to statehood. If the criterion is the use of constitutionalism as a tool for the geopolitical organisation of the world into the form of states,

[35] See R Albert, *Revolutionary Constitutionalism: Law, Legitimacy, Power* (Oxford, Hart Publishing, 2020) 1–424; G Jacobsohn and Y Roznai, *Constitutional Revolution* (New Haven, Yale University Press, 2020) 1–384; B Ackerman, *Revolutionary Constitutions: Charismatic Leadership and the Rule of Law* (Cambridge, MA, Belknap Press, 2019) 1–472; and M Belov and A Abat i Ninet (eds), *Revolution, Transition, Memory, and Oblivion. Reflections on Constitutional Change* (Cheltenham, Edward Elgar, 2020) 1–244.

[36] See P Blokker, 'Populism as a Constitutional Project' (2019) 17(2) *International Journal of Constitutional Law* 1; P Blokker, 'Populist Counter-constitutionalism, Conservatism, and Legal Fundamentalism' (2019) 15 *European Constitutional Law Review* 519; P Blokker, 'Varieties of Populist Constitutionalism: The Transnational Dimension' (2019) 20 *German Law Journal* 332; P Blokker, 'Populist Constitutionalism' in *Routledge Handbook of Global Populism* (New York, Routledge, 2018) 113; G Halmai, 'Populism, Authoritarianism and Constitutionalism' (2019) 20(3) *German Law Journal* 296, doi:10.1017/glj.2019.23; M Belov (ed), *Populist Constitutionalism and Illiberal Democracies: Between Constitutional Imagination, Normative Entrenchment and Political Reality* (Cambridge, Intersentia, 2021) 1–379.

[37] T Drinóczi and A Bień-Kacała (eds), *Illiberal Constitutionalism in Poland and Hungary: The Deterioration of Democracy, Misuse of Human Rights and Abuse of the Rule of Law* (Abingdon, Routledge, 2021) 1–224; T Drinóczi and A Bień-Kacała (eds), *Rule of Law, Common Values, and Illiberal Constitutionalism: Poland and Hungary within the European Union* (Abingdon, Routledge, 2020) 1–348; and M Belov (ed), *Courts and Judicial Activism under Crisis Conditions: Policy Making in a Time of Illiberalism and Emergency Constitutionalism* (Abingdon, Routledge, 2021) 1–236.

[38] O Pollicino, *Judicial Protection of Fundamental Rights on the Internet: A Road towards Digital Constitutionalism* (Oxford, Hart Publishing, 2021) 1–320; E Celeste, 'Digital Constitutionalism: A New Systematic Theorisation' (2019) 33(1) *International Review of Law, Computers & Technology* 76, doi:10.1080/13600869.2019.1562604.

regional unions or global constitutional architecture, then a distinction between Westphalian, post-Westphalian and neo-Westphalian constitutionalism[39] seem proper and adequate.

This book provides a typology of the different discourses of constitutionalism understood as a multilayered and multidiscursive phenomenon with manifestations in valid law, but also beyond it – in the realm of facts, practices and socio-legal implementation, and in the fields of ideas, imaginaries and psychological conceptualisations. Thus, the book explores textual, normative-institutional, rational, emotional, visual, performative and symbolic-imaginary constitutionalism through the prism and lenses of constitutional semiotics.

Quantum constitutionalism is not another type of constitutionalism as a multilayered and bulky phenomenon. It is not a substantial variant that can be adjusted to the overall typology of constitutionalism. It provides alternative account of constitutional law and the constitutional phenomena, looking at them from different, additional and unorthodox perspectives. It is not part of the classifications of the types of constitutionalism defined in accordance with the diverse criteria that have been outlined above. It is a methodological approach and an analytical strategy with paradigmatic importance rather than another type or subtype of constitutionalism.

The specific and distinct character of quantum constitutionalism also becomes clear in view of the fact that the conceptual antipode of quantum constitutionalism can in theory be 'predetermined constitutionalism', 'fully predictable constitutionalism' or 'stable constitutionalism'. Hence, potential synonyms of quantum constitutionalism can be 'indefinite constitutionalism', 'non-determined constitutionalism', 'fuzzy constitutionalism', 'mutating constitutionalism' or 'transitory constitutionalism'. However, these terms are less adequate than the term 'quantum constitutionalism' because they focus on specific aspects of quantum constitutionalism.

Moreover, the quantum metaphor is very powerful in relation to the intellectual revolution provoked by quantum physics. Quantum constitutionalism may induce comparisons with quantum physics in many aspects. It indicates the need to always take the indeterminacy in constitutionalism and constitutional law into account and to expect huge and various mutations of the actual performance of constitutional phenomena (values, principles, institutions and rights) on the ground, in the pragmatic socio-political interaction and in constitutional anthropology, especially when it is shaped as collective imaginaries expressed through constitutional semiotics and projected in the spheres of symbolic-imaginary and visual constitutionalism.

The main idea behind the concept of quantum constitutionalism is that each constitutional phenomenon (idea, principle, value, right or institution) has a certain potential that consists in a typical content, functional catalogue, system

[39] Belov (n 3) 13–54; and R Falk, 'Revisiting Westphalia, Discovering Post-Westphalia' (2002) 6 *Journal of Ethics* 311.

of elements and formal shapes and parameters. Thus, we have some initial knowledge about the phenomenon, but this is too abstract, vague and context-detached to predict with sufficient clarity how it will function in practice. More precisely, constitutional science and constitutional practice examined from historical and comparative perspectives provide us with some starting points for reflection and hints for the prediction of the performance and implementation of the constitutional phenomenon in the socio-legal practice, and for its acceptance in the ideal discourse of constitutionalism.

Thus, we know in principle what the overall design of the phenomenon is and what should be expected from it in theoretical, comparative and historical terms. In this sense, we are aware of its 'energy potential'. But we do not know for sure how this 'initial energy potential' will spread when the phenomenon materialises as part of the constitutional practice and constitutional politics. Even more problematically, we cannot predict with any more certainty how the phenomenon will internalise and make its mark upon the collective constitutional imagination of the socio-legal constitutionally framed community.

That is why each constitutional phenomenon brings with it both conceptual potential and a spectrum of possible variations of its practical performance and its intellectual perception. To an extent paradoxically, the more concrete information we have about the details of the phenomenon, the less we can see its broader shapes and parameters and the less we can predict the outcomes of its internalising as part of constitutionalism as socio-legal process and as mental process of collective constitutional psychology.[40]

The degree of uncertainty exists in all constitutional discourses. Thus, 'quantum constitutionalism' is an overarching concept that can be used as an analytical paradigm for all of them. This makes it a methodological device with huge epistemic value that transcends the classificatory distinctions and is applicable to constitutionalism both as a holistic phenomenon and to its particular forms and manifestations.

Nevertheless, there are some forms of constitutionalism which are more prone to indeterminacy. Their evolution and unfolding in the particular context is less predictable than other types of constitutionalism. In that regard, quantum constitutionalism as a methodological and epistemic paradigm is much more useful in constitutional discourses with a higher degree of abstractness and dependency on meta-legal factors. It gives a more adequate account of forms of constitutionalism that are prone to indeterminacy and are intertwined with anthropology, ethics, arts and, last but not least, semiotics – that is, symbolic-imaginary, visual, emotional, and performative constitutionalism.

On the contrary, the exploring of rational constitutionalism and to lesser degree textual constitutionalism through the prism of quantum constitutionalism

[40] On the conceptual parameters of this paradox that predetermines post-modern thinking and the post-modern versions of truth, see F Liotard, *The Postmodern Condition: A Report on Knowledge* (Minneapolis, University of Minnesota Press, 1984) 1–144.

can achieve more limited analytical results. However, we should take into account the fact that textual constitutionalism, if approached through the lenses of the open texture paradigm and the deconstructivist and narrative-based critical studies and understood as a range of narratives produced by authoritative speakers of the community, is also prone to indeterminacy.[41] In that regard, it might also be a valid object of quantum constitutionalism.

Similarly, normative-institutional constitutionalism as a form of rational constitutionalism may be closer to quantum constitutionalism and may be conceived as such if the constitutional institutions are not understood as static and eternal categories that are immutable and in possession on permanent logic. If institutions are understood as 'shells'[42] inhabited by different office holders with divergent tasks that evolve and adapt their institutional logic and dynamics according to their political goals, social considerations and plans and following collective imaginaries, then normative-institutional constitutionalism is also a valid epistemic target of quantum constitutionalism.

[41] For a critical approach to narratives, see A Abbott, 'Against Narrative: A Preface to Lyrical Sociology' (2007) 25 *Sociological Theory* 67.

[42] On the concept of institutions as shells inhabited by different office holders, see G Tsebelis, *Veto Players: How Political Institutions Work* (Princeton/New York, Russell Sage Foundation/Princeton University Press, 2002) 8.

3

The Rationalist Entrapment of Constitutional Modernity

Rationalism is one of the most important normative paradigms of Western modernity. It denominates both its formative period and its complex system of normative ideologies. Rationalism is a historical phase of the development of the West that merged with the Enlightenment. Thus, in terms of structuring history into phases of its development, rationalism is frequently subsumed under the age of the Enlightenment.[1] Nevertheless, it is an independent paradigm that also spreads beyond the Enlightenment. Its historical roots date back to antiquity and it is also one of the decisive normative ideologies of modernity. Rationalism is the philosophy which differentiates Western modernity from both the pre-modern period of development of the West and the non-Western societies and their political orders. Hence, rationalism is both a theory and a conceptual paradigm, and a historical period in the development of Western societies.

In that regard, rationalism was the most influential and fundamental normative ideology on modern law in general and constitutionalism in particular during its formative period – the 'long nineteenth century'[2] and afterwards. It is still among the pillars of contemporary constitutional civilisation revered in the West and praised as the only possible foundation of law and order in the East.

Thus, we can speak of the 'rationalist entrapment of constitutional and legal modernity', a metaphor that also highlights the deep dependence of constitutionalism and constitutional law on rationalism and the Enlightenment as normative intellectual paradigms. Rationalism predetermines the targets and objects of normative regulation and their theoretical assessment. It significantly influences the methodology of law and the overall predisposition of legal scholarship to a point of extreme dependence on rationalism as an ideology and a methodology. This leads to systematic negligence of the role of images,

[1] See Z Drozdowicz, *Faces of the Enlightenment Philosophical Sketches* (Berlin, Peter Lang, 2020) 1–200.

[2] E Hobsbawm, *The Age of Revolution: 1789–1848* (New York, Vintage, 1996) 1–368.

imaginaries,[3] performances and emotions in constitutionalism and constitutional law.[4]

Rationalism and humanism are the central constructive axes around which modern constitutionalism circulates. Rationalism emerged somewhat earlier than humanism. Nevertheless, both mutually reinforced their reformist claim at establishing a new type of socio-political and, later on, constitutional order.[5] In contrast to the medieval order, the new modern political order should have been based not on faith in God and the transcendental and metaphysical aspirations for eternity in the outer world and the divine origin of the earthly order, but on trust in human reason to deconstruct, construct and reconstruct socio-political relations, to reform the state, society and human relations on the basis of a rational and logical plan.[6] The centre of this plan should be organised through rational devices – the constitution and the laws – with the aim of establishing humanist society preconditioned upon eternal and supreme principles of humanism, rationality and justice.

Rationalism emerged as a philosophical concept that has been massively influenced by the advance of natural sciences. If it was possible to systematise the universe, the chemical elements, the constitution of the human body and the laws of nature, then why not use the same human reason to describe social behaviour, the laws that regulate the human relations and thus the political order? Moreover, the daring claim has been made to use human reason not only to describe and systematise the socio-political relations, but also to prescribe the perfect or at least the appropriate political order in the form of a master plan for organising society and its political framework, eg, in the form of a written and codified constitution.

Rationalism has shaped our understanding of history. History has been transformed from a static and eternal divine order into a dynamic process of permanent assent from darkness into light. It has been conceptualised as a process of restoration of 'eternal truths' gained in antiquity and reborn in modernity. History has been understood as a dialectical process leading to increasing social prosperity building on the heritage of the Greco-Roman civilisation. Moreover, rationalism

[3] 'But in the syllogisms of modern life the premises borrow their content from the imaginary; and the prevalence of the syllogism as such, the obsession with "rationality" unconnected with anything else constitutes a second-order imaginary. Modern pseudorationality is one of the historical forms of the imaginary; it is arbitrary in its ultimate ends to the extent that these ends themselves stem from no reason, and it is arbitrary when it posits itself as an end, intending nothing but a formal and empty "rationalization".' See C Castoriadis, *The Imaginary Institution of Society* (Cambridge, Polity Press, 1987) 156.

[4] For a critical approach to these extreme forms of rationalist overburdening of legal thought, see RM Unger, 'Legal Analysis as Institutional Imagination' (1996) 59(1) *Modern Law Review* 6.

[5] For an excellent analysis of the emergence and development of rationalism and humanism in the context of legal modernity seen from the perspective of post-modern critical legal studies, see C Douzinas, P Goodrich and Y Hachamovitch (eds), *Politics, Postmodernity and Critical Legal Studies: The Legality of the Contingent* (Abingdon, Routledge, 1994) 1–240.

[6] On the legitimacy issues stemming out of the secularisation of law during the constitutional age, see V Depaigne, *Legitimacy Gap: Secularism, Religion, and Culture in Comparative Constitutional Law* (Oxford, Oxford University Press, 2017) 1–240.

also massively influenced modern political philosophy and, later on, constitutional theory, suggesting universal ordering and an explanatory paradigm for constitutionalism.

Rationalism plays a central role in organising, explaining and legitimating modern constitutionalism and constitutional law. It is a key normative ideology of constitutionalism and constitutional law since their emergence in Western modernity.[7] It is the main organising matrix of constitutional design. It predetermines both the general framework of the constitutional model and the design of the system of human rights and duties, the institutional system of the meditative institutions of the public sphere and the system of the institutions of public power.

Rationalism is a normative ideology of modern and Western constitutionalism. It has emerged in the context of the general pathos of Western modernity to rationalise, structure and order the world in general and in terms of socio-legal relations in particular. Thus, rationalism as a paradigm is not limited to constitutional law or law in general. It is part of the overall trend of social sciences and humanities to construct proper and desired models of socio-political relations which are frequently based on two opposite but mutually dependent processes – construction and deconstruction.

The constructivist discourse is the predominant discourse in law in general and in constitutional law in particular. Modern constitutions do not only describe the socio-political reality. They are not just reflections of socio-political constellations. Constitutions also try to prescribe and reform, to create new worlds frequently based on holistic versions of truth, perfect abstract models of axiological and institutional design, and ultimate visions for socio-political improvement. Constitutions map out socio-political realities. They are holograms of existing power and interest schemes. The holographic characteristic of the constitutions is an important part of their semiotic nature and clearly demonstrates their semiotic importance. At the same time, constitutions contain systematised normative prescriptions forming normative programmes. Their normativity is derived from the authority of the lawgiver, the adequacy of the reformist plan they contain and the persuasiveness of the vision for 'the better world' they impose on society.

Constructing a 'brave new world'[8] based on logic, rationality and order, and systematically reshaping states, societies and people is a daring and ambitious project.[9] It became the leading theme of modern constitutionalism. Thus, rational and constructive constitutionalism, resulting in imposing reformist programmes on the people and society, gradually overshadowed the descriptive discourse even within rational constitutionalism. The constitutions started to be conceived much more as radical tools for rational reform (unilaterally imposed or negotiated) and

[7] On the concept of normative ideology, see pt III, ch 5 of this book.

[8] See A Huxley, *Brave New World* (New York, Harper Perennial, 2006).

[9] See D Lee, *Popular Sovereignty in Early Modern Constitutional Thought* (Oxford, Oxford University Press, 2016) 16.

even for constitutional engineering[10] rather than as reflections of interest constellations or descriptions of socio-political relations.

Nevertheless, the constructivist approach of modern constitutions, which is based upon their rationalist impetus, is frequently paralleled – implicitly or overtly – by the deconstructive approach.[11] In that regard, constitutional design is frequently a result of selective and, at least in theory, rational deconstruction of previous constitutions and socio-political constellations. The systematic and logical construction of new constitutional models was supposedly preceded by the systematic and rational deconstruction of preceding models.

Constitutional deconstruction implies reflective and critical engagement with the past.[12] It presupposes a selective approach to historical experience. Sometimes this may mean a combination of deconstruction and reconstruction of constitutional models forming a distinct national constitutional tradition on the basis of 'cherry-picking'. However, this may also result in an attempt to deliberately avoid path dependency and wrong constitutional-political choices. Extreme forms of constitutional deconstruction combined with rational reconstruction of the constitutional model on the basis of selective choice of constitutional design are the unamendable and entrenched clauses.[13]

In many cases, the deconstruction and reconstruction of constitutional heritage and the constitutional past involves the construction of constitutional myths and mythologies, even utopias, the launching of normative ideologies and ideas, and the shaping of constitutional dreams and memories.[14] In other words, rational constitutionalism, the rationalist deconstruction of the constitutional past and the construction of the constitutional future necessarily also involves, invokes and produces collective constitutional imaginaries triggering emotions and requiring instruments for their public exposure.[15] Hence, rational constitutionalism – despite or perhaps because of its claim to be a universal instrument for the creation of

[10] G Sartori, *Comparative Constitutional Engineering: An Inquiry into Structures, Incentives, and Outcomes* (New York, New York University Press, 1994) 1–229; and X Contiades (ed), *Engineering Constitutional Change: A Comparative Perspective on Europe, Canada and the USA* (Abingdon, Routledge, 2012) 1–490.

[11] On the deconstructivist paradigm and its impact on the social sciences and the humanities, see P Salmon, 'How to Deconstruct the World', *Psyche*, https://psyche.co/guides/how-to-deconstruct-the-world-by-thinking-like-jacques-derrida?fbclid=IwAR1nVvSqfBr8VYxsDbQJdYct2k7B8QTgOwKmpB_zX2DhY-9rAvmNmRxgRA4.

[12] See G Teschner and F McCluskey, 'The Deconstruction of the First Amendment: Philosophical Reflections on the Foundation of the City in Speech' in R Kevelson (ed), *Law and Semiotics*, vol 2 (New York, Plenum Press, 1988) 329–41.

[13] For more information about the eternity and entrenched (or entrenchment) clauses, see M Hein, 'Entrenchment Clauses in the History of Modern Constitutionalism' (2018) 86(3–4) *Tijdschrift voor Rechtsgeschiedenis/Revue d'Histoire du Droit/ Legal History Review* 434, https://doi.org/10.1163/15718190-08634P06.

[14] On the instrumentality of the past, see B Lincoln, *Discourse and the Construction of Society: Comparative Studies of Myth, Ritual, and Classification* (Oxford, Oxford University Press, 1992) 27–29.

[15] On the role of art in the representation of the past, see F Haskell, *History and its Images: Art and the Interpretation of the Past* (New Haven, Yale University Press, 1993).

constitutional and socio-legal reality – is to an extent paradoxically also a producer of symbolic-imaginary, emotional, visual and performative constitutionalism.[16]

Hence, the processes of the deconstruction, construction and reconstruction of constitutional content and matter that is imaginary organised in the forms of constitutional past,[17] present and future are dialectically intertwined.[18] The construction of constitutional design is usually preconditioned by the deconstruction of previous constitutions and constitutional tradition (or socio-political relations in the case of the first constitutions). Sometimes it results in the immediate or postponed reconstruction of constitutional design. In all cases, the deconstruction, construction and reconstruction of constitutional design is based upon the general rationalist paradigm and is accomplished within the framework of rational constitutionalism. Indeed, in many cases, constitutional reform and the choice of constitutional design are predetermined by interests and historical experience instead of pure rational choice, by the imposition of interests that are external to the community or by feelings, emotions, subconscious and unconscious choices.[19] Nevertheless, they are concealed by the predominance of rational constitutionalism in the constitutional discourse with all normative supportive ideologies that belong to it.

The rationalist discourse in constitutional theory is so influential, durable and overwhelming that it is frequently perceived not just as the predominant but in fact the only possible way of ordering socio-political systems and for explaining constitutional orders. Some of the most important theories of constitutional law such as legal normativism, legal positivism, legal institutionalism, the theory of communicative and discursive action and, of course, rational choice overemphasise rational constitutionalism. In fact, they are durably entrenched in and entirely preconditioned on rational constitutionalism. In other words, it is impossible for the modern approach to the constitution, constitutional law and constitutionalism to be detached from rationalism. These cannot be analysed without admitting their deep entrenchment in rationalism and in the rationalist tradition of Western modernity.

This all means that contemporary constitutionalism is deeply rooted in rationalist and Enlightenment traditions. Rationalism predetermines its ontology, teleology and methodology. Thus, we have to face the challenges stemming from this 'rationalist entrapment' of modern constitutional law, which also leads to the

[16] On the rationality of belief, see T Williamson, 'Ambiguous Rationality' (2017) 14(3) *Episteme* 263.

[17] On the constitutional past, see M Belov, 'Constitutional Memories: How Do Constitutions Cope with Constitutional Past' in M Belov and A Abat i Ninet (eds) *Revolution, Transition, Memory, and Oblivion: Reflections on Constitutional Change* (Cheltenham, Edward Elgar, 2020) 107–26; and C Bottici, *Imaginal Politics: Images Beyond Imagination and the Imaginary* (New York, Columbia University Press, 2014) 127–61.

[18] On the imaginary dimensions of time, the philosophical and social institution of time, and the distinction between identitary and imaginary time and between time of social representing and time of social doing, see Castoriadis (n 3) 186–221.

[19] See J Lachs, 'Law and the Importance of Feelings' in Kevelson (n 12) 221–29.

'rationalist path dependency' of all constitutional discourses (scientific, political, legislative, judicial etc) and produces the 'rationalist entrenchment' of constitutionalism as a multidiscursive project. Such a proper assessment of rationalist constitutionalism must not lead to its negation or rejection; it has to broaden our analytical and conceptual horizons for other constitutional discourses – symbolic-imaginary, emotional, visual and performative – that have been overshadowed by rational constitutionalism.[20] The exposure of these 'shadow constitutionalisms' mainly through the prism of constitutional semiotics is among the main aims of this book.

[20] For a similar claim, see K Abrams and H Keren, 'Who's Afraid of Law and the Emotions?' (2010) 94(6) *Minnesota Law Review* 1997, available at: https://ssrn.com/abstract=2434251.

4

The Concept of Rational Constitutionalism and the Need to Turn to 'Shadow Constitutionalisms' on the Basis of the Semiotic Approach

After clarifying the rationalist entrapment of constitutional modernity and its impact on organising the constitutional discourse in intellectual, normative and conceptual terms, let us now turn to the concept of rational constitutionalism and the functions it performs. This is a necessary precondition for the conceptual counterposition of rational and symbolic-imaginary constitutionalism that lies at the core of the analysis of this book. One of the key ideas in this book is to show that the visual, performative and intellectual tools for the representation of constitutionally relevant meaning are actually stretched between rational and symbolic-imaginary constitutionalism. The tools themselves are provided by textual, normative-institutional, visual and performative constitutionalism. Thus, a short outline of the main features of rational constitutionalism is a precondition for exploring the role it plays in the overall process of constitutional semiotics.

Several elements are typical of rational constitutionalism and thus give it its overall form. Many of them are relevant for the proper understanding of constitutional semiotics as a paradigm for the signification of meaning stretched between several constitutional discourses. They shed light on the role played by the constitution as an object, channel and tool of constitutional semiosis, and thus for the representation of constitutional meaning.

The constitution is conceptualised as a universal and quasi-omnipotent instrument for the rational ordering, shaping and framing of the socio-political reality. It is a universal tool for the construction of constitutionally relevant meaning. It is also the main instrument for the expression and representation of socio-political meaning. Thus, it is the logical, systemic and conceptual epicentre of constitutional semiotics generated through recourse to rationality. The construction and expression of meaning should be based on pure rationality. This must follow predictable patterns logically and permanently established by rational agents of constituent power. Thus, constitutional codes, metaphors,[1] allegories, myths,

[1] On the role of metaphors in law, see M Del Mar, *Artefacts of Legal Inquiry: The Value of Imagination in Adjudication* (Oxford, Hart Publishing, 2020) 278–330.

mythologies, normative ideologies and ideas, and even utopias and anti-utopias must entail and include predetermined rational meaning. They must by necessity offer rational explanations to the world, while the emotions and imaginaries are merely derivative side effects of the socio-legal performance of rational constitutionalism and byproducts of the rational and logical performance of constitutional law resembling permissible, possible and feasible but non-systemic hallucinations of secondary importance that have no epistemic value.

Constitutionalism was born in the age of rationalism and the Enlightenment. It is a phenomenon that initially emerged in Western modernity as part of the general codification movement, which had two aims – to legitimise a new political regime with its new legal order based upon rationality and to create a semi-autonomous legal matrix of the new socio-political order that emerged after the great revolutions that marked the transition to legal and constitutional modernity. Hence, since the late eighteenth and early nineteenth centuries, the constitution has become a code, a rationalising matrix and a universal legal framework for political life. It has been the culmination of the long tradition of the law as 'ratio scripta'.[2]

In this regard, the concept of the rational, systematic, logical and written constitution with the subsequent characteristics of constitutionalism is a symbol itself. It symbolises the intellectual power and the pre-eminence of Western modernity.[3] It is both a signifier of socio-legal truth, wisdom and durable patterns of behaviour compressed in the normative-institutional design of rational constitutionalism and a signified mythologeme of the age of rationalism and the Enlightenment.

The constitution as a written, codified, systematic and rational supreme law of the land can be understood, used and put into practice only by free rational agents.[4] Thus, rationalist constitutionalism is also dependent on the existence of interested and active office holders and citizens who are capable of understanding both the constitution and their constitutional interests, competences and rights.[5] Moreover, they should be capable of making active and rational choices in terms of maximising their benefits and constitutional positions.[6] The rational, written and codified constitution is of use and can be real and not fictitious only in the context of rational and enlightened society. Moreover, there should be a critical mass of citizens able to make rational choices based on the constitutional text. This statement seems a self-evident central feature of modern rational constitutionalism.

[2] See T Vesting, *Legal Theory and the Media of Law* (Cheltenham, Edward Elgar, 2018) 1–656.

[3] For a very reasonable criticism of Western-centric constitutionalism and the overemphasis of Western approaches and values in constitutionalism, see G Frankenberg, *Comparative Constitutional Studies: Between Magic and Deceit* (Cheltenham, Edward Elgar, 2018) 1–360.

[4] On the concept of free will, see R Kane, *A Contemporary Introduction to Free Will* (Oxford, Oxford University Press, 2005) 1–208; and M Balaguer, *Free Will* (Cambridge, MA, MIT Press, 2014) 1–152.

[5] For a critical approach to the concept of people as rational agents, see T Williamson, 'Ambiguous Rationality' (2017) 14(3) *Episteme* 265.

[6] P Weithman, *Religion and the Obligations of Citizenship* (Cambridge, Cambridge University Press, 2004) 106.

In that regard, the capability for the rational cognition and reconstruction of the world by the addressees of the constitution is a fundamental precondition for the proper functioning of constitutional semiotics. From a rationalist perspective and the viewpoint of rational constitutionalism, constitutional semiosis is a rational process based on a logical and systematic structure of construction, deconstruction and reconstruction of meaning entrenched in textual form in the forms of normative-institutional design of the constitutional world. There is a rational logic that always binds the nodes of the semiotic process which is permanently available for giving the reason – overt or hidden – for the constitutional signification of meaning. Thus, the constitutional fairytale based on myths, codes, allegories and constitutional imaginaries is or should always be reasonable. It has to be accessible to human reason. In any case, emotions, visuals, performances and imaginaries have to be reducible to a rational and logical content that is intentionally implied in the constitutional text and texture or is at least unintentionally but reasonably existent as a quasi-natural element of rational and normative-institutional constitutionalism and resulting in essentially rational or at least rationally represented constitutional stories.

Rational constitutionalism has many further concrete manifestations apart from the general paradigmatic functions it performs in terms of predetermining the outlook of the institutional design. Instead of inherited historical institutions justified by long-lasting tradition or by sacred experience, modern constitutions provide for rationally constructed institutional design conceptualised on the basis of explicitly written procedures and constructed with a view to abstract rational criteria.[7] Furthermore, rational constitutionalism presupposes a huge degree of commonality between people and societies, since it is grounded in the suggestion of universal rationality underlying the socio-political experience and aims of humankind. Hence, rational constitutionalism justifies universal constitutional transplantation in different forms – the reception or transplantation of institutions and the migration of normative ideas.[8] In that regard, constitutional semiotics must also be grounded in universal reasoning and universally recognisable processes of signification and representation of meaning. From the perspective of rational constitutionalism, it should be possible to construct rational and universal typologies of signified, signifiers and the overall process of signification of constitutionally relevant meaning.

Thus, rational constitutionalism creates several normative expectations which seem to be rather demanding if they are taken for granted and if they are expected to exist in such an absolute form. One of these is the claim of absolute rationality of constitutions and constitutionalism.[9] Another is the need for predominantly

[7] See M Weber, *Soziologie. Weltgeschichtliche Analysen. Politik* (Stuttgart, Kröner Verlag, 1968) 151 et seq.

[8] See A Watson, *Legal Transplants: An Approach to Comparative Law* (Athens, GA, University of Georgia Press, 1993) 1–144.

[9] See L Wintgens and A Daniel Oliver-Lalana, *The Rationality and Justification of Legislation: Essays in Legisprudence* (Dordrecht, Springer, 2013) 1–202.

rational agents as ultimate maximisers of constitutional rights, competences and capacities.[10] Yet another is the existence of universal and absolute constitutional truths that are transplantable to different socio-legal contexts. Together, they produce absolutist rationalism as a supreme intellectual normative paradigm of constitutionalism and constitutional law.

Such an extremely rational approach to constitutionalism may be very dangerous, since it is rather misleading. It underestimates the role that emotions and the collective imagination play in terms of both the understanding and the functioning of constitutions and constitutionalism. In general, it does not sufficiently take into account the normativity of collective feelings and emotions as driving forces for mastering, using and misusing the constitutional axiology and constitutional design. Moreover, the predominance of rationalist discourse conceals the important role performed not only by emotions, but also by the collective constitutional imagination. It omits to recognise the impact of constitutional myths and mythologies, normative ideas, constitutional symbols and imaginaries, and thus of the constitutional imagination for the constitutional organisation of socio-political relations.

According to G Frankenberg:

> Constitutions are fraught with ideas, ideals and ideology. So they hardly render an accurate description of social reality, nor can they be read as manuals instructing their readers about the actual working of the institutional arrangement they lay out. At best, they indicate how societies – rather their constitutional elites – envision coping with or camouflaging the business of establishing and exercising authority and bringing about social cohesion. If written in good faith, they can be commanding or at least aspirational texts, however definitely not blueprints.[11]

The label of rationality has been induced and extensively used as a structural principle in the theoretical, legal and socio-legal (empirical) dimensions of the constitution and constitutionalism. In other words, rationality is supposed to be the key for explaining and understanding the system of constitutional normative ideologies, valid constitutional law and the way in which we understand its practical functioning.[12] And, indeed, rationality is an extremely important pillar of Western modernity and of constitutionalism as a Western and modern phenomenon. Rationality has played a huge role in terms of improving and reforming the political and social order during modernity by giving it a rational constitutional foundation.

However, there are two main problems connected with the domination of rational constitutionalism as a paradigm for explaining and ordering the

[10] On the rational agents as power and interest maximisers, see some of the relevant rational choice literature such as D Farrell, 'Utility-Maximizing Intentions and the Theory of Rational Choice' (1993) 21(10) *Philosophical Topics* 53.

[11] See Frankenberg (n 3) 14–15.

[12] On the importance of practical semiotic narratives and their dependence on both rational construction and intellectual prejudice based on emotional perception and imaginary input, see M Landqvist, 'Semiotic Spaces in Antidiscriminatory Political Discourse: Naming Practices as Indexes' (2019) 48 *Language in Society* 721, doi:10.1017/S0047404519000459.

constitutional order. The first is that rationality has been transformed from a method and a viewpoint into a normative ideology, and from a normative ideology into a dogma. The second is that the rationalist dogma presents a rather one-sided reality and even stigmatises the proper understanding of the functioning of the constitutional ideology and especially of the constitutional axiology and institutional design.

The 'rationalist entrapment' of constitutional modernity, the reduction of constitutionalism to rational constitutionalism as an exhaustive and de facto only version of constitutionalism outweighs the existence of 'shadow constitutionalisms'. Such 'shadow constitutionalisms' are emotional, visual, performative and symbolic-imaginary constitutionalism. This hinders the proper understanding of the functioning of the constitutional order in general and its particular institutions.

It has been clarified that rational constitutionalism is the mainstream constitutionalism which has dominated constitutionalist discourse since its emergence. It has overshadowed other aspects of constitutionalism which have a partially autonomous role for ordering and explaining the constitutional order. Moreover, these other aspects may have an important explanatory role in terms of understanding the performance of rational constitutionalism.

These 'alternative' constitutional discourses, which exist in parallel to rational constitutionalism, may be defined as 'shadow constitutionalisms'. This is due to their marginal recognition by the traditional constitutional theory, which underestimates their role for organising the compliance of the socio-legal performance and behaviour with the formal, normative-institutional constitutional model and for understanding the shapes that rationally constructed constitutional institutions gain in constitutional practice and in the constitutional imagination.

The 'shadow constitutionalisms' co-exist with rational constitutionalism. They contain the imprints of normative-institutional design stemming from rational constitutionalism and exposed in constitutional texture that are moulded in performative, visual and symbolic-imaginary discourses. Thus, they are containers of a range of signifiers of meaning derived from rational, textual and normative-institutional constitutionalism. These signifiers have a different nature. They may consist in socio-legal behaviour and performative acts, but also visual imprints of constitutional content, codes and allegories, and the shared beliefs entrenched in the anthropology and the collective imaginaries of the constitutionally framed socio-legal community. Thus, these signifiers are important for decoding the way in which the rational constitutional matrix is implemented and further developed by the actors of the constitutional game.

There are several 'shadow constitutionalisms': emotional, symbolic-imaginary, performative and visual constitutionalism. They are independent phenomena with their own core content and their own system of typical features. Moreover, they perform autonomous functions for the constitutional order. Last but not least, these 'shadow constitutionalisms' play an important role in the signification of a range of constitutional phenomena with strategic importance for constitutional axiology and constitutional design.

Hence, emotional, symbolic-imaginary, performative and visual constitutionalisms are separate constitutional phenomena, but which are mutually interrelated and intertwined. The joint analysis of these 'shadow constitutionalisms' increases the explanatory potential for the general features of constitutionalism perceived as a holistic phenomenon and for the typical performance of specific elements of the constitutional design.

Moreover, emotional, symbolic-imaginary, performative and visual constitutionalisms are, to an extent paradoxically, also related to rational constitutionalism. This relationship is mutually reflective and even mutually reinforcing. While rational constitutionalism orders and explains the rational matrix of the socio-political relations constituting the core of the state and its relationship with the citizen, 'shadow constitutionalisms' shed light on other aspects of the functioning of the state, civil society and the people, which are not limited to expected rational behaviour. They expose the role of constitutional semiotics as a concept that focuses on the multiple ways in which constitutionally relevant meaning is constructed, deconstructed and reconstructed, and, even more importantly, represented and signified in the realms of the collective imagination, emotions, shared visual codes and symbolic constitutionally relevant performance.

In that regard, constitutional semiotics can be used as a tool of constitutional epistemology. It must be operationalised as a common approach to the ways in which rational meaning stemming from rational constitutionalism is signified in the other constitutional discourses. More precisely, constitutional semiotics may serve the important role of acting as a common analytical paradigm that explains the transfer and signification of meaning derived from rational constitutionalism in symbolic-imaginary, visual and performative constitutionalism. The process of constitutional semiosis may proceed directly from rational to symbolic-imaginary, visual and performative constitutionalism. However, much more frequently, this is done through the medium of textual and normative-institutional constitutionalism. Hence, this book will try to offer a systemic account of how constitutionally relevant meaning is constructed, represented and signified using semiotic tools belonging to the above-mentioned constitutional discourses and plains for the semiotic representation of constitutional content.

5

The Structure of Constitutional Semiotics

Signifiers, Signifieds and the Signification of Constitutional and Constitutionally Relevant Meaning

Constitutional semiotics is entrenched at the point of intersection of constitutional epistemology, constitutional anthropology, constitutional social psychology, socio-legal studies, and general and legal semiotics. It is embedded in studies of memory,[1] visual[2] and emotional politics,[3] and is inspired by semiotic and epistemological studies of text and texture. Thus, it is a phenomenon and field of research allocated at the crossroads between rational, normative-institutional, textual, visual, performative and symbolic-imaginary constitutionalism. It also has important emotional repercussions that are reflected in emotional constitutionalism.

A proper understanding of constitutional semiotics as a theory and a meta-theory should be based on an analysis of the structure of the constitutional semiosis, its determinants and elements, and its impact on the overall concept of constitutionalism. This scientific endeavour also demands a reconceptualisation

[1] Z Wang, *Memory Politics, Identity and Conflict: Historical Memory as a Variable* (London, Palgrave Macmillan, 2017) 1–126; S Kaasik-Krogerus, L Čeginskas and N Sääskilahti, 'Politics of Memory and Oblivion: An Introduction to the Special Issue' (2020) 21(3) *European Politics and Society* 271; P Ricoeur, *La memoire, l'histoire, l'oubli* (Paris, Seuil, 2000); and M Belov and A Abat i Ninet (eds), *Revolution, Transition, Memory, and Oblivion. Reflections on Constitutional Change* (Cheltenham, Edward Elgar, 2020) 1–244. Bottici offers an original 'politics of the past'; see C Bottici, *Imaginal Politics: Images Beyond Imagination and the Imaginary* (New York, Columbia University Press, 2014) 127–143.

[2] R Bleiker, *Visual Global Politics* (Abingdon, Routledge, 2018) 1–390; B Hooks, *Art on My Mind: Visual Politics* (New York, The New Press, 1995) 1–240; M McLagan and M McKee (eds), *Sensible Politics: The Visual Culture of Nongovernmental Activism* (Princeton, Zone Books, 2012) 1–664.

[3] N Demertzis, *Emotions in Politics: The Affect Dimension in Political Tension* (Basingstoke, Palgrave Macmillan, 2013) 1–322; S Ahmed, *The Cultural Politics of Emotion* (Abingdon, Routledge, 2014) 1–276; P Ioanide, *The Emotional Politics of Racism: How Feelings Trump Facts in an Era of Colorblindness* (Stanford, Stanford University Press, 2015) 1–288; and E Kidd White, 'On Emotions and the Politics of Attention in Judicial Reasoning' in A Amaya and M Del Mar (eds), *Virtue, Emotion and Imagination in Law and Legal Reasoning* (Oxford, Hart Publishing, 2020) 101–19.

of constitutionalism. Constitutionalism should be perceived not just as a rational and systematic order and a normative phenomenon entrenched in textuality safeguarded by the state authority; it also has to be conceived as an imaginary reality based on social trust, emotions and psychological perceptions generated through the signification of meaning by recourse to all instruments of semiotic expression and representation of constitutional content.[4] Thus, constitutionalism, perceived as a negotiated multidiscursive legal order justified on the basis of criteria stemming from collective constitutional imaginaries, becomes a necessary and proper object of constitutional semiotics.

Hence, constitutionalism can be intellectually framed as a system or, more appropriately, a range of imaginaries generated in the process of constitutional semiosis. These imaginaries have a divergent ontology and teleology, and somewhat diverse structural and functional characteristics. Thus, they are not always and are frequently not even capable of being framed as a coherent system. But they have one fundamental common feature: they construct constitutionalism as a semiotic process of representation of meaning and thus as a 'game of collective constitutional imaginaries'. These imaginaries are represented and shared with the constitutionally framed socio-political community textually, visually and performatively.

'Constitutionalism as a game of imaginaries' is an advancement in terms of grasping the complexity of constitutionalism as a multidiscursive and composite phenomenon that includes not only the legal order, but also its determinants and imprints in social relations and in the collective imagination and anthropology of the constitutionally framed socio-political community. Hence, constitutionalism conceived as a 'game of constitutional imaginaries' is a conceptual bridge, precursor and promoter of 'constitutionalism beyond rationality' and 'constitutionalism beyond positivism'. Again, this should not be understood as an assertion for the detachment of constitutionalism from rationalism as one of its main normative ideologies. Nor this is a claim for the promotion of some kind of 'constitutionalism without law'. On the contrary, it is rational to assume that the proper understanding of the valid constitutional law as a rationally and textually entrenched phenomenon is to broaden the analytical horizon with the intellectual and socio-legal dimensions of constitutionalism.

Constitutional semiotics seems to be a very appropriate analytical platform for grasping the phenomena of signification of meaning through the expression of constitutional imaginaries via textual, visual and performative constitutionalism, and thus has huge epistemic value. Constitutional semiosis can be a provocative but enlightening process that may serve as a paradigm for exploring the ways for the deconstruction, constitution, reconstruction and finally, for the representation and signification of meaning transported from the system of valid constitutional

[4] See A Amaya and M Del Mar (eds), *Virtue, Emotion and Imagination in Law and Legal Reasoning* (Oxford, Hart Publishing, 2020) 1–275.

law in collective constitutional imaginaries and social practices through recourse to the toolkit of textual, visual and performative constitutionalism.

In that regard, constitutionalism can even be conceived as a game of images,[5] performances and textual interpretations, and ultimately as a 'game of semiotic codes'. This chapter will first outline the main determinants of constitutional semiosis – signifiers, signifieds and the range of signification – before going on to explain why constitutionalism can be metaphorically constructed, imagined and explained as a 'game of semiotic codes'.

Each semiotic system requires a definition of three main variables serving as determinants of the semiotic process. The theoretical and normative interrelation and the practical interplay between them predetermines the overall design, scope and characteristics of the semiotic system. The conceptual parameters of constitutional semiotics should also be defined on the basis of the joint impact of these three determinants.

The first determinant of the semiotic process is the system of signifiers used in the process of signification.[6] The concept of the constitutional semiotic signifier must not necessarily be an exhaustive or strict one; it is permissible to have descriptive and all-encompassing definitions as well. Such definitions do not determine the scope of signifiers in rigid terms. They do not exclude additional signifiers that may appear in the de facto performance of the semiotic system.

Constitutional semiotic signifiers are tools for the signification and expression of meaning. They are phenomena that are capable of symbolising the objects of their signification in condensed, synthetic and emotionally and imaginary appealing ways. Efficient signifiers must be able to portray the symbolic representation of constitutional and constitutionally relevant meaning. At the same time, they should be capable of producing constitutionally relevant emotions shared in the constitutionally framed socio-political community. And, most importantly, they must be visually appealing to the same community which is also the addressee of the valid constitutional law.

[5] On the role of images in law, see A Wagner and W Pencak (eds), *Images in Law* (Farnham, Ashgate, 2006) 1–318; C Spiesel, R Sherwin and N Feigenson, 'Law in the Age of Images: The Challenge of Visual Literacy' in A Wagner, T Summerfield and F Benavides Vanegas (eds), *Contemporary Issues of Semiotics of Law* (Oxford, Hart Publishing, 2005) 231–57.

[6] On the concept of signifiers, signification and signifieds, see F de Saussure, *Course in General Linguistics* (London, Forgotten Books, 2018) 1–260' C Peirce, *Collected Papers of Charles Sanders Peirce, Volumes I and II: Principles of Philosophy and Elements of Logic* (edited by C Hartshorne and P Weiss) (Cambridge, MA, Belknap Press, 1932) 1–962; C Peirce, *Peirce on Signs: Writings on Semiotic* (edited by J Hoopes) (Chapel Hill, University of North Carolina Press, 1991) 1–294; N Howser and C Kloesel (eds), *The Essential Peirce, Volume 1: Selected Philosophical Writings (1867–1893)* (Bloomington, Indiana University Press, 1992) 1–448; and Peirce Edition Project (ed), *The Essential Peirce, Volume 2: Selected Philosophical Writings, 1893–1913* (Bloomington, Indiana University Press, 1998) 1–624; R Barthes, *Elements of Semiology* (New York, Hill & Wang, 1977) 35–54; D Chandler, *Semiotics: The Basics* (Abingdon, Routledge, 2017) 1–352; T Sebeok, *Signs: An Introduction to Semiotics* (Toronto, University of Toronto Press, 2001) 1–216; T Sebeok, *A Sign is Just a Sign* (Bloomington, Indiana University Press, 1991) 1–170; U Eco, *A Theory of Semiotics* (Bloomington, Indiana University Press, 1978) 1–368; M Bergman, *Peirce's Philosophy of Communication: The Rhetorical Underpinnings of the Theory of Signs* (London, Bloomsbury, 2011) 1–206.

Indeed, not all signifiers may be visually appealing (eg, textual signifiers), but most of them are. This is particularly true for visual and performative signifiers of meaning. It should be noted that the visual and emotional appeal of the constitutional semiotic signifiers is an important quality for their practical efficiency and empirical relevance for the process of constitutional semiosis. Nevertheless, the low capacity and levels of such an appeal does not necessarily deprive the signifier of its overall conceptualisation as a constitutional semiotic signifier; it merely determines its capacity to convey meaning in a way that can enchant the public and have a lasting impact on its collective constitutional imaginaries.

The determination of the constitutional signifiers of meaning depends on the methodological approach to the constitution and constitutionalism. Legal positivism methodologically allows only textual signifiers of meaning. Thus, constitutional semiotics will be limited to textual and normative-institutional constitutionalism, while visual and performative signifiers of constitutional and constitutionally relevant meaning will be excluded. The same is true of legal realism,[7] the only difference being that it broadens the scope of textual constitutionalism with the case law of courts (especially constitutional and supreme courts) and is prone to looking for textual signifiers in judicially created sources of law.[8]

A broader socio-legal approach to the constitution, constitutionalism and constitutional law expands the realm of constitutional semiotics beyond valid law. It may also include within its scope the empirical performance of constitutional phenomena and institutions, and their perception in the individual and collective constitutional imagination and in constitutional anthropology. Hence, the range of constitutional signifiers looks rather different if it is approached from a socio-legal perspective. Depending on the focus of the socio-legal approach which might be more sociologically oriented, or psychologically, anthropologically or culturally inclined and biased, constitutional signifiers can be contained in symbolic-imaginary, visual, performative or even emotional constitutionalism.

If this approach is followed, then signifiers of constitutional and constitutionally relevant meaning may be sought and found among textual codes, symbols and metaphors. They can also be detected in textually expressed forms of symbolic-imaginary constitutionalism with huge signification potential, such as normative ideologies and ideas, constitutional utopias, and constitutional myths and mythologies. Furthermore, visual symbols of constitutional phenomena and the performative representation of constitutional meaning should also be considered as an important part of constitutional semiotics.

[7] On the relationship between legal realism and legal semiotics, see M Saltman, 'Legal Realism in a Cross-cultural Context' in R Kevelson (ed), *Law and Semiotics*, vol 2 (New York, Plenum Press, 1988) 293–307.

[8] For more on the structure and process of textual signification of meaning, see D Klinck, *Word of the Law: Approaches to Legal Discourse* (Ottawa, Carleton University Press, 1992) 46–87. For more on the relevance of the choice of sources of law for the semiotic analysis of law, see E Menezes de Carvalho, *Semiotics of International Law: Trade and Translation* (Dordrecht, Springer, 2011) 28–37.

Consequently, constitutional semiotic signifiers are all possible bearers of constitutionally relevant meaning that are capable of its synthesis and symbolic representation. Constitutional relevance is predetermined by the methodological approach of the analyst. Thus, it may be limited to valid law and forms of normative-institutional and textual constitutionalism, or may go beyond this traditional restraint of the scope of constitutional relevance.

The second determinant of the semiotic process is the range and scope of signification. The main issue here is the delimitation between the epistemic (cognitive) and the semiotic (symbolic-expressive and denoting) part of the construction, deconstruction and reconstruction of meaning. All forms of representation of meaning contain epistemic and semiotic components. This is a result of the fact that the cognition and signification, understanding or implying of meaning and representation of meaning are intrinsically intertwined but still separate phenomena.

This is the reason why this book is grounded in a mixed epistemological-semiotic approach. Regardless of whether meaning is contained in textual, normative-institutional, visual, performative or symbolic-imaginary constitutionalism, it requires both understanding and expression in a way that combines rational, emotional and imaginary approaches. Furthermore, the deconstruction, construction and reconstruction of meaning can best be achieved through a combination of epistemology and semiotics.

Nevertheless, this book is entitled *Constitutional Semiotics* and not *Constitutional Epistemology*, despite its huge epistemic potential and its wide engagement with issues of constitutional epistemology. The reason for this is that the phenomenon which frames the analysis is the way in which constitutional meaning is expressed, represented and signified by constitutional narrators, visualisers and performers.

Hence, constitutional semiotics is the scientific framing paradigm that generally defines the object and scope of the analysis. Indeed, the broader phenomena explored in this book – namely textual, symbolic-imaginary and visual constitutionalism – are epistemic entities and containers of meaning. However, the book focuses on the modalities and instruments through which this meaning is signified, represented and expressed, and is not preoccupied with the achievement of meaning per se as substantial category and a core of constitutional epistemology.

In summary, constitutional semiotics is explored as a conceptual phenomenon with normative, theoretical, and pragmatic implications. It is defined as a paradigm that is capable of grasping in a coherent and systematic way the process of the signification of meaning in constitutionalism perceived as a multitude of discourses ranging from rational, normative-institutional and textual to visual, performative, emotional and symbolic-imaginary constitutionalism. In that regard, constitutional semiotics is a theory (and a meta-theory) that explores the multidiscursive process of the constitutional signification of meaning (constitutional semiosis) through a range of collective imaginaries expressed via different semiotic tools for signification (constitutional signifiers).

The third and final determinant of the semiotic process is its signification focus consisting of the range and scope of signified objects and targets of representation of meaning – in other words, the range of constitutional signifieds. This element of practical constitutional semiosis, which is a constitutive element of constitutional semiotics as a conceptual paradigm, is again largely dependent on the same methodological concerns and determinants related to the choice of theoretical approach that have already been discussed above in relation to the system of constitutional semiotic signifiers.

To put it another way, the scope of constitutional signifieds, which are detected and determined as forms of constitutional signification, may vary from purely normative-institutional phenomena entrenched in textual constitutionalism to a broader range of objects belonging to the empirical and imaginary reality. In this latter case, the object of signification (the constitutional signified) may be the socio-legal imprints of constitutional institutions and other constitutional phenomena or their projections in the realms of collective constitutional imaginaries and constitutional anthropology.

Hence, from the viewpoint of the latter symbolic-imaginary dimension of constitutionalism, the object of constitutional signification and thus the range of constitutional signifieds is twofold. Constitutional signifieds may either be normative-institutional phenomena belonging to the sphere of valid law or empirical (socio-legal) phenomena. Thus, the signifieds may be part of normative-institutional constitutionalism. Nevertheless, they may also stem from law in action. In this case (when the signifieds are part of law in action), they can be either the imprints of legal institutions on the plain of empirical reality or the durable patterns of behaviour that have gained de facto constitutional approval and constitutional relevance. They may be signified in the realm of collective imaginaries and made available to the individual or collective imagination through significations and signifiers belonging to textual, visual, performative or symbolic-imaginary constitutionalism.

In other words, the constitutionally relevant signifieds may be signified via text, speech, image or performance. Most frequently, constitutional semiosis is accomplished through textual, performative and visual acts, while the semiotic representation of meaning via verbal acts is something of a rarity. This is for two reasons: the volatility and perishability of the verbal act, and its low capacity and ability for the semiotic signification of meaning.

The perspective used in this book is socio-legal in its broadest sense. Consequently, the theory of constitutional semiotics which I am proposing here is socio-legal, extensive and inclusive. This means that, in my view, the range of constitutional signifieds includes phenomena that belong not only to textual but also to symbolic-imaginary, visual and performative constitutionalism.

PART II

Textual Constitutionalism and its Role in Constitutional Semiotics

1

The Concept of Textual Constitutionalism

In this part, I will explore the constitutional text, constitutional texture and constitutional narratives as a means for unfolding and constructing of textual constitutionalism and their importance for constitutional semiotics. This part assesses the semiotic importance of constitutional texture. It explores the semiotic potential of the constitutional text and defines it as a repository of semiotic meaning.[1] Furthermore, it problematises the tension between the holistic nature of the constitution as a semiotic and epistemic project that is textually embedded and entrenched, and its discursive features that deconstruct the textual constitutionalism into a range of constitutional narratives and stories.[2] It is devoted to constitutional texture and the semiotic representation of textually encoded constitutionally relevant meaning. In that regard, it also explores the problems relating to constitutional narratives and authoritative constitutional narrators.[3]

A book devoted to constitutional semiotics must pay special attention to constitutional text and texture.[4] This is due to the fact that the semiotic representation of meaning requires instruments for its accomplishment, and the constitutional text and texture fulfil that function. They are the *conditio sine qua non* for constitutional semiotics, since they are containers of semiotic figures with strategic importance for constitutionalism and constitutional law. The textuality of constitutionalism is demonstrated by the constitutional entrenchment of semiotic figures in the constitutional text and texture. Thus, they are bearers of semiotic signification.[5] Conversely, the textuality of constitutionalism and the textual entrenchment of constitutional semiosis require their textual description, deconstruction, systematisation and explanation, which results in the production of new forms of textual

[1] For more on the importance of textualisation, textualism and the narrative construction of meaning for its signification and representation, see W Kelber, 'In the Beginning were the Words: The Apotheosis and Narrative Displacement of the Logos' (1990) LVIII(1) *Journal of the American Academy of Religion* 69, https://doi.org/10.1093/jaarel/LVIII.1.69.

[2] See P Brooks, 'Legal Stories, the Reality Effect and Visual Narratives. A Response to Simon Stern' in M Hanne and R Weisberg (eds), *Narrative and Metaphor in the Law* (Cambridge, Cambridge University Press, 2018).

[3] For the relationship between the narrator, narratee, narrated and narratives, see D Klinck, *Word of the Law: Approaches to Legal Discourse* (Ottawa, Carleton University Press, 1992) 291–323.

[4] J Broekman and L Cata Backer, *Lawyers Making Meaning: The Semiotics of Law in Legal Education II* (Dordrecht, Springer, 2013) 64.

[5] See also Kelber (n 1).

representation of meaning with constitutional relevance. These are the theoretical texts that form constitutional doctrine in general and the theory of constitutional semiotics and of symbolic-imaginary constitutionalism in particular.

Hence, the textuality of constitutionalism, its textual entrenchment, and its structuring and framing in texts and texture produce two types of semiotic processes of signification of constitutionally relevant meaning. First, signifieds from the socio-political reality and the empirical world are represented in the constitutional text through constitutional signifiers provided by the apparatus of constitutional law and belonging to the realm of the valid axiological and institutional design enshrined in the written constitution. Second, the constitutional text containing the provisions of the valid constitutional law contains signifieds that are further represented by signifiers of the socio-legal realm producing constitutional textures that have huge symbolic and imaginary importance. Moreover, they are represented in the process of their theoretical conceptualisation through signifiers of constitutional theory and constitutional meta-theory.[6]

Consequently, the constitutional text is the medium through which multiple processes of semiotic signification are accomplished. These are processes for signification of meaning produced within the empirical reality in the normative reality of the valid law and subsequently emerging from the latter, resulting in new representations and significations in the constitutional imagination, constitutional doctrine and constitutional anthropology. In that regard, constitutional text is the fundamental and irreplaceable link between the socio-political, normative-institutional and ideal-imaginary aspects of constitutionalism.

The overall phenomenon reflecting, denominating and exploring the strategic importance of constitutional text for the above-mentioned multitude of representations of constitutionally relevant meaning is textual constitutionalism. In a sense, it may seem that constitutionalism is in principle a textual phenomenon, since valid constitutional law is expressed via legal texts. This is not absolutely true because the symbolic-imaginary and socio-legal aspects of constitutionalism are largely separate from its textually entrenched normative-institutional dimension. Moreover, constitutional institutions have empirical manifestations which are dependent on their textually prescribed frames, but also possess a degree of autonomy from them based on the normativity of the factual behaviour.[7] Thus, there is a need for the conceptualisation of a specific category of constitutionalism – textual constitutionalism – focusing on the textual dimension of constitutional law.

Here it should be noted that textual constitutionalism is not limited to constitutional semiotics. It does not include only significations relating to symbolic-imaginary constitutionalism. Moreover, it is an independent and separate

[6] Constitutional theory explains the normative, institutional and socio-legal dimensions of constitutional law. Constitutional meta-theory is a theory about constitutional theory. It structures, orders and explains constitutional theory, offering constructive and deconstructive conceptual and methodological insights. The theory of constitutional geometry that I am proposing here is an example of constitutional meta-theory.

[7] J Stalev, *The Normative Power of the Factual* (Sofia, Feneya, 2007) 1–280 (in Bulgarian).

phenomenon and concept that should be distinguished from symbolic-imaginary constitutionalism. Textual constitutionalism frames and explores the role of constitutional text and texture for constitutional law. Symbolic-imaginary constitutionalism conceptualises the collective constitutional symbols and imaginaries relating to constitutional epistemology and constitutional semiotics. Nevertheless, textual and symbolic-imaginary constitutionalism are interrelated because of the huge relevance of constitutional text and texture for constitutional semiotics. It has been said that constitutional semiotics is to an extent a textually entrenched phenomenon. This is due to the fact that constitutional semiosis unfolds on textual, visual and performative plains that are mostly created by authoritative writers, narrators, visualisers and performers, and are maintained by the collective constitutional imaginaries of the constitutionally framed socio-legal community.

The written constitution is a key instrument for the regulation and framing of phenomena relating to constitutional imaginaries. The constitutional text is the venue for the unfolding of the semiotic processes of representation of meaning structured around signifiers conceptualising the signified with constitutional relevance in the course of constitutional signification.[8] The constitutional text is a strategic device for structuring symbolic-imaginary constitutionalism. It is the basis for the organisation of semiotic meta-theories such as constitutional geometry aiming at explaining the semiotic structures of the constitutional order.

Hence, there is a need for a separate conceptualisation of constitutional texture, its role in symbolic-imaginary constitutionalism and its semiotic importance. This can be done on the basis of a theory which can be defined as textual constitutionalism. Thus, textual constitutionalism is the intellectual and conceptual bond between several concepts with strategic importance for constitutionalism and constitutional law. These are the concepts of the written constitution, constitutional symbols, constitutional ideology and constitutional imaginaries.

Textual constitutionalism should be conceived as a form of constitutionalism emphasising the centrality of text and texture for the constitution and constitutional law. It shows the role of text and texture as fundamental prerequisites for the unfolding of constitutionalism as an overall socio-political, legal and intellectual phenomenon. They provide for and constitute a strategic discourse for the representation and signification of meaning in textual form. Textual constitutionalism is a discourse of constitutionalism that exposes the textual dependence of the constitution and constitutional law, offering insights into the signification of the constitutionally relevant signified and thus serving as a background for a semiotic approach to constitutional phenomena. Textual constitutionalism is a paradigm for the conceptualisation of the constitution and constitutional law as textually entrenched phenomena prone to the semiotic conveyance of meaning and thus to exploration via recourse to constitutional semiotics.

[8] For an interesting analysis of the structure of textual signification of legal and legally relevant meaning, see T Panji Nugraha and S Na'afi, 'Legal Semiotics Approach: Understanding Asymmetrical Symbols Behind Text of Positive Legal Norms' (2021) 1(1) *Indonesian Journal of Legal Thought* 67.

Textual constitutionalism brings to the fore the conceptual and strategic importance of the constitutional text as a basis and framework for structuring the constitutional reality. In that sense, textual constitutionalism should be considered as interrelated with two main trends in the history of ideas: the textually related and textually oriented theories of law (especially theories of legal interpretation) and the conceptual approaches relating to the so-called 'linguistic turn' in the social sciences and humanities.[9] In that regard, textual constitutionalism is a phenomenon that is placed at the intellectual crossroads between constitutional semiotics, constitutional hermeneutics and constitutional epistemology. It takes inspiration from all three branches of textually related constitutional studies.

Textual constitutionalism is based on the signification and representation of meaning in textual form and on the deconstruction, reconstruction and construction of meaning by textual means. Such means frequently have huge semiotic importance. This stems from the fact that textual constitutionalism (and the constitutional text itself) contains constitutional codes, constitutional memories, constitutional dreams and all other forms of constitutional imaginaries, all of which aim at the representation and signification of meaning in a semiotic process.

This process is a constitutional semiotic process – a semiotic process that is constitutionally relevant – for several reasons. It is accomplished on the basis of constitutional text and constitutional texture. It conveys meaning through semiotic means. It is relevant for constitutionalism in all of its dimensions – theoretical, imaginative, symbolic, normative, institutional and socio-legal. And it is structured around constitutional phenomena belonging to the constitutional axiology or the constitutional design.

Textual constitutionalism exposes the nature of the constitution as a textual phenomenon – as a power phenomenon entrenched in text. In this way, it demonstrates the key role of the constitutional text for the organising, preserving and conveying of meaning. Thus, textual constitutionalism is closely interrelated with constitutional epistemology and constitutional semiotics. Both the constitutional text and the constitutional texture are, from a semiotic perspective, containers of semiotic signification and a representation of meaning accomplished through constitutional narratives, constitutional imaginaries and constitutional symbols. They are organised in the form of constitutional codes, constitutional symbols, constitutional myths and other means of constitutional semiotics. In this regard, textual constitutionalism is a discourse for the expression of constitutional mythology and normative constitutional ideology as key aspects of symbolic-imaginary constitutionalism. This shows the interrelation of constitutional semiotics, textual constitutionalism and symbolic-imaginary constitutionalism.

[9] See R Rorty (ed), *The Linguistic Turn: Essays in Philosophical Method* (Chicago, University of Chicago Press, 1992) 1–416; K Hirschkop, *Linguistic Turns, 1890–1950: Writing on Language as Social Theory* (Oxford, Oxford University Press 2019) 1–337; and B Alderman, *Symptom, Symbol, and the Other of Language: A Jungian Interpretation of the Linguistic Turn* (Abingdon, Routledge, 2015) 1–161.

2

Constitutional Communication Perceived through the Semiotic Perspective of Textual Constitutionalism

Constitutional communication is a form of political communication. Hence, it possesses all the features of general political communication. However, it differs from this in three main respects: the content; the forms of and methods for their expression; and the degree of legal institutionalisation.

Constitutional communication is political communication that relates to constitutionally relevant issues. It is political communication that concerns the constitutional foundations of the human status (human rights or duties), the institutions of the public sphere (political parties, non-governmental organisations, the media etc), the institutions of public power, and the overall constitutional axiology and constitutional design. All these issues are constitutionally relevant elements of both the constitutional and the political order. Thus, they are objects of constitutional communication and as such are targets for deliberation, exploration and communicative deconstruction, construction and reconstruction of meaning. Some of these discursive practices have semiotic importance and are relevant for constitutional semiotics.[1]

The discursive construction, deconstruction[2] and reconstruction of the information contents of constitutional communication are carried out via institutionalised and non-institutionalised means. Constitutional communication differs from political communication, especially with regard to its institutionalised forms and instruments. These are the legal and the political acts issued or adopted by state institutions. Hence, institutionalised constitutional communication is contained not only in political acts (declarations, addresses, messages etc), but also in draft legal acts and in legal acts (whether individual or normative) which are adopted

[1] On the symbolic dimension of legal and political communication, see J Přibáň, *Constitutional Imaginaries: A Theory of European Societal Constitutionalism* (Abingdon, Routledge, 2020) 90.

[2] See P Salmon, 'How to Deconstruct the World', *Psyche*, https://psyche.co/guides/how-to-deconstruct-the-world-by-thinking-like-jacques-derrida?fbclid=IwAR1nVvSqfBr8VYxsDbQJdYct2k7B8QTgOwKmpB_zX2DhY-9rAvmNmRxgRA4.

and have entered into force. At the same time, the political acts are communicative devices for both political and constitutional communication, but they differ with regard to the first criterion, namely the content.

Political communication may be accomplished by virtue of different means, which may be verbal, textual, non-verbal, performative, visual etc. Indeed, constitutional communication in a proper sense is mainly contained and expressed in verbal and textual forms. However, it may also be detected and decoded in non-verbal, performative, and visual acts when it merges with political communication.

In all cases, both political and constitutional communication are used for the representation and signification of meaning.[3] In that regard, they are of key importance for constitutional semiotics and for semiotic studies of the constitution, which is perceived as a discursive act with projections in the realm of the symbolic-imaginary, the visual and the performative. Thus, constitutional communication is one of the keys for understanding symbolic-imaginary, visual and performative constitutionalism. It is also relevant for emotional constitutionalism because it is a powerful device (or more precisely a set of tools) for the modelling and mastering of constitutional emotions. The forms of constitutional communication are the strings on which the constitutional melody is played,[4] thus enchanting or annoying the constitutional public by provoking constitutionally relevant emotions and activating constitutional imaginaries.[5]

The constitution itself as a textual intellectual project may also be perceived as a form of constitutional communication. To be more precise, it is a container of messages, codes, symbols and information content that may be used in constitutional communication as well as in political communication. Such communication may be instrumental and pragmatic, but also substantial. An underestimated aspect of the constitutional communication based on the text, textuality and texture of the constitution is its symbolic-imaginary dimension.

One of the main tasks of constitutional semiotics is to expose the nature of the constitution as a result of the semiotic process of representation of socially relevant constitutional content frequently accomplished in forms that are specific bearers of semiotic signification of meaning. These are constitutional myths and mythologies, constitutional codes, constitutional dreams, constitutional memories, the constitutional ideal and ideologies, and constitutional utopias.[6]

The constitution is the starting point of visual constitutionalism. It is a criterion for the relevance of textuality and its forms as bearers of constitutional

[3] See J Broekman and L Cata Backer, *Lawyers Making Meaning: The Semiotics of Law in Legal Education II* (Dordrecht, Springer, 2013) 9–11 and 21.

[4] For the concept of the law's melody, see J Sammons, 'The Law's Melody' (2010) 55 *Villanova Law Review* 1143.

[5] See A Amaya and M Del Mar (eds), *Virtue, Emotion and Imagination in Law and Legal Reasoning* (Oxford, Hart Publishing, 2020) 1–275.

[6] E Black, *Our Constitution: The Myth That Binds Us* (Boulder, Westview Press, 1988); and O Tans, 'Imagined Constitutionality: Rethinking Democratic Citizenship with the Aid of Fiction Theory' (2019) 15(2) *Law, Culture and the Humanities* 1.

semiotic information. Indeed, visual constitutionalism is not limited to the constitution, but manifests itself mainly in the constitutionally relevant performances and instantiations in the socio-legal context,[7] including in forms of art. However, the constitution frequently contains information about the visual symbols of the state and society. This overlapping of the symbolic-ritual and the visual elements of imaginary constitutionalism is also the starting point of visual constitutionalism.

The constitutional imaginaries are also initial references that may trigger discourses of constitutional communication. Constitutional myths and mythologies, ideals and ideologies, codes, symbols and taboos are sources of constitutional argumentation, 'wells and fountains' of socio-legal and semiotic knowledge relating to constitutional archetypes and collective imaginaries, as well as pillars of strategic and tactical constitutional communication.

It is exactly these elements of symbolic-imaginary and visual constitutionalism, which are the object of constitutional communication, that are placed at the core of constitutional semiotics. Thus, they can be explained from multiple analytical angles, namely from the viewpoint of constitutional epistemology, constitutional communication and constitutional semiotics. This is the crossing point between discursive-communicative studies, linguistic studies and constitutional semiotics.

In a sense, the constitution lies at the core of the constitutional and political debate in both authoritarian and democratic societies. It is the node of transgenerational dialogue on constitutional issues. The dialogue is usually considered to be related to rational constitutionalism. It is frequently defined in terms of a rational reaction to previous constitutional models and of imposing rationality for the future. Constitutional drafting and constitutional reforms are conceived and presented as a result of public reason, rational deliberation and rational decision-making. Thus, the constitution and its amendments are supposed to be strategic sources of rational legitimacy.[8]

However, the constitutional dialogue with the past, present and future generations rooted in the constitution and performed implicitly through entrenchment in the constitutional texture or explicitly by virtue of subsequent semiotic interpretation in the scientific, jurisprudential or legisprudential[9] discourses, or through recourse to constitutional communication, is also grounded in myths, mythologies and ideologies. It is dependent on codes and metaphors signifying encoded semiotic content. In that regard, the constitution is the codification of the fears, dreams and hopes of both the past and the future.[10]

[7] See D Law, *Constitutionalism in Context* (Cambridge, Cambridge University Press, 2021).

[8] See, eg, J. Patty and E Penn, *Social Choice and Legitimacy: The Possibilities of Impossibility* (Cambridge, Cambridge University Press, 2014) 1–224.

[9] For more on legisprudence, see L Wintgens and A Daniel Oliver-Lalana, *The Rationality and Justification of Legislation: Essays in Legisprudence* (Dordrecht, Springer, 2013) 1–202.

[10] M Belov and A Abat i Ninet (eds), *Revolution, Transition, Memory, and Oblivion: Reflections on Constitutional Change* (Cheltenham, Edward Elgar, 2020), 1–244; R Kosellek, *Futures Past: On the Semantics of Historical Time* (New York, Columbia University Press, 2004) 205–22.

The singularity of the constitutional moment is verbally constructed, visually demonstrated and performed (and thus to an extent also consumed) in discursive acts of constitutional and political communication. It is textually enshrined and, moreover, encoded in the constitution as a transtemporal, transgenerational and intergenerational semiotic project. The constitution is a form of reworking the past and a tool for modelling and even predicting the future. It is a transgenerational textual semiotic project in the sense that it not only has contextual meaning relevant for the epoch and generation in question, but also has or pretends to possess universal meaning. This meaning is supposed to be and usually claims to be typical for the distinct nation taken as a transtemporal constitutional community. It is intergenerational because it binds different generations by reflecting (in a positive or negative way) the achievements of the past and also tries to serve as guidance for the people to come in the future. Either way, the constitution represents meaning and signifies constitutionally relevant signifieds, which are then communicated to the constitutional semiotic community by its authoritative speakers, narrators and storytellers.[11] This usually implies the deconstruction of codes, myths, dreams, fears and other bearers of symbolic meaning through constitutional semiotics, which is then exposed and transmitted to the semiotic discursive community by virtue of constitutional communication.

Thus, the constitutional present is always constructed discursively and dialogically. It is constructed by the authoritative narrators on the basis of the constitution as authoritative text and a container of semiotic representation of meaning. The constitutional text (the linguistic-textual fixed nature of representations and significations of constitutionally relevant information) and the constitutional texture (the broader composition of signs and symbols in the socio-legal context that have constitutional semiotic relevance) are permanently negotiated via constitutional communication.

This shows that the constitution is an act of power and order, and constitutional law and constitutionalism are about power, authority, will and interest. But the constitution is also a reservoir of information, including a container of bearers of semiotic meaning (codes, myths etc). Thus, constitutionalism and constitutional law are also about information, communication, representation and the signification of meaning. In that regard, constitutionalism can also be defined as a process of generating, processing, transmitting and preserving of information. A very special and important part of constitutionalism-as-communication-and-information is the representation and signification of symbolic meaning through constitutional semiosis. This is a phenomenon and process that predetermines and shapes the symbolic-imaginary, textual and visual, but also performative and to an extent emotional constitutionalism.

Hence, from the viewpoint of constitutional semiotics, the constitutional present is nothing more than the concrete instantiation in the sense of a temporal

[11] The impact of narrated law on the representation of legal phenomena is well explored in H White, 'The Value of Narrativity in the Representation of Reality (1980) 7 *Critical Inquiry* 5.

stabilisation of meaning objectivised in the constitutional text, the constitutional texture and constitutional gesture (constitutional performance). Such a stabilised representation and signification of meaning is possible only in the presumably static moment of the constitutional present. The constitutional future and the constitutional past are permanently discursively negotiated in the form of constitutional stories and constitutional narratives by the authoritative speakers of the constitutionally framed discursive and semiotic community.[12]

The constitutional intergenerational dialogue may be explicit or implicit. It is explicit when there are direct references to previous or future generations in the constitution. This is usually done in the constitutional preamble.[13] In that regard, the preamble may be conceived as a dispatching point in the intergenerational dialogue. It sets the constitution on the temporal continuum composed of the constitutional past, constitutional present and constitutional future and the narratives related to constitutional dreams, memories, hopes and fears.

The dialogue is implicit when the constitution contains hidden messages that signify meaning related to the past or the future.[14] In such cases, this meaning requires systematic interpretation in order to be exposed and explained. While one can think of such an intellectual exercise as a form of 'digging out of meaning' enshrined by the constitutional legislator and inherited from the past, in practice it is much closer to the 'carving out' of meaning or shaping of meaning by the players of constitutional communication and mainly by the constitutional narrators.

The digging metaphor is bound to the idea that the meaning is already vested in the text by the original narrators – the constitutional legislator or, even more powerfully, the people as a sovereign – while the subsequent readers must only discover the entrenched representations and significations of constitutionally relevant signifieds. Such modest, historically true interpretative activity is at most reconstructive; it can never be deconstructive or constructive. The semiotic phenomena are vested once and forever and are simply waiting to be (re)discovered by the subsequent readers and writers – in other words, interpreters belonging to the semiotic discursive community. It does not matter whether they are ordinary communicative agents or authoritative narrators, speakers or storytellers.

The carving out metaphor, on the other hand, inspires a more dynamic, procedural and prospective approach to the constitution as a semiotic container and textual framework of constitutional signifiers of meaning. The digging out metaphor is static because it focuses on a concrete and specific moment of constitutional creation and of representation and signification of meaning fixed within the

[12] See P Brooks, 'Legal Stories, the Reality Effect and Visual Narratives: A Response to Simon Stern' in M Hanne and R Weisberg (eds) *Narrative and Metaphor in the Law* (Cambridge, Cambridge University Press, 2018); and D Klinck, *Word of the Law: Approaches to Legal Discourse* (Ottawa, Carleton University Press, 1992) 232–91.

[13] M Belov, 'The Preamble of the Constitution in the European Constitutionalism' (2013) 20 *Revista General de Derecho Romano*.

[14] On the symbolic construction of the social and political community through the symbolic signification of its past, see A Cohen, *Symbolic Construction of Community* (Abingdon, Routledge, 1985) 99–104.

quasi-magical moment of the constituent situation. It is retrospective because for it, what counts are the semiotic entities enshrined and, in a non-formal sense, even entrenched in the constitutional text in the foundational constituent moment. Such entrenchment is informal because it demonstrates the conservative-retrospective attitude of the proponents of historical interpretation of constitutional semiotics. Thus, it has to be differentiated from the entrenched and the unamendable clauses of the constitutions which concern the procedure for constitutional amendment.

The historical interpretation of constitutional semiotics suggests that semiosis exists only in the constituent moment. The political foundations of the state and their formal-legal inauguration in the form of a constitution (or constitutional amendment, reform or revolution) are given in a concrete historical moment, which also limits the process of semiotic representation and signification of meaning. This meaning should be retrospectively discovered or rediscovered and 'dug out' of the constitutional text as a historically pre-given artefact fixing static the semiotic landscape.

This historical, retrospective and static interpretation of constitutional semiotics, represented by the 'digging out' metaphor, has one advantage: it brings to the fore the fact that the constitutional legislator encodes, engraves and entrenches semiotic heritage, messages and thresholds. These should serve as normative criteria for the subsequent epistemological efforts in their discovery and interpretation, and have to determine the semantic core of the semiotic phenomena that will be prone to deconstruction or reconstruction in the future. Such an entrenched semiotic landscape, engraved in the foundational or reformist constitutional moments,[15] provides a degree of objectivity and stability in the constitutional semiotic forms. It requires constitutional scholars to admit the existence of foundational constitutional semiotics providing for an encoded signification-representative constitutional alphabet of signs and symbols.

However, such a static, formalistic, retrospective and conservative approach, understanding the constitution as a pre-given legal but also as a semiotic order, deprives it of the ability to adjust to the evolving socio-legal context. Moreover, this is not the way in which the constitutional semiotics is understood and practised by members of the constitutional semiotic community. Indeed, the constitution predetermines the framework of the semiotic process. It serves as a core for the epistemic discovery of semiotic heritage. But it also has to be admitted that members of the constitutional semiotic community engage in explicit and implicit practices for constitutional discussion. They deliberate on constitutional semiotic figures carved out in constitutional text and rediscover them in constitutional texture while speaking, writing and even staging and performing the constitution.

The constitutional text is prone to evolution and to the semantic expansion of its semiotic landscapes by members of the semiotic community, but especially by

[15] See B Ackerman, *We the People: Foundations* (Cambridge, MA, Harvard University Press, 1991) 266.

authoritative interpreters, narrators and storytellers.[16] However – and what is even more exciting – the constitution is also evolving beyond its text in the constitutional texture of symbols, signs and forms that demonstrate and represent meaning in a performative way. Thus, constitutional semiotics is an essentially dynamic and prospective concept that has evolved in different ways, both within and beyond textual constitutionalism. This is done in symbolic-imaginary, visual and performative constitutionalism as well. In any case, central role for such a 'carving out' of meaning, frequently represented as the 'digging out' of semiotic figures inherited from the past, is performed by constitutional narrators as authoritative speakers of the constitutional semiotic community.

[16] See also D Cornell, The Problem of Normative Authority in Legal Interpretation in R Kevelson (ed), *Law and Semiotics*, vol 1 (New York, Plenum Press, 1987) 149–59.

3

The Constitution as a Discursive Semiotic Project

Constitutional Narratives, Constitutional Narrators and the Constitutional Semiotic Community

In this chapter, I will briefly clarify what is meant by 'discursive community' and 'semiotic community'. The clarification of these concepts is necessary because the semiotic process based on the written constitution and written constitutional law traditionally unfolds within the confines of a specific and distinct group of participants. This group is framed by the language in which the constitution and constitutional law are written and in which the constitutional narratives and stories are written and told.[1] Thus, the scope of the semiotic community is linguistically predetermined. Consequently, this makes the semiotic community also a discursive community. However, not all discursive communities are also semiotic communities, as will be clarified below.

Indeed, symbolic-imaginary and visual constitutionalism may also be performed, played, told, imposed, demonstrated, negotiated or implemented by virtue of non-verbal acts. The performative dimension of constitutionalism is largely underestimated in constitutional theory. It is driven to the periphery of knowledge and scientific interest by the predominant textual constitutionalism grounded in the concept of the linguistic and textual entrenchment of constitutional phenomena and constitutional law. That is why certain parts of this book will be devoted to symbolic-imaginary, visual and performative constitutionalism.

It is true that textual constitutionalism if of paramount importance for constitutionalism. Modern constitutional law is written law. The modern concept of the constitution is intrinsically bound within its written and codified character.[2]

[1] For more on the constitutional 'narratives of magic and deceit', see G Frankenberg, *Comparative Constitutional Studies: Between Magic and Deceit* (Cheltenham, Edward Elgar, 2018) 11–13. For a critical approach on narratives in law, see P Brooks, 'Narrative Transactions: Does the Law Need a Narratology?' (2006) 8(1) *Yale Journal of Law & the Humanities* 1. On the relationship between myth and language, see E Cassierer, *The Myth of the State* (New Haven, Yale University Press, 2009) 16–23.

[2] J-L Halperin, *Five Legal Revolutions since the 17th Century: An Analysis of a Global Legal History* (Dordrecht, Springer, 2014) 35–73.

Hence, modern constitutionalism is textual constitutionalism. Yet, premodern political orders were relying to a great extent on political imaginaries,[3] symbolic representations and performative symbolic acts. Now, with the rise of social media, the medialisation of constitutionalism and constitutional law, and the enhancement of symbolic politics in the context of the information and communication revolution, we are seeing the rising importance of visual, symbolic-imaginary and performative constitutionalism.

The exclusiveness of textual constitutionalism is rock-solid only if constitutionalism is understood as limited to valid constitutional law, to the law in books and, more precisely, to the system of sources of written constitutional law. However, if we broaden our horizons beyond written law and also include the intellectual, symbolic-imaginary realm of constitutionalism within the scope of research, the projection of constitutional law in the human mind, consciousness, subconsciousness and imagination, as well as its manifestations and instantiations in the socio-political reality (the law in action), then constitutionalism goes beyond textual constitutionalism. It also includes performative constitutionalism describing and encompassing the implementation of constitutional law, its functioning on the ground, the shapes of 'law in action' and the durable patterns of constitutionally relevant factual behaviour. A large part of this performative dimension of constitutionalism has semiotic potential and projects itself not only in performative constitutionalism, but also in symbolic-imaginary and visual constitutionalism.

The implications of constitutional law and constitutionalism in art should also be taken into account. The symbolic-visual representations of national symbols,[4] constitutional heroes, founding fathers and mothers, constitutional myths, mythologies, dreams,[5] codes, ideas and even taboos are important elements of visual constitutionalism.[6] They are the binding node between symbolic-imaginary and visual constitutionalism. They are based on a specific texture and specific language

[3] For a thorough analysis of political imaginaries, see C Bottici, *Imaginal Politics: Images Beyond Imagination and the Imaginary* (New York, Columbia University Press, 2014) 1–253; R Geuss, *Politics and the Imagination* (Princeton, Princeton University Press, 2010) 31–42; and J Grant, 'On the Critique of Political Imaginaries' (2014) 13(4) *European Journal of Political Theory* 408.

[4] According to Fitzsimmons, this requires 'a new language of politics and a new political imagery based on the new ideology of the nation'. His analysis concretely concerns the shift towards political modernity in France, but is applicable to all forms of political modernisation in the form of nationalism. See M Fitzsimmons, *The Remaking of France: The National Assembly and the Constitution of 1791* (Cambridge, Cambridge University Press, 2002) 59.

[5] On the representation of dreams, including dreams with socio-political relevance, via arts, see K Walton, *Mimesis as Make-Believe: On the Foundations of Representational Arts* (Cambridge, MA, Harvard University Press, 1993) 1-480.

[6] In fact, heroes and heroism can be represented not only in traditional heroic forms being carved out in the official pantheon of the nation; more recently, legal and constitutional ideas, including constitutional myths and mythologies and heroic narratives, have also been represented through visual signifiers belonging to pop culture. See T Giddens, 'Lex Comica: On Comics and Legal Theory' and G Ferris and C Lunt, 'Devil's Advocate: Representation in Heroic Fiction, *Daredevil* and the Law' in *Graphic Justice: Intersections of Comics and Law* (Abingdon, Routledge, 2015) 8–17 and 36–54 respectively.

of visual signs and symbols[7] depicting symbolic representations of constitutional narratives and stories.[8] Indeed, they tell the visual history of constitutionalism from a national and comparative perspective.

Consequently, performative constitutionalism and visual constitutionalism also have their own specific language. This comprises context-specific forms of semiotic representation, as well as regionally and universally readable and understandable semiotic significations. Such significations and representations may be relevant within a specific context (temporal, geographical, geopolitical, ideological etc) or may have the potential and capacity to reveal universally appealing and comprehensible meaning.

Thus, performative constitutionalism and visual constitutionalism, while not textually enshrined and not based on textual constitutionalism entrenched in a specific language, are still expressed on the basis of texture – a range of signs, shapes and forms for the representation and signification of meaning. However, this texture is not a text. Thus, it remains external to textual constitutionalism and the textual semiotic representation of constitutionally relevant meaning.

From a semiotic viewpoint, performative and visual constitutionalism and the stories they convey or tell are disadvantaged in the sense that they are deprived of official language that is universally and formally recognised. Without such language – and without a textual dimension – they are not supported by valid law. Nevertheless, this language is not always as objective and stable as it is often supposed to be. It is prone to interpretation, contextual adjustments and further development and negotiation of the meaning it carries and signifies.[9] On the other hand, performative and visual constitutionalism may have broader transboundary, transterritorial and transtemporal dimensions precisely because they offer universal insights and semiotic representations, and are freed from the burden of textual entrenchment and the need to refer to a specific discursive and semiotic community.

This allows for the establishment of a new branch of constitutional science devoted to the study of the performative and visual semiotics of constitutionalism. Such research can be accomplished from a comparative perspective or a historical perspective, or may be carried out with regard to law in context and subsequent exemplary case studies. The analysis may be devoted to the semiotic representation of constitutional content in official constitutional and political culture, in popular culture and even in critical, deconstructive, pop art and revolt movements. Such research must be provided by studies of visual constitutionalism, which are indeed

[7] J Broekman and L Cata Backer, *Lawyers Making Meaning: The Semiotics of Law in Legal Education II* (Dordrecht, Springer, 2013) 143–46.

[8] See also M Wolf, *Building Imaginary Worlds: The Theory and History of Subcreation* (Abingdon, Routledge, 2012) 1–394.

[9] On the phenomena of 'linguistic relativity', see D Klinck, *Word of the Law: Approaches to Legal Discourse* (Ottawa, Carleton University Press, 1992) 12–46.

on the rise.[10] But it can also be used to explore the field of performative constitutionalism devoted to the semiotic representation of meaning through human behaviour, for example, by the 'authoritative performers' of the community.

Nevertheless, it should be admitted that the textual representation of constitutional meaning is still rather central for our constitutional orders. Visual and performative imaginaries have an increasingly important role to play in our societies and in terms of the constitutional and political acculturation of the people. And, as noted above, they are transterritorial and transtemporal, playing the role of natural transmitters of constitutionally relevant content. Thus, perhaps the future of comparative constitutional law is in the comparative research of visual, symbolic-imaginary and performative constitutionalism from both an epistemic and a semiotic viewpoint.[11] It may be the case that comparative constitutional law will be supplemented by comparative constitutional semiotics and comparative constitutional anthropology. But the role of textual constitutionalism is still very important. So, textual constitutionalism is a key strategic playground for constitutional semiotics that both allows and requires the discursive and linguistic representation of meaning. That is why here I devote special attention to the following concepts: the discursive community, the semiotic community, constitutional stories and narratives, and constitutional narrators or storytellers.

'Discursive community' means a linguistic community structured around normative text, in which members engage in discursive interactions and performances with a textual basis and a linguistic core. 'Semiotic community' is a variant of this. It is a discursive community which conveys, signifies and communicates meaning through semiotic figures. A semiotic community is based upon text and texture expressed through discursive semiotic means. The semiotic community deliberates, expresses and exchanges meaning encapsulated in symbols. These might be geometric or more abstract figures, signs, myths, ideals, dreams or more complex and less visually expressive forms of signification, such as ideologies and mythologies that are in fact systems of elements with imaginary and visual significance, relevance and importance.

It is not necessary that all members of the semiotic and discursive community are permanently active and engage in performative acts of semiotic importance. It is sufficient that they are all exposed to, confronted with and participate in the communicative maintenance, construction, deconstruction and reconstruction of a common semiotic order. Thus, a constitutional semiotic community potentially includes all members of the constitutionally framed socio-political community. Indeed, it should also be taken into account that some of the members of the constitutional community may not feel enchanted and bound by its imaginary-visual,

[10] See, eg, J Bainbridge, 'Visual Law: The Changing Signifiers of Law in Popular Visual Culture' in A Wagner and J Broekman (eds), *Prospects of Legal Semiotics* (Dordrecht, Springer, 2010) 193–215.

[11] This approach is used in Frankenberg (n 1) 1–360.

symbolic and semiotic dimensions, while others who are not members of the constitutional community but are legal outsiders belonging to other constitutional community may feel this way. However, this is an empirical possibility, while from a legal viewpoint, normatively, all members of the constitutional community are potential members of the semiotic constitutional community that serves as a group for semiotic exchange of constitutional content. Here, the constitutional community denominates the range of people united by their legal status of belonging to a constitutional order. It should be noted that the question of what is the binding link to the constitutional community – the citizenship, the capacity of being the addressee to the valid constitutional law or a range of pre-legal social characteristics – is the subject of some dispute in constitutional theory.

Indeed, the most important semiotic and discursive impact on the constitutional semiotic community can be expected to be produced by the authoritative narrators. However, the mostly passive acceptance of the results and outcomes of the semiotic process by the other members of the semiotic community and their adherence to established and recognised semiotic schemes and common constitutional imaginaries also plays a fundamental role, for example, in the establishment of the constitutional anthropology and the constitutional culture of that group.

Proper and intense scientific discussion of the discursive representation and signification of meaning through constitutional semiotics in the constitutional text and texture is still underdeveloped in constitutional theory. Such discussion has to take into account not only the constitutional story but also the constitutional storytellers. The problems of constitutional stories and constitutional storytellers are interrelated, but still separate. Thus, they deserve attention both separately and in conjunction with one another.

This is exactly the aim of this part of the book. It will try to look at the constitution in a twofold way. First, I will explore it as a monolithic and holistic outcome of the sovereign will possessing quasi-magical status and elevated as part of the national pantheon of constituent myths, mythologies and normative ideologies.[12] Second, I will analyse it as a multilayered discursive product of a range of constitutional narratives (or constitutional stories) told by the authoritative speakers of the community.[13] Hence, here I will explore the textual constitutionalism as both a holistic project and as a system of constitutional narratives. More precisely, I will focus on the importance of textual constitutionalism as a container of semiotic meaning represented in both a holistic and a discursive way.

The definition of constitutional narratives (stories) and constitutional storytellers (the authoritative narrators or speakers of the community) and the exploration of the constitution through the lenses of these two separate but mutually related paradigms are especially relevant for the semiotic approach to the constitution and

[12] See Z Oklopcic, *Beyond the People: Social Imaginary and Constituent Imagination* (Oxford, Oxford University Press, 2018) 1–416.

[13] This approach to law is defined by Brooks as 'narratology'. See Brooks (n 1).

constitutional law.[14] It is methodologically important because such approach offers explanation how constitutional semiotic figures with huge relevance for visual and imaginary constitutionalism are produced through their textual representation and even entrenchment in textual constitutionalism. This is also conceptually important because it demonstrates the combination of static and dynamic ways of production, reproduction, construction, deconstruction and reconstruction of constitutional signification-symbolic systems.[15] In brief, constitutional semiotic phenomena can be result of the quasi-sacred process of constitution making presented as a holistic phenomenon or may be triggered by a multitude of discursive practices stemming from a range of constitutional narrators – the authoritative speakers of the constitutionally framed socio-legal discursive community.

Since the 'linguistic turn',[16] the importance of the text for the understanding, conveying, symbolising, constructing and deconstructing of meaning in the social sciences and the humanities has risen. Since the 'death of the author' and the 'birth of the interpreter',[17] the same has happened in relation to the discursive and dynamic understanding of the text as a product of the interplay between objective and subjective meaning, and between the sign and signified in the process of their signification.[18]

The post-modern turn[19] has shown that the very concept of single, stable, imminent, permanent and, in this sense, objective meaning is somewhat questionable.[20] Nevertheless, even if we consider texts (and, more precisely, constitutional texts) as objective phenomena and as bearers of stabilised, normative and thus to an extent objective meaning, we have to take into account the fact that the initially enshrined objective meaning can be evolved, developed, deconstructed, reconstructed and upgraded. This is done in an evolutionary manner by all members of the constitutionally framed socio-legal community, which is at the same time also a discursive and semiotic constitutional community. Such evolution of meaning is based on the pragmatic informal negotiation of meaning through a range of narratives[21] in the course of the accomplishment of socio-legal practices based

[14] Klinck (n 9) 291–323; D Cornell, 'The Problem of Normative Authority in Legal Interpretation' in R Kevelson (ed), *Law and Semiotics*, vol 1 (New York, Plenum Press, 1987) 149–59.

[15] On law as a symbolic system, see P Kahn, 'Comparative Constitutionalism in a New Key' (2003) 101(8) *Michigan Law Review* 2677.

[16] See R Rorty (ed), *The Linguistic Turn: Essays in Philosophical Method* (Chicago, University of Chicago Press, 1992) 1–416; K Hirschkop, *Linguistic Turns, 1890–1950: Writing on Language as Social Theory* (Oxford, Oxford University Press 2019) 1–337; and B Alderman, *Symptom, Symbol, and the Other of Language: A Jungian Interpretation of the Linguistic Turn* (Abingdon, Routledge, 2015) 1–161.

[17] R Barthes, *Image-Music-Text* (New York, Hill & Wang, 1978) 142–49.

[18] See U Eco, *Semiotics and the Philosophy of Language* (Bloomington, Indiana University Press, 1986) 14–46.

[19] For the so-called 'narrative turn' which is also post-modern and linguistic at the same time, see M Hyvärinen, 'Prototypes, Genres, and Concepts: Travelling with Narratives' (2012) 2(1) *Psychology* 10.

[20] See M Foucault, *Aesthetics, Method and Epistemology*, vol 2 (New York, The New Press, 1998) 205 et seq.

[21] Richardson defines this phenomenon as 'postmodern narratology'. See B Richardson, 'Recent Concepts of Narrative and the Narratives of Narrative Theory' (2000) 34 *Style* 168.

on the constitutional text. In other words, the meaning may evolve in the course of social interaction that also includes constitutional daydreaming, the chasing of constitutional myths, imaginary redefinition or confirmation of the constitutional shapes of space[22] and time[23] (especially the collective constitutional sublimation of the past), and the construction and reproduction of the symbolic, visual and imaginary constitutional pantheon of the socio-legal community.

Such analysis is related to the 'law as a culture'[24] and 'law and literature'[25] approaches. It is explored by constitutional and political anthropology and goes beyond the scope of the discussion in this volume.

However, the central and decisive role in evolving the sense of constitutional texture and in the explicit implication of meaning and shaping constitutionally relevant signifieds in a process of signification and encoding in constitutional text and texture through semiotic means is played by the authoritative storytellers – the authoritative constitutional narrators. Thus, special attention must be paid to their explicit creative and interpretative activity, focusing on the representation of meaning in constitutional texture through codes, myths, and symbols in the form of constitutional stories or narratives.[26]

The constitutional story is the objective (although dynamically unfolding) process of the textual, visual or performative representation of meaning having important semiotic implications and thus affecting not only rational but also symbolic-imaginary constitutionalism. Constitutional stories can be told and thus developed orally. They may be performative acts resulting in symbolic behaviour. In both cases, of most relevance for constitutionalism are the verbal and performative acts and activities of the office holders – the institutionalised constitutional players. Nevertheless, the discursive-performative engagement of other, even informal, agenda-setters (those whose opinions shape public opinion, influencers etc) may also be important for the development of the symbolic-imaginary, visual and emotional discourses of constitutionalism.

[22] See, eg, M Belov, 'Territory, Territoriality and Territorial Politics as Public Law Concepts' in M Belov (ed), *Territorial Politics and Secession: Constitutional and International Law Dimensions* (London, Palgrave Macmillan, 2021) 15–45.

[23] See, eg, J Balkin, *The Cycles of Constitutional Time* (Oxford, Oxford University Press 2020) 1–256.

[24] See, eg, J Thomas, 'Legal Culture and the Practice: A Postmodern Depiction of the Rule of Law' (2001) 48 *UCLA Law Review* 1495. A thorough semiotic analysis of legal culture is offered by Menezes de Carvalho, who explores legal culture in a twofold way: legal culture as a system of signification and legal culture as communication. See E Menezes de Carvalho, *Semiotics of International Law: Trade and Translation* (Dordrecht, Springer, 2011) 3–37.

[25] A pioneering work in the scientific exploration of legal imagination in the context of law and literature is J Boyd White, *The Legal Imagination* (Chicago, University of Chicago Press, 1985) 1–334. A novel approach to 'law and literature' with special emphasis on the signification of legal and legally relevant meaning and which offers an original 'law and comics' approach can be found in Giddens (n 6) 36–54.

[26] According to Frankenberg ((n 1) ix), 'reading and comparing constitutions should be geared towards finding and conveying these narratives, at times uncovering and decoding them – or at least pointing out where, under the textual surface, one may come upon context.'

However, usually the most important constitutional stories are textually entrenched. They have normative-institutional standing, being part of valid law – typically the constitution – or are included and objectivised within authoritative texts belonging to constitutional theory or political theory literature.

Hence, constitutional stories have a textual dimension (as part of constitutional or constitutionally relevant texts) or textuality dimensions (being an element of visual-imaginary narratives that are unfolding in the socio-political discourse). They have projections in all constitutional discourses – textual, rational, emotional, normative-institutional, intellectual, imaginary, performative, visual and factual. They may unfold asymmetrically through different constitutional discourses and may be represented via divergent means of symbolic representation. When constitutional stories are told (or written) by official and institutionalised constitutional narrators, they are framed and formed as part of their legal or political acts. Thus, their semiotic content acquires formalisation through textual representation as part of textual constitutionalism. Otherwise, when included in verbal, performative or visual acts, they are part of a constitutionally relevant texture composed of imaginary forms that also frequently have an emotional appeal.

Constitutional stories are discourses about constitutional law based on constitutional texts and constitutional texture. They may be told by all members of the semiotic discursive constitutional community. However, the constitutional stories told by the constitutional narrators who are the authoritative speakers of the community are of most relevance. This is because they have a certain normativity that is binding on the members of the community. There are a range of constitutional narrators, who have different levels of institutional standing in the constitutional order and varying importance in the imaginary and socio-legal constitutional discourse.

That is why focused analysis should also be carried out on the concept of constitutional narrators in the context of the open constitutional texture.[27] Special attention should be paid to the figure of the authoritative constitutional narrators as authoritative speakers of the political community. This is due to the fact that they are the legitimate producers of normative constitutional meaning. Such production of meaning also includes involvement in the process of signification and representation of meaning related to constitutionally important phenomena.

Here it will be shown how and why the constitutional narrators as authoritative speakers of the community are key factors in the development of constitutional semiotics. Moreover, they are strategic players in the process of production of semiotic figures and semiotic meaning based on the constitutional texture. The constitutional texture is conceived as both a holistic project and a phenomenon that is 'sliced' into constitutional discourses, narratives and stories.

[27] On the open texture of law, see HLA Hart, *The Concept of Law* (Oxford, Oxford University Press, 1997) 124–36.

Many of these constitutional stories have semiotic importance. Some of them are related to constitutional memories and the constitutional conceptualisation of time – especially the past.[28] There are also semiotic constitutional narratives that address constitutional sentiments[29] and emotions, and build up the emotional discourse in constitutionalism and constitutional law.[30] They can and should be organised around the concept of emotional constitutionalism. Furthermore, constitutional stories are also epistemic containers for constitutional mythology and constitutional ideology.

The famous quotation of Roland Barthes reads as follows: 'the author enters his own death, writing begins'.[31] Indeed, this statement is devoted to the 'ordinary' writing of literature and not 'qualified' and 'conditional' writings, such as the writing of a constitution. The drafting of a constitutional text is preconditioned by specific forms and procedures. It has its own and rather specific ontology, teleology and axiology.[32] It can be accomplished only by specific authorised authors as institutionalised authoritative speakers of the constitutional community. In that sense, the author of the constitution never really dies 'entering its own death' *à la* Barthes, but rather persists as a latent constituent power. Hence, the drafting of a constitution is conditional in a formal-procedural sense and 'qualified' in both a formal and a substantial form. It is both a rational procedure for the imposition of reformist will framed as a socio-political contract[33] and a ritual moment of constitutional craftsmanship[34] triggering constitutional magic.[35]

Still, the constitution is a form of literature, albeit a specific and peculiar one.[36] And the constitutional founding fathers and mothers as well as the subsequent

[28] See M Belov, 'Constitutional Memories: How Do Constitutions Cope with Constitutional Past' in M Belov and A Abat I Ninet (eds), *Revolution, Transition, Memory, and Oblivion: Reflections on Constitutional Change* (Cheltenham, Edward Elgar, 2020) 107–26.

[29] See A Sajó, *Constitutional Sentiments* (New Haven, Yale University Press, 2011) 1–400.

[30] A Sajó, 'Emotions in Constitutional Institutions', *Emotion Review*, 2016, 8 (1) 44–49; A Sajó, 'Emotions in Constitutional Design' (2010) 8(3) *ICON* 354; S Bandes, J Madeira, K Temple and E Kidd White (eds), *Research Handbook on Law and Emotion* (Cheltenham, Edward Elgar, 2021) 1–640.

[31] See R Barthes, 'La mort de l'auteur', https://monoskop.org/images/3/38/Barthes_Roland_1968_1984_La_mort_de_l_auteur.pdf.

[32] On the semiotic determinants of legal drafting, see J Brkic and N Anderson, 'Drafting and Interpreting Legal Documents' in Kevelson (n 14) 87–105.

[33] On the mythological characteristics of the social contract, see R Holcombe, 'Consent or Coercion? A Critical Analysis of the Constitutional Contract' and P Boettke and A Fink, 'Agent Type, Social Contracts and Constitutional Mythologies' in A Marciano (ed), *Constitutional Mythologies: New Perspectives on Controlling the State* (Dordrecht, Springer, 2011) 9–25 and 25–39 respectively.

[34] See S Rajagopalan and R Wagner, 'Constitutional Craftsmanship and the Rule of Law: Organizational Arrangement, Moral Imagination, and the Separation of Powers', *GMU Working Paper in Economics*, 2013 (13-08), available at: https://ssrn.com/abstract=2250935.

[35] On constitutional magic and the 'law as magic', see A Alvarez-Nakagawa, 'Law as Magic: Some Thoughts on Ghosts, Non-humans, and Shamans' (2017) 18(5) *German Law Journal* 1247. According to Frankenberg ((n 1) 10), 'for over 200 years constitutional projects have oscillated between the poles of magic and deceit, depending on how ideology, myth and the symbolic dimension came into play. Constitutional magic appears in different guises'.

[36] See also the specific approach on law and literature in R Dworkin, *A Matter of Principle* (Cambridge, MA, Harvard University Press, 1985) 146–81.

speakers of the constituent power's will are still the authors of a text, although one that is special, official, valid and in a sense magical. From the viewpoint of constitutional semiotics, the constitution is a system of signifiers expressed in textual form. Consequently, we can agree with Barthes that:

> [A]ll writing is itself this special voice [the voice of the writer], consisting of several indiscernible voices, and that literature is precisely the invention of this voice, to which we cannot assign a specific origin: literature is that neuter, that composite, that oblique into which every subject escapes, the trap where all identity is lost, beginning with the very identity of the body that writes.[37]

Hence, in the moment when the constitution is written and adopted, the author to a certain extent dematerialises, depersonalises, disappears and gives way to the further development of the constitution and constitutional law[38] on the basis of its 'open texture'.[39] Such further development is usually accomplished by the authoritative speakers of the community. And this is done explicitly, by the constitutional courts, or implicitly, by other narrators with de facto authority to engage in epistemic and in semiotic processes for the deconstruction, reconstruction and representation of meaning.

Again, Barthes suggests that 'the narrative is never undertaken by a person, but by a mediator, shaman or speaker, whose "performance" may be admired (that is, his mastery of the narrative code), but not his "genius"'. Transferring Barthes' idea to the field of constitutional law, one can suppose that the constitution is not a monolithic and entirely codified text even in the case of codified constitutions. It is a composite textual construction containing multiple narratives, including the text of the constitution and its interpretations by the authoritative speakers of the community – the constitutional, supreme and ordinary courts, the authoritative texts (including interpretative texts) produced by the constitutional theory etc. In that regard, the constitution comprises signifiers of meaning delivered in a multi-discursive way by these speakers, writers and interpreters.

Hence, the constitutional text contains 'narrative codes' in the manner of Barthes.[40] It can be presented as a rational and well-ordered system of norms and institutions. But it can also be conceptualised as a range of narratives representing meaning, producing signs and engaging in the signification of ideas, codes, figures and phenomena that have initially emerged in the legal and socio-legal reality. In this regard, the constitution is a range of coordinated (but at times even competing) narratives with huge epistemic and semiotic importance that construct not only the rational but also the visual, performative and symbolic-imaginary discourses of constitutionalism that also have an impact on the realm of emotional constitutionalism. Consequently, textual constitutionalism is the field, instrument

[37] See Barthes (n 31).
[38] See Foucault (n 20) 205 et seq.
[39] See Hart (n 27) 100.
[40] On the semiotic theory of Barthes, see R Barthes, *Elements of Semiology* (New York, Hill & Wang, 1977) 1–112.

and reality for the signification of meaning that has pivotal importance for other types or dimensions of constitutionalism. Thus, it plays a central role in and is of paradigmatic importance for constitutional semiotics.

Even in the birth of the constitutional text, we can observe the 'death of the author'[41] in the manner of Barthes and the birth of multiple readers, interpreters and writers. The depersonalisation of the authorship of the constitution, the loss of the concrete identity of the author of the text and the authoritative impact of the speakers of the community are imminent features in most cases of constitution-making. The loss of the author's monopoly – that is, the monopoly of the constituent power over the authorship of the constitutional text – can be observed especially in liberal-democratic societies with the increase of the dispersion of authority in the constitutional order. The clear ascription of authorship of the constitutional text is typically used in the case of old constitutions with huge symbolic importance for constitutional civilisation as well as in authoritarian and totalitarian regimes. An example of the former case is the US Constitution, where an explicit recourse to the 'founding fathers' is used not only as a legitimation and authority-building strategy, but also as a marker of the birth of a constitutional civilisation. In several constitutions belonging to the revolutionary or post-revolutionary constitutionalist model,[42] the recourse to political leaders as concrete authors or, much more frequently, sources of inspiration for constitution-making and constitutional reform is also an indicator of legitimacy, authority and tradition-building.[43]

In that regard, the recourse to 'founding fathers', founding mothers, founding ancestors and great leaders who have initiated the constitution and inspired the constitutional text is a signifier itself. It is used as a semiotic code in multiple ways according to the constitutional regime and the aims of the constitution-making process. Hence, the rebirth of the author of the constitutional text is a symbolic exercise with huge semiotic potential. The same is true of the 'death of the constitutional author' in relation to its de-personification, delusion and dispersion. General formulas of national or popular sovereignty, while lacking feasible shapes and forms, are used as triggers of meaning, as representations of normative ideas, as founding constitutional myths and as codes.[44] In other words, they serve as signifiers in symbolic-imaginary constitutionalism and as elements of constitutionalism perceived as 'game of codes, signs, symbols, myths, dreams and memories'.[45]

[41] Barthes (n 17) 142–49.

[42] On the revolutionary imaginaries in Caribbean constitutionalism, see K Olson, *Imagined Sovereignties: The Power of the People and Other Myths of the Modern Age* (Cambridge, Cambridge University Press, 2017) 110–44.

[43] See Belov (n 28) 107–26.

[44] For a very original and detailed exploration of constitutional imaginaries relating to sovereignty, constituent power and the people which challenges the traditional narratives, see Oklopcic (n 12) 43–121; and Olson (n 42) 1–215.

[45] See E Dale, 'Popular Sovereignty: A Case Study from the Antebellum Era' in Marciano (n 33) 81–107; and Oklopcic (n 12) 1-416.

Some definitional clarity should be provided on the concepts of authoritative constitutional speakers of the community and constitutional narrators. These two concepts must be defined and compared with each other. This should be done from the viewpoint of constitutional semiotics as an epistemic attempt at conceptualising constitutionalism through the prism of its visual-imaginary and emotional discourses.

From an epistemological viewpoint, the constitution can be conceptualised in two different ways, which are conceptual antipodes, but in practice are mutually supportive and build on each other. The first prototype is the constitution as a holistic project resulting from the will of the sovereign conceived as a monolithic phenomenon, while the second prototype is the constitution as a system of interrelated narratives produced by authoritative constitutional narrators.

The traditional theory of sovereignty that emerged in the early modern era postulates that there is only one authoritative narrator. This is the sovereign acting as constitutional legislator and creating a holistic constitutional project for the constitutional community. Consequently, there is also only one valid constitutional story – the constitution. Moreover, the constitution is a holistic project that contains internally coherent and mutually coordinated institutional narratives.[46]

In that first model, the process of the semiotic representation of meaning occurs only in the constituent moment when the constitution is adopted or in the course of explicit and formal constitutional amendments accomplished at a later stage. In this sense, this process is a rather singular event. Ideally, it occurs rarely, maybe once in a generation, or in a single moment of the life of a nation: the constitutional moment.[47] In practice, this happens more often, since constitutional amendments or even the adoption of a new constitution is required more frequently. Still, this is an exceptional and rare event. The semiotic representation is entrenched in a constitution that is stable and rarely changed. Thus, it is a mystical event – official, solemn and, in a sense, static. The semiotic representation process is static because it can be compared to a snapshot of the meaning grasped at the constituent moment. It is a singular and concrete event and not a process that unfolds in parallel with the evolution of the constitution and the constitutional order.

This early modern, static conceptualisation of the constitution as a monolithic story told by the sovereign in exclusive situations (constitutional moments) and containing the semiotic representation of meaning fixed in this very moment does not properly reflect the contemporary stance of constituent power and constitution-making as a mixed and complex process of combining revolutions and evolutions of meaning created by a range of constitutional narrators. Following the 'linguistic turn' in the social sciences and the humanities and the rise of critical, post-modern and socio-legal studies, a second model for analysis of

[46] See also Oklopcic (n 12) 43–121.

[47] See B Ackerman, *We the People: Foundations* (Cambridge, MA, Harvard University Press, 1991) 266.

the constitutional construction, deconstruction and representation of meaning has gained momentum. In the context of this model, the constitution is conceived not so much as a static and holistic project, but rather as a dynamic narrative project, framed in norms and secured by validity and legal sanction, which unfolds over time. This happens on the basis of the upgrading of the initial meaning implied by the constitutional legislator[48] in his or her capacity as the key narrator. The upgrading is accomplished by the range of authoritative speakers and authoritative narrators of the constitutional community.

Indeed, the constitutional legislator, acting on behalf of the de facto metaphysical subject – the sovereign – is a privileged narrator. The constitutional legislator is privileged in multiple ways. It is the agenda setter or the author of the initial story, giving a decisive push in the unfolding of the constitutional narratives that subsequently stem from this first, original and constitutive 'big story'. Furthermore, it can always change the story, give it a new direction and shift its overall shape, concrete design or direction. It can even abolish the story and make the constitutional narratives based on it redundant. The constitutional legislator's role is especially visible with regard to constitutional semiotics because it is the agenda setter of constitutional ideologies, constitutional myths and mythologies, and the overall constitutional imaginaries enshrined in the constitution.

Nevertheless, the original constitutional project evolves and is further developed by the authoritative constitutional narrators of the constitutionally framed socio-political community. These are the apex courts[49] (the constitutional and supreme courts) and, less visibly, the ordinary courts[50] and administrators, the parliament and the narrators who belong to the legal doctrine which are capable of producing texts and interpretations with de facto or sociological normativity. The constitution as a textual and semiotic project is developed through the construction, deconstruction and reconstruction of meaning in a discursive way. This post-modern, fragmented and selective semiosis conceptually competes but in practice supplements the modern concept of constitution as a holistic semiotic project entrenched in rationality and textuality and produced in exclusive historical moments. Thus, the role of authoritative speakers and narrators of the constitutionally framed socio-political community for the production and signification of meaning increases. This makes them central agents of constitutional semiotics.

[48] See J Manning, 'Textualism and Legislative Intent' (2005) 91 *Virginia Law Review* 419, available at: https://ssrn.com/abstract=2853690.

[49] On the concept of apex courts, see S Schlegel, 'Activism as Defence: The Role of Courts in Shaping the Relationship between Constitutions and International Law. A Comparison of the Apex Courts of Switzerland, Germany, and Austria' in M Belov (ed) *Courts and Judicial Activism under Crisis Conditions: Policy Making in a Time of Illiberalism and Emergency Constitutionalism* (Abingdon, Routledge, 2022) 43–61.

[50] See S Stern, 'Narrative in the Legal Text: Judicial Opinions and Their Narratives' in M Hanne and R Weisberg (eds), *Narrative and Metaphor in the Law* (Cambridge, Cambridge University Press, 2018) 121–39.

4

Constitutional Text and Constitutional Texture from a Semiotic Perspective

The Role of Open Texture for Constitutional Semiotics

Textual semiotics is an important part of general semiotics. The signification of meaning is largely based on text and texture. Symbols, signs and representations of meaning frequently have a textual dimension. Very often, texts are bearers of meaning, standing for concepts of the inner psychological world and the external realm of empirical facts and social interaction. The textual systems themselves are in fact semiotic systems. They are also epistemic orders offering cognition and ordering of the world in multiple and interrelated ways through textual construction and reconstruction of meaning. An important although underestimated part of their epistemic essence has a semiotic nature and relevance. The text is a system for the representation of meaning that sometimes occurs in symbolic form. Indeed, we have become used to using text conventionally as a medium of information, so we barely think about its semiotic nature. But semiotic meaning is part of all texts. This meaning is usually implied and contained in semiotic codes, images, imaginaries, representations and significations deliberately included in the text. Meaning is textually represented. Thus, the text itself is a semiotic system.[1]

This also holds true for the constitutional text. Semiotics is a topic of growing importance in literature and the visual arts. It has been conceived as an important branch for the achievement of new discourses of meaning within the social sciences and the humanities. However, it has been largely underestimated in the fields of constitutional law and constitutional theory, where semiotic means for the achievement of constitutionally relevant meaning have been rather scarcely used. Hence, constitutional semiotics must be advanced in order to cope with the development of the semiotic meaning of textually enshrined constitutional phenomena. Such a semiotic turn in constitutional law can be achieved through the fostering of a scientific analysis of textual and symbolic-imaginary constitutionalism.

[1] See G Long, 'The Written Story: Toward Understanding Text as Representation and Function' (1999) 49(2) *Vetus Testamentum* 165, https://doi.org/10.1163/156853399774228957.

The constitutional text has semiotic importance in three ways. First, it has been clarified that each textual system is potentially a semiotic system as well. It is prone to the representation of meaning, thus standing for signifieds derived from the imaginary, the emotional and the real. It contains signifiers grouped according to the logic of the particular constitutional ontology, teleology and axiology contained in the distinct constitution and constitutional order. Each text is an invitation for the semiotic interpretation of its encoded meaning and textually enshrined knowledge.[2] Hence, the constitutional text has semiotic importance in this general sense in its capacity as a text. However, there are also specific semiotic features of the constitutional text.

Thus, second, the constitutional text is the form and substance on the basis of which the written constitution is organised. The text is the main form through which the constitution manifests itself in the empirical reality, thus becoming intellectually available to and comprehensible by the constitutional semiotic community. The written constitution is a symbol itself.[3] It is a symbol of sovereignty, statehood, independence, authority and eventually, under certain circumstances, also of liberty. In that regard, the constitution is a signifier of all these phenomena. This is especially visible with regard to statehood. The constitution is the legal representation of statehood. It is a symbol of statehood in the legal domain and from a legal viewpoint. The first constitutions in the constitutional history of most countries are conceived as a form of 'birth certificates' of a new statehood or as symbolic documents for the legitimate restoration of statehood.

Third, and most importantly, the constitutional text is a container of constitutional semiotic phenomena. It contains semiotic codes, taboos, memories, dreams, images, ideas, myths and other phenomena related to the constitutional imaginary. It is the medium through which semiotic content can be objectivised, preserved, institutionalised and thus can become valid law. Hence, the constitutional text is the instrument and dashboard for signifying meaning in a durable, visible and normative way. This third aspect of the semiotic role of the constitutional text is the most important one because it shows the peculiar power of constitutional texture in terms of promoting a semiotic approach to constitutionalism and allows for the construction of semiotic schemes and the inclusion of semiotic codes with recourse to the established means of linguistics. These means have traditionally been important since the emergence of modern written and codified constitutions. However, they are especially powerful and convincing following the 'linguistic turn' in the social sciences in general and in legal theory in particular.

[2] On the relationship between language and knowledge, see C Belsey, *Poststructuralism: A Very Short Introduction* (Oxford, Oxford University Press, 2002) 1–128.

[3] See E Black, *Our Constitution: The Myth That Binds Us* (Boulder, Westview Press, 1988). According to Frankenberg, 'the term "constitution" has belonged to the prominent signs and ideological icons of modernity'. In his view, 'constitutions have been regarded as prominent signs, cherished documents and ideological icons of a better modernity. They came with a new vocabulary, and they became points around which epistemic communities could crystallize'. See G Frankenberg, *Comparative Constitutional Studies: Between Magic and Deceit* (Cheltenham, Edward Elgar, 2018) 13 and 26.

Is there a difference between constitutional text and constitutional texture from the viewpoint of constitutional semiotics? The answer to this is that it depends on the viewpoint in question. What we define as constitutional text is generally clear. This is the text as the system of words fixed in written form and connected on the basis of general linguistic rules and special rules of the normative language and normative grammar of constitutional law.[4] Thus, the constitutional text is a particular form of text addressing constitutional law problems. It serves as a means of textual representation of constitutional phenomena and as a material ground and instrument for the ascription of meaning and thus for signification. The constitutional text is a form of expression of semiotic content through written linguistic representation. It allows for the signification of constitutional and constitutionally relevant signifieds stemming from either the ideal constitution and the symbolic-imaginary constitutionalism or from the socio-legal reality of the empirical world of government, power and human political interactions. Sometimes constitutional text contains signifiers that signify at the same time the imaginary, the normative and the real.

We must distinguish between the texts of valid constitutional law and the texts that contain constitutional information but are part of constitutional theory. Moreover, differentiation must be made between the text of the constitution and the texts of the other sources of constitutional law. In that regard, one can distinguish between constitutional texts in a strict or narrow sense (those provided by valid constitutional law) and constitutional texts in a broader sense that also include the texts of constitutional theory (and eventually also constitutionally related texts in print media).

The concept of constitutional texture is much more complex. Two main concepts of constitutional texture can be distinguished. The first is a simpler and, it could be said, even a reductionist one. It reduces constitutional texture to the form of constitutional text. It treats constitutional text and constitutional texture as synonymous concepts. According to it, constitutional text and constitutional texture are the same: forms and plains for the representation of the constitutional law. They are the linguistic dimension of the constitutional order in written form representing and signifying the other dimensions of constitutionalism through textual constitutionalism. Constitutional text and constitutional texture are the bricks through which the so-called 'fabric of constitutionalism' achieves its most important material substantiation.

The second concept is a more complex one. It is particularly important for the semiotic analysis of constitutionalism, constitutional law and their textual dimensions. This is especially true for authors and theories accepting and promoting theories of visual constitutionalism and symbolic-imaginary constitutionalism. In a sense, these concepts imply the distinction of constitutional text from constitutional texture and are reliant on both of them.

[4] On the concept of legal grammar and its application in the sphere of international law, see M Koskenniemi, *From Apology to Utopia: The Structure of International Legal Argument* (Cambridge, Cambridge University Press, 2006) 563–615.

According to this second understanding, constitutional texture is broader than constitutional text. It includes all forms of semiotic representation of constitutional phenomena by virtue of all possible means of signification of meaning. Hence, constitutional texture includes not only textual semiotic forms but also forms for semiotic signification produced by other means of visual expression, including the visual arts, the visual representation of constitutional institutions and constitutionally relevant phenomena, and constitutional symbols. Constitutional texture includes all signification systems capable of representing constitutional and constitutionally relevant content.

Hence, it can be claimed that textual constitutionalism is focused on the constitutional text while visual constitutionalism and symbolic-imaginary constitutionalism are broader concepts exploring, assessing and ordering both the constitutional text and constitutional texture. In that regard, constitutional texture is of key importance for visual constitutionalism. This is due to the fact that visual constitutionalism is based on a symbolic representation of constitutional meaning in and through constitutional texture understood as a broader concept than the constitutional text. Constitutional texture is also important for symbolic-imaginary constitutionalism because it contains forms and instruments for the signification of meaning that play a key role in forming constitutional imaginaries, and triggering and shaping constitutional imagination, offering incentives for symbolic behaviour based on chains of the visual-symbolic representation of constitutionally relevant signified objects.

In this book, I use the concept of constitutional texture in this second and broader sense. The obvious reason for this is that I am trying to develop a theory of symbolic-imaginary and visual constitutionalism that encompasses not only the semiotic processes and phenomena within the constitutional text, but also the broader symbolic signification of constitutional meaning based on all possible signification systems. In my account, constitutionalism is a wide phenomenon that has not only textual but also social-legal and – most importantly – intellectual aspects and implications. Constitutionalism includes constitutional imaginaries that are produced through narratives and narration, and textual representation, but also via the symbolic manifestation of meaning. Together, these processes produce constitutional imaginaries and constitutional semiotic structures that are based on both constitutional text and constitutional texture, and jointly form symbolic-imaginary and visual constitutionalism.

Constitutionalism is produced by a range of practices that have linguistic, textual or performative modalities for formal expression in the material world. Most of them are entrenched in patterns of durable constitutional behaviour or are conceived as full or partial anti-system deviations. Thus, only some of these practices have normative relevance and contribute to the production of the normative foundations and the normative framework of constitutionalism. Constitutionalism is heavily dependent on factual behaviour, but it still remains a textual phenomenon. Thus, the textual dimension of constitutionalism – its fixing in the text of the constitution and the texture of constitutional law – remains of fundamental importance.

Constitutional texture is the ultimate foundation and imaginary dashboard for the unfolding of constitutional phenomena and constitutional developments. It is the playground of the constitutional imagination and the tool for materialisation and substantiation of collective constitutional imaginaries. Constitutional texture is the clay for shaping constitutional imaginaries and for their public exposure. It is both a key tool for expression and the ultimate signification boundary and limitation for constitutional semiotics.

Modern constitution has always been primarily conceptualised as a text. Modern constitutionalism is bound to the concept of written and codified constitution. This is one of the key contributions of modern constitutionalism to legal modernity.[5] The concept of the constitution as a reasonable, systematic, written and codified project, together with the separation between 'public and private', the territoriality of power, and the hierarchy and pyramid-like structure of the constitutional order are the key markers and normative pillars of modernity. They determine the transition from the pre-modern (medieval) to the modern political world. The crisis of these fundamental concepts for modern constitutionalism is visible in the context of the transition to post-modernity in our age.

The constitution is the text with the highest political importance and legal validity. It is an authoritative text which results from the ultimate authority recognised by the socio-political community.[6] The ultimate authority of constitutional text rests upon several normative conditions: the nature of the constitution as a result of sovereign will, the truthfulness of the constitution as a textual manifestation of the rational, systematic and consistent political project, and the emotional appeal of the constitution to the socio-political community it frames and whose behaviour it regulates. Thus, the acceptance of the constitution as the ultimate normative criterion for socio-political behaviour given in textual form is heavily dependent on both its rational qualities and its emotional appeal. Hence, the recognition of the standing of the constitution as the supreme authoritative text is stretched between rational, emotional and symbolic-imaginary constitutionalism. The constitution is authoritative due to the fact that it provides rational rules for political behaviour. It is also authoritative because it engages the collective imagination of the community, refers to the constitutional ideal, contains constitutional memories, includes constitutional imaginaries and semiotic codes, and provides for constitutional dreams.

Thus, the constitutional texture is the medium through which the constitution as both a holistic and a discursive project unfolds and projects itself in rational, emotional and symbolic-imaginary constitutionalism. The constitution is a textual container of constitutional ontology, constitutional teleology and constitutional

[5] Frankenberg stipulates that 'constitutionalism introduced a new vocabulary for, mindset and mode of establishing, legitimizing and limiting political authority as well as founding of a polity'. See Frankenberg (n 3) 14.

[6] See J Derrida, 'Force of Law: The "Mystical Foundation of Authority"' in D Cornell, M Rosenfield and D Carlson (eds), *Deconstruction and the Possibility of Justice* (London, Routledge, 1992) 3–67.

axiology, but also of constitutional memories, constitutional dreams, constitutional symbols, and semiotic codes and constitutional imaginaries.

In that regard, the constitutional texture is a place where rational constitutionalism encounters emotional constitutionalism and symbolic-imaginary constitutionalism. Indeed, the rationalist project of the constitution is immediately visible from the constitutional text, while the imaginary and emotional implications of the constitution require interpretation. But they are both grounded in the constitutional text, while also having projections in the constitutional texture. Thus, they are relevant not just for textual constitutionalism, but also for visual constitutionalism. Their textual embeddedness is a requirement of their constitutionality.

Thus, the constitutional text serves as an objective determinant for the interpretative development of the symbolic-imaginary and emotional projects stemming from the constitution. The constitutional text is an object of constitutional interpretation accomplished through the means of constitutional epistemology and constitutional semiotics. At the same time, it is also the ultimate limitation to constitutional interpretation and to the unfolding of the interpretative projects of the authoritative narrators shaping the multitude of constitutional narratives on which symbolic-imaginary and emotional constitutionalism discourses are grounded. Hence, the constitutional text is a key criterion for judging and justifying the spread of its symbolic-imaginary and emotional aspects in the constitutional context, and in the range of alternative interpretative projects developed by the authoritative speakers of the community.

Rational constitutionalism is the main object of constitutional texture. It is a holistic project enshrined in the constitution that is also further developed through constitutional interpretation. In contrast, symbolic-imaginary and emotional constitutionalism are usually not provided by the constitution as holistic projects. Typically, the constitutional text partially institutionalises them by providing for certain aspects or issues belonging to symbolic-imaginary and emotional constitutionalism in a rather fragmented, incidental and particular manner. Thus, there is a need for interpretative tools which one can use to reconstruct the symbolic-imaginary and emotional projects deeply enshrined in the constitution. We need instruments for the deconstruction of constitutional texture that may bring to light its symbolic-imaginary and emotional dimensions. We have to decode the semiotic codes entrenched in the constitutional texture in order to expose and make operational the constitutional memories, constitutional dreams and constitutional vision, and overall the constitutional imaginaries hidden behind the rationalistic project of the constitution.[7] Such tools for the deconstruction and decoding of the constitutional texture are offered by constitutional epistemology and especially by constitutional semiotics.[8]

[7] According to Frankenberg, 'disenchantment is one of the important tasks of comparative constitutional studies'. Thus, he suggests the recourse to 'disenchanted hermeneutics' of comparative constitutional studies. See Frankenberg (n 3) 12.

[8] See M Colmegna, 'Decoding the Code' in R Kevelson (ed), *Law and Semiotics*, vol 2 (New York, Plenum Press, 1988) 135–43.

How does the textuality of the constitution relate to its holistic or discursive-narrative nature? What does it mean to say that the constitution is a holistic textual project, while also being at the same time a discursive project that contains a range of sometimes even competing constitutional narratives? Is the claim for a holistic worldview provided through constitutional texture not a logical and practical contradiction of the fragmented viewpoints behind the multitude of constitutional discourses? Let us answer these important and proper questions one by one.

Textuality is one of the most important features of modern constitutions. This is the feature which distinguishes them from pre-modern political orders based on de facto constitutions as socio-legal projects. Textuality may be open, partially open and closed. Closed textuality means that not only can the text not be subject to further modifications, but also that it cannot be subject to further interpretation. This type of textuality is typical for sacred texts that claim to be complete and perfect. Extreme versions of textual originalism may be witnessed in conservative interpretations of the Bible, the Talmud and the Koran. However, even these have been exposed to further interpretation, which was necessary in order to clarify their meaning or to adapt the text to the shifting and evolving context. Thus, no sacred text is capable of surviving in isolation from the socio-political reality. Hence, a text can never fully escape its context and absolutely closed textuality is a mere fiction.

The same is true for the absolute openness of textuality. The text always offers some epistemic certainty. The text is objective, fixed (until it is not amended) and entrenched in the factual reality through the rules of written language. Indeed, the text may and in many cases should be interpreted. It can be also changed or destroyed. But if meaning has to be textually represented, there will always be a degree of certainty in the mere fact of the existence of the text.

The text represents meaning. It stands for imaginary reality. It contains symbols, codes and imaginaries. Thus, the text is construed and is further developed. It is given by its author while emancipating from it after its creation. Thus, it is objective and pre-existing but also interpreted, and in that regard prone to subjective understanding and further development.[9]

This also holds true for the constitutional text and the constitutional texture. The text is the most visible dimension of the constitution. While other constitutional dimensions – the ideal, the material and the factual constitution – are complex imaginary phenomena requiring intellectual reconstruction and multilayered negotiation of their content and meaning, the written constitution is an immediate reality which can be directly comprehended by its reader. Simultaneously, it is also an imagined world and a representation of reality. Thus, the constitutional text that composes the written constitution and the normative-institutional dimension of constitutionalism is both a reality and representation of reality. It is text that constitutes textual reality and representation of ideas, ideals, concepts,

[9] In this regard, see also R Barthes, *Image-Music-Text* (New York, Hill & Wang, 1978) 142–49.

codes and legally shaped socio-legal phenomena. Thus, to an extent paradoxically, the written constitution is text that represents objective phenomena, but also text that signifies a higher reality composed of symbols, codes, ideas and ideals, and myths and mythologies. Hence, it is a textual container of collective constitutional imaginaries. In that regard, the constitutional text performs two representative functions. It stands for the ideal reality and the socio-legal reality, and thus acts as a tool for the representation of the symbolic-imaginary and the socio-legal dimensions of constitutionalism.

That is why constitutional texture can be neither completely closed nor completely open. It is grounded in written text with a high degree of stability due to the complex procedures required for constitutional amendment. However, this text can also be formally amended and is prone to constitutional interpretation by the authoritative speakers of the community – the official constitutional narrators. Consequently, there is a sense of 'shades of grey' between the extreme poles of closed and open texture. In fact, all texts are allocated somewhere along the range between these poles, and their place on the scale is not reserved forever, but evolves over time and with a view to the context and the interpretative output and activity of the authoritative speakers and interpreters of the community. The texts are being adjusted to the context by the authors and the authoritative narrators. In that regard, the constitutional texture is also prone to change, being a permanently evolving artefact of constitutional reason and constitutional imagination through the will of the constitutional legislator (the official authors of the constitutional text) and the constitutional interpreters (the authoritative narrators and the authoritative speakers of the community). Both the constitutional legislator and the constitutional interpreters (constitutional authoritative narrators) are agents of constitutional change and instruments for the adaptation of the constitutional text to the constitutional context.

5

The Concept of Authoritative Constitutional Text and its Functions for Constitutional Semiotics

The concept of authoritative constitutional text in general and from a semiotic perspective in particular should also be clarified. At first glance, it seems that the concept is to an extent ridiculous, internally controversial and nonsensical. This is due to the fact that from a predominant legal positivist perspective, all constitutional texts and all parts of the constitutional text are authoritative in the sense of being valid. The constitution is obviously authoritative because it is the supreme and fundamental legal act that predetermines the foundations of the legal order. But the other sources of constitutional law are also authoritative from a legal positivist viewpoint, since they are all valid and possess the ultimate authority derived from the will of the state expressed by the constitutional or the ordinary legislator.

This firm and clear position can be softened and partially relativised from a semiotic perspective. Indeed, it has to be admitted that all sources of constitutional law are authoritative in the sense of being normative and valid legal texts. However, from a semiotic perspective, the range of authoritative texts is not limited to valid law. Constitutional semiotics is interested in the symbolic-imaginary dimension of constitutionalism as represented through shapes and forms with semiotic importance. The semiotic phenomena may be entrenched in the collective mentality, in the constitutional anthropology of the community and in its constitutional imaginaries. Together, they are formed not only by the valid law, but also by previous constitutional sources of law that have been abolished. Thus, abolished acts that are no longer valid law may also contribute to the symbolic-imaginary dimension of constitutionalism and thus may shape the range of forms of constitutional semiotics lying at its core.

Moreover, the role of authoritative texts may also be performed by semiotic forms represented by constitutional texture in the second or broader sense explained above. This means that normative representations forming the emotional, symbolic-imaginary and visual discourses of constitutionalism can exist, as signified through various signification systems. These representations may even serve as key signifiers of constitutional meaning without being explicitly provided by valid constitutional law. Nevertheless, they must have some reference to valid constitutional law and at least implicit constitutional standing within the constitutional texture of the constitutional order.

Finally, doctrinal texts may also be in a position to serve and be conceived as authoritative constitutional texts. Indeed, they are not authoritative in the sense of being legally valid. They do not possess the authority of law. However, they may be authoritative in the sense of being of key importance for understanding and explaining as well as shaping the semiotic order of the constitutional community. In fact, constitutional theory contributes significantly to the shaping and forming of symbolic-imaginary, visual and emotional constitutionalism. This is done in parallel with the other constitutional discourses of strategic semiotic importance (the media discourse, the official protocol discourse, the representative-symbolic behaviour of the state institutions and other key constitutional players etc). Constitutional theory makes the people imagine the constitutional order, its institutions and its rules in a distinct way. It shapes constitutional anthropology, constitutional culture and thus also the collective constitutional imaginaries. Hence, key constitutional theoretical texts may also perform the function of authoritative constitutional texts in the broader sense of this concept.

Constitutional doctrine in its manifestation as a collection of authoritative constitutional texts represents semiotic content with constitutional relevance. Thus, it has normativity in a broad sense. This means that despite the fact that the texts produced by the constitutional doctrine are not and have never been valid law, they still may determine the way in which the constitutional players – office holders, other stakeholders and the other members of the constitutionally framed socio-political community – understand the law and perceive its imaginary, symbolic, visual and emotional aspects. In this sense, constitutional theory possesses strong intellectual (but not legal) normativity and significantly influences the way in which the society constructs its semiotic order related to the constitution, constitutionalism and constitutional law. Hence, constitutional doctrine is frequently engaged via its authoritative and intellectually binding texts in the process of the semiotic representation of meaning and in the course of the constitutional signification of constitutionally relevant phenomena within the framework of symbolic-imaginary constitutionalism.

The authoritativeness of the constitutional text stems from several main reasons. The first reason is constitutional ontology. The constitutional text is a product of the sovereign will and thus enjoys special standing within the constitutional and political order. This can be qualified as the ontological authoritativeness of the constitutional text. Second, the constitutional text is further developed by the authoritative narrators – the authoritative speakers of the community. Thus, they invest their own authority in the constitutional text and in the overall process of constitutional signification and representation of meaning. This is the discursive authority of the constitutional text. Third, constitutional texts can enjoy a high level of relevance in the political process of the collective creation of meaning with a view to the socio-political and imaginary performance of constitutional institutions. Hence, this is a performative-pragmatic authority of the constitutional text.

Finally, the constitutional text can be authoritative itself. It may be convincing due to its substantial characteristics. This is the substantial authority of the constitutional text.

The concept of authoritative constitutional text should be analysed in conjunction with the concept of the authoritative constitutional narrator. It should be made clear that the constitutional text is not a tabula rasa; it has a degree of objectivity. But, on the other hand, its meaning is also negotiated through a multitude of social practices. Some of these relate to the socio-political behaviour of the constitutional actors on the ground adjusting the meaning of the constitutional text to the constitutional context and dispersedly implying meaning in textually encoded symbols and signifiers through the prism of collective practices and collective imaginaries with deep anthropological implications. Other practices – in fact, the most important of them – are the result of the interpretative activity of the authoritative narrators of constitutional stories. Their activity has a normative impact on semiotic structures on the ground and in the collective imagination. They are authoritative because they can imply meaning on a textual and an imaginary level on the basis of the open texture of the constitution and the openness of the collective imaginaries. This demonstrates the interrelation and interdependence of constitutional semiotics, the openness of the constitutional texture, and the activity of the authoritative speakers of the community.

The representational character of the constitutional texture for both the symbolic-imaginary and the socio-legal reality has a deep, important and lasting semiotic impact. It consists in the fact that the constitutional text contains codes, symbols and representations of meaning reflecting and standing for either the imaginary-ideal or the empirical reality. Thus, the constitutional text is in a sense a bridge between the different dimensions of constitutionalism – ideal, legal and socio-legal. The constitutional text is a container of meaning that is relevant for understanding not only the immediate object of the constitutional texture providing for the institutional design and the normative structure of the constitutional order, but is also the most important tool for the sharing, revealing and mastering of semiotic meaning with implications for both the constitutional imagination and constitutional pragmatics.

Thus, the constitutional text performs representative and bridging functions for constitutionalism and its different dimensions. The constitutional text contains epistemic entities which are also direct or indirect bearers of semiotic meaning. The constitution claims to represent the socio-political reality, its institutions, institutional relations, power schemes and parameters of dependence and liberty, authority and compulsion. At the same time, the constitution aims to regulate socio-political relations by offering a comprehensible and comprehensive legal framework. The medium by virtue of which the constitution regulates the social reality and simultaneously reflects the social reality is the constitutional text. Thus, the constitutional text represents and stands for social and political phenomena, and mediates the interplay between the legal (normative-institutional) and socio-legal (empirical, sociological) dimensions of constitutionalism. In fact, this is a complex scheme of constitutional signification that includes signifiers entrenched in constitutional texture and signified phenomena of the socio-political reality. Thus, we are exposed to a permanent process of the semiotic representation of empirical political and constitutional reality through constitutional phenomena entrenched in the normative-institutional dimension of the constitution, valid constitutional law and constitutionalism, and signified by recourse to semiotic means provided by the constitutional texture.

The constitutional text also plays representative and bridging functions at the crossroads between the imaginary-ideal and normative-institutional discourses of constitutionalism and constitutional law. The constitutional text contains legal provisions textually shaping rules, principles and values that are related to rational constitutionalism. These form the rational model of authority and power, and thus also play a semiotic role in the process of constitutional signification. At the same time, the constitutional text is a repository of constitutional semiotic codes. It contains rules that directly or, much more frequently, indirectly shape constitutional symbols and constitutional imaginaries. Thus, the constitutional text is both a source of objects of representation in the constitutional imagination (textual phenomena as signified) and a container of meaning and signification.

Subsequently, there is a multidimensional process of representation and signification of meaning that is frequently mediated by the text of the constitution. Hence, the constitutional text plays a central role in constitutional semiotics as a preserve of meaning, a tool for the representation and transportation of meaning (especially symbolic meaning), and a container of signifiers and signifieds, depending on the context in the process of constitutional signification. In that regard, constitutional semiotics is to an extent textually entrenched, and constitutional texture is of crucial importance for constitutional semiotics.

PART III

Symbolic-Imaginary Constitutionalism

1

The Concept of Symbolic-Imaginary Constitutionalism

This part of the volume addresses the need to theoretically conceptualise the phenomena of the constitutional imagination,[1] constitutional imaginaries and the role of collective symbolic-imaginary attitudes and practices for constitutionalism and constitutional law. This will be done through the prism of a novel paradigm: symbolic-imaginary constitutionalism.[2] The main task of this part is to outline the core of this concept and its scope, meaning and relationship to other theoretical constructs that I will propose and discuss as part of my theory of constitutional semiotics.

Naturally, this book cannot address all issues relating to social imaginaries.[3] It cannot explore in detail either the whole range of theories relating to social imaginaries or their practical implications. There is a vast amount of literature devoted to collective social imaginaries in a multitude of scientific discourses – behavioural sciences and social psychology, anthropology, political philosophy etc.[4] A book on constitutional semiotics cannot engage in detail with

[1] On the concept of constitutional imagination, see M Loughlin, 'The Constitutional Imagination' (2015) 78(1) *Modern Law Review* 1.

[2] On the interrelation between the symbolic, the imaginary and their institutional projections, see C Castoriadis, *The Imaginary Institution of Society* (Cambridge, Polity Press, 1987) 115–65. The 'symbolic constitution of the society' concept was launched in constitutional theory by Přibáň. See J Přibáň, *Constitutional Imaginaries: A Theory of European Societal Constitutionalism* (Abingdon, Routledge, 2020) 4.

[3] For a powerful analysis of social and political imaginaries and a theory of the imaginal, see C Bottici, *Imaginal Politics: Images Beyond Imagination and the Imaginary* (New York, Columbia University Press, 2014) 1–253. For a critique of theories of social and political imaginaries with special emphasis on the theories of C Taylor, M Warner and C Bottici, see J Grant, 'On the Critique of Political Imaginaries' (2014) 13(4) *European Journal of Political Theory* 408.

[4] For some of the most important theoretical approaches to constitutional imaginaries, see Přibáň (n 2) 1–251; J Přibáň, 'A Social Theory of Constitutional Imaginaries: Beyond the Unity of "Topos-Ethnos-Nomos" and its European Context' in U Belavusau and A Gliszczyńska-Grabias (eds), *Constitutionalism under Stress: Essays in Honour of Wojciech Sadurski* (Oxford, Oxford University Press, 2020) 175–90; J Komárek (ed), *European Constitutional Imaginaries: Between Ideology and Utopia* (Oxford, Oxford University Press, 2021); and J Komárek, 'Political Economy in the European Constitutional Imaginary: Moving beyond Fiesole', *Verfassungsblog*, 4 September 2020, https://verfassungsblog.de/political-economy-in-the-european-constitutional-imaginary-moving-beyond-fiesole. There are also several projects devoted especially to constitutional imaginaries. One of the most visible among them is 'IMAGINE – European Constitutional Imaginaries – Utopias, Ideologies and the Other'

all theoretical approaches and scientific contributions addressing the issues of social imaginaries. It has a much more modest aim, namely to provide an outline of the constitutional imaginaries produced by the constitutional imagination which shape and form a specific constitutional discourse – symbolic-imaginary constitutionalism. More precisely, this analysis will be performed through the specific prism of constitutional semiotics. Hence, this part of the book will focus on the constitutionally relevant manifestations of collective social imaginaries and their role in constitutional semiotics and in the signification of constitutionally relevant meaning.[5]

The definition and analysis of symbolic-imaginary constitutionalism has to be accomplished in parallel with the exploration and delimitation of its components and other relevant phenomena. Hence, it is strategically important to define in advance: what is constitutional imagination;[6] who can create imaginary constitutionalism grounded in the semiotic manifestations of constitutional imagination; what are the legal basis, framework, scope and functions of constitutional imagination; has constitutional imagination any legal validity, is it relevant and how for constitutional law and, in the event of a positive answer, under which circumstances; is it possible to consider the existence of constitutional imagination beyond legal validity – as a socio-legal and not as a strictly legal phenomenon, and, if so, how can we differentiate valid constitutional imagination from non-valid but empirically important constitutional imagination? It is also necessary to define what the relationship is between constitutional imagination and symbolic-imaginary constitutionalism, as well as how symbolic-imaginary constitutionalism relates to other variants and forms of constitutionalism. These issues will be the central focus here.

It should be noted that some forms of symbolic-imaginary constitutionalism are also explored in other parts of this book. This is done in the context of outlining and developing the concept of visual constitutionalism, especially with a view to constitutional allegories and visual constitutional geometry. Most importantly, Part V of this book is devoted to constitutional geometry as a specific and autonomous phenomenon of constitutional semiotics which is related mainly to symbolic-imaginary constitutionalism. In other words, in parallel to its very important textual, visual and performative manifestations, constitutional geometry is deeply embedded in symbolic-imaginary constitutionalism.

https://imagine.sites.ku.dk. This is a project led by Komárek and is devoted to the research of European constitutional imaginaries. On the relationship between virtue, emotion, imagination and reasoning in law and legal theory, see A Amaya and M Del Mar, 'New Horizons for the Study of the Legal Mind: Relating Virtue, Emotion and Imagination' in A Amaya and M Del Mar (eds), *Virtue, Emotion and Imagination in Law and Legal Reasoning* (Oxford, Hart Publishing, 2020) 1–25.

[5] On the role of imaginary significations and the process of signification of social imaginaries, see Castoriadis (n 2) 127–65.

[6] See Loughlin (n 1).

Imagination is reserved for human beings.[7] It can be practised individually or collectively, in big or small groups.[8] The imagination capabilities of animals or artificial intelligence will not be considered or discussed in this book. This is due to the fact that its object is constitutional imagination and, at least for now, animals and AI are considered to be excluded from the range of subjects of constitutional law, and thus belong to its objects.[9] Hence, so far, constitutional imagination remains limited to human communities.[10]

This part of the book addresses the collective constitutional imagination. It will not engage in an analysis of the way in which individual imagination regarding constitutional institutions, constitutional memory[11] and constitutional perspectives is formed or expressed.[12] The constitutional culture, constitutional consciousness and motivation as factors for the establishment and development of constitutional imagination and thus of constitutional imaginary practices will also not be explored here.[13]

More precisely, this part discusses one very specific form of collective social imagination. This is the constitutional imagination as a phenomenon which lies at the core of symbolic-imaginary constitutionalism as an important but still underestimated form of constitutionalism. One of the aims of this book is to bring symbolic-imaginary constitutionalism to the fore of the constitutional debate, to shed some light on its essence, functions and components, and to highlight the huge relevance of symbolic-imaginary forms of conceptualisation

[7] According to Cornelius Castoriadis, 'man is an unconsciously philosophical animal, who has posed the questions of philosophy in actual fact long before philosophy existed as explicit reflection; and he is a poetic animal, who has provided answers to these questions in the imaginary'. See Castoriadis (n 2) 147.

[8] For an extensive and telling research on imagination, see E Brann, *The World of the Imagination: Sum and Substance* (Lanham, MD, Rowman & Littlefield, 2017) 1–810.

[9] There are many claims that constitutional law has to be less speciesist and must also grant a degree of subjectivity to animals and AI. See, eg, A Peters, 'Liberté, Égalité, Animalité: Human–Animal Comparisons in Law' (2016) 5(1) *Transnational Environmental Law* 25; R Ryder, *Animal Revolution: Changing Attitudes towards Speciesism* (Oxford, Berg, 2000); M Vinding, *Speciesism: Why it is Wrong and the Implications of Rejecting it* (CreateSpace Independent Publishing Platform, 2015), T Milligan, 'Speciesism as Variant of Anthropocentrism' in R Boddice (ed), *Anthropocentrism: Humans, Animals, Environments* (Leiden, Brill, 2011) 223ff. Nevertheless, there is no appeal for admitting that entities other than human beings can have socially relevant imagination. Thus, for the moment, the sphere of constitutional imagination seems to be reserved only for human beings.

[10] See M Belov, 'Post-human Constitutionalism? A Critical Defence of Anthropocentric and Humanist Traditions in Algorithmic Society' in M Belov (ed), *The IT Revolution and its Impact on State, Constitutionalism and Public Law* (Oxford, Hart Publishing, 2021) 15–41.

[11] For the interrelation between imagination and memory, see M Del Mar, *Artefacts of Legal Inquiry: The Value of Imagination in Adjudication* (Oxford, Hart Publishing, 2020) 132–36.

[12] For a different approach, see A Sajo, 'Emotions in Constitutional Design' (2010) 8(3) *ICON* 354.

[13] There are an increasing number of publications relating to these issues; however, these mostly focus on emotional constitutionalism. See A Sajo, 'Emotions in Constitutional Institutions' (2016) 8(1) *Emotion Review* 44; Sajo (n 12); S Bandes, J Madeira, K Temple and E Kidd White (eds), *Research Handbook on Law and Emotion* (Cheltenham, Edward Elgar, 2021) 1–640.

of the constitutional order for constitutional epistemology.[14] The part will demonstrate why this is best done through the analytical lens of constitutional semiotics.

Constitutional imagination is the process of the establishment and maintenance of collective perceptions of constitutionally relevant phenomena and their preservation in the form of constitutional imaginaries. Constitutional imagination is a psychological process of individual and collective assessment, conceptualisation and understanding of the constitutional reality in all its facets – normative-institutional, textual, visual, performative, ideal etc.[15] Its scope includes all constitutional and constitutionally relevant phenomena which are considered to be rationally or emotionally appealing and thus able to result in durable imprints on the collective constitutional conscious, subconscious or unconscious of the constitutionally framed socio-political community. Thus, constitutional imagination has a specific object – the range of constitutional and constitutionally relevant phenomena – which is not limited to valid constitutional law. It also encompasses 'constitutional law-as-performance', 'constitutional law-as-visualisation' and 'constitutional law-as-imagination'.

Constitutional imagination leads to the establishment of constitutional imaginaries which can be individual and collective;[16] in the latter case, we speak of the collective constitutional imagination. Together, the collective constitutional imaginaries form the overall concept of symbolic-imaginary constitutionalism.[17] They shape the constitutional semiotic landscapes and thus contribute to the semiotic approach to the constitution, constitutionalism and constitutional law. Metaphorically, the constitutional imagination is the paintbrush for the signification of constitutional and constitutionally relevant meaning and the drawing of constitutional semiotic landscapes that are contained in symbolic-imaginary constitutionalism and are expressed and represented in the forms of and via the figures provided by textual, visual and performative constitutionalism.

Constitutional imagination expresses the imaginary, emotional and dreamy aspects of constitutionalism. It is evidence that constitutional law is not the only rational device for the performance of pragmatic operations, but is also an imaginative enterprise with deeper symbolic, emotional and inspirational layers. It is not just a system of rationally ordered and textually expressed rules providing for

[14] On the importance of the imaginary approach for the epistemology of constitutional normativity, see O Tans, 'Imagined Constitutionality: Rethinking Democratic Citizenship with the Aid of Fiction Theory' (2019) 15(2) *Law, Culture and the Humanities* 14–15.

[15] For an excellent and innovative exploration of imagination and its various dimensions and models, see Del Mar (n 11) 125–95.

[16] According to Přibáň, imaginaries also do not belong to either the substructure of material power or the superstructure of hegemonic ideology or symbolic order. They need to be distinguished from cultural myths and economic or political dogmas and cannot be treated as mere residues of mythological and ideological imaginations operating in otherwise functionally differentiated systems and falsely constituting idealisations of social unity and totality. See Přibáň (n 2) 2.

[17] For the interplay between the institution and the imaginary and for the social imaginaries, see Castoriadis (n 2) 115–21.

institutions, forms and procedures, but also a form of the collective art of joint constitutional remembering, dreaming, hoping, fearing, hating and loving, which produces collective constitutional imaginaries in conscious, partially conscious or unconscious ways.[18]

The range and forms of collective imagination can vary, but it is possible to dream big on a massive scale – in social groups, nations or even whole regions marking the borders of civilisations. The triggers of imagination, its scope, the possibility of defining its social and socio-political boundaries, the process of its emergence and unfolding, and the preservation of stable socio-political imaginaries are fundamental interdisciplinary questions. They require thorough and in-depth analysis using the latest achievements of psychology, anthropology, theory of mind, epistemology and cognitive sciences. Such analysis obviously goes beyond the scope of a book devoted to constitutional semiotics. Thus, here I will simply briefly discuss the main features of constitutional imaginaries which are relevant for the structuring, understanding and defining of the concept of symbolic-imaginary constitutionalism as one of the pillars of my approach for proposing a theory of constitutional semiotics.[19]

There are different factors that trigger and stimulate the collective imagination and sustaining collective images and imaginaries,[20] but they will not be examined here. What is important to note is that social imagination is key for social cohesion. It produces normative ideologies, normative ideas and founding, and conceptual myths which contribute substantially to the establishment, maintenance and evolution of social communities. Social imagination is of pivotal importance for the authority, efficiency and legitimacy of social institutions.[21] Constitutional imagination is the invisible but feasible glue that binds together the particles of quantum constitutionalism[22] in the form of cloud constitutionalism.[23] Symbolic-imaginary cloud constitutionalism – the dispersed clouds of constitutional meaning – facilitates the spread of the imaginary potential of the community and preserves in a durable but usually non-structured and non-institutionalised way the substance and the potentiality of the constitutional order. An exception here is constitutional geometry, is based on structured constitutional imaginaries, as will be shown in Part V below.

[18] See O Tans, 'The Imaginary Foundation of Legal Systems: A Mimetic Perspective' (2014) 26(2) *Law & Literature* 127, doi:10.1080/1535685X.2014.888204.

[19] Symbolic-imaginary constitutionalism rests very much on the idea that the constitution and constitutional law perform symbolic functions for the people and society. See M Lerner, 'Constitution and Court as Symbols' (1937) 46(8) *Yale Law Journal* 1290.

[20] On the difference and relationship between images and imaginaries, see Castoriadis (n 2) 127 et seq.

[21] See J Derrida, 'Force of Law: The 'Mystical Foundation of Authority' (1989–90) 11 *Cardozo Law Review* 920–1045; and J Přibáň, 'Constitutional Imaginaries and Legitimation: On Potentia, Potestas, and Auctoritas in Societal Constitutionalism' (2018) 45(1) *Journal of Law and Society* 30, who also speaks of 'the constituent power of social imaginaries' impacting constitutional legitimacy.

[22] See pt I, ch 2 of this book.

[23] See pt V, ch 7 of this book.

In other words, the potential that is entrenched in valid constitutional law can be fully realised only if it is emotionally appealing to the people while triggering their collective understanding of constitutional phenomena. The collective constitutional imaginaries are accessible not just through reason and intelligence, but also via intuition that relies upon the dispersed process of constitutional semiosis. In that regard, constitutional semiosis is preconditioned upon the quantum symbolic characteristics of the constitutional order and its capability to sustain imaginaries in a collective and dispersed way.

Thus, the constitutional imagination and symbolic-imaginary constitutionalism play an important role for the proper understanding of constitutional law, which is rather underestimated, being considered a meta-legal problem of history, anthropology or social psychology. It improves constitutional epistemology relating to constitutional memories, hopes and dreams.[24] It offers an original glimpse into the issues of constitutional remembrance, constitutional memory politics and the constitutional management of collective emotions. Finally, it is of huge importance for the proper understanding of the ways in which constitutional law is perceived and practised by the members of the constitutionally framed socio-political community and by this community taken as a joint actor, producer and addressee of constitutional semiosis.

To sum up, constitutional imagination and the constitutional imaginaries produced by it impact the way in which people understand and apply the constitution and constitutional law. Hence, they are determinants of constitutionalism as a socio-legal paradigm, shaping its pragmatic outlook and the symbolic-imaginary forms through which it is conceived and practised. Consequently, constitutional imagination and the constitutional imaginaries require proper and focused scientific research accomplished on the basis of a theoretical paradigm that is capable of giving them substantial analytical depth and legitimate scientific standing. This is the symbolic-imaginary constitutionalism perceived as a specific analytical and explanatory paradigm belonging to the realm of constitutional semiotics.

Constitutional imagination may belong to real or 'imagined communities'[25] that are structured, defined and ordered according to different criteria. Constitutional imagination is produced and maintained by individuals. Nevertheless, it is not reducible to the individual imagination of the members of the community. Conversely, it is not a mere sum of individual imaginations. The collectives and communities of people imagine in a different manner from individuals, despite being dependent on individual imagination as a structural prerequisite and being holders and producers of the collective imagination and imaginaries. They dream big, but the shapes of their imagination are less clear than those of the imagination of the individuals from which they are composed.

[24] See M Belov, 'Constitutional Memories: How Do Constitutions Cope with Constitutional Past' in M Belov and A Abat i Ninet (eds), *Revolution, Transition, Memory, and Oblivion: Reflections on Constitutional Change* (Cheltenham, Edward Elgar, 2020) 107–26.

[25] See B Anderson, *Imagined Communities: Reflections on the Origin and Spread of Nationalism* (New York, Verso, 2016) 1–256.

Luckily, constitutions and constitutional law contain imprints of constitutional imagination making symbolic-imaginary constitutionalism a legal phenomenon relating to valid law. These are the collective dreams, traumas, hopes and fears[26] structured as constitutional myths and mythologies, normative ideologies and ideas, constitutional utopias and constitutional codes. Nevertheless, collective constitutional imaginaries are not reducible to their legal imprints and constitutionally entrenched shapes. Their societal and socio-legal projections in a range of constitutional discourses – visual, performative and textual – go well beyond the legal core of constitutional imagination. Hence, constitutional semiotics as instrument for decoding, understanding and systematising symbolic-imaginary constitutionalism as a framing concept of collective constitutional imaginaries is definitely not a purely legal concept, but is rather a socio-legal phenomenon.[27]

Moreover, there are competing choices relating to the problem of what can be defined as the collective constitutional imagination. This is rarely a statistical phenomenon – an entirely measurable and quantifiable entity. In fact, the collective constitutional imagination is a phenomenon that is partially autonomous and detached from the aggregation of individual consciousness, despite their empirical contribution to its formation. The collective constitutional imagination is a socio-cultural artefact and a socio-legal determinant of the constitution and constitutional law, and an interpersonal, dispersed and 'cloud' concept spread through the constitutionally framed socio-political community that is not reducible to either valid law or the individual consciousness of its bearers. It is dependent on the existence of cloud constitutionalism.[28]

In that regard, the collective constitutional imagination is an interpersonal, meta-legal concept sustained by individual and collective consciousness. It has its imprints and manifestations in various constitutional discourses – textual, rational, normative-institutional, performative, emotional and visual – but is not reducible to them. It is entrenched in symbolic-imaginary constitutionalism as a concept of constitutional semiotics, while the rest of constitutional discourses serve as important epistemic plains for its discovery and reconstruction through semiotic tools.

There might be a range of partially overlapping collective imaginations, some of which claim the status of predominant, official, proper or representative imaginations. They form a dynamic picture that evolves according to a range of factors. The most important of them are formal constitutional change, the evolution of the

[26] See M Belov, 'The Role of Fear Politics in Global Constitutional "Ernstfall": Images of Fear under COVID-19 Health Paternalism' in M Belov (ed), *Populist Constitutionalism and Illiberal Democracies: Between Constitutional Imagination, Normative Entrenchment and Political Reality* (Cambridge, Intersentia, 2021) 187–221; G Frankenberg, *Comparative Constitutional Studies: Between Magic and Deceit* (Cheltenham, Edward Elgar, 2018) 24; and A Bianchi and A Saab, 'Fear and International Law-Making: An Exploratory Inquiry' (2019) 32 *Leiden Journal of International Law* 351, doi:10.1017/S0922156519000177.

[27] M Colmegna, 'Decoding the Code' in R Kevelson (ed), *Law and Semiotics*, vol 2 (New York, Plenum Press, 1988) 135–43.

[28] Cloud constitutionalism is a phenomenon that will be explained in pt V, ch 7 of this book.

constitutional model, including developments in constitutional anthropology, the migration, reception and transplantation[29] of normative ideas, ideologies, myths, mythologies, codes, utopias and other forms of symbolic-imaginary constitutionalism, and the shifting socio-political and ideal contexts. Together, these factors produce a range of constitutional imaginaries in the process of the symbolic representation of meaning.

This means that constitutional semiosis is not a unilateral process with a clear and single direction; rather, it is a multidiscursive, multilayered and unstructured process. It may be based on different projections of 'law's melody'[30] in symbolic-imaginary constitutionalism: synchronic or diachronic, synthetic or antithetic, symphonic, coordinated and orchestrated or counter-punctual.[31] This all leads to a rather fragmented, multilayered and pluralistic picture of symbolic-imaginary constitutionalism and the range of constitutional imaginaries encompassed by it.

Consequently collective constitutional imaginaries do not necessarily form a coherent system. On the contrary, frequently there are a range of collective constitutional imaginaries that are to an extent contradictory, while co-existing in the collective constitutional consciousness. The logical-rational contradiction does not diminish their joint contribution to forming the realm of symbolic-imaginary constitutionalism.

There are multiple examples of matching normative ideologies which were initially conceptually mutually contradictory and rationally inconsistent with each other. Some of the most important of these are the merger of representation and democracy in the concept of representative democracy;[32] the belief in holistic representation of the nation by Members of Parliament in the context of competitive party democracy; the myth of the co-existence of representative democracy with huge areas of party political impartiality, such as the judiciary and the public administration; and the myth of the neutral role of the head of state in the context of parilamentarism.[33]

Social and constitutional imagination requires the involvement of one or more human beings. The minimal prerequisite of the collective imagination is the existence of many individuals grouped together on the basis of certain criteria. In the case of the constitutional imagination, this criterion is belonging to the same

[29] A Watson, *Legal Transplants: An Approach to Comparative Law* (Athens, GA, University of Georgia Press, 1993) 1–144.

[30] J Sammons, 'The Law's Melody' (2010) 55 *Villanova Law Review* 1143.

[31] M Poiares Maduro, 'Contrapunctual Law: Europe's Constitutional Pluralism in Action' in N Walker (ed), *Sovereignty in Transition* (Oxford, Hart Publishing, 2003) 501–38; and M Poiares Maduro, 'Three Claims of Constitutional Pluralism' in M Avbelj and J Komarek (eds), *Constitutional Pluralism in the European Union and Beyond* (Oxford, Hart Publishing, 2012) 67–84.

[32] M Brito Vieira and D Runciman, *Representation* (Cambridge, Polity Press, 2008) 29–63.

[33] B Constant, *Principes de politiques applicables à tous les gouvernements représentatifs* (HACH. LIVRE-BNF, 2016) 1–333; S Baume, 'De l'usage des pouvoirs neutres' (2012) 143(4) *Pouvoirs* 17; P Rolland, 'Comment préserver les institutions politiques? La théorie du pouvoir neutre chez B Constant' (2008) 27(1) *Revue Française d'Histoire des Idées Politiques* 43.

socio-political community, which is framed on the basis of the normative ideology, axiology and imaginaries provided by the constitution.

This does not preclude the fact that collective constitutional imaginaries can migrate and be the object of reception and transplantation[34] beyond the borders of specific constitutional jurisdictions. The people become increasingly inspired by content that is signified through constitutional and constitutionally relevant signifiers beyond state borders and at a regional and universal scale. The new means of transportation and especially of communication facilitate, promote and foster the speedy and intense exchange of symbols, myths, images, ideas etc. Thus, they contribute to the forming of composite and rather cosmopolitan constitutional imaginaries. This is especially true for digital and internet-based forms of constitutional communication resulting in the digitalisation of constitutional semiotics. They trigger multiple processes that are related to the spread of symbolic-imaginary constitutionalism – globalisation, universalisation, harmonisation and approximation of constitutional signifiers – as well as their grouping into distinct semiotic networks organised on the basis of a particular logic. Thus, the shaping of contemporary symbolic-imaginary constitutionalism is a result of the creative clash, interception and mutual approximation of local, subnational, national, international, transnational and global constitutional imaginaries.[35]

In such a context, constitutional semiotics must be considered to be a multi-layered approach to a range of constitutional imaginaries at all levels of the constitutional imagination. It has to develop skills and toolkits for understanding local constitutional imaginaries at the subnational and national levels, while also enhancing its capacity to propose a regional and universal semiotic grammar applicable to supranational and global symbolic-imaginary constitutionalism. Constitutional semiotics has to be conceptually allocated to the realm of comparative constitutional cultures.[36] It is a sophisticated instrument for the comparison of the symbolic-imaginary, visual, textual and performative cultures of the different constitutional civilisations.

The constitutional imagination is a form of collective social imagination. It is characterised by several specific features. Its main determinant as a subtype of the collective social imagination is its object. It targets constitutional phenomena, elements of social life which relate to the constitution, constitutional law and constitutionalism in general.

The constitutional imagination may relate to written constitutional law – the constitutional institutions or distinct elements of constitutional law, such as

[34] Watson (n 29) 1–144.

[35] On the important issues of constitutional imagination applied in the sphere of global and supranational constitutionalism, see O Angeli, 'Global Constitutionalism and Constitutional Imagination' (2017) 6(3) *Global Constitutionalism* 359.

[36] See G Frankenberg, *Order from Transfer: Comparative Constitutional Design and Legal Culture* (Cheltenham, Edward Elgar, 2013) 1–384; Frankenberg (n 26) 1–360; and M Steger, *The Rise of the Global Imaginary: Political Ideologies from the French Revolution to the Global War on Terror* (Oxford, Oxford University Press, 2008) 129–249.

constitutional values, constitutional principles, constitutional aims, human rights[37] or components of the institutional design. Thus, it may address constitutional ontology, constitutional axiology, constitutional teleology or constitutional design.

From the viewpoint of legal positivism, it seems logical that the social imagination, if it claims to be constitutional imagination, should focus on valid constitutional law. However, even in this case, the constitutional imagination might be disqualified as an 'extra-legal', paralegal, meta-legal or even non-legal phenomenon. A positivist answer to this positivist criticism might be that there are many instances in which the constitutional imagination is explicitly or implicitly enshrined and encoded in written constitutional law, and especially in constitutions.

Many constitutions contain national mythologies about the emergence of the state, the role of national heroes for the establishment or preservation of independence and statehood, the cultural roots of the constitutional order, the national aims for the establishment of a better society, frequently with an imaginary and even a utopian character etc. This is especially true for the communist constitutional tradition, but is also visible in many constitutions in Africa, Asia and Latin America that heavily emphasise the socio-cultural embeddedness and role of constitutional law. These constitutions dream, hope and fear through constitutional memories,[38] constitutional myths and mythologies, and imaginary trajectories based on quantum constitutionalism. Utopian societies – past, present and future – are part of the normative object of emotionally oriented constitutions planning their imaginary outlook through norms of valid law. Thus, it is certain that at least constitutional imagination in a narrower sense – that which is written down in constitutional provisions – is a valid and legitimate object of research for legal science.

Nevertheless, constitutional imagination may also be focused on the ideal, theoretical[39] and socio-legal discourses of constitutionalism. This is the constitutional imagination in a broader sense which can be derived from constitutional theory, public opinion and socio-political practices. Constitutional imagination may be enshrined in valid law, embedded in social practices, and justified and conceptually shaped in constitutional theory. In all three discourses – legal, socio-legal and ideal – constitutional imagination produces a process of encoding and decoding of meaning which requires a constitutional semiotic approach.[40]

Hence, constitutional imagination justifies the existence of a separate discourse in constitutionalism: symbolic-imaginary constitutionalism. Symbolic-imaginary

[37] On the impact of political imagination on human rights, see Bottici (n 3) 161–203.

[38] See Belov (n 24).

[39] On the role of theory in shaping constitutional imagination and for original conceptualisation of theory as imagination, see Z Oklopcic, *Beyond the People: Social Imaginary and Constituent Imagination* (Oxford, Oxford University Press, 2018) 1–37.

[40] Colmegna (n 27).

constitutionalism – like other forms and types of constitutionalism – has ideal, legal and socio-legal dimensions. Some of its forms are encoded in valid constitutional law; others are derived from socio-legal practices based on the collective imaginary and even the collective unconscious. Finally, there is the phenomena of symbolic-imaginary constitutionalism, which serves as a meta-theory capable of explaining and ordering the constitutional order into macro- and meso-shapes and forms. This is especially true of constitutional geometry as a form of constitutional semiotics bridging the gap between rational and symbolic-imaginary constitutionalism.

Constitutions, of course, cannot literally imagine, dream or remember. They are products of the human imagination practised, structured, procedurally framed and coordinated in a collective way. They are triggers of constitutional imagination and the results of human imagination. Thus, they are artefacts of legal inquiry[41] and containers of semiotic signification and epistemic knowledge about symbolic-imaginary constitutionalism.

Constitutions, as perceived in the theoretical discourse and as a social practice, stem from the collective or collectively perceived and appreciated imagination. This is the imagination of the author (encoder) of meaning, the imagination of the interpreter, the imagination of the implementing subject, the imagination of the addressee of constitutional provisions and collective constitutional imaginary constructs etc. The imaginary constitutionalist constructions and theories launched in the constitutional doctrine are collectively perceived and appreciated. They are a product of the permanent presentation, representation and interpretation of constitutionally encoded or theoretically or socially constructed collective imaginaries adjusted in accordance with the valid constitutional law.

Hence, constitutions are institutional containers of constitutional imagination when they provide normative ideologies, normative ideas, constitutional mythologies, constitutional memories, constitutional dreams and other forms of imaginary constitutionalism. They are also the occasion, trigger and pretext for imagination – theoretical imagination constituting imaginary constitutionalism as a theory and the collective social imagination forming imaginary constitutionalism as practice.[42]

Thus, constitutions can metaphorically 'imagine' via subjects allowed to imagine on their behalf. Constitutional imagining on behalf of the community may mean two different things: it may consist in adopting valid legal provisions containing imaginary constitutionalism or in de facto shaping the collective constitutional imaginary of the constitutionally framed socio-political community. In the former case, we have constitutional imagination enshrined in valid constitutional law and thus imaginary constitutionalism in a strictly legal and narrow sense. In the latter case, we can speak of imaginary constitutionalism in

[41] See Del Mar (n 11) 1–484.

[42] Original and insightful analysis of theoretical imagination and theory as imagination can be found in Oklopcic (n 39) 1–37.

a broader sense – as theoretical discourse or social practice. It may contribute significantly to the collective imagination on constitutional themes, but does not possess any legal validity.

There are subjects which are officially allowed to imagine on behalf of the constitutionally framed community. This means that they can officially 'invest' constitutional imagination in the legal order by enacting constitutional provisions or provisions of other sources of constitutional law containing such imagination. Investing legally valid constitutional imagination means enshrining normative ideologies, normative ideas, constitutional memories, constitutional dreams and constitutional myths and mythologies in the text of the constitution, but also in other important sources of constitutional law.

The powerful position of grand masters of valid constitutional imagination – constitutional imagination enshrined in valid constitutional law – is typically granted to the constitutional legislator. The constitutional legislator is supposed to be the demiurge of symbolic-imaginary constitutionalism, making semiotic order out of visual, performative, significatory and imaginary disorder. In practice, however, the constitutional legislator simply creates the initial text and thus sends an invitation for constitutional semiosis to all members of the semiotic community, but especially to the authoritative narrators, interpreters, performers, visualisers and creators of the collective constitutional imagination. In that regard, the power to participate in the process of mastering symbolic-imaginary constitutionalism with projections in valid law and thus in legally valid constitutional semiosis is typically also vested in the constitutional or supreme courts. These courts may shape the legal foundations of collective constitutional imaginaries through their decisions. This is done by accomplishing 'virtual amendment and further development of the constitution'[43] on the basis of its 'open texture'.[44]

Much less frequently, such a role is played by Parliament and the government. It is very unlikely that the acts of Parliament or government can contain constitutional imaginaries and thus contribute to symbolic-imaginary constitutionalism. They are pragmatic acts bound to rational constitutionalism and possess teleology that is rather different from the pathos of symbolic-imaginary constitutionalism. This has to be taken into account when accomplishing semiotic research in national or comparative constitutional law. It should also be noted that the parliaments and governments of authoritarian and totalitarian regimes or highly ideologically indoctrinated political regimes are keener to produce and promote collective constitutional imaginaries than their counterparts in more pragmatic and less dogmatically impacted regimes. Moreover, the appetite of parliaments and governments to engage in constitutional imaginary discourses increases during times of political turbulence, change and transition.

[43] E Tanchev and M Belov, 'Constitutional Gradualism: Adapting to EU Membership and Improving the Judiciary in the Bulgarian Constitution' (2008) 14(1) *European Public Law* 3.

[44] See HLA Hart, *The Concept of Law* (Oxford, Oxford University Press, 1997) 124–36.

Again, the principal 'investor' of constitutional imaginary and, hence, the main subject shaping symbolic-imaginary constitutionalism in a strictly legal sense is the subject to which the constituent power belongs. It is well known that the constituent power may impose or negotiate constitutions. Hence, symbolic-imaginary constitutionalism and the manifestations of the constitutional imagination (normative ideologies, normative ideas, constitutional mythologies, constitutional myths and constitutional memories) may either be negotiated or imposed.

However, in most cases, symbolic-imaginary constitutionalism and the collective constitutional imaginaries it contains are shaped by a multitude of narratives. Constitutional imaginaries are usually a product of semiotic waves of narratives triggered and mastered by different actors – constitutional legislators, authoritative interpreters of the constitution, and authoritative speakers and performers of the community. The latter can be both formal (courts, parliaments, leading office holders etc) and informal (opinion leaders, influencers etc). Symbolic-imaginary constitutionalism is also affected by the range of visualisers and performers of constitutionalism and constitutional law, and by its social and psychological internalisation through collective constitutionally relevant emotions. Hence, symbolic-imaginary constitutionalism is also connected to visual, performative and emotional constitutionalism.

Consequently, there are a multitude of factors, including theorists and key de facto authorities of the community (eg, past leaders), that may shape the constitutional imagination via normative statements and involvement in normative practices. They form symbolic-imaginary constitutionalism in a broader sense – as theory and practice and not as valid law. Nevertheless, symbolic-imaginary constitutionalism in a broader sense (imaginary constitutionalism as theory or practice) may have varying degrees of influence over imaginary constitutionalism in a stricter sense (imaginary constitutionalism as valid law and the legal institutionalisation of constitutional imagination). It may influence the interpretative attitude of the subjects that should apply valid imaginary constitutionalism. It may form the legal consciousness and public opinion or even the general constitutional anthropology of the community. And it may have an impact on the process of signification and communication of symbolic-imaginary constitutionalism in a stricter sense that is enshrined and encoded in constitutional texture, thus having an important semiotic dimension.

This part of the book is focused predominantly on the 'institutionalised constitutional imagination'. This is constitutional imagination which is based on and can be derived from explicit constitutional texts or can be implicitly extracted from the constitution. Nevertheless, it also provides analysis based on key supportive normative ideologies, especially with regard to constitutional geometry conceived in its quality as an explanatory scheme of constitutional law. It also includes scientific inquiries devoted to the projections of constitutional imagination in visual and, to a much lesser extent, emotional and performative constitutionalism. In other words, the analysis also extends to imaginary constitutionalism in a broader sense.

The analysis is largely based on a semiotic approach exploring the process of signification via constitutional institutionalisation, textualisation, visualisation[45] and empirical demonstration. Indeed, the proper understanding of symbolic-imaginary constitutionalism requires its theoretical conceptualisation based on the deconstruction and reconstruction of its constitutional institutionalisation from national, historical and comparative perspectives. Epistemological and anthropological approaches may be very productive as well, especially with regard to symbolic-imaginary constitutionalism in a broader sense. This is due to the fact that symbolic-imaginary constitutionalism has projections in valid law, but also in socio-political practices of collective imagination and in representative theoretical 'standard works'.

Nevertheless, imaginary constitutionalism is bound to images, textually institutionalised representations and collective imaginaries related to ideas, ideologies, utopias, myths, mythologies, codes, memories, dreams and taboos.[46] The textual representation of ideas and their signification via constitutional images, constitutional codes and other semantic nodes in the web of institutionalised constitutional imagination necessitate the use of constitutional semiotics. Hence, the extensive application of constitutional semiotics serves the explanation of constitutional imagination within the framing paradigm of symbolic-imaginary constitutionalism, but also beyond it – as part of visual, textual and performative constitutionalism.

It has already been noted that imagination implies subjectivity and the involvement of the human personality. Imagination requires the existence of a subject as both source and recipient of information structured as images, dreams, memories, hopes etc. Imagination is produced by people. In its capacity as an interpersonal and social phenomenon, it is intermediated by different communicative media. All of these are produced by people and directed towards people. Subjects are also involved as bearers and mediators of imagination, which in the case of constitutional law imagination is largely transmitted through constitutional text and texture. Nevertheless, it is also spread in the form of cloud constitutionalism.

Thus, constitutional imagination has to be approached and analysed from a semiotic perspective. It is an object of constitutional semiotics. This is due to the fact that the constitutional imagination is objectivised via a process of signification that is either institutionalised in the constitution itself, thus producing symbolic-imaginary constitutionalism in a stricter sense, or reflected in other forms of

[45] On the process of the establishment of social imaginaries through visualisation, see M Wolf, *Building Imaginary Worlds: The Theory and History of Subcreation* (Abingdon, Routledge, 2012) 253–57.

[46] According to Mulcahy: 'Images are generally taken to be more anarchic than text or numbers … When we observe an image, we may well grasp the simultaneous presence of many disparate things within one frame. The result is that images have the potential to reveal a "multiplicity of othernesses and differences" which are for the most part silenced in texts.' See L Mulcahy, 'Sociology of Legal Images' in J Přibáň (ed), *Research Handbook on the Sociology of Law* (Cheltenham, Edward Elgar, 2020) 4.

shared communicative and signification experience forming part of symbolic-imaginary constitutionalism in a broader sense.

Hence, imaginary constitutionalism is loaded with a degree of subjectivity. This is due to the fact that an imagining subject is required in order to trigger, produce, transmit and maintain constitutional imagination, which is at the core of symbolic-imaginary constitutionalism. In general, the construction, deconstruction, observance and further development of the constitutional order is based on human imagination. In particular, memories about constitutional history and dreams for the constitutional future are based on constitutional imagination. Thus, to an extent, they are doomed to be subjective and dependent on the human imagination and on the strengths and limits of the human mind. The constitutional institutionalisation of imagination depends on official narratives of the past and the future,[47] the human condition, human society and the state.

However, constitutional imagination is neither entirely subjective nor purely speculative. The very moment that people start to collectively dream, imagine or memorise, their individual consciousness expands beyond the 'prison of individuality' and the solipsistic nature of the self. Hence, collective imagination, collective memories and collective dreams are subjectively predetermined, but at the same time are also inspired by and result in objective phenomena – or at least in phenomena that are generally perceived as having a substantial degree of objectivity.

In that regard, the constitutional imaginaries exist to an extent autonomously from the individual consciousness. They are scientifically provable by social sciences such as history, social psychology or anthropology precisely because of their objectiveness. Memories, dreams and imagination may be proven, criticised, deconstructed, reconstructed and scientifically researched (analysed, typified etc.) because they materialise in constitutionally relevant visuals, texture or performance. Such materialisation is of vital importance for the process of the formation of cloud constitutionalism,[48] which is to an extent produced as a result of constitutional semiosis.

It has been noted that one can differentiate between symbolic-imaginary constitutionalism in a stricter or narrower sense and symbolic-imaginary constitutionalism in a broader sense. The former concerns only the institutionalisations detectable directly or indirectly, explicitly or implicitly in written constitutional law, while the latter also comprises the manifestations and instantiations of constitutional imagination in the legal literature and theory, in practice, in arts and architecture, and in the collective imagination of the constitutionally framed socio-legal community.

Hence, while symbolic-imaginary constitutionalism in a stricter sense can be explored via legal methodology, symbolic-imaginary constitutionalism in

[47] See C Kølvraa, 'Past and Future in the Construction of Communal Identity: Collective Memory and Mythical Narratives' (2015) 6(3) *Scandinavian Studies in Language* 62; and B Lincoln, *Discourse and the Construction of Society: Comparative Studies of Myth, Ritual, and Classification* (Oxford, Oxford University Press, 1992) 38–53.

[48] See pt V, ch 7 of this book.

a broader sense mostly requires the use of social psychology, sociological and anthropological methods. In both cases, the use of semiotic methods is advisable and necessary in order to gain a better understanding of the phenomenon. This is due to the fact that symbolic-imaginary constitutionalism is based on two mutually dependent processes. The first of these consists in enshrining and encoding imaginary concepts in the constitution by subjects empowered to do so and of sharing and mutually shaping such concepts in the collective imagination, memories and dreams. The second results in the decoding,[49] deciphering and understanding of imaginary concepts objectively encoded in law or social reality via the first process by communicative actors belonging to the semiotic community or in the form of external observers, researchers etc. Both processes consist of signification and interaction between signs, signifiers and signified. Hence, they are semiotic processes that, due to their object, namely constitutional and constitutionally relevant phenomena, fall within the scope of constitutional semiotics.

The constitutional relevance of social imaginaries is a result of two main factors. The first pf these is objective. It is the added political value of the social phenomenon – in this case, the form of collective imagination. Constitutionally relevant imaginaries are those forms of collective imagination which concern the common interest of the socio-political community for the establishment and maintenance of a well-ordered society. Constitutional imagination may encompass traumas, fears, taboos, memories and inherited institutions from the past, dreams, aims and hopes for the future,[50] or conceptualisations of the human being, society, human organisations and the institutions of public power which have been, are or will be central for the political organisation of society in a constitutional form.

The second factor for constitutional relevance might be defined as subjective. This is the will of the constitutional legislator and the authoritative constitutional narrators, visualisers and performers. The constitution is a product of the will of the 'constitutional legislator', being itself a framework concept that may include the monarch, the constituent assembly, the Parliament or the people. Moreover, as mentioned above, constitutional imaginaries are also shaped, formed and moulded by the constitutionally framed socio-political community and its authoritative narrators, visualisers and performers.

Thus, constitutional imagination is a twofold concept. It may denominate the collective imagination of the socio-political community as well as the collective imagination as enshrined in the written constitution by the constitutional legislator on behalf of the socio-political community ('the people', 'the nation' etc).[51] In its first, sociological, socio-legal or societal sense, it is a form of collective imagination

[49] Colmegna (n 27).

[50] On the imaginary use (and misuse) of the future for political purposes, see Lincoln (n 47) 38–53.

[51] According to Frankenberg, 'the term constitution launched a new way of imagining political reality, to wit, a political imaginary that crystallized around the political existence of a social collective – people, nation, Volk, pueblo – as an "imagined community"'. See Frankenberg (n 26) 24.

that resembles other phenomena of societal constitutionalism,[52] such as public opinion and the general will.[53] The socio-legal aspect of constitutional imagination is organised on the basis of cloud constitutionalism.

In its second sense, constitutional imagination is a strictly legal phenomenon. It encompasses the legal projections of constitutional imagination as enshrined in the written constitution and eventually in the other sources of constitutional law. It is anchored in textual constitutionalism. Thus, it is related to the constitutional institutionalisation of the collective social imagination in the text of the constitution.

Hence, constitutional imagination encompasses those elements of social imagination which have constitutional relevance produced by their added political value as defined by the will of the constituent power or the range of authoritative narrators, performers and visualisers of the constitutionally framed socio-political community. Consequently, it has objective shapes and forms institutionalised by constitutional law in general and the constitution in particular. It is enshrined in the constitutional texture – the text of the written constitution and the other written sources of constitutional law – but also in the other systems for the representation and signification of constitutional and constitutionally relevant meaning.

As such, constitutional imagination is a historical artefact, a sociological phenomenon, a physiological process and an anthropological finding. It is a phenomenon which has projections in the past, the present and the future. Constitutional imagination is a historical fact documented in historical sources and in theoretical research, but is also enshrined in historical constitutional texts. It is a sociological phenomenon, being a product of the shared memories, dreams and beliefs of the members of the socio-political constitutionally framed community. It is a product of social psychology being based on the political and constitutional anthropology of the community.

What is particularly important from a constitutional viewpoint is that constitutional imagination is a semiotic phenomenon for the signification and communication of important symbolic ways of perceiving constitutional phenomena. It frames and reflects a semiotic process of constitutional signification that involves the constitutional legislator and the authoritative speakers of the community, including the formative doctrine – the works of authors who intellectually master, frame and determine our understanding of the constitutional order.

Hence, we can speak much more of a multitude of narratives presenting different pictures of 'objective meaning' enshrined in the constitutional texture than of one single and objective meaning of the constitutional imagination. Some of these narratives are enshrined in valid law and thus produce constitutional imagination

[52] On constitutional imagination as a central element of societal constitutionalism, see Přibáň (n 21); and Přibáň (n 2) 1–251.

[53] On the ideological, utopian and mythological characteristics of the general will, see P Hallward, 'General Wish or General Will? Political Possibility and Collective Capacity from Rousseau through Marx' in S Chrostowska and J Ingram (eds), *Political Uses of Utopia: New Marxist, Anarchist, and Radical Democratic Perspectives* (New York, Columbia University Press, 2016) 126–61.

that possesses legal validity. These are the narratives of the constituent power or of constitutional institutions empowered to adopt valid sources of constitutional law. Other narratives have intellectual persuasiveness. They make us imagine constitutionalism and constitutional reality in a way which is not necessarily explicitly prescribed by law and thus legally valid. They have intellectual normativity based on their capacity to convince, persuade and shape collective constitutional beliefs. Finally, there are a fuzzy and broad but tangible range of narratives constituting public opinion on the imaginary discourse of society and its constitutional foundations that are organised as cloud constitutionalism.

2

Constitutional Semiosis via Symbolic-Imaginary Constitutionalism at the Crossroads between the Collective Conscious, Subconscious and Unconscious

Symbolic-imaginary constitutionalism is a holistic phenomenon. It is a separate constitutional discourse and a specific type of constitutionalism with a distinct logic, intellectual structure, conceptual apparatus and organisation. It performs specific functions and plays its own role in the overall process of constitutional semiosis. Thus, it is entrenched in systemic relations with the other constitutional discourses – textual, rational, normative-institutional, visual, emotional and performative constitutionalism.

Nevertheless, symbolic-imaginary constitutionalism is also a complex and composite paradigm. It is fragmented and inclusive. It can be disassembled into several main composite elements. These elements are complex and composite structures themselves. At the same time, symbolic-imaginary constitutionalism serves as a framing paradigm that arranges and binds them all into a broader and inclusive set of phenomena adjusted through common logic, functionality and interdependence. Hence, it is composed of a range of phenomena that are mutually interconnected by its general logic, but which also have a distinct existence, particular parameters and semi-autonomous importance, role and functions.

This complex and composite nature of symbolic-imaginary constitutionalism imposes an important analytical task upon legal science. Constitutional theory must provide a semiotic scheme for ordering the elements of symbolic-imaginary constitutionalism. This scheme has to fulfil several important conditions. It must be comprehensive, consistent and clear. It should be just and adequate to the peculiarities of the overall phenomenon (symbolic-imaginary constitutionalism) and to the particularities of its elements. It must allow for comparison between the classified phenomena and the exposure of their commonalities and differences. Last but not least, it should serve as an ordering matrix that is compatible with both the general logic of the broader phenomenon (symbolic-imaginary constitutionalism) and the specific features of the classified elements.

The semiotic approach to constitutional law also predetermines additional requirements to the classification of the elements of symbolic-imaginary constitutionalism. More concretely, the classification scheme of its components must give a proper explanation of their semiotic role, function and performance. It should bring to the fore the semiotic relevance of the forms of symbolic-imaginary constitutionalism and their particular role in constitutional semiosis.

In principle, all forms of symbolic-imaginary constitutionalism are intellectual constructions with an internal logic, scheme and structure. Nevertheless, they are not entirely rational, but possess huge emotional potential and capacity for visual representation and imaginary signification. In that regard, they are dependent on collective emotions and imaginaries. They signify constitutionally relevant objects relating to constitutional ontology, teleology, axiology and institutional design in ways that are emotionally appealing and that trigger chains of symbolic-imaginary representations.

Thus, what unites the forms of symbolic-imaginary constitutionalism is their role as bridges between the constitutional imagination and the rest of the constitutional discourses. They are instruments for the representation of ideas in textual and normative-institutional constitutionalism that stem from the realm of collective constitutional imagination. Some of them are also signified through art, architecture and performance, and thus are also relevant for visual and performative constitutionalism. On the other hand, the forms of symbolic-imaginary constitutionalism are tools for the signification of meaning originating in valid law or in 'law in action' – in the cloud of symbolic-imaginary constitutionalism – that are grouped and stored there through their organisation as normative ideologies and ideas, constitutional myths and mythologies or constitutional utopias,[1] and signified through constitutional codes.

Hence, constitutional myths and mythologies, normative ideas and ideologies, and constitutional utopias are expressions of common intellectual effort. This effort relates to and results in the pursuit of constitutional enchantment of the addressees of constitutional law in emotionally appealing and symbolically persuasive ways. This is also the need for the symbolic representation of intellectual constellations with strategic importance for the functioning of 'constitutional law-as-imagination' through the expressive means of textual, visual and performative constitutionalism. They are tools for the activation not only of the conscious, deliberate and rational behaviour of the constitutional actors, but also of the subconscious attitudes of self-affiliation and self-identification, obedience, inclusion and pursuit of aims grounded in collective constitutional imaginaries. Hence, the forms of symbolic-imaginary constitutionalism are projections of the ideal and the imaginary on the rational plain.[2]

[1] See also M Wolf, *Building Imaginary Worlds: The Theory and History of Subcreation* (Abingdon, Routledge, 2012) 1–394.

[2] For further arguments based on the theory of C Castoriadis, see C Gilleard, 'From Collective Representations to Social Imaginaries: How Society Represents itself to itself' (2018) 5(3) *European Journal of Cultural and Political Sociology* 320.

The above-mentioned tasks and goals have a rational core. Nevertheless, they are achieved in rational and irrational, and conscious, unconscious and subconscious ways. Hence, the forms of symbolic-imaginary constitutionalism are provided by the constitutions in a dubious way in order to trigger two effects. First, they are supposed to be rationally accessible, justifiable and convincing. They must be able to be constructed, deconstructed and reconstructed through human reason and through the use of rational methods of constitutional interpretation of constitutional text and texture. Second, they must also be able to trigger feelings and imaginations, to subconsciously and unconsciously promote ideas and ideals, and to enchant and convince through recourse to archetypes,[3] collective dreams, memories, traumas, aspirations etc.

Consequently, the forms of symbolic-imaginary constitutionalism are intellectual bridges between the conscious, unconscious and subconscious plains of constitutionalism. They stand at the crossroads between reason and emotions, intellect, intuition and feeling. Moreover, they are not simply a passive result of the interplay between these dichotomic concepts used for ordering the interplay and balance between the rational, emotional and symbolic-imaginary world. They are also active factors for mastering those interrelations that play the role of the magmatic subterrain of constitutionalism and constitutional law.[4] There active role is twofold.

On the one hand, the forms of symbolic-imaginary constitutionalism are channels for the expression of the collective subconscious and unconscious, and for its moulding in the shape of symbolic-imaginary constitutionalism engineered through the means of textual, rational and normative-institutional constitutionalism. They are symbolic eruptions of constitutional imagination that have crystallised in terms of their constitutional texture, have acquired an institutional outlook and have gained validity through normative institutionalisation in the constitution.

In this first sense, the forms of symbolic-imaginary constitutionalism have an evidential and, to an extent, a documentary character. They signify mental processes, intellectual achievements and tendencies, and conceptual phenomena that have been created in the collective constitutional imagination and even in the depths of the constitutional subterrain of the collective unconscious.[5]

The task of the forms of symbolic-imaginary constitutionalism is to expose collective imaginaries and collective normative beliefs that sculpt the shapes of terrain of the constitutional psychology of the constitutionally framed socio-political community. In this process, the methods and forms of textual, rational

[3] CG Jung, *Four Archetypes* (London, Routledge, 2003) 1–216. On the constitutional archetypes, see also the approach in G Frankenberg, *Comparative Constitutional Studies: Between Magic and Deceit* (Cheltenham, Edward Elgar, 2018), 27 et seq.

[4] See C Castoriadis, *The Imaginary Institution of Society* (Cambridge, Polity Press, 1987) 160–65.

[5] CG Jung, *The Archetypes and the Collective Unconscious* (Princeton, Princeton University Press, 1990).

and symbolic-imaginary constitutionalism have an instrumental role to play. They are the tools for the expressing of meaning that is frequently accomplished through semiotic signification, resulting in various forms of symbolic-imaginary constitutionalism. These forms are the signifiers of signifieds derived from the depth of the collective emotional and imaginary heritage and the container of collective constitutionally relevant feelings (hopes, fears, dreams etc) of the constitutionally framed socio-political community.[6]

The semiotic process of signification is directed from the realm of the symbolic-imaginary to the realm of textual and normative-institutional constitutionalism. Sometimes it manifests itself through the signifiers of visual and performative constitutionalism. In that regard, the forms of symbolic-imaginary constitutionalism appear as reflections and projections of the collective imaginaries on the plain of textual and normative-institutional constitutionalism drawn with the help of rational constitutionalism. Hence, this aspect and direction of the semiotic process is dependent on the plausibility of the belief in the transformative force of rational constitutionalism – more precisely, it rests on its capacity to grasp, deconstruct, construct and transform collective imaginaries, making them into constitutional imaginaries. It is also dependent on the trust in the capability of textual, visual, performative and normative-institutional constitutionalism to represent meaning generated in the collective unconscious and subconscious, and to signify imaginary content in reliable, recognisable, stable and formal ways.

On the other hand, the forms of symbolic-imaginary constitutionalism are tools for the structuring of the collective imaginaries according to the strategic imperatives of constitutional engineering[7] and constitutional politics. They are the strings strained by the constitutional legislator and tuned up by the authoritative narrators, speakers, writers, interpreters, visualisers and performers of the community, and that politicians can then pull and play with. Thus, they can activate collective imaginaries and guide the melody of the socio-political orchestra oscillating between the multitudes of variations. These variations are stretched between the conceptual extremities of conscious-subconscious-unconscious, rational-emotional, real-imaginary and textual-visual-performative.

In that regard, the semiotic significations of symbolic-imaginary constitutionalism through textual, visual and performative means resemble an iceberg or a mountain rising above a sea of fog.[8] The range of these significations framed as symbolic-imaginary constitutionalism is provided by the constitution. Hence, the institutionalised part of symbolic-imaginary constitutionalism is its peak standing above the water of the subconscious archetypal constitutional depth. This peak

[6] See also J Lachs, 'Law and the Importance of Feelings' in R Kevelson (ed), *Law and Semiotics*, vol 2 (New York, Plenum Press, 1988) 221–29.

[7] G Sartori, *Comparative Constitutional Engineering: An Inquiry into Structures, Incentives, and Outcomes* (New York, New York University Press, 1994) 1–229; and X Contiades (ed), *Engineering Constitutional Change: A Comparative Perspective on Europe, Canada and the USA* (Abingdon, Routledge, 2012) 1–490.

[8] The iceberg comparison is frequently used in psychoanalytical literature.

is accessible through traditional forms and methods of rational constitutionalism and constitutional rationality entrenched in textual and normative-institutional constitutionalism. At the same time, the peak is grounded in constitutional emotions, feelings, imaginaries, hopes, fears, memories and dreams. They are visually or performatively represented or concealed under the waters of collective constitutional irrationality and subconsciousness. They are accessible only intuitively and are prone to discretional and, to an extent, provocative and speculative interpretation.

The dubious, fuzzy and twofold character of the forms of constitutional imagination requires a special type of constitutional studies and constitutionalism to be devoted to them. This should be focused on their exploration, intellectual examination and scientific exposure. This is the role of symbolic-imaginary constitutionalism perceived as a semiotic phenomenon and partially constructed through recourse to the methods of constitutional semiotics.

3

Constitutional Semiotic Landscapes

The Teleology and Functionality of Symbolic-Imaginary Constitutionalism as a 'Game of Constitutional Semiotic Imaginaries'

Constitutionalism is a battlefield for the hearts and minds of people.[1] It is a playground for winning compliance, obedience, authority and power on the basis of trust and legitimacy.[2] The power game is played by the official rules of normative-institutional constitutionalism, but it has deeper dimensions: emotional and imaginary. Constitutionalism is rational and pragmatic, but also metaphysical and transcendental. The constitutional power game is played in the realm of the conscious through the rules and by virtue of the tools of rational and normative-institutional constitutionalism. It is also played at the levels of the collective subconscious and unconscious. The rules of the game on the plain of the collective unconscious, the imaginary and the transcendental are less clear and definitely under-researched. They include the formal rules of rational and normative-institutional constitutionalism, which are deconstructed, reconstructed, redesigned, renegotiated and internalised on the basis of emotional and symbolic-imaginary constitutionalism.

The constitutional power game is signified on both plains – conscious-rational and subconscious-emotional-imaginary – through a range of constitutional signifiers provided by textual, visual, performative and symbolic-imaginary constitutionalism. Taken together, these collective constitutional imaginaries organise and form constitutional semiotic landscapes which are the main object of research in constitutional semiotics. Thus, constitutional power games are transformed by constitutional semiosis in 'symbolic-imaginary games'. These are games of constitutional codes, myths and ideas signified through structured or unstructured imaginaries spread across constitutional texture and in cloud constitutionalism. They can be explained via a range of analytical approaches – psychological, psychoanalytical,[3] anthropological and socio-legal. Nevertheless, the specific issue

[1] See A Sajó, *Constitutional Sentiments* (New Haven, Yale University Press, 2011) 1–400.

[2] J Derrida, 'Force of Law: The "Mystical Foundation of Authority"' (1980–90) 11 *Cardozo Law Review* 920.

[3] See, eg, P Goodrich, 'Psychoanalysis in Legal Education: Notes on the Violence of the Sign' in R Kevelson (ed), *Law and Semiotics*, vol 1 (New York, Plenum Press, 1987) 193–215.

of how the rules, procedures and constellations of these constitutional power games are signified and projected in the sphere of the ideal and the symbolic-imaginary, and what is the significatory essence and potential of the constitutional symbolic-imaginary landscapes can only be explored, assessed and explained via recourse to constitutional semiotics. Thus, the constitutional power games are also 'games of constitutional semiotic imaginaries'.

The formal rules of the game do matter a great deal for the official players. The constitutional chessboard is set for institutional play entrenched in the normative network of valid law. It is played by institutional rules processed via officially recognised interinstitutional channels carefully ordered in the constitutional text. However, in parallel to the official institutional game, there are also unofficial processes of constitutional enchantment, inspiration and persuasion. These unfold implicitly and to a great extent unconsciously without clear rules being known in advance. These parallel constitutional games of feelings and emotions are played in several settings – the collective conscious, but also the collective subconscious and unconscious. These are also games of imaginaries the goal of which is to enchant and make people believe in constitutional constellations related to constitutional ontology (the origin of the constitution), constitutional axiology (values and principles), constitutional teleology (the goals and aims of the constitution) and constitutional design.

An important part of these imaginary constitutional games is formed by a specific semiotic game which aims at signifying key imaginaries in a condensed and laconic but symbolically strong and emotionally persuasive way. This is the game of semiotic codes. It is played on the basis of the constitutional codes enshrined in, stemming from, developed on the basis of and sometimes even entrenched in the constitution. The constitutional codes have their rational explanation and background, but are predominantly elements of symbolic-imaginary constitutionalism.

Constitutional codes possess a range of possible meanings. In a narrower sense, they are signifiers of meaning belonging to textual, visual and performative constitutionalism which signify constitutionally relevant signifieds in condensed, symbolically appealing and partially concealed ways. In a wider sense, all forms of symbolic-imaginary constitutionalism may be perceived as constitutional codes. This is due to the fact that they are signifiers of condensed symbolic meaning, which has two sides: rational, rationally accessible and explicit; and symbolic-imaginary, intuitively accessible and implicit. Thus, the forms of symbolic-imaginary constitutionalism conceived as constitutional codes establish the specific semiotic language of signification of meaning, which has its textual roots but is generally spread and contained in cloud constitutionalism. They are also prone to expansion or limitation of meaning in the course and as a result of constitutional semiosis. They are important tools for the interpretative and multidiscursive development of meaning in the course of constitutional semiosis based on the concept of quantum constitutionalism.[4]

[4] On the concept of quantum constitutionalism, see pt I, ch 2 of this book.

In this context, the task of constitutional semiotics in general and of symbolic-imaginary constitutionalism in particular is to explain and order constitutionalism conceived as a 'game of imaginaries' and a 'game of constitutional codes'. It has to give scientific grounds and an explanation of these phenomena, which already exist in the socio-legal dimensions of constitutionalism, having their fragmented manifestations in the system of valid constitutional law. The proper understanding of the performance of the constitutional order in the realms of the collective subconscious and unconscious requires a semiotic approach to the range of constitutional signifiers of symbolic-imaginary meaning allocated in the field of semiotic constitutional landscapes. In that context, the functional analysis of symbolic-imaginary constitutionalism plays an important epistemic role.

Symbolic-imaginary constitutionalism has several functions – epistemic, symbolic-signification, enchanting, programming, foretelling (future constructing) and transcendental –which are accomplished through its forms. Constitutional myths and mythologies also have remembrance and tradition-building functions which are related to the constitutional conceptualisation of time, constitutional memory politics and the constitutional signification of the past and the future. In addition to the above-mentioned general functions, normative constitutional ideologies and ideas also perform an ordering (organisation) function, which is a variant and upgrade of the programming function (see above) that is typical of all forms of symbolic-imaginary constitutionalism.

These functions are interrelated and together expose the combined epistemic-semiotic importance of the elements of symbolic-imaginary constitutionalism. At times, they appear in an intertwined and symbiotic way, asserting joint effects that frequently trigger constitutional semiosis. These functions, taken jointly or separately, have huge explanatory potential for the role of the forms of symbolic-imaginary constitutionalism performed within the constitution and the constitutional order and outside of it in the field of empirical socio-legal relations and in the collective constitutional imaginaries and the constitutional anthropology of the constitutionally framed socio-political community. Thus, they are epistemic tools of constitutionalism in general and symbolic-imaginary constitutionalism in particular. The forms of symbolic-imaginary constitutionalism, being part of the symbolic-imaginary landscapes, are also of great relevance for constitutional semiotics.

The epistemic function of symbolic-imaginary constitutionalism is important for all its dimensions (theoretical, legal, socio-legal etc). Constitutional communication and the conveying of meaning is impossible without proper systems for its signification. These systems must be understandable for the addressees of constitutional law and constitutional messages, who should be able to encode, decode and communicate meaning.[5] The range of components of symbolic-imaginary

[5] In the words of Frankenberg, 'constitutions, like any other legal text, have to be read, decoded and converted into plausible arguments, which have to be defended against other plausible arguments'. See

constitutionalism that together make up constitutional semiotic landscapes are in fact condensed forms of constitutional meaning. They are simultaneously rationally construable tools for the signification of meaning that is accessible through reason. At the same time, they are proxies to collective constitutional imagination that can be accessed through both intellect and intuition.[6]

The epistemic function of symbolic-imaginary constitutionalism unfolds through its forms. It consists in the production of epistemic proxies to the information about the collective constitutional imaginaries contained in normative ideologies, constitutional mythologies, constitutional utopias, codes and taboos that are expressed in semiotic forms. All these forms tell stories about the symbolic-imaginary fields of constitutionalism in the concrete national constitutional model, in the region or from a comparative perspective. Thus, the forms of symbolic-imaginary constitutionalism may be used for the creation of both national and comparative typologies of constitutional imaginaries based on the semiotic approach.

The symbolic-signification function is the most natural and evident of these. The signification of constitutional and constitutionally relevant meaning through symbols represented by the expressive means of textual, visual and performative constitutionalism is the main task of the forms of symbolic-imaginary constitutionalism. It is deeply embedded in all forms of symbolic-imaginary constitutionalism.

The forms of symbolic-imaginary constitutionalism also achieve a programming function. This consists in the determination of long-term performance of the constitutional order in the context of constitutional semiosis. The normative ideologies, constitutional mythologies, codes and utopias frame the process of constitutional semiosis. They impose the parameters for the accomplishment of constitutional semiosis, determining the design of the system of semiotic signifiers of constitutionally relevant meaning, the scope of the constitutional signifieds and the framework of the overall process of constitutional signification. Normative ideologies are also capable of imposing ordering schemes on constitutional axiology and constitutional design. Thus, their programming function is intertwined with and upgraded by their ordering function.

The foretelling function stems from the aim of the forms of symbolic-imaginary constitutionalism to signify and thus to symbolically construct the future in the realm of the collective constitutional imagination. This signification is performed through signifiers that are mainly available in textual constitutionalism. The construction of a bright constitutional future and a 'brave new world'[7] is part of the reformist plan of all constitutions. The role of the forms of symbolic-imaginary constitutionalism in this plan is to enchant the public and to appeal to

G Frankenberg, *Comparative Constitutional Studies: Between Magic and Deceit* (Cheltenham, Edward Elgar, 2018) 16.

[6] See H Bergson, *The Creative Mind: An Introduction to Metaphysics* (New York, Dover Publications, 2010) 1–240; and G Deleuze, *Bergsonism* (Princeton, Zone Books, 1990) 13–37.

[7] A Huxley, *Brave New World* (New York, Harper Perennial, 2006).

the collective constitutional imagination using constitutional metaphors, symbols and signs demonstrating normative ideologies and constitutional mythologies. Naturally, the most suitable forms for shaping the constitutional future are the constitutional utopias. Conversely, constitutional mythologies are the least future-oriented forms of constitutional imagination. They are usually oriented backwards and are entrenched in the past, although they possibly also construct imaginary bridges with the present and the future. Constitutional codes are forms of semiotic transtemporal dialogue. They are signifiers of encoded transtemporal messages.

The function for the production of constitutional enchantment is shared by all forms of symbolic-imaginary constitutionalism. It is part of the battle for hearts and minds described above.[8] The promotion of the collective constitutional imagination via forms of symbolic-imaginary constitutionalism and through recourse to constitutional semiotics entrenched in constitutional text and texture is the key for securing the legitimacy of the constitutional order.[9] People behave on the basis of rational rules and procedures when they trust the system in a rational way; however, they also need to believe in the system. The system of collective beliefs is grounded in normative ideologies and ideas, constitutional myths and mythologies, constitutional codes and, last but not least, constitutional utopias.

It should be stressed that the function of constitutional enchantment is deeply interrelated with the transcendental function of the forms of symbolic-imaginary constitutionalism. Constitutionalism is based on rationality. Rationality is one of the pillars of constitutionalism. This is a product of the overall social movement for rationalism promoted initially in Western civilisation and then globally since the Enlightenment. Rationalism is a great achievement of modernity. Nevertheless, there are excesses of rationalism which have been discussed earlier in Part I, Chapters 3 and 4. People need to believe. People are not only rational maximisers of interests making permanent rational calculations, but are also emotional beings, entrenched in imaginaries, and thus need to be believers. However, modern law that is preconditioned on rationality, logic, presumed objectivity and systematic thinking deprives them of grounds for belief beyond this rational 'bed of Procrustes'. The forms of symbolic-imaginary constitutionalism aim at partially compensating for this shortage of beliefs and emotional-imaginary enchantment. They offer grounds for normative beliefs that are both part of the valid constitutional law and of collective constitutional imagination. They serve as channels for the opening of the constitutional and legal order to hopes, dreams, beliefs, fears and other possible feelings, emotions and perceptions framed as collective constitutional imaginaries. They are textually embedded and legally valid versions of constitutional imagination.[10]

[8] See Sajó (n 1) 1–400.

[9] See J Přibáň, 'Constitutional Imaginaries and Legitimation: On Potentia, Potestas, and Auctoritas in Societal Constitutionalism' (2018) 45(1) *Journal of Law and Society* 30; and J Přibáň, *Constitutional Imaginaries: A Theory of European Societal Constitutionalism* (Abingdon, Routledge, 2020) 1–251.

[10] On the problem of hyper-rationality produced by the divorce between law and morality seen from the perspective of post-modern and critical legal studies, see C Douzinas and R Warrington, *Justice Miscarried: Ethics and Aesthetics in Law* (Edinburgh, Edinburgh University Press, 1997) 1–326.

Normative ideologies, constitutional mythologies and constitutional utopias are composite phenomena. They are intellectual frameworks consisting of a range of normative ideas, myths or other phenomena capable of the signification of meaning in a symbolic-imaginary appealing way. Usually normative ideas belong in a standard and typical way to normative ideologies. In other words, each normative ideology typically contains a particular and specific set of normative ideas that concretise and further develop it, giving it a clearer shape and a distinctive outlook. In that regard, there is huge and typical interdependency between the normative ideologies and the normative ideas maintained through a range of different links: logical, normative and semiotic. This interdependence also has repercussions that are relevant for their functional performance.

This is not necessarily the case with constitutional myths and the composite elements of constitutional codes and constitutional utopias. These are less systematically ordered and are combined in a way that is premised upon collective imaginaries as derived from the collective conscious, subconscious and unconscious. Constitutional mythology has roots which are deeply anchored in the collective unconscious. They are embedded in collective archetypes and in the emotional and imaginary path-dependency of thinking, feeling, dreaming and remembering differently from normative ideologies and constitutional utopias. This is due to the fact that normative ideologies and constitutional utopias have powerful symbolic-imaginary aspects, but are also rational plans for the imposition of a perfect model of the constitutional order based on rationally defined principles, priorities and structures.[11] Thus, the programming and ordering functions are much more visible in the case of normative ideologies and constitutional utopias compared to constitutional mythologies.

There is a certain implicit logic in the construction of the design of normative ideologies that predetermines the range, system and scope of the normative ideas they contain. This logic is based on ontological, conceptual and pragmatic preconditions. In other words, normative ideas are the result of the choice of normative ideologies forming the symbolic-imaginary constitutionalism of the distinct constitutional order. They are a consequence of this choice and are predetermined by it. The selection of normative ideologies and normative ideas depends on socio-legal and intellectual-anthropological preconditions, but also on the political choice of the constitutional legislator and the formative influence of the authoritative speakers, visualisers and performers of the constitutionally framed socio-political community. This choice and selection is made with a view to the ordering, symbolic-signification, programming and ideological functions of normative ideologies and ideas.

Constitutional utopias and constitutional mythologies are also based on constructivist logic. This is the logic of the imposed collective imaginaries aiming at explaining and ordering the world from the viewpoint of the augmented reality of the magical and surreal, offering partial or holistic alternatives to the present

[11] On the semiotic role of archetypes, see U Eco, *Semiotics and the Philosophy of Language* (Bloomington, Indiana University Press, 1986) 144–47.

derived from the past or the future. In that regard, constitutional mythologies, normative ideologies and constitutional utopias offer a glimpse into the realm of the imaginary. They propose salvation in a perfected constitutional world that once existed or has to be constructed through the common efforts of all members of the constitutionally framed socio-political community. And it is based on the combined effects of their symbolic-signification, foretelling (future constructing) and transcendental functions.

People need to believe in order to follow rules, obey authority and perform in a systemic manner. Public compliance is dependent on the enchanting power of collective constitutional imaginaries. These imaginaries have to be signified in a rationally, emotionally and imaginary convincing manner. Hence, the signification of constitutional order has to address the conscious, subconscious and unconscious predispositions of the members of the constitutionally framed socio-political community. The power of the elements of symbolic-imaginary constitutionalism to convince is dependent on their capacity to enchant and persuade and to create a convincing range of signifiers.

Moreover, constitutions and other sources of constitutional law frame the system of normative ideas included in normative ideologies in a normative way. Normative ideologies spread through the system of valid law, gaining its security and authority.[12] Hence, suggesting that a certain constitutional system has a distinct normative ideology means proving that its constitutional order and especially the constitution contain its typical set of normative ideas. This is possible only if they represent a higher axiological and normative order serving as channels for the translation of meta-legal normativity and charm into the constitutional order. In fact, this is the transcendental function served by constitutional utopias, normative ideologies and constitutional mythologies. The constitutional codes also serve as proxies for meta-legal normative orders and transcendental reality. Last but not least, the beliefs in the constitutional order are also grounded in the capability of its semiotic signifiers to give an indication of future developments. The constitutional semiotic landscapes should not only enable the transcending of the constitutional Dasein[13] and its connection with a higher reality of collective unconscious and subconscious; they must also be able to transcend the constitutional order in a temporal perspective and to project it into the past and the future as imagined and semiotically signified plains for the unfolding of constitutional semiosis. This capacity is related to the foretelling (future constructing) function of the forms of symbolic-imaginary constitutionalism.

From a structural and systematic perspective, the normative ideologies and normative ideas are the most logical and systematic elements for ordering the symbolic-imaginary dimension of constitutional order. Constitutional utopias follow an inherent logic implied by their creator. Nevertheless, they have an

[12] Derrida (n 2).

[13] See M Heidegger, *Being and Time* (New York, Harper Perennial, 2008) 1–608; and N Zuckerman, 'Heidegger and the Essence of Dasein' (2015) 53(4) *Southern Journal of Philosophy* 493.

enhanced degree of symbolism, mysticism and imaginary discretion in terms of describing and prescribing the proposed augmented reality created through the symbolic signification of meaning. The random character of constitutional mythology is comparable to those of constitutional utopias. Both constitutional mythology and constitutional utopias are less rationally ordered and much more dependent on the symbolic signification of meaning and the imaginary construction of the world grounded in collective constitutional unconscious[14] than normative ideologies. In that regard, constitutional utopias and constitutional mythologies have greater semiotic potential than normative ideologies, but a reduced ordering capacity. They are based much more on the symbolic and semiotic signification of meaning than normative ideologies. Hence, constitutional utopias and constitutional mythologies are much more prone to constitutional semiosis and to the semiotic approach to constitutional epistemology than normative ideologies. They perform the transcendental, symbolic-signification and enchanting functions better, but are less capable of accomplishing epistemic, programming and foretelling (future constructing) functions in comparison to normative ideologies.

The most synthetic devices for the semiotic signification of meaning are the constitutional codes. They are the purest examples of constitutional semiotic tools belonging to symbolic-imaginary constitutionalism. Thus, they are the perfect signifiers of meaning and the natural device for accomplishing symbolic-signification and enchanting functions. Naturally, this reduces their capacity to order the constitutional order in a systematic way and thus to perform programming, not to speak of ordering functions. It has already been mentioned that constitutionalism perceived and conceptualised as a 'game of codes' cannot really be a systematic phenomenon. Thus, constitutional codes promote quantum constitutionalism as a form of constitutionalism based on certainty about the uncertainty of the practical and concrete unfolding of the constitutional order and constitutionalism in general, and the process of constitutional semiosis in particular.

If we allocate constitutional imaginaries to the comparative plain of constitutional semiotic landscapes, we will discover that the elements with the highest semiotic potential for symbolic signification of meaning are the constitutional codes, followed by the constitutional myths, mythologies and utopias, whereas the most rational and least symbolic-synthetic-significatory elements are the normative ideologies and the normative ideas.[15] Normative ideologies and ideas are supposed to be coherent rational concepts for ordering constitutional axiology and constitutional design which possess a huge degree of abstraction and by necessity aim at the establishment of the imaginary realm, comprising ideal visions for the past, the present and the future. Thus, the ordering and programming function of normative ideologies prevails over their symbolic-signification function.

[14] For a counter-position between constitutional archetypes and the constitutional unconscious, see Frankenberg (n 5) 30.

[15] On the relationship between political myths, ideologies and utopias, see C Bottici, *A Philosophy of Political Myth* (Cambridge, Cambridge University Press, 2007) 177–200.

The constitutional myths and mythologies are less rational and much more dependent on abstraction, fiction[16] and the symbolic representation of meaning than normative ideologies.

Constitutional codes are signifiers of meaning based on constitutional semiosis in the purest sense. This is due to the fact that constitutional codes are shortcuts to social imaginaries. They are containers of condensed symbolic meaning with strategic importance extracted through interpretation of the constitutional text. Constitutional codes may have projections and also materialise in other constitutional discourses based on text and texture. They may even be demonstrated through visuals and performance. Constitutional codes are usually enshrined in the constitutional text or in the texture of constitutionalism structured around different constitutionally relevant significations of meaning in the socio-political reality. They may also be generated by constitutional theory.

Hence, constitutional codes may stand for, symbolise and represent phenomena enshrined in the text of the constitution, but also in 'constitutional law in action'. Thus, we can differentiate between constitutional codes provided by textual constitutionalism and constitutional codes representing factual phenomena stemming from visual or performative constitutionalism. Hence, constitutional codes are contained in constitutional text and texture and are signified via a range of signifiers – textual, art and architecture forms or performative acts consisting in durable symbolic patterns of behaviour or in concrete symbolic gestures. In all cases, the establishment, understanding and classification of constitutional codes is mediated by interpretation, which requires a semiotic approach to the problem.

The interpretation of normative ideologies and ideas, constitutional myths and mythologies, and constitutional codes can be made by all addressees of constitutional law. However, not all of them can impose legally valid meaning derived through interpretation on the constitutionally framed socio-political community. In fact, the interpretation of the constitution and constitutional law by the authoritative speakers of the community prevails.[17] It has legal validity based on admitting the possibility for virtual amendment of the constitution and constitutional law due to its open texture. Since the authoritative speakers of the community are not always aware, prepared or willing to engage in constitutional law as a 'game of codes', it is usually constitutional theory that is the main source used for understanding which are the constitutional codes in the widest sense (including ideologies, myths and other forms of symbolic-imaginary constitutionalism) that are enshrined in a distinct constitutional order. Constitutional theory has a pivotal

[16] On the constitution as a product of the collective imagination and fictions, see O Tans, 'Imagined Constitutionality: Rethinking Democratic Citizenship with the Aid of Fiction Theory' (2019) 5(2) *Law, Culture and the Humanities* 1. On the role of fictions in law, see M Del Mar and W Twining (eds), *Legal Fictions in Theory and Practice* (Dordrecht, Springer, 2015) 1–449; M Del Mar, *Artefacts of Legal Inquiry: The Value of Imagination in Adjudication* (Oxford, Hart Publishing, 2020) 235–78; and L Fuller, *Legal Fictions* (Stanford, Stanford University Press, 1967) 1–158. On the interplay between narrative, fiction and imagination, see D Matravers, *Fiction and Narrative* (Oxford, Oxford University Press, 2017) 1–192.

[17] See pt II, ch 3 of this book.

role to play in the understanding of constitutional codes produced by authoritative narrators, writers, interpreters, visualisers and performers, and enshrined in textual, visual and performative constitutionalism. This can only be properly done on the basis of a semiotic approach to 'constitutional codes in books' and 'constitutional codes in action'.

Hence, constitutional semiotics is the main epistemic device for understanding constitutionalism as a game of imaginaries and a game of codes. Thus, the forms of symbolic-imaginary constitutionalism have huge epistemic potential and may perform the epistemic function mentioned above well. However, an important precondition for this is the development of a theory of constitutional semiotics that can cope with constitutionalism as a 'game of codes' based on quantum constitutionalism and organised around the construction, deconstruction and reconstruction of symbolic-imaginary forms of condensed meaning.

Hence, a central role for the discovery, exposure and critical assessment of constitutionalism as a 'game of constitutional imaginaries' and a 'game of constitutional codes' has to be played by constitutional theory organised on the basis of constitutional semiotics. Theory should be able to provide additional meaning extracted from the semiotic structures enshrined in the constitution or detected as phenomena that shape and form visual, performative and emotional constitutionalism, thus also having an impact on symbolic-imaginary constitutionalism. Here the forms of symbolic-imaginary constitutionalism play an important role in their capacity as semiotic structures whose meaning can be grasped, distilled, exposed, analysed and classified by constitutional theory.

In that regard, constitutional theory has de facto monopolised the task of decoding constitutional law. The official constitutional players typically abstain from engaging in semiotic practices. Some of them – Parliament, the government and the administrative institutions – are not well equipped for this task. They do not have the incentives and motivation and are not interested in or willing to engage in constitutional semiosis.

This is not the case with the courts and especially the apex courts (constitutional and supreme courts). They are used to participating in interpretative games, exploring, further developing and even investing meaning in constitutional text, and coping with the interpretative challenges posed by the open texture of constitutional law. This is particularly true for activist courts. However, the courts are also not frequent participants in the process of constitutional semiosis. They are not used to working with symbolic-imaginary constitutionalism as an overarching paradigm and more precisely with constitutional codes and constitutional mythologies. The apex courts work mostly with normative ideologies and ideas, and less frequently with constitutional myths and mythologies, and rarely engage with constitutional codes. Sometimes their jurisprudential activity is entrenched in constitutional utopias perceived as normative ideologies, thus making the courts their unconscious promoters. Actually, the apex courts engage in interpretative semiotic games and thus in 'imaginary semiotic games', but these are much more 'games of normative ideologies' than 'games of codes'.

Constitutional codes, normative ideologies, constitutional mythologies and constitutional utopias are generalisations of content stemming from rational and normative-institutional constitutionalism. However, they differ with regard to the degree of abstraction, the detailed or condensed methods for the signification of meaning and some of their tasks. This chain of abstraction and representation of condensed meaning culminates in constitutional codes.

All elements of symbolic-imaginary constitutionalism are signifiers of a range of signifieds, including constitutional phenomena contained in normative-institutional and rational constitutionalism. Furthermore, they are themselves turned into signifieds that are represented through text, visuals and performance via signifiers belonging to textual, visual and performative constitutionalism.

Consequently, normative ideologies and normative ideas, constitutional myths and mythologies, constitutional codes and constitutional utopias are elements in a chain of semiotic production, reproduction, construction, deconstruction, reconstruction and representation of meaning. They participate in constitutional semiosis and thus have a fundamentally semiotic character. They are strategic nodes in the process of constitutional semiosis and are part of the semiotic signification and representation of meaning.

There are several determinants of the constitutional semiotic landscapes which define the overall outlook of constitutionalism as a 'game of imaginaries' and a 'game of constitutional codes'. These are the historical, ideological, intellectual and socio-psychological determinants, constitutional anthropology, but also external factors such as foreign domination and the imposed transplantation of constitutional axiology, institutional design and normative imaginaries after wars, geopolitical shifts and catastrophes, foreign domination etc. Hence, normative ideologies and ideas, constitutional myths and mythologies, constitutional codes and constitutional utopias are based on rationality that might be intrinsic and implied in their own history and internal logic or that is imposed from outside and stems from reasons external to the constitutional order.

The intermediate conclusion is that normative ideologies are ordering schemes and ordering frameworks for normative ideas. This is also true for constitutional mythologies as composite phenomena encompassing a range of constitutional myths. They are also containers of meaning belonging to both rational and symbolic-imaginary constitutionalism expressed in a textual, visual or performative way. In particular, normative ideologies and ideas assert systematising and ordering effects on the points of overlap between rational, normative institutional and symbolic-imaginary constitutionalism. They frame the process of constitutional semiosis and offer – frequently in conjunction with myths, codes, taboos and utopias – points of rational access to collective imaginaries, constitutional anthropology and social constitutional psychology. This is a clear example of the interconnectedness and mutual intertwining of all functions of the forms of symbolic-imaginary constitutionalism. They jointly contribute to the production of composite intellectual products based on the symbolic and condensed representation of meaning and accessible through the means of constitutional semiotics.

Normative ideologies and normative ideas and, to a lesser extent, constitutional myths, mythologies and utopias spread, influence and are logically further developed and in a sense decomposed in the constitution and its subsystems (the human rights system, the institutional system etc). They impose certain institutional logic, constitutional philosophy and constitutional design on the constitutional order. They predetermine its outlook, shapes and institutions.

Thus, the forms of symbolic-imaginary constitutionalism, but especially the normative ideologies perform an ordering function for the constitution and the constitutional order. They not only require a certain and specific organisation of the normative-institutional constitutionalism expressed in a textual form, but also predetermine the constitutional imaginaries that guide the behaviour of the members of the constitutionally framed socio-political community.

Normative ideologies and the normative ideas, frequently in conjunction with other forms of symbolic-imaginary constitutionalism, signify core imaginary meaning. They create a distinct meta-legal system for the signification and representation of constitutionally relevant meaning. Thus, they order meaning in an expressive way that impacts the other elements of symbolic-imaginary constitutionalism – constitutional myths and mythologies, constitutional utopias and constitutional codes.

All forms of symbolic-imaginary constitutionalism contain valuable information about the overall outlook of the constitutional order. They are epistemic containers that contain information mostly from the realms of symbolic-imaginary and normative-institutional constitutionalism, expressed through textual, visual and performative constitutionalism, and impacting emotional constitutionalism. Thus, they are a combination of rational, emotional and imaginary components signified through various semiotic signifiers.

Nevertheless, they also have a powerful rational core which imposes a particular form of organisation of the constitutional order and the constitutional architecture. They are rationally accessible and rationally explainable. This makes them a proper object of scientific exploration, especially if the analysis is based on a semiotic approach to the constitution and constitutional law.

Normative ideologies and normative ideas, constitutional myths and mythologies, and constitutional utopias inform us about the original constitutional strategies of the constitutional legislator for shaping symbolic-imaginary constitutionalism. In that regard, they are instruments for structuring and organising the collective constitutional imaginaries. At the same time, they are also explications of the normative interpretations of the ideological design of the constitution given by the authoritative speakers, narrators and performers of the community. Thus, they are epistemic tools for the exploration of the constitution as a multidiscursive narrative intellectual project that is written, interpreted, further developed, visualised and performed by a range of constitutional narrators, performers and visualisers.

Consequently, the epistemic function of the forms of symbolic-imaginary constitutionalism is neatly interrelated with their semiotic capacity as preserves of constitutional significations. The greater their semiotic potential, the greater their epistemic value. In other words, the proper and adequate understanding of symbolic-imaginary constitutionalism is necessarily connected to the exploration of the signification systems used by it for the representation of constitutional meaning in a condensed and symbolic way.

We gain information about the forms of symbolic-imaginary constitutionalism mostly from textual constitutionalism comprising both the text and texture of constitutional law (especially the constitution) and the constitutional theory. This is due to the fact that normative ideologies and ideas, constitutional myths and mythologies, constitutional utopias and, to a lesser extent, constitutional codes are promoted, preserved and imposed through valid law in textual form. Nevertheless, they are also objects of signification of visual and performative constitutionalism. Clear examples of this are the architectural representations of transparency, democracy, rationality, humanism, authority, justice and many other normative ideologies and ideas in the official buildings of state institutions – on their overall structure and design, on their facades etc. This is especially true for the Parliament and court buildings. Thus, the signifiers of visual constitutionalism are used for the signification of elements of symbolic-imaginary constitutionalism. In this case, these are the normative ideologies and normative ideas.

Hence, the epistemic function of the forms of symbolic-imaginary constitutionalism is by necessity supported, completed and further developed by their symbolic-signification function. The symbolic-signification function is a complex and composite one. It has to be subdivided into three sub-functions. These are the function for the triggering of constitutional imagination (the constitutional enchantment function), the function for the signification of meaning (the signification function) and the function for the intermingling of rational constitutional content with emotional and imaginary inspiration (the imaginary mixture function). The constitutional enchantment function may also be defined as a separate function, as has been done above in the context of the outline of the functional catalogue of the forms of symbolic-imaginary constitutionalism.

The constitutional enchantment and its signification is extremely important from the viewpoint of symbolic-imaginary constitutionalism. Hence, it is mainly due to the symbolic-signification function that some of the forms of symbolic-imaginary constitutionalism, such as the normative ideologies and normative ideas, are included as part of symbolic-imaginary and not, for example, of rational or normative-institutional constitutionalism. It has been mentioned that they do possess rational features, pursue rational targets and are deliberately created by the constitutional legislator. Hence, normative ideologies and normative ideas have rational ontology and teleology. Moreover, as already explained, normative ideologies and normative ideas have an impact on constitutional architecture and institutional design. They are further developed by constitutional institutions and spread in constitutional design. In that regard, they are also intermingled with normative-institutional constitutionalism.

However, the main aim of normative ideologies and ideas is not to organise the normative system or to structure the constitutional design. Their strategic and inherent goal is to make people believe in the constitution and to follow its commands voluntarily on the basis of their free will and free choice. The same is true for all forms of symbolic-imaginary constitutionalism.

Thus, the constitution has to allow for the proper and context adequate mixing of rational constitutional content with emotional and imaginary inspiration (the imaginary mixture function), expressing it through forms of textual constitutionalism, highlighting the most inspirational parts through semiotic signification provided by textual but also by visual and performative constitutionalism (the signification function) and, finally, producing constitutional enchantment. The normative ideologies and ideas provide both rational and emotional guidance for the members of the constitutionally framed socio-political community. The normative ideologies and ideas allow people to act in accordance with the constitution, to perform its commands, transforming them into 'law in action', to deliberate, interpret and communicate constitutional text and texture, and to express it through constitutional visuals on the basis of shared beliefs in the ideological meta-structure of the constitutional order. The constitutional actors, interpreters, visualisers and performers should also be believers. The messages of their normative belief that stem from the constitution in its capacity as the core of constitutionalism perceived as an ideology and a secular religion are conveyed through a range of methods.[18] A central role in this process of signification and communication of meaning is played by constitutional semiotics.

Normative ideologies and ideas and also, to a lesser extent, constitutional myths and mythologies and constitutional codes also have an opening function for meta-legal normative orders. They opening the constitutional order to meta-legal standards, values, beliefs, symbols and imaginaries. Thus, they provide a degree of transcendental plausibility to the constitution and the constitutional order.[19] This transcendental plausibility consists in the attachment of certain emotional, inspirational and imaginary value of the constitutional order for the members of the constitutionally framed socio-political community based on shared normative beliefs. These abstract ideas are transformed into normative beliefs and then into collective imaginaries through multiple and multilayered processes of constitutional signification of meaning based on a range of signifiers belonging to textual, visual and performative constitutionalism.

Thus, the opening of rational constitutionalism results in the decompression of the legal order through allowing meta-legal imperatives and standards

[18] In that regard, see also Cornelius Castoriadis, according to whom 'the institution of law is the institution of legal "objects" and "relations" – it cannot exist unless it is a specific institution of legal legein; but the state of affairs is no different in the case of magic, religion or even art'. See C Castoriadis, *The Imaginary Institution of Society* (Cambridge, Polity Press, 1987) 256–57.

[19] On the need for restoring the link between law, moral, ethics and aesthetics, see C Douzinas and R Warrington, *Justice Miscarried: Ethics and Aesthetics in Law* (Edinburgh, Edinburgh University Press, 1997) 1–326.

as well as normative imaginaries to influence the behaviour of the addressees of normative-institutional constitutionalism. In this context, symbolic-imaginary representation of meaning through semiotic signification plays an important role. Hence, the opening and transcendental function of the forms of symbolic-imaginary constitutionalism also intermingles with their ordering, explanatory and symbolic-signification functions, producing complex constitutional imaginaries and engaging in the process of representation of ideals and signification of meaning.[20]

Normative ideologies and ideas order the relations between pragmatic constitutional discourses (such as rational, textual and normative-institutional constitutionalism) and transcendental constitutional discourses (such as symbolic-imaginary constitutionalism). Thus, in conjunction with other forms of symbolic-imaginary constitutionalism, they remedy the extreme rationality of normative-institutional, positivist and legal realist constitutional discourses in order to provide transcendental foundations for the constitutional order and to create a form of secular religion enshrined in the constitution.[21]

The forms of symbolic-imaginary constitutionalism shape the symbolic-imaginary landscapes whose roots are in the solid ground of textual, rational and normative-institutional constitutionalism, while their peaks grow upwards into the transcendental reality of meta-legal concepts. Many of these meta-legal sources of inspiration are fuzzy and uneasy to grasp by virtue of the traditional legal methods belonging to rational constitutionalism. Thus, it is constitutional semiotics which makes them accessible through recourse to quasi-intuitive, partly emotional and, to an extent, rational processes of signification of meaning representing these transcendental phenomena via the expressive forms of textual, visual and performative constitutionalism.

Indeed, the broken connection to transcendental reality is characteristic of modern and post-modern society. The individual and collective 'gaze beyond' the horizon of rationalism, pragmatism and empiricism, which was foundational and thus carefully maintained in pre-modern ages, as well as the pluralism of imagined realities typical of the age of baroque[22] have been replaced by an emphasis on the present empirical well-being grounded in hyper-rationalism.[23] The hypertrophic reliance on empiricism, pragmatism and blunt rationalism deprived the

[20] The transcendental functions of imagination have been explored in I Kant, *Critique of Pure Reason* (Cambridge, Cambridge University Press, 1999); and Castoriadis (n 19) 175.

[21] The problem of extreme secularism of constitutional law stemming from the modern detachment of law from any religious basis and connotations has been detected by many authors. See, eg, C Schmitt, *Politische Theologie: Vier Kapitel zur Lehre von der Souveränität* (Berlin, Duncker & Humblot, 2015) 1–65; M Borowski and S Paulson (eds), *Die Natur des Rechts bei Gustav Radbruch* (Heidelberg, Mohr Siebeck, 2015) 1–270; and V Depaigne, *Legitimacy Gap: Secularism, Religion, and Culture in Comparative Constitutional Law* (Oxford, Oxford University Press, 2017) 1–240.

[22] R Sherwin, *Visualizing Law in the Age of the Digital Baroque: Arabesques and Entanglements* (Abingdon, Routledge, 2011) 1–256.

[23] For a post-modern critique of hyper-rationalism in law, see Douzinas and Warrington (n 20) 1–326.

constitution and constitutional law of any metaphysical foundations. It limited the scope for the performing of the constitutional play to the 'here-and-now' physical situation. Thus, it has curtailed the time-space continuum, limiting it to the present unfolding of events. The past and the future were compressed and gained merely secondary importance, being formally attached to the imperial dimensions of the present. Furthermore, the present was detached from supra-, meta- or extra-legal foundations, principles and sources of justification.

The broken connection to transcendental reality has been underlined by many philosophers as an overall feature of our time and the zeitgeist in which we live. The transcendental emptiness and the crisis of extreme detachment of constitutional law from meta-legal normative systems and transcendental sources of existential inspiration has also been emphasised by a range of legal scholars from different ideological and conceptual backgrounds.[24]

In that sense, the forms of symbolic-imaginary constitutionalism perform this role of bridging constitutional pragmatism with constitutional transcendentalism, which seems rather strange at first glance. This linking role may also be conceptualised from the particular analytical viewpoint as part of their ordering function. Normative ideologies and normative ideas, to lesser extent constitutional myths and mythologies, constitutional utopias and constitutional codes order the relationship between rational and normative-institutional constitutionalism on the one hand, and symbolic-imaginary constitutionalism on the other. They impose the intellectual framework for the penetration of transcendental and meta-legal concepts, values and phenomena in the constitutional order.

In order to fulfil their ordering function at the crossroads between constitutional transcendentalism and constitutional pragmatics, the forms of symbolic-imaginary constitutionalism require instruments for the signification of meaning.[25] Thus, they are involved in the process of the signification of transcendental concepts mostly through the tools of textual constitutionalism.

Nevertheless constitutional signification of the forms of symbolic-imaginary constitutionalism through the instruments of visual and performative constitutionalism also occurs quite frequently. Examples might include the ceremonial elements of parliamentary procedures, procedures for the appointment of high-ranking office holders, and judicial procedures. The opening ceremonies of newly elected parliaments or of new parliamentary sessions, speeches given by monarchs in parliaments in parliamentary and constitutional monarchies, ceremonies for the appointment of new governments, and ceremonies where high-ranking officials are sworn in are excellent examples. The opening ceremony of the Westminster Parliament, the speech of the British monarch at the opening of Parliament, the inauguration ceremony of the US President are simply the most obvious examples,

[24] See J Haskell, *Political Theology and International Law* (Leiden, Brill, 2018) 1–98; Schmitt (n 22) 1–65; Borowski and Paulson (n 22) 1–270; and Depaigne (n 22) 1–240.

[25] See also J Balkin, 'Transcendental Deconstruction, Transcendental Justice' (1994) 92 *Michigan Law Review* 1131.

with the former demonstrating the normative ideologies, constitutional mythologies and visual codes of parliamentary monarchy and the latter those of the presidential republic.

Judicial procedures are fully organised in a symbolic-imaginary way in order to demonstrate the normative ideologies of justice and the rule of law.[26] The architecture of the courtroom,[27] the elevated podium for the court, the custom for participants to stand up when the judges enter, the allocation of the participants in the trial according to the biblical division of sinners and saints on the 'left-right' axis', the judge's hammer, the colours of the robes of the judges and the state prosecutors etc are all signifiers of these key normative ideologies, constitutional mythologies and constitutional codes of contemporary constitutionalism. They represent and shape the collective constitutional imaginaries through the joint means of visual and performative constitutionalism. Thus, they are signifiers of normative ideologies and ideas deeply entrenched in both rational and symbolic-imaginary constitutionalism.

[26] See A Mooney, 'The Drama of the Courtroom' in A Wagner and W Pencak (eds), *Images in Law* (Farnham, Ashgate, 2006) 71–89.

[27] See L Mulcahy, *Legal Architecture: Justice, Due Process and the Place of Law* (Abingdon, Routledge, 2011) 1–244; L Mulcahy and E Rowden, *The Democratic Courthouse: A Modern History of Design, Due Process and Dignity* (Abingdon, Routledge, 2020); L Nead, 'Visual Cultures of the Courtroom: Reflections on History, Law and the Image' (2002) 3(2) *Visual Culture in Britain* 119; J Resnik and D Curtis, *Representing Justice: Invention, Controversy, and Rights in City-States and Democratic Courtrooms* (New Haven, Yale University Press, 2011) 1–720; and A-K Hubrich, 'Multilayered Functions of Early Modern Courtroom Equipment: Luneburg for Example' in S Huygebaert, G Martyn, V Paumen, E Bousmar and X Rouseaux (eds), *The Art of Law: Artistic Representations and Iconography of Law and Justice in Context, from the Middle Ages to the First World War* (Dordrecht, Springer, 2018) 149–67.

4

Constitutional Codes

Important issues relating to the nature and the essence of constitutional codes[1] and their functional characteristics have already been discussed. This has been done in comparison with the other forms of symbolic-imaginary constitutionalism. In that regard, constitutional codes have been allocated in the realm of constitutional semiotic landscapes. This chapter will be devoted mainly to the analysis and exposure of the semiotic nature of constitutional codes.

Constitutional codes are representations of social imaginaries which have emerged in the empirical reality – the realm of facts.[2] They have been transcended and transformed in the realm of shared beliefs, encoded in the constitutional text and represented in constitutional theory. This line of representation is accomplished either directly or through their crystallisation in visual and performative constitutionalism.

There are also constitutional codes which have been directly encoded in textual constitutionalism without preceding empirical manifestations. They are the product of constitutional engineering relating to symbolic-imaginary constitutionalism. In both cases, constitutional theory extracts them from the significatory encoding in the constitutional text and texture, and then transposes them into the realm of symbolic-imaginary constitutionalism. In all cases, constitutional codes are imprints of constitutional imagination shaping the constitutional semiotic landscapes.

Hence, constitutional codes exist as formal imaginaries of textual constitutionalism, as structured imaginaries of visual constitutionalism or as structured or dispersed imaginaries of performative constitutionalism. In the latter case, they are provided in the form of cloud constitutionalism and are signified through a behavioural signification system or on the basis of visual signifiers enshrined in the constitutional texture.

The fact that constitutional codes are provided in a more or less organised way in the constitutional text and texture and are contained in a dispersed way,

[1] On the concept of code, see U Eco, *Semiotics and the Philosophy of Language* (Bloomington, Indiana University Press, 1986) 164–89; and D Chandler, *Semiotics: The Basics* (Abingdon, Routledge, 2017) 177–222. The concept of legal code is explored in E Menezes de Carvalho, *Semiotics of International Law: Trade and Translation* (Dordrecht, Springer, 2011) 138–45.

[2] On the role of collective imaginaries for the representation of social meaning, see C Gilleard, 'From Collective Representations to Social Imaginaries: How Society Represents itself to itself' (2018) 5(3) *European Journal of Cultural and Political Sociology* 320.

being spread in cloud constitutionalism, means that they are both textual phenomena relating to the constitutional text and constitutional texture, and socio-legal phenomena based on shared constitutional imaginaries of the members of the constitutionally framed community. In the latter case, they stem from various manifestations of symbolic-imaginary constitutionalism and are entrenched in the collective constitutional conscious, subconscious and unconscious of the community. Hence, constitutional codes must be researched as complex and multidimensional phenomena that have projections in reality with its performative, visual and emotional dimensions, in textuality, in normativity and in the symbolic-imaginary dimensions of constitutionalism and constitutional law.

Traditionally, textual constitutionalism is a central object of constitutional semiotic analysis and a plain for the allocation of constitutional signifieds, including constitutional codes. This is a result of the prevalent textual character of law and the predominance of legal positivism, legal institutionalism and, more recently, of legal realism as methodological approaches to constitutionalism and constitutional law. Indeed, the constitutional text is a very important source of semiotic information because it has a monopoly over the framing and containment of valid constitutional law. The constitutional text is the focus of semiotic representation and is the only source of valid legal arguments. Hence, constitutional semiotics should pay special attention to textual constitutionalism, looking for explicit or implicit constitutional codes enshrined in the text of the constitution and the constitutional law or provided in non-binding forms of constitutional texture in the wider sense, such as constitutional theory and textually explicated constitutional imaginaries.

However, performative and visual constitutionalism are also important sources of constitutional codes which themselves are elements of symbolic-imaginary constitutionalism. Thus, the conceptualisation of constitutionalism and constitutional law as 'game of codes' has to take into account not only textual but also performative and visual constitutionalism. Such a complex, extensive and inclusive approach is necessary for the proper and adequate elaboration of the semiotic concept of the constitutional code as a form of symbolic-imaginary constitutionalism.

Textual constitutionalism must be deciphered and decoded via recourse to constitutional semiotics, and constitutional codes are key elements of constitutional semiosis. An important paradigm for extracting constitutional codes as signifiers of constitutional and constitutionally relevant meaning from textual constitutionalism is constitutional archaeology. Constitutional archaeology is an analytical approach which is to an extent based on Michel Foucault's concept of the archaeology of knowledge.[3] In that regard, constitutional archaeology may help constitutional semiotics to dig out and excavate epistemic phenomena encoded in

[3] M Foucault, *The Order of Things: An Archaeology of the Human Sciences* (New York, Vintage, 1994) 1–416; and M Foucault *The Archaeology of Knowledge: And the Discourse on Language* (New York, Vintage, 1982) 1–256.

the constitutional text and forming part of the symbolic-imaginary constitutionalism. Constitutional semiotics is an excellent tool of constitutional archaeology, especially with regard to constitutional codes.

Consequently, constitutional codes perceived as textually dependent phenomena of constitutional signification that bridge the gap between textual constitutionalism and symbolic-imaginary constitutionalism. Constitutional codes are textually enshrined and textually dependent, but they also symbolise, represent and stand for social imaginaries which have textual imprints. There are also constitutional codes which are allocated in the realm of the visual and performative signification of constitutional information.

Constitutional codes may be defined as second-grade signifiers. The signifieds are the objects of constitutional law derived from 'law in books' or 'law in action'. They are those parts of reality which the historical experience, the political will and the intellectual discretion of the power centres that assumed the position of constitutional legislators or have acquired the position of authoritative narrators, writers, performers or visualisers define as being in need of constitutional regulation.

Constitutional codes gain constitutional shape in a twofold way: through constitutional textualisation and via constitutional institutionalisation. Constitutional textualisation consists in providing constitutional codes in constitutional texts or other forms of constitutional texture. Constitutional institutionalisation stems from the approval of constitutional codes as constitutional institutions on the basis of their provision in valid law or by being recognised by the constitutional actors, including the authoritative narrators, visualisers, interpreters, performers and encoders, and by the socio-political constitutionally framed community.

Constitutional codes are one of the elements of symbolic-imaginary constitutionalism. They are tools for the symbolic, emotionally appealing shaping of meaning, structuring of information and channelling of understanding. They stand for the values, principles and ideas of constitutionalism and constitutional law, and represent them in symbolic-imaginary constitutionalism. Thus, they serve as second-grade constitutional signifiers forming the meta-texture and meta-language of constitutional law. They build upon the first-grade signifiers – the constitutional principles, values, aims, rights, duties and institutions – which are enshrined in the texture of constitutional law, its normativity and its institutional design.

This first degree of signifiers provided explicitly in the constitutional texture seems to be sufficient for the more traditional approaches to constitutional law, limiting it to institutionalism and focusing on its purely legal positivist dimension. The constitutional text is an important medium for constitutional communication. It is a tool for the sharing and depositing of constitutional information. It is the container of the normativity of constitutional law. It is the immediate tool for the representation and for the negotiation and establishment of meaning.

However, there is also a second layer of signifiers. This layer builds upon the first level of signifiers, stands for it and represents it. It contains the elements of symbolic-imaginary constitutionalism and in this regard also constitutional codes as the most abstract form of constitutional signification. Thus, constitutional codes are elements of symbolic-imaginary constitutionalism. They are part of this second-level system for constitutional signification. They are the core object of study of constitutional semiotics. This is due to the fact that they are signifiers of the initially signified objects of constitutional law and the constitutional institutions enshrined in constitutional textuality which represent them on a first, immediate and more direct level of ideal and conceptual representation.

Thus, the first level system of signification, based on the representation of ideas and concepts via constitutional textualisation and constitutional institutionalisation, is a precondition for the second-level system of constitutional signification comprising the elements of symbolic-imaginary constitutionalism, including the constitutional codes as nodes in the signification system based on symbolic abstraction. The second-level system of signification invests new meaning in the first-level system. It allows for the abstract symbolic representation not only of principles, values and institutions, but also of constitutional normative ideologies and constitutional myths and mythologies. In that regard, constitutional codes are signifiers not only of elements of textually entrenched forms of normative-institutional constitutionalism, but also of the components of symbolic-imaginary constitutionalism that may be signified through text and texture, constitutionally relevant visuals and performance.

In that regard, constitutional coding, encoding and decoding is a multilayered process of the semiotic signification of meaning.[4] It denominates the complex and multifaceted process of constitutional semiosis through the use of constitutional codes in a wider and a narrower sense. It is interesting and important to note that constitutional codes are tools for both the demonstration and concealing of constitutional and constitutionally relevant meaning. They show, demonstrate and signify, while simultaneously requiring semiotic keys for their decoding and the decompression of the condensed symbolic meaning they contain. In that regard, constitutional codes are ambivalent, chameleonic phenomena based on intrinsic dialectics of revealing and concealing of meaning requiring the parallel processes of its symbolic compression and decompression via decoding and deconstruction.[5] They exist because of the need to partially conceal meaning, to render it readable only through the lenses of a particular semiotic grammar known and redefined by the authoritative semiotic players of the constitutionally framed socio-political community. The revealing of meaning is only in symbolic form due to the need to demonstrate it in laconic, condensed and compressed form, which itself requires recourse to semiotic procedures for the signification of constitutional and constitutionally relevant meaning.

[4] On the process of semiotic deconstruction of meaning in international law and international relations, see S Tiefenbrun, *Decoding International Law: Semiotics and the Humanities* (Oxford, Oxford University Press, 2010) 1–559.

[5] See also M Colmegna, 'Decoding the Code' in R Kevelson (ed), *Law and Semiotics*, vol 2 (New York, Plenum Press, 1988) 135–43.

Constitutional codes are also ambivalent concepts in another sense. They are explicit or implicit, textual or non-textual (contained in other symbolic systems[6] such as art and architecture). They may be detected in and also extracted from the symbolic behaviour of constitutionally relevant players. These may be the office holders of the state institutions, or the people and citizens performing their ascribed constitutional roles. In this case, constitutional codes are also provided by symbolic-performative constitutionalism.

Symbolic-performative constitutionalism is a result of the demonstration of constitutional codes in constitutional practice by constitutional actors. This behaviour may consist in the application of codes and symbolic roles or the producing of normative patterns of behaviour with symbolic importance which engage the collective constitutional imaginary of the constitutional community. The latter case is an expression of the 'normativity of the factual'[7] performance of symbolic behaviour and demonstrates the repercussions that the socio-legal discourse may have on the normative or strictly legal discourse of constitutionalism.

Constitutional codes presuppose the ability of the constitutional order for the representation of the world via its projection in a system of signifiers, and the capacity of the people and especially of the authoritative narrators, visualisers, performers and interpreters to decode encoded constitutional meaning. Constitutional codes always require interpretation of the signifiers, which is intrinsically semiotic and always leads to constitutional semiosis. This interpretation itself may be creative, assembling or disassembling, constructing, deconstructing or reconstructing meaning.

Constitutional codes serve as nodes of the symbolic-imaginary representation of meaning via distillation and abstraction in this second-level system of signification in constitutional law. They are bearers of indeterminacy and are potentiality entrenched in quantum constitutionalism. They are contained in text and texture, but are also spread in the collective subconscious and unconscious in the form of cloud constitutionalism. They neither describe nor ascribe; they represent, stand for and symbolise. They are distillates of meaning signifying the overall meaning of assemblages of provisions, institutions and norms.[8] Thus, constitutional codes go beyond the rational aspect of constitutionalism. They are not necessarily logical, rational and systematic. There is no rational grid of codes with universal or even contextually universal meaning.

In fact, to an extent, constitutional codes even go against the idea of codification. The concept of codification is tied to rationalism. It is one of the main manifestations of rationalism in law. Codification is correlated and deeply intertwined with

[6] On law as a symbolic system, see P Kahn, 'Comparative Constitutionalism in a New Key' (2003) 101(8) *Michigan Law Review* 2677.

[7] J Stalev, *The Normative Power of the Factual* (Sofia, Feneya, 2007) 1–280 (in Bulgarian).

[8] Here it should be clarified that I am using the word 'assemblage' in a sense which is different from the meaning implied by Deleuze and Guattari. See J Broekman and L Cata Backer, *Lawyers Making Meaning: The Semiotics of Law in Legal Education II* (Dordrecht, Springer, 2013) 116–22.

systematisation, with the logical and uncontroversial ordering of the world within the perfectly calibrated framework of valid law. Constitutional codes are symbolic representations of ideas. They are at the crossroads between the conscious and the collectively unconscious in law. They are the binding nodes of rational and symbolic-imaginary constitutionalism. They are unevenly distributed within the texture of constitutional law and in the otherwise systematically ordered grid of normative and institutional design. In particular, they play a role in relation to phenomena with huge emotional appeal, loaded with imaginary, symbolic and signification potential. They are of lesser importance for the more technical and pragmatically oriented parts of the constitution and constitutional law.

That is why constitutional codes are not systematic but random phenomena. The main source of systematisation of constitutional codes is constitutional theory, the theoretical deconstruction of constitutional textuality and normativity, and their symbolic-imaginary reconstruction via constitutional codes.

That is why symbolic-imaginary constitutionalism cannot offer an uncontroversial system of well-ordered codes in a logical and rational network. It is not a new 'Begriffsjurisprudenz', but a 'game of codes' in the realm of the symbolic-imaginary. Consequently, symbolic-imaginary constitutionalism is not 'counting with codes', in contrast to the way in which some of the main proponents of Begriffsjurisprudenz defined law as 'Rechnung mit Begriffe', 'counting with concepts'.[9] Constitutional codes trigger the perception and conceptualisation of constitutional law as a 'game of codes'. It is a game, there are rules and common features, and there is a framework, but not full determinacy. It is a game with the imaginary and thus the 'game of codes' engages with both the collective conscious and the collective unconscious.

Consequently, constitutional codes are not logical and systematic explanatory schemes; they are merely incentives to think, feel, deliberate and be inspired by constitutionalism. They are invitations to look at the constitutional order from a different viewpoint. They stimulate the reconceptualisation of constitutional law as a simultaneously rational and emotional phenomenon that appeals to both our consciousness and to the unconscious. They are key strategies for constitutional enchantment. Constitutional codes serve for symbolisation instead of ordering and for the representation of ideas, instead of postulating immediate decisions and requiring concrete results.

It has already been explained in the previous chapter that constitutional codes have important epistemic value. They are containers of condensed meaning. They may serve as deliberative nodes in a form of constitutional law conceived as a multidiscursive framework of shared imagination. They reflect the context-specific

[9] This approach to law is also defined by Unger as 'relentless category-grinding'. See RM Unger, 'Legal Analysis as Institutional Imagination' (1996) 59(1) *Modern Law Review* 1. See also M Heidemann, *Bernhard Windscheid und die „Begriffsjurisprudenz". Die Pandektendogmatik im späten 19. Jahrhundert* (Munich, GRIN Publishing, 2015) 1–56.

diversity of national symbolic-imaginary constitutionalism. At the same time, they also allow for the creation of comparative schemes. Indeed, a comparative constitutional approach to constitutional codes allows for the enhancement of knowledge on the commonalities and differences in the symbolic perception and representation of the constitutional order expressed textually by different constitutional cultures and in different constitutional orders. Such comparative analysis of constitutional codes or, more precisely, an exploration of the presence of specific important constitutional codes is not possible here due to space constraints and because of the fact that this book is devoted to the methodology of constitutional semiotics, including its projections in symbolic-imaginary constitutionalism, and the conceptual issues stemming from this approach.

A brief consideration of the ontology of constitutional codes from a semiotic perspective also needs to be given. Constitutional codes may be ascribed to the will of the constitutional legislator; indeed, in many cases, it is the constitutional legislator, which is in a position to make use of the constituent power to shape collective constitutional imaginaries through textual semiosis, which encodes meaning in the constitutional text. It is not uncommon for the constitutional legislator to make overt, explicit and deliberate recourse to constitutional codes and to choose concrete codes in order to represent and symbolise constitutional meaning.

However, an approach based on the concept of the 'death of the author' of the constitution à la Barthes,[10] on a discursive and narrative approach to constitution à la Foucault and on the concept of dispersed linguistic sovereignty shared by a multitude of authoritative speakers of the community allows for a pluralistic, dispersed, less intentional, less centred and less rational explanation of constitutional codes. If constitutional codes are open for interpretation by the multitude of authoritative narrators, speakers, writers and interpreters of the community, and if they are bearers of meaning on a symbolic level, serving as nodes of symbolic communication open for a multidiscursive mastering of meaning based on the deconstruction, construction and reconstruction of signifiers and signifieds in a process of signification through narratives, then they are also prone to subjectivism.

However, this is not a problem, but rather an advantage. This increases the epistemic openness of constitutional codes and their semiotic importance. If constitutional codes may be used as elements of a superstructure of intercultural communication via symbolic representation, then they allow for a broader interpretation of constitutional law as civilisation and a cultural phenomenon entrenched not only in the normativity of rules, but also in the normativity of the collective imaginaries, the collective consciousness and even the collective unconsciousness. The random character of constitutional codes and the openness for their interpretation and reconstruction by a multitude of authoritative speakers

[10] R Barthes, *Image-Music-Text* (New York, Hill & Wang, 1978) 142–49.

and by multiple discourses does not deprive them of either their epistemic value or their rationality.

Finally, it should be clarified that there are several meanings of the 'constitutional code' concept. The first and most general one concerns constitutional language as a specific code.[11] Indeed, legal language in general and constitutional language in particular are particular linguistic discourses that include metaphors, allegories,[12] synthetic and symbolic expressions which are based on the encoding of meaning. They are based on textual semiosis with huge implications and importance for the construction of constitutional meaning.

It is too general and imprecise to state that constitutional language is a container of codes and plays an important role in constitutional semiosis. It is true that constitutionalism is in a sense based on constitutional semiosis and is a kind of 'game of codes' and a process of 'constitutional encoding', representation and symbolic expression of meaning. But it is precisely the encoding of forms of symbolic-imaginary constitutionalism that matters. Hence, in a second and again rather broad sense, all these forms – constitutional myths and mythologies, normative ideas and ideologies, constitutional utopias and anti-utopias etc – are instruments for the symbolic-imaginary, semiotic representation of meaning and thus for its 'constitutional encoding'.

This does not necessarily mean that all forms of symbolic-imaginary constitutionalism are themselves constitutional codes, but sometimes they are. The organisation of constitutional imaginaries as constitutional codes depends mainly on contextual factors such as the specific history, anthropology and collective psychology of the constitutionally framed socio-legal community or the contextual determinants of the will of the constitutional legislator. The constitutional legislator may decide to signify a myth, idea, value, principle or even certain specific objects of protection, such as the nature or particular parts of constitutional heritage, the history and the constitutional and political pantheon through constitutional codes and via the process of constitutional encoding. These may be codes for civilisational or cultural belongingness, codes for inclusion or exclusion in the realm of constitutional memories or the constitutional community, codes for the signification of importance or for the ascription of a particular value and, conversely, for departure from path-dependency and adherence to previous tradition etc.

Hence, all forms of symbolic-imaginary constitutionalism are actually dependent on constitutional codes and constitutional encoding. This is due to the fact that constitutional normative ideologies and ideas, myths and mythologies, and

[11] On language as code, see C Castoriadis, *The Imaginary Institution of Society* (Cambridge, Polity Press, 1987) 237–44. In his view, 'language is langue to the extent that it signifies, that is to say, to the extent that it refers to a magma of significations. Language is a code to the extent that it organizes and organizes itself in an identitary manner' (at 238).

[12] For a general analysis of the concept and role of allegories, see V Brljak (ed), *Allegory Studies: Contemporary Perspectives* (Abingdon, Routledge, 2021) 1–290.

utopias are encoded in visual, textual and symbolic-imaginary constitutionalism. They are expressed via codes, some of which have universal meaning, while others are important and meaningful only in a particular type of constitutional system or a specific region, a culture or tradition, and even in a concrete constitutional jurisdiction and order. In that regard, the constitutional encoding of meaning is the main technique for the semiotic representation of all semiotic approaches to constitutionalism and constitutional law– textual, visual, performative, emotional and symbolic-imaginary.

5

Normative Ideologies and Ideas

Normative ideologies are tools for the signification of abstract and purposeful meaning which stands for cohesive complexes of institutional and axiological architectures representing them in a conceptual way.[1] They are composed of normative ideas serving as nodes of condensed meaning. Both normative ideologies and normative ideas signify models of governance with their underlying values, principles and aims, and with the goals that the institutions must pursue from an axiological, functional and normative perspective. They are assemblages of representations of structural models with an organising role for the whole constitutional design.

The cohesion of normative ideologies and normative ideas is a complex one. It is based on rational bonds between their elements supplemented with huge emotional potential and imaginary-inspirational capacity. The vitality of normative ideologies and normative ideas is assured not only by the convincingness of their rational arguments, but also by their intellectual charm, emotional appeal and symbolic-imaginary attractiveness for the addressees of the constitution and constitutional law, namely the constitutionally framed socio-political community. Hence, normative ideologies and normative ideas must not only have a rational core and structure, and aim at reasonable legal or socio-legal goals; they must also be capable of drawing imaginary trajectories in the collective consciousness of the nation, produce emotionally appealing messages, and signify inspirational and emotionally desirable constitutional targets. They have to produce signifiers with imaginary and emotional potential capable of being vividly represented through the means of visual and performative constitutionalism. Last but not least, they must be capable of textual representation through linguistic codes and other signifiers of meaning: visual, performative or textual.

Thus, normative ideologies and normative ideas exist at the crossroads between rational, emotional, symbolic-imaginary, visual, performative and textual constitutionalism. They are the targets of multidiscursive and multifaceted representation of meaning through textual, visual and performative signifiers. This fact makes normative ideologies and normative ideas not only elements of symbolic-imaginary constitutionalism with projections in the aforementioned alternative

[1] For more on the concept of 'ideological signs' that links political and constitutional ideologies to the semiotic signification of meaning, see P Kotiaho, 'A Return to Koskenniemi; or the Disconcerting Co-optation of Rupture' (2012) 13(5) *German Law Journal* 483.

constitutional discourses; it turns them into an object of multiple semiotic significations. Normative ideologies and normative ideas are important phenomena of constitutional semiotics due to their capacity to trigger constitutional imagination. The concrete shaping of constitutional imagination requires its organisation on the basis of signifiers, signifieds and signification, producing chains of semiotic representation of constitutional and constitutionally relevant meaning. In that regard, normative ideologies and normative ideas are constitutional semiotic phenomena.

Normative ideologies represent in an idealised way phenomena of normative-institutional and factual constitutionalism. Clearly, normative ideologies are idealised versions of the world.[2] They serve for the abstract signification of signifieds which exist in legal and factual reality. The process of signification always requires textual means, but may also include visual and performative signifiers. The range of signifieds varies from fact to values, principles and institutions that are typically represented in a systematic and interrelated way. Thus, semiotic signification based on normative ideologies and ideas spreads through a range of constitutional discourses. It generates emotional understanding and symbolic-imaginary figures that become entrenched in constitutional and political anthropology. In this way, normative ideologies and normative ideas impose intellectual normativity on the collective imaginaries of the constitutionally framed socio-political community.

In that regard, normative ideologies are constitutive elements of an augmented reality organised around dreams, memories, imaginaries, utopias and anti-utopias, codes and intellectual-emotional teasers. Constitutional ideologies and ideas form the realm of 'constitutional imaginary fair' that must be able to guide, enchant, convince and inspire the public. This is an artificial world that contains imagined shapes and forms and idealised models of constitutional phenomena derived from the empirical reality or from valid law.

Thus, normative ideologies are intellectual models of augmented reality based on the constitutional signification of meaning.[3] They serve as substitutes, reflections and imprints of normative-institutional and empirical constitutionalism in the realm of collective imaginaries and symbolic-imaginary constitutionalism. This reveals the importance of normative ideologies not just for constructing the rational system of valid law and for guiding the behaviour of the implementers of the law, but also for shaping the realm of symbolic-imaginary constitutionalism. Hence, normative ideologies can be explored not only rationally, through their usefulness for the rational discourse of constitutional law, but also by virtue of an analysis of constitutional imaginaries and the symbols, significations and abstract models used for the depiction and representation of the semiotic imprints of rational constitutional phenomena.

[2] For a detailed analysis of ideologies, see K Mannheim, *Ideology and Utopia: An Introduction to the Sociology of Knowledge* (Eastford, Martino Fine Books, 2015) 55–109.

[3] They should be understood in the context of the theory on social imaginary significations. See C Castoriadis, *The Imaginary Institution of Society* (Cambridge, Polity Press, 1987) 340–74.

Consequently, normative ideologies and ideas should also be conceptualised as semiotic phenomena and as a legitimate object of research by constitutional semiotics. They stand for constitutionally relevant signifieds existing in the factual reality or in normative discourse. Thus, they can be signifiers of constitutional phenomena that are facts or that are themselves the result of intellectual conceptualisation and ideal representation in the sphere of norms and institutions.

Clear cases of this are the normative ideologies relating to space and time conceived as both empirical and legal phenomena, such as the normative ideologies relating to different concepts of territoriality (fixed, 'container-like' territoriality,[4] fluid territoriality,[5] transversally bordered spaces, cities,[6] global cities[7] etc). These are semiotic signifiers of both territory as fact and territory as a legal (constitutional, administrative and public international law) institution.

More concretely, space and time have three main dimensions. They are facts that belong to the empirical reality. They have legal shapes that are conceptualised by different branches of law. The concepts of 'state territory', 'state of institutional jurisdiction' (for example, of courts or administration), 'institutional seat' and 'capital city' are legal models for the representation of territory as fact in the sphere of law. The overall concept of territoriality is an intellectual construction which performs a twofold signification of meaning: it signifies territory as fact into the realm of law; and it also signifies territory as fact and norm into the realm of intellectual concepts sustaining the legal and constitutional order.[8]

In this last aspect, territoriality as a semiotic signifier of territory and as an element of both rational and symbolic-imaginary constitutionalism is an object of semiotic constitutional engineering. It is a target of intellectual deconstruction, reconstruction and construction, and is at the core of a range of normative ideologies. The most abstract among them are the normative ideologies sustaining the theories of territoriality, post-territoriality and aterritoriality of public power. Some of the most important concrete ideologies underlying territoriality as a

[4] PJ Taylor, 'The State as Container: Territoriality in the Modern World-System' (1994) 18 *Progress in Human Geography* 2; PJ Taylor, 'Beyond Containers: Internationality, Interstateness, Interterritoriality' (1995) 19 *Progress in Human Geography* 1; and N Brenner, 'Beyond State-Centrism? Space, Territoriality and Geographical Scale in Globalization Studies' (1999) 28(1) *Theory and Society* 39.

[5] M Belov, 'Territory, Territoriality and Territorial Politics as Public Law Concepts' in M Belov (ed), *Territorial Politics and Secession: Constitutional and International Law Dimensions* (London, Palgrave Macmillan, 2021) 21.

[6] See G Prakash and K Kruse (eds), *The Spaces of the Modern City: Imaginaries, Politics, and Everyday Life* (Princeton, Princeton University Press, 2008) 1–472.

[7] For transversally bordered spaces and global cities, see S Sassen, *The Global City* (Princeton, Princeton University Press, 2001) 1–480; S Sassen, 'When Territory Deborders Territoriality' (2013) 1(1) *Territory, Politics, Governance* 23; and S Sassen, 'From National Borders to Embedded Borderings: One Angle into the Question of Territory and Space in a Global Age' in W de Been, P Arora and M Hildebrandt (eds), *Crossroads in New Media, Identity and Law* (London, Palgrave Macmillan, 2015) 17.

[8] M Belov, 'Territory, Territoriality and Territorial Politics as Public Law Concepts' in Belov (ed) (n 5) 15–43.

constitutional semiotic signifier of territory are the concepts of fixed, 'container-like' territoriality,[9] open territoriality and fluid territoriality.

The same is true for time as an existential, philosophical and empirical category having significant implications for law in general and constitutional law in particular. Time has different institutional representations in normative-institutional constitutionalism. It is part of rational constitutionalism and is textually provided and entrenched, thus also being framed by textual constitutionalism. Nevertheless, time is also an element of normative ideologies and ideas. Thus, it is also a feature of symbolic-imaginary constitutionalism.

Time is an object of constitutional semiotic significations bridging the gap between empirical, normative-institutional and symbolic-imaginary realms of constitutionalism. Time-as-fact is represented in multiple ways in valid constitutional law. Thus, time-as-norm is based on a range of normative significations of time-as-fact. And time-as-imagination, which consists of normative ideologies, myths, mythologies and utopias, stands for both time-as-fact and time-as-norm.

Examples of legal instantiations of time-as-fact that transform it into time-as-norm are the different provisions relating to constitutional timing. These are provisions for a range of terms and deadlines that should be met within the different constitutional procedures – parliamentary procedure in general, legislative procedure, parliamentary control procedure, budgetary procedure, court procedure, referendum procedure etc.

Time-as-imagination consists of representations of facts, normative phenomena and institutions in the realm of collective constitutional imaginaries. Examples of normative ideologies related to time-as-imagination are the temporal separation of powers, the democratic alteration in office, and the concepts of 'constitutional cycle', 'constitutional moment'[10] and 'constitutional transition'. In fact, the past and the future are very powerful sources of constitutional imagination. They are extremely appealing objects of constitutional semiotics with a high degree of constitutional institutionalisation. However, the past and the future are mostly organised as constitutional memories and constitutional dreams, the former being mainly structured as constitutional myths and mythologies, with the latter frequently having the character of either myths and mythologies or constitutional utopias.

Thus, the constitutional past and the constitutional future are indeed important parts of symbolic-imaginary constitutionalism. They are the object of signification via constitutional semiosis. Nevertheless, they are mostly a part of other elements of symbolic-imaginary constitutionalism – myths, mythologies and utopias. Hence, it is mostly the constitutional present which assumes the shape of normative ideologies and ideas, some of which have been mentioned above.

[9] Taylor, 'The State as Container' (n 4); Taylor, 'Beyond Containers' (n 4); and Brenner (n 4).

[10] See B Ackerman, *We the People: Foundations* (Cambridge, MA, Harvard University Press, 1991) 266.

In that regard, normative ideologies are based on rational strategies for the organisation of the constitutional system, but also trigger, promote, provoke and result in collective imaginaries and ideal conceptualisations of the constitutional world. These imaginaries and ideal conceptualisations are organised through recourse to the symbolic and semiotic signification of meaning.

Therefore, the utopian character of normative ideologies is not a rarity and cannot be excluded. Thus, normative ideologies are intrinsically bound to constitutional utopias, but also to constitutional myths and mythologies. Nevertheless, normative ideologies, constitutional utopias and constitutional mythologies remain closely related, but still different elements of symbolic-imaginary constitutionalism. They are conceptual denominators of different phenomena belonging to the range of symbolic-imaginary constitutional landscapes.[11]

Normative ideologies are pillars for the organisation of meaning that have a formative role for the constitutional order and indirectly also for the whole legal order.[12] For example, the normative ideologies relating to the rule of law, authority and justice have important effects beyond the constitutional system. They spread through the whole legal order and are of special relevance for public law. Thus, normative ideologies are containers of rational meaning generated through the convincingness of fundamental concepts and ideals. At the same time, their normativity is grounded in their emotional and imaginary appeal to the collective constitutional consciousness of the constitutionally framed socio-political community. The rational power of normative ideologies is entrenched in constitutional imaginaries. It is triggered by the desire of people to believe in higher values with legal relevance, in permanent and supreme epistemic schemes that provide some sort of external legitimacy to the legal and constitutional order and a necessary metaphysical underpinning of constitutional rationality.[13]

In that regard, normative ideologies are stretched between the rationality of their core content and the imaginaries that they trigger and rest upon. They possess huge symbolic power. They stand for aggregations of constitutional elements that jointly assert formative force over the way in which people – office holders and stakeholders, but also the different constitutionally relevant groups and the public and citizenry in general – perceive, comprehend and imagine the constitutional order.

Normative ideologies shape and form the constitutional consciousness, and determine intellectual normative parameters and perimeters for the

[11] On the relationship between normative ideologies and social imaginaries, see also M Steger, *The Rise of the Global Imaginary: Political Ideologies from the French Revolution to the Global War on Terror* (Oxford, Oxford University Press, 2008) 1–19.

[12] On the normative ideologies underpinning the EU legal order, see J Komárek, 'European Constitutional Imaginaries: Utopias, Ideologies and the Other', *University of Copenhagen Faculty of Law Research Paper*, 2019 (2020-88), available at: https://ssrn.com/abstract=3477160 or http://dx.doi.org/10.2139/ssrn.3477160.

[13] See J Přibáň, 'Constitutional Imaginaries and Legitimation: On Potentia, Potestas, and Auctoritas in Societal Constitutionalism' (2018) 45(1) *Journal of Law and Society* 30; and J Přibáň, *Constitutional Imaginaries: A Theory of European Societal Constitutionalism* (Abingdon, Routledge, 2020) 1–251.

conceptualisation of constitution, constitutionalism and constitutional law. They impose intellectual normativity based on their convincing character and power to grasp and form the collective imagination of the constitutionally framed socio-political community. Their normativity results from the capacity to contain compressed meaning with formative relevance for constitutionalism and constitutional law in a durable and condensed way.

Thus, normative ideologies must be able to preserve, but also to update meaning and adjust it to the socio-political context and to the changes in the legal and constitutional order. They should be intellectually convincing, emotionally engaging, fascinating and rationally plausible.

What is particularly important here is to emphasise that normative ideologies have a strong but generally underestimated semiotic relevance. This is due to several factors. First, traditionally the semiotic approach to constitutionalism is rarely used and is thus rather exotic. Second, normative ideologies are also rarely explored. They are still to a great extent considered as obscure phenomenon with doubtful relevance for constitutional law. Third, even when they get into the analytical focus of constitutional science, normative ideologies are considered in a twofold way: as ideas-principles and as framing concepts. They are understood as conceptual pillars of the socio-political community that are of immense importance for the structuring and organising of the constitutional order. Alternatively, they are also considered to be intellectual frameworks serving as overall concepts for framing constitutionally relevant meaning. However, in both cases, normative ideologies are perceived as rational categories embedded in constitutional texts. They are supposed to be the fundamental reasons that impose the intellectual outlook of the constitutional system and the constitutional order.

These are indeed proper considerations and legitimate viewpoints on normative ideologies; however, they cannot exhaust their full meaning. Such routine understanding of normative ideologies excludes them from the realm of symbolic-imaginary landscapes and undermines their proper conceptualisation as mixed phenomena on the border between several constitutional discourses. Last but not least, it prevents a semiotic approach from being applied to them.

Hence, the main task of this chapter is to clarify the concept of normative ideology and the normative idea, but especially to allocate them in the intellectual power field of symbolic-imaginary constitutionalism and to bring their semiotic role and importance to the fore. Thus, this chapter defines the normative ideologies as elements of symbolic-imaginary constitutionalism.

The semiotic relevance of normative ideologies consists precisely in their essence as part of the range of elements that belong to symbolic-imaginary constitutionalism. Normative ideologies organise meaning in a twofold way: rationally and symbolically. Rationally they aim at providing holistic or partial models for organising constitutional content according to underlying values, aims and principles. Symbolically they signify rational content in condensed, emotionally appealing and intellectually provoking ways. Thus, they are instruments of constitutional epistemology that organise the constitutional reality both in a rational and in a symbolic-imaginary way. The same is true of the role of normative ideologies as explanatory paradigms with rational and symbolic-imaginary aspects.

Hence, normative ideologies are both epistemic and semiotic tools for the organisation and explanation of constitutionalism and the constitutional order. They are devices for the signification of constitutional phenomena via recourse to fundamental organising ideas with normativity stemming from their emotional and symbolic-imaginary power to enchant while conveying meaning.

Normative ideologies are textually enshrined in the authoritative constitutional texts and also in the texts produced by constitutional theory. Thus, they are contained in a partial, fragmented, syncretic and austere way in the constitution and other sources of constitutional law. They are provided by the authoritative texts of valid law in a limited or a more extensive way. However, they are usually further developed by different authoritative speakers of the community, especially the constitutional and supreme courts, and by other constitutional narrators. The most important role here is played by constitutional theory in conjunction with political theory and philosophy. The theoretical narrators expand upon the meaning implied in constitutional texts that are part of valid law. They broaden meaning, order and systematise elements of normative ideologies, expand normative ideas and shape their overall outlook.

In a sense, the normativity of constitutional ideologies rests upon their textuality. Constitutional texts and texts belonging to constitutional theory are the key means of the fixation, signification and communication of normative ideologies in a universally comprehensible and structured way. They are the main intermediaries between the signified constitutional phenomena (a complex epistemic content composed of axiological and institutional elements) and the signifier (the normative ideology or idea) in the process of the constitutional signification of meaning. Thus, the semiotic potential and the role of normative ideologies rest upon textual constitutionalism.

Nevertheless, this semiotic potential is not limited to textual constitutionalism or only confined within it. It is also applicable to emotional and symbolic-imaginary constitutionalism. In addition, normative ideologies are also rational phenomena and thus have many of the features of rational constitutionalism. Hence, they are, like most of the elements of symbolic-imaginary constitutionalism, complex phenomena that include different aspects belonging to the whole range of constitutionalism – textual, rational, symbolic-imaginary and emotional.

Normative ideologies are also represented by visual constitutionalism, although to a lesser extent than constitutional myths and mythologies and the constitutional codes. The visual representation of normative ideologies and normative ideas is mostly accomplished through visual metaphors expressed via allegories and visual symbols, signs and codes. Sometimes they are signified and visually represented in conjunction with constitutional myths, mythologies and codes. Thus, constitutional myths, mythologies and codes frequently serve as proxies for the visual signification of normative ideologies and normative ideas.

Normative ideologies possess emotional potential and are thus related to emotional constitutionalism. However, this potential is highly dependent on the extent to which textually expressed normative ideologies are also integrated into the collective constitutional symbolic pantheon and the collective constitutional imaginaries of the constitutionally framed socio-political community. The greater the impact of normative ideologies on the way in which people, stakeholders and office holders perceive constitutional phenomena, organise their life in accordance with or in contrast to the constitutional model and structure socio-political reality in constitutional terms through the prism of normative ideologies and ideas, the stronger their relevance for emotional and symbolic-imaginary constitutionalism.

Normative ideologies are intellectual products imposed by intellectual and political elites on society. Hence, they are always elitist products resulting from constitutional engineering.[14] Nevertheless, the hierarchical, imposed and elitist character of normative ideologies and ideas does not preclude the negotiation of their meaning. Such negotiation may be the result of elitist bargaining signified as social contract. Typical examples are the normative ideologies relating to parliamentarism and especially to its monarchical forms, namely constitutional and parliamentary monarchy. In particular, the doctrines of mixed government, based on the blending and creative cross-fertilisation between the doctrines and ideologies of the monarchy and the parliamentary government, are the most visible models of negotiated normative ideologies. They combine normative ideologies and ideas typical of the monarchy (the divine (supra-communitarian or extra-communitarian) right of the monarch, his or her impunity, his or her role as supreme and neutral moderator of the political process that represents the nation as a holistic community and his status as an institution beyond party political divisions and above party politics, defined as a 'neutral moderating power'[15] or 'patriot king'[16] with normative ideologies and ideas belonging to the realm of (bourgeois) parliamentarism.[17] Examples of the latter are the normative ideas of representative, responsible, responsive and limited government.

Furthermore, normative ideologies and ideas are also negotiated by constitutional conversations between the authoritative speakers of the community and the range of constitutional narrators. Such deliberative negotiation of their meaning is

[14] On the concept of constitutional engineering, see G Sartori, *Comparative Constitutional Engineering: An Inquiry into Structures, Incentives, and Outcomes* (New York, New York University Press, 1994) 1–229.

[15] B Constant, *Principes de politiques applicables à tous les gouvernements représentatifs* (HACH. LIVRE-BNF, 2016) 1–333; S Baume, 'De l'usage des pouvoirs neutres' (2012) 143(4) *Pouvoirs* 17; P Rolland, 'Comment préserver les institutions politiques? La théorie du pouvoir neutre chez B Constant' (2008) 27(1) *Revue Française d'Histoire des Idées Politiques* 43.

[16] H Bolingbroke, *The Idea of a Patriot King: With Respect to the Constitution of Great Britain. By a Person of Quality* (Gale Ecco, 2018) 1–170.

[17] On bourgeoisie imaginaries and their role in constructing and stabilising socio-political relations, see S Maza, *The Myth of the French Bourgeoisie: An Essay on the Social Imaginary, 1750–1850* (Cambridge, MA, Harvard University Press, 2009) 1–272.

performed through the expressive forms of textual constitutionalism using textual signifiers. However, they are reflected in the realm of symbolic-imaginary constitutionalism shaping the collective constitutional imaginaries. A special role in this second type of negotiation of meaning is played by constitutional theory and is reflected in theoretical texts.

Moreover, the pure imposition of normative ideologies and ideas is not sufficient, since they also require wide social acceptance in order to be able to assert their intellectual normativity. Winning over minds and souls requires engaging them voluntary in the constitutional ideological project. In line with George Orwell's Big Brother, people must not only understand and obey, but also have emotional affiliation with the imposed normative ideologies and ideas.[18] Hence, these normative ideologies and ideas must also comply with the political and cultural anthropology of the socio-political community. This compliance or non-compliance also explains the success or failure of the practical implementation of normative ideologies.

Normative ideologies are central elements of the ideal constitution comprising the ideal, anthropological and theoretical dimensions of constitutionalism. They are also bridges between rational and symbolic-imaginary constitutionalism. Their role is to predetermine the socio-political behaviour of the subjects of constitutional law, making them apply constitutional law in a specific way and in accordance with the prescribed model of life. Normative ideologies produce an intentionally biased understanding of constitutionalism by durably and profoundly persuading the members of the constitutionally framed socio-political community to follow their imperatives and by triggering normative beliefs stemming from and related to the constitutional order. The semiotic signification of meaning plays an important role in this production of imagined reality.

Normative ideologies usually consist of a typical set of normative ideas. Hence, each normative ideology comprises a distinctive set of normative ideas capable of comparative classification. The normative ideas explain, frame and influence specific discourses of the broader constitutional object underlying the normative ideology. Both the normative ideologies as framing and overarching paradigms and the normative ideas through which they are further developed and concretised predetermine the constitutional design of human rights and constitutional duties as well as of the state institutions. If properly entrenched in the constitutional anthropology of the constitutionally framed socio-political community, they also influence constitutional practice.

Thus, it is of pivotal importance for the proper understanding of constitutional civilisation, constitutional tradition and constitutional order to define, outline and systematise their leading constitutional normative ideologies. This should be done in conceptual, comparative and contextual ways. In other words, the normative ideologies and normative ideas can be explored with a view to their

[18] See G Orwell, *Nineteen Eighty-Four* (New York, Signet Classics, 1961) 1–328.

abstract features, through comparative typologies and via case studies. Usually a proper understanding of both normative ideologies and normative ideas requires deconstruction.

This book focuses on constitutional semiotics. Thus, it explores normative ideologies and ideas mainly as part of symbolic-imaginary constitutionalism conceived as a complex and composite phenomenon with huge importance for constitutional semiotics. Hence, further detailed elaboration of comparative typologies and a presentation of a range of important case studies of normative ideologies and ideas are beyond the scope of both this chapter and this book. What has been given so far in this chapter is the presentation of the concept of normative ideologies and normative ideas with its abstract characteristics and core content. Special emphasis has been placed on the role of normative ideologies and ideas for constitutional semiotics. In the remainder of this chapter, some of the most important normative ideologies and ideas will be presented. This brief outlining of concrete normative ideologies and ideas neither aims to offer exhaustive comparative overview nor to focus on all relevant and important normative ideologies and ideas;[19] the goal is simply to provide some concretisation and substance to the conceptual analysis.

Each constitutional civilisation has its own distinct set of normative ideologies and normative ideas. The difference exists not only with regard to the institutional design of the main constitutional prototypes, but especially with a view to the normative ideologies which underlie constitutional ontology, teleology, axiology and pragmatics.

All forms of constitutionalism are based on their own normative ideologies. In fact, they are a mixture of values, principles and institutions structured around key normative ideologies and ideas. These are the pillars for the organisation of constitutional axiology, constitutional teleology and institutional design structured around rational concepts with huge symbolic-imaginary and emotional appeal that are expressed textually and signified in both the constitutional text and the constitutional texture. They concern all aspects of constitutional design – the institutional architecture, the concept of an ideal and perfect state and society, the societal constitution,[20] as well as the perfect human being and citizen, and the human image of the constitution.[21]

The normative ideologies which are pillars of liberal constitutionalism[22] are the minimal state, the free and rational individual aiming at and capable of achieving

[19] An interesting analysis of the 'grand ideologies' that are also of fundamental importance for constitutionalism and constitutional law is given in Steger (n 11) 19–129.

[20] According to Příbáň, 'societal constitutions enhance power through specific knowledge regimes and imaginaries transform them into generally shared systems of rules and norms'. See Příbáň, 'Constitutional Imaginaries and Legitimation' (n 13).

[21] On the concept of the human image of the constitution, see, eg, U Becker, *Das 'Menschenbild des Grundgesetzes' in der Rechtsprechung des Bundesverfassungsgerichts* (Berlin, Duncker & Humblot, 1996) 1–121.

[22] On the main ideological differences between liberal, democratic, illiberal and populist constitutionalism, see P Blokker, 'Populism as a Constitutional Project' (2019) 17(2) *International Journal*

personal liberty, emancipation and prosperity, the liberty-maximising and liberty-striving individual and society, the clear public-private divide, the separation of powers, the possibility for the establishment of 'islands of political impartiality' in the case of courts and public administration, the inherent character of human rights which are natural, pre-given and alienable, and the absolute value of the human being with his or her personal and political rights.

The core of the normative-ideological design of liberal constitutionalism includes several key normative ideas structured around the fundamental normative ideology of liberty. These are the normative ideas of free will, free choice, moral autonomy and personal autonomy. Liberty has several aspects. It is conceived as free market competition, but also as liberty to make unrestrained personal and moral choices, including choices relating to religion or atheist beliefs. Furthermore, liberty includes power polycentrism, and social, political, economic and cultural pluralism. It also contains the ideas of formalism,[23] proceduralism, an open path for the pursuit of happiness, and entrenched checks and balances in relation to public power.

The normative ideologies of democratic constitutionalism are based on a range of ideas such as equality, fraternity, political empowerment and communitarian inclusion. The supremacy of the majority will and the existence of the common will capable of detecting the common good of society are key normative ideologies of democratic constitutionalism which have been launched at the earliest stages of the emergence of constitutional modernity and have been developed and refined thereafter. They are based on the ideas of solidarity and the inclusive state governed for the benefit of all in the name of all and by all. This concept is clearly expressed in the famous 'Gettysburg formula' of US President Abraham Lincoln.

Unitary concepts of state and society are grounded in ideas of the collective pursuit of happiness requiring extensive political rights and duties. Thus, the main normative ideas that are visually and performatively expressed are solidarity, community, homogeneity and inclusion. In contrast, the visual and performative signification of liberal constitutionalism is centred on the idea of liberty.

The big manifestations of the demonstration of solidarity on important national and international holidays are the clearest examples of the semiotic signification of these core ideas of democratic constitutionalism through the means of performative constitutionalism. From a comparative perspective, manifestations in liberal constitutionalism demonstrate much more discontent, dissent, conflict and public

of Constitutional Law 1; P Blokker, 'Populist Counter-constitutionalism, Conservatism, and Legal Fundamentalism' (2019) 15 *European Constitutional Law Review* 519; P Blokker, 'Varieties of Populist Constitutionalism: The Transnational Dimension' (2019) 20 *German Law Journal* 332; P Blokker, 'Populist Constitutionalism' in *Routledge Handbook of Global Populism* (New York, Routledge, 2018) 113–28.

[23] On the 'culture of formalism', see M Koskenniemi, *The Gentle Civilizer of Nations: The Rise and Fall of International Law 1870–1960* (Cambridge, Cambridge University Press, 2004) 494–510; Kotiaho (n 1) 491–94; J Klabbers, 'Towards a Culture of Formalism? Martti Koskenniemi and the Virtues' (2013) 27(2) *Temple International and Comparative Law Journal*, 417.

checks in relation to state power than solidarity and equality. The raised fist is also an appealing symbol and signifier of unity and decisiveness for collective action in the realm of visual constitutionalism of more radical, leftist and protest-oriented forms of democratic constitutionalism.

It should be noted that some of the signifiers of democratic constitutionalism are borrowed from or are at least similar to some forms of authoritarian solidarism and egalitarianism. The red colour, the celebrations for International Labour Day (1 May) and the fist are common elements of visual constitutional semiotics for both democratic and communist constitutional orders. Some novel protest movements are also borrowing heavily from the whole range of socialist, social-democratic, egalitarian or even communist constitutionalism.

Communist constitutionalism is largely based on extreme forms of solidarity and equality combined (to an extent in an anti-systemic manner) with hierarchy. It is grounded in revolutionary traditions frequently based on revolutionary myths and mythologies.[24] Its revolutionary threats and characteristics are signified via a range of myths of modern martyrdom, but especially by the red colour in state symbols and especially in flags. The self-sacrifice of national and class heroes, the resistance against oppression and the striving for socio-economic emancipation are common objects of signification in communist, revolutionary and post-colonial constitutionalism, and is detectable in many post-colonial constitutions in Africa, Asia and Latin America.[25] Frequently it is combined with national and ethnocentric constitutional myths and mythologies, as demonstrated through official state visuals and acoustic signifiers such as flags,[26] anthems and coats of arms, and via unofficial signifiers of visual and performative constitutionalism.

Monarchical constitutionalism has developed an extensive system of signifiers of its normative ideologies and ideas. The hierarchy, authority, order, continuity and supra-communitarian extraordinarity and excellence of the monarchical power underline the ideological design of monarchical constitutionalism. Since monarchical constitutionalism is a bulky concept, these ideas and ideologies may vary greatly according to the concrete model to which they are applied. Nevertheless, they are signified through a range of well-established and extensively developed signifiers of visual and performative constitutionalism expressed through the means of art, architecture and official state ceremony.

It should be noted that colour is an important signifier of belongingness in many international constitutionally relevant communions. These are not only the communist and the agrarian internationals being more traditional international organisations, but also green and ecological movements, regimes produced during the spread of neoliberal globalism etc. The signification of normative ideologies,

[24] See K Olson, *Imagined Sovereignties: The Power of the People and Other Myths of the Modern Age* (Cambridge, Cambridge University Press, 2017) 110–44.

[25] M Belov and A Abat i Ninet (eds), *Revolution, Transition, Memory, and Oblivion: Reflections on Constitutional Change* (Cheltenham, Edward Elgar, 2020) 107–26

[26] See A Wagner and S Marusek (eds), *Flags, Color, and the Legal Narrative: Public Memory, Identity, and Critique* (Dordrecht, Springer, 2021) 1–745.

myths, mythologies and utopias through colour[27] is explored in Part IV of this book, which is devoted to visual constitutionalism.

Moreover, all constitutional regimes develop official ceremonials which structure and organise the signification of normative ideologies and ideas via performative constitutionalism. Some of these ceremonies are largely elitist and are organised and performed in a closed semiotic plain for the signification of constitutional and constitutionally relevant meaning (parliaments, courtrooms etc). Others are extensively democratic, aiming at the performative signification of meaning via mass events such as manifestations, gatherings, national holidays and celebrations.

There are numerous examples of signifiers of normative ideologies and ideas in visual and performative constitutionalism. They derive their normative core from textual constitutionalism and express it in both an institutionalised and legally binding and in an unrestrained and legally unregulated manner. This conclusion is valid for the normative ideologies and normative ideas of all variants of constitutionalism, irrespective of the ideology on which it is based. For historical reasons, the signifiers of liberal, democratic, monarchical and communist constitutional orders are most widespread in visual and performative constitutional semiotics.

Neoliberal constitutionalism impacts the constitutional semiotic orders at the national, supranational and international levels. For example, visual signifiers of liberal constitutionalism influence the flags of some newly established or re-established states such as Bosnia and Herzegovina, and Kosovo. The blue-yellow design of their flags stems from the liberal palette of colours as signifiers of constitutionally relevant meaning, which is also visible in the flags of the European Union and the Council of Europe, both of which are examples of neoliberal visual semiotics at the supranational and international levels. The visual signifiers of globalism are also clearly visible in the official insignia of all international organisations – especially the UN and its organisations.

Illiberal constitutionalism has the least clear visual signification due to its relatively novel character and its intermingling with the symbolism of both democratic and authoritarian constitutionalism. Another reason for this is that it has emerged and unfolded more as negation – as denial of liberalism and neoliberalism – and as a kind of return to traditional values frequently in the form of 'invented tradition'[28] than as an entirely new form of constitutionalism. It is precisely the elements of illiberal constitutionalism relating to its 'invented tradition' that are most symbolically appealing and thus capable of semiotic signification. This is, for example, the case for the return to religious symbols and symbolism with constitutional relevance, and thus to religious constitutional semiotics in Putin's Russia or Erdogan's Turkey.

[27] On the role of colour as a signifier of meaning and on visual codes relating to flags and colours, see ibid.

[28] E Hobsbawm and T Ranger (eds), *The Invention of Tradition* (Cambridge, Cambridge University Press, 2012) 1–324.

6

Constitutional Myths and Mythologies

This chapter is devoted to constitutional myths and constitutional mythology. It will explore the origin, concept and nature of constitutional myths and mythologies, as well as their structure, logic, functions and role for symbolic-imaginary constitutionalism and constitutional semiotics.[1] The aim here is to offer concise but structured and telling analysis of the main aspects of the phenomena in question. Hence, the task is to provide the basics of a theory of constitutional mythology, giving insights about their ontology and teleology from a semiotic perspective.[2]

Constitutional myths and constitutional mythology have already been allocated on the map of symbolic-imaginary constitutional semiotic landscapes. The conceptual analysis of the role and functional impact of constitutional myths and constitutional mythology on constitutional semiotics and their comparison with other phenomena that belong to symbolic-imaginary constitutionalism has already been done in the previous chapters in this part, especially in Part III, Chapter 3.

I will explore constitutional myths and constitutional mythology as phenomena that belong mainly to symbolic-imaginary constitutionalism. However, their reflections in visual and performative constitutionalism, their importance for emotional and rational constitutionalism as well as their entrenchment in textual constitutionalism will also be assessed.[3] This chapter will also contain a classification of the types of constitutional myths and constitutional mythologies.

It has already been noted that this book is devoted to a general theory of constitutional semiotics. It also includes a range of theories and meta-theories exploring and explaining specific aspects of the process of signification of constitutional

[1] For an excellent and enlightening analysis of the role of myths and mythologies, see R Barthes, *Mythologies* (New York, Noonday Press, 1972). For a social choice and public choice approach to the problem, see A Marciano (ed), *Constitutional Mythologies: New Perspectives on Controlling the State* (Dordrecht, Springer, 2011) 1–176. For an excellent analysis of founding and foundational constitutional myths, their conceptual grounds and their relationship to revolutionary constitutionalism in a post-colonial context, see K Olson, *Imagined Sovereignties: The Power of the People and Other Myths of the Modern Age* (Cambridge, Cambridge University Press, 2017) 1–215. A fundamental analysis of state-centred political mythology with huge constitutional relevance is given in E Cassierer, *The Myth of the State* (New Haven, Yale University Press, 2009) 1–303. Cassierer thoroughly explores the history and philosophy of state-related myths and mythologies.

[2] One of the most influential and well-developed theories of political mythologies is given in C Bottici, *A Philosophy of Political Myth* (Cambridge, Cambridge University Press, 2007) 1–286.

[3] For interesting research on the semiotic performance of legal myths, see D Manderson, 'The Metastases of Myth: Legal Images as Transitional Phenomena' (2015) 26(3) *Law and Critique* 207.

and constitutionally relevant meaning and the production of collective constitutional imaginaries. In line with this general logic, this chapter will offer a concise theory of constitutional myths and mythology. It will not provide either comparative research or case studies. It will tackle concrete constitutional myths and will outline the basics of typologies only when this is necessary as an illustration of the theoretical arguments.

First, it should be clarified what will be considered here as constitutional myths and constitutional mythologies. Definitions always restrict reality, being artificial and thus in a way reductionist and misleading. In any case, the introduction of novel concepts such as constitutional myths and mythologies always requires at least some general and preliminary definition.

Constitutional myths are stories at the crossroads between rational, emotional and symbolic-imaginary constitutionalism. They are concise symbolic stories containing a range of interrelated narratives which are open to further development, modification and adjustment to the socio-legal context. They are textual and linguistic narratives which are capable of visual and performative representation.[4] The textual, visual and performative signification of constitutional myths and mythologies is semi-autonomous and only partially mutually dependent. Actually, it is usually the visual and performative signification of constitutional myths and mythologies which is dependent on their projections in textual constitutionalism.

Constitutional myths and mythologies are representations of symbolic-imaginary meaning carved out in constitutional text and texture, sometimes presented via art, architecture and performance, and durably imprinted in the collective constitutional consciousness, but also in the collective constitutional subconscious and unconscious. Thus, the containers of constitutional meaning moulded in the shapes of constitutional mythology are the signification systems of visual, performative and textual constitutionalism and the oral constitutional tradition, as well as cloud constitutionalism.

The constitutional mythological stories and narratives are quite telling about the constitutional culture and constitutional anthropology of the constitutionally framed socio-political community.[5] This is due to the fact that usually they reflect the culture and anthropology of the society, and offer transcendental projects with semiotic potential that have to enchant the public, capture the public imagination and engage it in emotionally appealing symbolic-imaginary games. The epistemic importance and semiotic power of constitutional myths stem from their allocation at the border between the rational, the emotional, the real, the imaginary and the ideal.

Constitutional myths and mythologies may also be imposed on the community by reformist political elites. They may be part of projects for social modernisation and reform or, conversely, for conservative 'back to the roots' projects frequently

[4] On the relationship between myth and language, see Cassierer (n 1) 16–23.

[5] For an excellent historical overview of a range of important and telling constitutional and legal myths, see Manderson (n 3).

presented in the form of invented tradition.[6] In such cases, constitutional myths and mythologies are not a reflection of the constitutional culture and constitutional anthropology, but rather serve as tools for the rupture and dismantling of mythological path-dependency and for the promotion of mythological constitutional engineering.

Constitutional myths and mythologies are symbolic-imaginary stories with rational elements and emotional appeal, and have huge semiotic potential. This is due to several interrelated reasons. Constitutional myths are both emotionally and symbolically appealing. They are the perfect object for the symbolic representation of meaning because they contain narratives about the origin, the distinctive features, the past and the future of the constitution and the constitutional order. They offer stories of heroes and villains, saints and sinners, collective and individual bravery, heroic or tragic predestination, tragedies, redemption and salvation etc.

Constitutional myths and mythologies may be based on stories of historical existential confrontations that have a class, race, religious, ethnic or ideological character. They provide a glimpse into how the community conceptualises its historical predestination, cultural embeddedness and imaginary shapes from a constitutional semiotic perspective.[7] Constitutional myths and mythologies typically concern the ontology, teleology and axiology of the community. They contain narratives about authority,[8] justice, leadership, and the origin, faith and predestination of the very concept of the constitutionally framed community.

Narratives of victories and defeat, glory and oppression are abundant in non-pragmatic, ideological constitutions that use constitutional semiotics, symbolic-imaginary constitutionalism and especially constitutional myths and mythologies as a toolkit for the signification of the great regularities that drive the history of the constitutionally framed socio-political community.[9] The time-space continuum as a constructed reality structured in the past, the present and the future is the big drawing board for the mythological picture painted by the instruments of constitutional semiotics.

In that regard, the constitutions of many Asian, Latin American and African states, as well as many revolutionary, radical democratic, populist and communist constitutions depart from the rational-textual core of constitutional modernity and enter the magical world of heroism, idealism and historical predetermination, where constitutional myths and mythologies are the signifiers of a quasi-magical reality. In this jungle of constitutional magic, constitutional myths and mythologies

[6] On the concept of 'invented tradition', see E Hobsbawm and T Ranger (eds), *The Invention of Tradition* (Cambridge, Cambridge University Press, 2012) 1–324.

[7] See C Bottici, *A Philosophy of Political Myth* (Cambridge, Cambridge University Press, 2007) 203–26.

[8] J Derrida, 'Force of Law: The "Mystical Foundation of Authority"' (1989–90) 11 *Cardozo Law Review* 920.

[9] See, eg, G Frankenberg, *Comparative Constitutional Studies: Between Magic and Deceit* (Cheltenham, Edward Elgar, 2018) 1–360; and Olson (n 1) 1–215.

serve as epistemic pillars of symbolically represented meaning. They offer guidance and expose the intention of the grand architects of the semiotic puzzles structured around a range of forms of symbolic-imaginary constitutionalism where constitutional myths and mythologies play a pivotal role.

Constitutional myths and mythologies make relative what has to be firm and sound by introducing magic and deceit[10] into normative-institutional and rational constitutionalism. And, conversely, they provide an argumentative basis, offer structured stories and serve as epistemic containers for the discursive stabilisation of meaning via its negotiation by the authoritative narrators, visualisers and performers of the community in the labyrinth of the ideal and the imaginary allocated in the sea of the collective unconscious and subconscious.

Thus, constitutional myths and mythologies can grasp not only the mind but also the heart and the imagination of the members of the constitutionally framed socio-political community. They are inspirational, adorable and capable of being signified through different signifiers belonging to textual, visual and performative constitutionalism.[11]

In that regard, constitutional myths and mythologies can be conceived as first-grade signifiers. They assign key persons and landmark events with strategic importance for the incitement of pride and honour, structuring the collective constitutional imaginaries and belonging to the constitutional pantheon. They represent partial or general stories about the origin, the past and the future of the state and society. At the same time, they are themselves signified by second-grade signifiers belonging to the toolkit of textual, visual and performative constitutionalism. Allegories depicted through textual, art and architectural means and performance, textual and linguistic metaphors, and a wide range of constitutional codes are the signifiers through which constitutional myths and mythologies are signified.

Thus, from a semiotic viewpoint, constitutional myths and mythologies are entrenched in a long process of constitutional semiosis originating in rational and normative-institutional constitutionalism, expressed via textual, visual and performative constitutionalism, contained in symbolic-imaginary and cloud constitutionalism, and affecting emotional constitutionalism. In this complex semiotic process, constitutional myths and mythologies are both signifiers and signifieds, as explained above.

Constitutional myths are contained in constitutional mythologies. Conversely, constitutional mythologies are systems of constitutional myths. Hence, constitutional myths are the building blocks and the elements of constitutional mythologies, in a similar way to how normative ideas are the constructive parts of normative ideologies. This does not mean that each constitution has an extensive constitutional mythology. Many constitutions do not, because they are pragmatic tools

[10] Frankenberg (n 9) 1–360.

[11] For a very interesting analysis of feminist mythologies that shape our constitutional understanding of the feminine in law, see C Bottici, *A Feminist Mythology* (Oxford, Hart Publishing, 2021) 1–216.

concentrated on rational and normative-institutional constitutionalism. However, more ideologically open constitutions – those which have long preambles that tell semiotic stories and are open to the semiotic representation of meaning – contain a multitude of constitutional myths which are fully or partially ordered as part of the constitutional mythology.

An important question which needs to be answered is who can create constitutional myths? This is the problem of constitutional mythogenesis. Beyond the realm of constitutionalism, in folklore tradition or in other oral and written cultural traditions, myths are usually not created by a specific person. They are typically the anonymous result of a long tradition of the inheritance of collective imaginaries.[12] Of course, myths can be systematised, analysed and further developed by specific narrators. Mythology can be invented by trusted narrators who are capable of presenting mythological systems in a structured, coherent and appealing way that can be comprehensible and adequate for grasping the imaginaries of the audience.[13] Nevertheless, beyond the realm of law in general and constitutionalism and constitutional law in particular, even these personified narratives build upon pre-existing mythological traditions based on inherited, dispersed and anonymous mythological narratives.

Hence, apart from constitutional law, mythology does not stem from a concrete constitutive will for mythogenesis. It is a result of a dispersed, impersonal but at the same time interpersonal process for the imaginary self-organisation of the constitutionally framed socio-political community. Naturally, mythology can be attributed to an idealised narrator or an initial mythological demiurge, which is typical of religious mythology, but in most cases such ascription of the mythological ontology is largely fictitious. In such cases, the supposed author or initial constitutive narrator is actually a signifier of the constitutive myth related to the ontology of the mythological system, thus being itself also part of semiotic ontology.[14]

This is not the case with constitutional myths and mythologies. Constitutions, with the notable exception of the unwritten British constitution, have 'birth certificates' and concrete mothers and fathers. They are product of the will of the constitutional legislator imposed in a fixed constitutional moment.[15] Hence, it is

[12] On the relationship between myths and imaginaries, see G Bouchard, *Social Myths and Collective Imaginaries* (Toronto, University of Toronto Press, 2015) 7–23.

[13] For example, pre-existing mythology can be systematised or new mythological stories may be invented on the basis of pre-existing diffuse popular mythology. The invented and authored mythology builds upon and further develops the popular mythology and integrates its key figures and narratives. Good examples are the collation of ancient Greek mythology by Kuhn and the different collations of folk tales largely modified by their concrete authors, eg, the Brothers Grimm and the imaginary world of JRR Tolkien.

[14] See R Barnett, 'Constitutional Legitimacy' (2003) 103 *Columbia Law Review* 113; Z Oklopcic, *Beyond the People: Social Imaginary and Constituent Imagination* (Oxford, Oxford University Press, 2018) 1–416; and Olson (n 1) 1–215.

[15] See B Ackerman, *We the People: Foundations* (Cambridge, MA, Harvard University Press, 1991) 266.

the constitutional legislator who is supposed to have the monopoly to perform as the official demiurge of constitutional mythology. Consequently, constitutional myths and mythologies can be ascribed to the will of the specific constitutional legislator – the monarch, the parliament, the constituent assembly etc.

A more dynamic, discursive and post-modern understanding of constitutions based on their open texture also assumes that the authoritative narrators of the constitutionally framed socio-political community can engage in the creation, mastering and evolution of their constitutional mythology. Thus, the authoritative interpreters (eg, the constitutional and supreme courts) can also engage in interpretative games for the semiotic signification of meaning shaped in the forms of constitutional myths and mythologies.[16]

Going beyond textual constitutionalism, as this book suggests, means that producers of constitutional mythology can also be the authoritative performers and visualisers of the constitutionally framed socio-political community. They can signify mythological content through allegories, visual (art and architecture) metaphors and codes, official ceremonies, symbolic performative demonstrations etc. This means that even the people as a whole can engage in the symbolic representation of mythological meaning demonstrated through behaviour. Traditional celebrations of political and historical events that have an official constitutional standing or an informal but substantial constitutional relevance can be signifiers of mythological content and meaning.

Last but not least, it should be noted that constitutional theory can also be an important source of constitutional myths and mythology. It can base its mythological narratives on the already existing legal discourse, eg, on constitutionally provided or otherwise authoritatively demonstrated myths and mythologies. However, the theory can also create its own myths and mythologies as partially autonomous constitutional discourse. In both cases, the theoretical production of myths and mythologies is frequently interrelated with the discursive development of other forms of symbolic-imaginary constitutionalism such as normative ideologies and ideas and constitutional utopias. This process is largely semiotic since it results in the symbolic-imaginary production, representation and signification of meaning.

It should be mentioned that constitutional myths can be developed into mythologies and discursively modified by authoritative speakers, narrators, performers and visualisers because they carry huge semiotic potential in condensed form. The potentiality of constitutional myths and their character as epistemic containers of condensed and symbolic meaning links them with the concept of quantum constitutionalism. All forms of symbolic-imaginary constitutionalism have enhanced quantum potential for discursive development in comparison to the more institutional, procedural and technical parts of the constitution. However, constitutional codes and constitutional myths are most prone to extensive

[16] See J Frank, *Courts on Trial: Myth and Reality in American Justice* (Princeton, Princeton University Press, 1949).

epistemic evolution via interpretation. They are open for further development through semiotic means.

Hence, an interim conclusion can be reached: although constitutional myths and mythologies, in contrast to their extra-legal and non-legal counterparts, typically have specific authors, they may also be produced by a range of authoritative narrators, interpreters, performers and visualisers. The interpretative evolution of constitutional myths is based on a complex, multidiscursive, asymmetric and asynchronous process of signification of meaning by a range of mythological storytellers. Hence, they are engaged in a process of constitutional semiosis which targets constitutional myths and constitutional mythology.

Another important issue which is worthy of attention concerns the question of where the constitutional myths are contained. The problem is how do we detect and define the containers of constitutional mythology and thus how do we discover its locus? This problem has two dimensions. The first, broader and more conceptual aspect concerns the question of which are the forms of constitutionalism that allow for semiotic signification of meaning via constitutional myths and mythologies. The second, narrower and more technical aspect relates to the structure of the constitution. It can be subsumed under the following question: which are the structural parts of the constitution that are the usual and typical containers of constitutional myths and mythologies?

Let us start with addressing the first aspect. Constitutional myths and mythologies are initially textual phenomena. They have their normative anchors in valid constitutional law. Typically they are contained in the constitution. Not all constitutions contain constitutional myths and mythologies; this is a property of the more transcendentally oriented, programmatic, semantically and ideologically open constitutions.[17] The pragmatic and more technical constitutions do not contain extensive ideology and axiology. They reduce constitutionalism to its normative-institutional and rational forms. Thus, they are not especially prone to the signification of meaning via constitutional semiosis and do not constitute the typical textual context for the unfolding of constitutional myths and constitutional mythology.

Hence, the initial container of constitutional myths and constitutional mythology is textual constitutionalism. Nevertheless, constitutional allegories are frequently represented in constitutionalism beyond constitutional law or more precisely beyond its textual dimension. In that regard, visual constitutionalism and performative constitutionalism are replete with constitutional allegories and a range of visual and performative constitutional codes signifying constitutional myths, constitutional mythologies or simply some aspects of them. Performative constitutionalism is a field of constitutional semiosis where the multitude of mythological narratives are demonstrated both in structured and institutionalised

[17] On the subject of normatively undetermined constitutions, see E Tanchev, *Introduction to Constitutional Law* (Sofia, Sibi, 2003) 195–97 (in Bulgarian).

form via official ceremonies and in a non-institutionalised way, dispersedly, intuitively and through informal signification acts and performance.

In that regard, constitutional myths and constitutional mythology are contained not only in constitutional text and constitutional texture. The formal systems for the constitutional signification of meaning – official or unofficial – are not the only containers of constitutional myths and constitutional mythology. This is due to the fact that they can also be contained as part of cloud constitutionalism. In that sense, constitutional myths and constitutional mythology are part of the constitutional culture, the constitutional anthropology and the constitutional heritage of the constitutionally framed socio-political communities. This exposes the socio-psychological, archetypal and anthropological nature and essence of constitutional myths.

The second and more technical aspect of the question of where the constitutional myths and mythologies are contained has structural implications. Constitutional myths and mythologies are necessary elements of many constitutions, especially the less pragmatic and more ideological and programmatic ones. Actually, all constitutions require founding myths and underlying mythologies; nevertheless, not all of them provide these in an explicit manner. In fact, most constitutions outline the myths and mythologies in an incremental and implicit way, suggesting their existence in relation to constitutional ontology and constitutional teleology, giving hints in the preambles and pinpointing their elements through the constitutional text.

Usually and typically, it is the constitutional preamble that is the main container of constitutional myths and mythologies. The long, detailed and passionate ideologically oriented preambles of many African, Asian and Latin American constitutions are the typical place where constitutional myths and mythologies exist. Many communist, revolutionary and radical democratic constitutions have extensive constitutional mythology provided by their preambles as well. Less frequently, elements of constitutional myths and mythologies may also be provided by the normative text of the constitution.

Constitutions are typically conceived as rational phenomena. It has already been explained in detail that they are entrenched in textuality and rationality. They are based on forms and procedures that are unified by inherent logic and are systematically ordered through the devices of normative-institutional constitutionalism. Both textuality and rationality are conceived as key characteristics of modern constitutional law. Constitutions are not only written and rational; they are also systematic, normative and institutional. They are prescriptive authoritative texts providing for rational paths for the future and remedying the mistakes of the past.

Is it possible then that such rational phenomena contain constitutional myths and mythologies? Aren't myths and mythologies irrational, non-systematic, illogical and impossible to include in a normative text belonging to valid law? Wouldn't myths and mythologies destroy or at least question the authoritative character of the constitution as a normative text and a container of institutional logic?

Can myths and mythologies be rationally ordered as part of a constitutional project that aims at offering clear and indisputable visions of the future? Is it not the case that myths and mythologies rest upon emotions, thus making them vulnerable, fluid and fuzzy? Last but not least, where do constitutional myths and mythologies derive their validity, convincing power and legitimacy to be part of the constitutional project conceived as both a conceptual phenomenon of modernity and as a concrete instantiation of a legally framed political project for the rational and authoritative government of the state and society?

Constitutional myths and mythologies are devices for the rational reworking and sublimation of constitutionally relevant phenomena that have eventually occurred in the history of the constitutional community and have been deliberately transformed and reshaped by the constitutional legislator in the form of constitutional myths. They can also be precursors of the future, offering symbolic-imaginary proxies with huge signification and emotional potential.

In other words, the implicit rationality of constitutional myths and mythologies consists in their ability to serve as tools for the sublimation of traumas, fears, anger and anxiety. Even better, they are able not only to suppress negative feelings, but also to promote and channel them in a direction that is preferred by the constitutional legislator and is subsequently moulded by the a range of narrators, performers and visualisers. Hence, constitutional myths and mythologies are tools for the sublimation of the past and for modelling the future in terms of the politics of evil, hate and other negative feelings. Thus, they can be part of constitutional fear politics[18] and thus contribute to the promotion and establishment of 'dark' or 'fear' constitutionalism.

Conversely, constitutional myths and mythologies can also be triggers for positive feelings. They may promote pride, hope and striving at perfection according to the postulates of 'invented tradition',[19] a real or imaginary 'glorious past' or a better and perfected future world that can be expected. In the last case, constitutional myths and mythologies are part of or may contribute to the promotion of a constitutional utopia. Hence, they may be constitutive elements and semiotic signifiers not only of 'dark' or 'fear' constitutionalism, but also of the 'bright' constitutionalism of pride, joy and happiness. In all cases, they are proxies of collective ideals, imaginaries and emotions entrenched in the realm of reality through provision in valid constitutional law and thus via textual constitutionalism or signified by

[18] On the concept of fear politics and some of its manifestations, see M Belov, 'The Role of Fear Politics in Global Constitutional "Ernstfall": Images of Fear under COVID-19 Health Paternalism' in M Belov (ed), *Populist Constitutionalism and Illiberal Democracies: Between Constitutional Imagination, Normative Entrenchment and Political Reality* (Cambridge, Intersentia, 2021) 187–221. On fear politics and anger politics, and their impact on constitutional imaginaries, see T Koncewicz and L Strother, 'The Role of Citizen Emotions in Constitutional Backsliding – Mapping Out Frontiers of New Research', *Verfassungsblog*, 21 March 2019, https://verfassungsblog.de/the-role-of-citizen-emotions-in-constitutional-backsliding-mapping-out-frontiers-of-new-research.

[19] E Hobsbawm and T Ranger (eds), *The Invention of Tradition* (Cambridge, Cambridge University Press, 2012) 1–324.

virtue of other systems for the semiotic signification of constitutional and constitutionally relevant meaning.

Hence, constitutional myths and mythologies are semiotic signifiers at the crossroads between emotional, symbolic-imaginary and rational constitutionalism. They are channels for the linking of rational constitutional law to transcendental levels of constitutional imagination through the semiotic signification of constitutional and constitutionally relevant meaning. They make constitutional law more emotional, passionate, imaginative and even heroic, introducing a degree of irrationality usually subsequent to a rational plan.

Thus, it seems that the irrationality of constitutional myths and mythology is in most cases rationally conceptualised and organised. This is due to the fact that constitutional myths and mythologies are transcendental projects with a symbolic-imaginary core, emotional appeal and a capacity for textual, visual and performative signification that are included in the overall rationalist constitutional project. They require rationality for the sake of being included in the generally rational constitutional order, but also a degree of irrationality in order to be emotionally and symbolically appealing.

Last but not least, a brief and concise typology of constitutional myths and mythology needs to be outlined. I cannot offer an extensive comparative typology of constitutional myths and mythology here due to both space constraints and my plans to develop it in a precise and detailed way in the future. Nevertheless, here I will provide a short outline of the main features of such a typology.

Initially it is necessary to distinguish between a range of myths with regard to their role in relation to the whole constitutional project. Thus, we have to differentiate myths relating to constitutional ontology, myths relating to constitutional axiology, myths relating to constitutional teleology and myths relating to constitutional design. Ontological constitutional mythologies offer insights about the origins of the constitution, the founding subject, the original context, and the uniqueness of the foundational moment and its actors through the lens of symbolic-imaginary constitutionalism that usually provides for the semiotic signification of constitutional meaning.[20] Similarly, teleological constitutional mythologies use the instruments of constitutional semiotics to signify the constitutional foundations. However, in contrast to ontological constitutional mythologies, the teleological constitutional mythologies signify strategic goals that have to be achieved by the constitutional community and its institutions through the means of the constitution. Such goals usually concern the establishment of a better society defined in terms of the imposed constitutional ideology. Such aims often have a utopian character. This is especially the case when the striving for the achievement of a better society takes place in a revolutionary and

[20] On the role of foundational imaginaries and fictions in constitutional law, see O Tans, 'Imagined Constitutionality: Rethinking Democratic Citizenship with the Aid of Fiction Theory' (2019) 15(2) *Law, Culture and the Humanities* 1.

post-revolutionary context or is part of a populist, revolutionary or any other form of radical constitutional project.

Constitutional mythologies may also be focused on elements relating to the constitutional principles and values or the constitutional architecture and design. In this case, we distinguish between axiological constitutional myths and institutional constitutional myths. Axiological constitutional myths usually concern some of the most 'heroic' and emotional principles of constitutional law. These are sovereignty (especially the monarchy and popular sovereignty as forms that are more appealing to the collective imaginaries) and democracy or, more precisely, democracy in its more radical and even revolutionary forms. In that regard, axiological constitutional mythologies may be interrelated with ontological constitutional mythologies.

The second field for the comparative allocation of myths concerns their attitude to the fundamental preconditions for the existence and functioning of the constitution and the constitutional order. Here we can distinguish between temporal constitutional myths (or constitutional myths relating to the past, the present and the future) and spatial constitutional myths,[21] which concern territory, territoriality and territorial politics.[22]

Temporal myths can be subdivided into two main groups. The first group includes the retrospective temporal mythologies which are bound to constitutional memories. They include historical artefacts with a personal and substantial character which shape the constitutional memory politics largely grounded in symbolic-imaginary constitutionalism and the semiotic signification of the past. The second group includes the prospective temporal mythologies, which relate to constitutional goals and constitutional dreams and plans for the future. Some of the most important prospective temporal mythologies are based on normative ideologies and ideas such as the pursuit of happiness, the construction of an egalitarian, fair and just society or its specific version – the establishment of communist society or the establishment of ecological equilibrium based on archetypal ethno-ecological figures such as Mother Nature (Pacha Mama in Bolivia and Ecuador).

Temporal mythologies may be organised on the basis of several modalities. The most typical of these are constitutional mythologies relating to antiquity, ancient roots, enduring identity and glorious ancient civilisations; long revolutionary

[21] On the use of temporal, territorial and spatial anomalies, eg, 'places outside space' and 'moments outside time', see B Lincoln, *Discourse and the Construction of Society: Comparative Studies of Myth, Ritual, and Classification* (Oxford, Oxford University Press, 1992) 160–62.

[22] For a special analysis of the semiotic signification of spatiality and territoriality, see M Belov, 'Territory, Territoriality and Territorial Politics as Public Law Concepts' in M Belov (ed), *Territorial Politics and Secession: Constitutional and International Law Dimensions* (London, Palgrave Macmillan, 2021) 15–45. On the imaginary properties of spatiality, see also E Brann, *The World of the Imagination. Sum and Substance*, (Lanham, MD, Rowman & Littlefield, 2017) 581–84. For fundamental considerations about spatial and temporal mythology, although general and thus to an extent different from constitutional mythology, see E Cassierer, *The Philosophy of Symbolic Forms, Vol 2: Mythical Thought* (New Haven, Yale University Press, 1965) 105–66.

struggle; revolutionary detachment from the past; redemption of ancestors' omen and realising constitutive dreams from the past.[23]

The third way in which we can distinguish between constitutional myths and systematise them is in the field of conflictual constitutionalism. It is entrenched in the critical reassessment of the past with a view to fundamental political, social, cultural, religious or economic conflicts with strategic importance for constitutional politics, constitutionalism and constitutional law. Hence, the focus here is on phenomena which can be broadly labelled constitutional myths and mythologies that are entrenched in critical and conflictual constitutionalism. These are the myths relating to race, religion,[24] gender, class, colonialism and post-colonialism,[25] slavery, different forms of oppression and servitude, and more recently also ecology. These myths are usually focused on the constitutional heritage and thus on structural conflicts with systemic importance from the past. Nevertheless, some of them in parallel promote specific constitutional teleology, frequently with a utopian character, for a better constitutional future. Hence, this third group of myths is closely related to constitutional ideology and constitutional utopia.

Fourth, there is also a range of constitutional myths that are structured around concrete historical figures, collective experiences and artefacts. Some of these myths relate to heroes, martyrs and saints, villains, occupiers and oppressors. They can be defined as personal myths. Others concern events having pivotal importance in the history of the community. They serve different functions, but usually aim at a symbolic break with the past or at starting or a dismantling of path-dependencies. There are also myths grounded in facts and artefacts deeply entrenched in collective constitutional archetypes,[26] triggering constitutional pride and constitutional prejudice[27] with huge symbolic, imaginary and semiotic potential.

Indeed, there is no strict line dividing up these four groups of constitutional myths. Personal myths and myths about crucial events and other artefacts with huge symbolic-imaginary appeal are also temporal myths. They can also be myths that relate to sacred spaces, places and territories. Myths of constitutional ontology may also be temporal myths or can relate to personal myths. All of these myths frequently also have an ideological dimension. Even liberal myths of formal and

[23] See M Belov, 'Constitutional Memories: How Do Constitutions Cope with Constitutional Past' in M Belov and A Abat i Ninet (eds), *Revolution, Transition, Memory, and Oblivion: Reflections on Constitutional Change* (Cheltenham, Edward Elgar, 2020) 107–26.

[24] See, eg, N Rouhana and Nadera Shalhoub-Kevorkian, *When Politics are Sacralized: Comparative Perspectives on Religious Claims and Nationalism* (Cambridge, Cambridge University Press, 2021) 1–300.

[25] See Olson (n 1) 110–67; and U Kothari and R Wilkinson, 'Colonial Imaginaries and Postcolonial Transformations: Exiles, Bases, Beaches' (2010) 31 *Third World Quarterly* 1395.

[26] For an interesting analysis of constitutional archetypes, see D Law, 'Constitutional Archetypes' (2016) 95 *Texas Law Review* 153; and G Frankenberg, 'Comparing Constitutions: Ideas, Ideals, and Ideology – Toward a Layered Narrative' (2006) 4(3) *International Journal of Constitutional Law* 439, https://doi.org/10.1093/icon/mol012.

[27] See L Blum, '"Black Lives Matter": Moral Frames for Understanding the Police Killings of Black Males' in A Amaya and M Del Mar (eds), *Virtue, Emotion and Imagination in Law and Legal Reasoning* (Oxford, Hart Publishing, 2020) 121–38.

supposedly neutral constitutional ontology promote the specific ideological foundation of constitutional ontology. This is implicitly based on myths – eg, the myth of the social contract concluded under the 'veil of ignorance.[28]

In summary, constitutional myths and mythologies have to be organised into typologies. They may be grouped in comparative clusters. Nevertheless, this should not lead to either their 'sterilisation' and detachment from the socio-political and ideal-imaginary context in which they are produced and embedded, or to their proximities in textual, visual, performative and symbolic-imaginary constitutionalism being disregarded.

[28] On the 'veil of ignorance', see J Rawls, *A Theory of Justice* (Cambridge, MA, Belknap Press, 1999) 1–560. For a critical approach to the 'veil of ignorance' from the viewpoint of constitutional mythology, see L Imbeau and S Jacob, 'Is the "Veil of Ignorance" in Constitutional Choice a Myth? An Empirical Exploration Informed by a Theory of Power' in A Marciano (ed), *Constitutional Mythologies: New Perspectives on Controlling the State* (Dordrecht, Springer, 2011) 53–71.

7

Constitutional Utopias

The final chapter of Part III is devoted to constitutional utopias.[1] Its aim is to provide a brief and concise but telling analysis of the semiotic features of constitutional utopia as an element of symbolic-imaginary constitutionalism. It explores the role of constitutional utopias in the process of the semiotic signification of meaning using the toolkit of textual, visual and performative constitutionalism.[2] Hence, it will not go into detail on the nature of utopias,[3] their structure and general functions for law and legal science. Due to space constraints, it will not engage with the existing debate on the general impact of utopias on states, statehood and the functioning of public law.[4] The brief typology of utopias is limited to examples of conceptual importance which have the highest relevance for constitutional law and are sufficiently telling, especially with a view to the semiotic role of constitutional utopias. Hence, the list of groups of utopias given at the end of the chapter is included not as an exhaustive typology of constitutional utopias, but rather as a classification exemplifying the previous conceptual analysis and as a good starting point for any future work in the sphere of comparative constitutional law focused on the forms of symbolic-imaginary constitutionalism in general and constitutional utopias in particular.

[1] For different approaches to constitutional utopias, see, eg, S Herman, 'Constitutional Utopianism' (2016) 12 *UTOPIA500* 93, available at https://scholarlycommons.pacific.edu/utopia500/2016/events/12; R Nozik, *Anarchy, State, and Utopia* (New York, Basic Books, 2013) 297–335; J Komárek, 'European Constitutional Imaginaries: Utopias, Ideologies and the Other', *University of Copenhagen Faculty of Law Research Paper*, 2019 (2020–88), available at: https://ssrn.com/abstract=3477160; A Teršek, 'Political Alternatives for Constitutional Democracy: Between Utopia, Pandemic and Dystopia' (2021) 4 *Open Political Science* 45; S Chrostowska and J Ingram (eds), *Political Uses of Utopia: New Marxist, Anarchist, and Radical Democratic Perspectives* (New York, Columbia University Press, 2016) 1–331; and B Ashcroft, 'Constitution Hill: Memory, Ideology and Utopia' (2014) 51(2) *Tydskrif Vir Letterkunde* 94, http://dx.doi.org/10.4314/tvl.v51i2.8.

[2] On constitutional utopias and constitutional eutopias, and the constitutional imagination related to them, see Z Oklopcic, *Beyond the People: Social Imaginary and Constituent Imagination* (Oxford, Oxford University Press, 2018) 343–81.

[3] For an analysis of the nature, history and diversity of utopias as well as for their political application in a range of radical socio-political contexts, see K Mannheim, *Ideology and Utopia: An Introduction to the Sociology of Knowledge* (New York, Martino Fine Books, 2015) 55–109; and S Chrostowska and J Ingram (eds), *Political Uses of Utopia: New Marxist, Anarchist, and Radical Democratic Perspectives* (New York, Columbia University Press, 2016), 1–331.

[4] See, eg, E Brann, *The World of the Imagination. Sum and Substance* (Lanham, MD, Rowman & Littlefield, 2017) 714–24.

A constitutional utopia is a form of symbolic imaginary constitutionalism.[5] It offers a holistic project for the development of the constitutional order. The project is holistic because it includes more or less complete visions for the state, the society and the person in its capacity as both citizen and human being. Thus, typically constitutional utopias offer an extensive signification scheme, all of the phenomena which are regulatory objects of the constitution and constitutional law.

In most cases, constitutional utopias are not limited to institutional design. They offer an account of the preferable system of state institutions because they are the central object of each constitutional model. The institutional design is the more technical and strictly legal part of constitutional law. Thus, it is mainly a part of rational and normative-institutional constitutionalism. Nevertheless, constitutional utopias engage with institutions since it is the institutions which govern the people, the society and the state. Hence, they devote attention to the promotion of a 'better model' of government. If the perfection of the state, society and the human being has to be achieved, then there is a need for experiments with new systems of government as instruments for socio-political and economic advancement and cultural perfection. This predetermines the central role of institutional architecture for the construction of constitutional utopias.

Nevertheless, constitutional axiology (constitutional values and principles), human rights and the constitutional status of the human being are also of great importance for constitutional utopias. This is due to the fact that their constitutional modelling allows for the accomplishment of value-based constitutional engineering impacting the axiological core, the value consensus and the constitutional model of the human and the citizen.

Consequently, the holistic character of constitutional utopias is to an extent predetermined by their object. Constitutional utopias must provide a general picture of the world. Their task is to offer an image and vision of a better world with its perfect institutions, perfected humans and citizens and impeccable society. The model offered by constitutional utopias should not only be reasonable and rational, but also desirable and even adorable. This is achieved through the semiotic signification of meaning and engagement with collective emotions and especially collective constitutional imaginaries. That is why constitutional utopias are not limited to rational and normative-institutional constitutionalism, but are elements of symbolic-imaginary constitutionalism represented through the means of textual, visual and performative constitutionalism.

In that regard, constitutional utopias are holistic not only because they strive at providing an overall and all-encompassing model that conceptually frames

[5] According to E Balibar, 'the main problem facing us at the turn of the century consists of taking leave of utopia while setting free the powers of the imagination.' This statement is interesting because it creates a field of tension between utopia and imagination, notwithstanding the fact that they are mutually dependent phenomena. See E Balibar, 'After Utopia, Imagination?' in S Chrostowska and J Ingram (eds), *Political Uses of Utopia: New Marxist, Anarchist, and Radical Democratic Perspectives* (New York, Columbia University Press, 2016) 161.

and signifies ideals of the state, the society and the people; they are also holistic because they impact all forms of constitutionalism.[6] Constitutional utopias by necessity focus on symbolic-imaginary constitutionalism for the reasons provided above. They do concern rational constitutionalism because they provide constitutional models for governing the state and society, and thus have to offer rationally convincing forms, procedures, institutions and legally framed patterns of behaviour.

However, constitutional utopias are not just raw models for the establishment of mechanisms of an improved and even perfect state and society; they are also devices for winning the hearts and minds of their addressees, who are the members of the constitutionally framed socio-political community that is striving for utopian perfection. In that regard, constitutional utopias are key elements of symbolic-imaginary constitutionalism. They are instruments for constitutional enchantment and for triggering imaginary processes. Moreover, constitutional utopias not only start the process of constitutional imagination; they are not just an invitation for imagining a better constitutional future and a perfect constitutional world. They possess a huge degree of finality, being promises not only for the path to the better future, but also offering imaginaries for the concrete shapes and forms of this 'brave new constitutional world'.[7]

Constitutional utopias are signified through the whole range of constitutional signifiers. Like the other elements of symbolic-imaginary constitutionalism, they are provided by the constitutional text, but are in parallel also signified through the signifiers of visual and performative constitutionalism. The belongingness of constitutional utopias to textual constitutionalism is clearly proven by the fact that they are part of the general model of constitutional governance and are spread across all parts of the constitution relating to constitutional values, aims, principles, human rights, constitutional foundations of the society and the public sphere, and the system of constitutional institutions. The constitutional preamble is the typical location for all elements of symbolic-imaginary constitutionalism and constitutional utopias are no exception here. A peculiarity of constitutional utopias is their specific link to constitutional teleology; in other words, they are deeply interrelated with the system of constitutional goals due to their prospective, future-oriented character.

Constitutional utopias are also a perfect object of constitutional signification of meaning via signifiers belonging to visual and performative constitutionalism. They are intertwined with political ideology, which is perfectly manifested via signifiers of official visual constitutionalism, such as the colours and elements of

[6] For a semiotic approach to constitutional utopias applicable to Europe and the EU in particular, see A Ponzio, 'The European Constitution: A Semiotics Analysis of Ideology, Identity and Global Commun in Present-Day Europe' (2008) 21 *International Journal for the Semiotics of Law* 35, doi:10.1007/s11196-007-9055-z.

[7] I use the 'brave new world' coined by A Huxley in *Brave New World* (New York, Harper Perennial, 2006).

a nation's flag[8] and coat of arms. They are prone to signification through performance and even through music.[9] Good examples here are the text and the music of the national anthem or other official hymns played on official occasions and the performative-visual organisation of official or semi-official manifestations (especially in authoritarian and totalitarian regimes). Moreover, one should also take into account the performative signifiers which are being demonstrated through official or semi-official body language. This body language is typically arranged according to a scenario that aims to demonstrate the adherence to the imperatives of the predominant constitutional utopia. Furthermore, the official art depictions of state symbols and constitutional and constitutionally relevant phenomena and the architecture of state and public buildings are also important elements in the toolkit of visual constitutional semiotics devoted to constitutional utopias.[10] In parallel to these official or semi-official signifiers of constitutional utopia, we also should take into account the plurality of expressive forms belonging to unofficial art and architecture, music and the performing arts.

This all shows the huge semiotic importance of constitutional utopias and the extensive range of signifiers that can be used for their signification. From a symbolic-imaginary and semiotic perspective, they are the perfect object for the textual, visual, musical and performative signification of constitutional and constitutionally relevant meaning. This is due to the fact that they are inspirational and emotionally appealing phenomena which can be easily signified through a range of separate or interrelated signifiers belonging to multiple systems of signification of meaning.

Constitutional utopias are exciting because they offer a glimpse into the future.[11] Notably, their inspirational power acts in a opposite direction to that of constitutional myths, which mainly aim at the symbolic-imaginary and emotional representation of the past. In that regard, constitutional utopias and constitutional myths can be easily combined because they signify both the past and the future, offering inspiration that is simultaneously retrospective and prospective.

Constitutional utopias are also exciting due to the fact that they offer concrete legal shapes of an imaginary world and create an invented universe to serve as a pragmatic imperative of valid constitutional law. Thus, they are not just delusional

[8] A Wagner and S Marusek (eds), *Flags, Color, and the Legal Narrative: Public Memory, Identity, and Critique* (Springer, 2021) 1–745. On the flag as a symbol, see also C Castoriadis, *The Imaginary Institution of Society* (Cambridge, Polity Press, 1987) 131.

[9] See D Manderson, *Songs without Music: Aesthetic Dimensions of Law and Justice* (Berkeley, University of California Press, 2000) 1–299.

[10] On the semiotic role of court architecture, see L Mulcahy and E Rowden, *The Democratic Courthouse: A Modern History of Design, Due Process and Dignity* (Abingdon, Routledge, 2020) 1–370. For an informative case study of the architecture of the English courts, see C Graham, *Ordering Law: The Architectural and Social History of the English Law Court to 1914* (Abingdon, Routledge, 2003) 1–519.

[11] On the issues relating to the futurism of utopias, see R Saage, 'Is the Classic Concept of Utopia Ready for the Future?' in S Chrostowska and J Ingram (eds), *Political Uses of Utopia: New Marxist, Anarchist, and Radical Democratic Perspectives* (New York, Columbia University Press, 2016) 57–80.

fantasies derived from the theory of collective imagination, but have semiotic projections in constitutional text and textual constitutionalism which binds them to the authority of the state and its law.[12]

Constitutional utopias are also the perfect object of constitutional semiotics for three additional reasons. First, they are deeply interrelated with the other elements of symbolic-imaginary constitutionalism, which allows for their joint signification. The simultaneous representation of normative ideologies, constitutional myths and constitutional utopias through art, architecture and performance increases their power to convince. The multitude of interrelated signifieds strengthens the semiotic capacity of constitutional utopias and their symbolic-imaginary appeal. Constitutional utopias are conceptually intertwined, especially with normative ideologies and constitutional myths and mythologies. Hence, they are frequently interrelated in their representation in textual constitutionalism. This allows for the mutual reinforcement of their intellectual convincingness and symbolic capacity, triggering a range of combined significations in the various realms of visual and performative constitutionalism.

Second, constitutional utopias are the perfect signifieds for a range of signification systems – visual, musical, textual and performative. They attract the attention of the constitutionally framed socio-political community beyond the formal-procedural character of normative-institutional constitutionalism. Moreover, they are suitable for interrelated signification in all or most of these signification discourses. Thus, coordinated systems for their signification via both official and unofficial textual, visual and performative constitutionalism are largely used.

The possible signification of constitutional utopias in various signification systems has the following typical structure. Constitutional utopias are provided in constitutional text with their rational and normative-institutional components, but also with their ideological, mythological, futuristic, transformative and imaginary features. Simultaneously, they are represented in official and semi-official art forms, and are permanently demonstrated by the behaviour of state officials and citizens following procedures and formal routines that have a huge semiotic-signification impact on the perception of the characteristic of the utopia.

Since that moment, when a utopian action is practised or at least demonstrated with pragmatic behaviour, it is partially transformed into reality. Nevertheless, this is a multifaceted reality which has pragmatic but also ritual-like dimensions that appeal to collective constitutional archetypes and create or apply collective constitutional imaginaries.[13] In the course of its practical signification via performance and behaviour, constitutional utopias may not always have a radical, profound and all-encompassing transformative effect on the state, society and the human being;

[12] J Derrida, 'Force of Law: The "Mystical Foundation of Authority"' (1989–90) 11 *Cardozo Law Review* 920.

[13] For more on the interrelation between constitutional myths, constitutional rites and constitutional rituals, see J-M Rosselin, 'Making and Implementing the Rules of the Game: The Political Economy of Constitutional Myths and Rites' in A Marciano (ed), *Constitutional Mythologies: New Perspectives on Controlling the State* (Dordrecht, Springer, 2011) 171–74.

they may be just a façade. But this is an inspirational façade that has a potentially huge impact on collective emotions and collective constitutional imaginaries.

In that regard, constitutional utopias are much more dependent on constitutional semiotics and thus on symbolic-imaginary, visual and performative constitutionalism than on rational constitutionalism. This is because they may not become a fully fledged reality and in fact may even not be planned to be the grounds for a really new constitutional order.

At the same time, constitutional utopias have a deep transformative effect on constitutional culture and constitutional anthropology. They impact the way in which people believe, imagine and signify the utopian world.

Thus, constitutional utopias are closely related to the realm of the symbolic, the imaginary and the ideal, even if they are not well legally institutionalised, properly implemented and perform poorly on the ground. This is due to the fact that they shape the wide underground lake of the collective subconscious and unconscious, and mould constitutional archetypes which are then entrenched in cloud constitutionalism while simultaneously being demonstrated in official, semi-official and unofficial constitutional semiotics. They form the visible and feasible features of the systems for the signification of constitutional and constitutionally relevant meaning, deeply impacting not only symbolic-imaginary but also emotional constitutionalism.

It should be noted that there might be different logics for the representation of constitutional utopias in the various fields of signification which also predetermine reversed sequences for the signification of utopian content and meaning. Constitutional utopias may first be provided in the text of the constitution, being signified through the means of textual constitutionalism and textual semiotics, and only then represented in the other semiotic discourses via art, architecture, music or performance. Thus, the semiotic signifiers imposed by the constitutional legislator are subsequently further developed by the authoritative narrators, but also by informal and unofficial narrators, performers, visualisers etc.

Nevertheless, there might be also a second and reverse logic of semiotic representation. According to this, constitutional utopias might initially be launched in theory and especially in political, social and legal philosophy, and only then included in the constitution and constitutional law. In this case, textual constitutionalism is a reflection of the pre-legal parameters of constitutional utopias which are initially signified via meta-legal systems for the signification of constitutional and constitutionally relevant meaning.

It is also interesting to note that constitutional utopias are the only forms of symbolic-imaginary constitutionalism which can be signified via musical signifiers as well. Ideas, myths and mythologies have been a proper object of signification through music signifiers. These are mainly general philosophical and political ideas, some of which have metaphysical and even esoteric connotations.[14] Many of

[14] See Manderson (n 9) 1–299.

the works of Mozart and Wagner (and to a lesser extent Beethoven) are excellent examples of this. But music is less capable of signifying constitutional models in general or constitutional utopias in particular in a systematic way. Music forms can be used to represent constitutional ideas, ideals and utopias only as systems of signifiers with secondary and additional importance.

Indeed, this is quite rare and is difficult to be subsumed under a holistic model of constitutionalism serving for the signification of constitutional meaning defined, for example, as 'music constitutionalism', in contrast to the possibility for the definition and construction of textual, visual and performative constitutionalism as forms of constitutionalism distinguished on the basis of the type and system of signifiers, and the plain for the signification of constitutional and constitutionally relevant meaning. However, music is used for the signification of constitutional utopian content, although this is only done occasionally. The constitutional orders of authoritarian and totalitarian states clearly demonstrate that by systematically using the official musical repertoire for the demonstration of the constitutional utopias on which they are based, an emotionally appealing form for the signification of meaning through the musical signifiers can be provided. Such musical signifiers and the overall musically based signification of constitutional and constitutionally relevant meaning are typically used for political mobilisation and for the political self-identification of the public at large. This is also carried out in liberal and democratic regimes. For example, the utopia of universal brotherhood is signified via musical signifiers in Beethoven's 'Ode of Joy', which is the official anthem of the EU.

Third, constitutional utopias can be signified as holistic objects. They may be demonstrated via textual, visual, performative or even musical signifiers using an essentialist approach and focused on representing and transmitting the core ideas and the general message to the public. At the same time, constitutional utopias contain a range of elements which can be signified as separate objects of signification in the process of the constitutional signification of meaning. The fragmentation of the semiotic representation of constitutional utopias and the focusing of the semiotic process on their distinct features may be a result of pragmatic political reasons or may be used as a semiotic tactic for better semiotic exposure of the constitutional utopia both as a whole and of its parts. In practice, both approaches – the holistic and the partial, focused and fragmented representation of constitutional utopias – are used jointly in order to increase their overall emotional understanding and inspirational and symbolic impact on the collective constitutional imagination.

It should be mentioned that there is a partial overlap of the signifiers of constitutional utopias and other forms of symbolic-imaginary constitutionalism. This means that constitutional utopias are frequently signified in conjunction and even in a syncretic way with constitutional myths, normative ideologies and ideas, and constitutional codes. Sometimes they are represented together with stigmas, fetishes and taboos which frequently co-exist and interact in a rather complex way with constitutional utopias.

Constitutional utopias play an important role in symbolic-imaginary constitutionalism due to many reasons, three of which are of special importance and deserve additional attention. The first reason has already been analysed above – it consists in their huge semiotic potential and their ability to enchant and durably shape collective emotions and collective imaginaries in conjunction with their future-oriented prospective character, making them ideal instruments for representing the perfect future in constitutional terms and via constitutional semiotic signifiers.

The second reason is the need for the constitutional legislator to provide a holistic model for a better future. Thus, even relatively pragmatic and non-ideologically oriented constitutions use utopian elements and strategies or even provide soft versions of constitutional utopias. Indeed, the utopian features of the constitutional model stem from the need to offer a holistic version of the constitutional future to the addressees of constitutional law.

Each constitution needs to enchant and promise social and political reform. Thus, it has to be aspirational and even partially fictitious. If the constitution is a mere reflection of the factual socio-political constellations, then it is useless and purely descriptive. If it is entirely detached from reality and the concrete social, cultural and political determinants of the context, then it is purely fictitious, which may be the result of its utopian character. Nevertheless, a degree of mismatch between the imaginary-ideal and the real is necessary if the constitution is going to serve as a reformist plan and not as a descriptive or fictitious document. This partial mismatch inevitably entails a degree of utopian endeavour, which has to be signified to the public via the expressive means of constitutional semiotics.

The third reason is partially related to the second – it consists in the need to provide the constitutional project with a degree of transcendental attractiveness. Constitutional utopias are programmes for upgrading reality and for the achievement of a better or even a perfect constitutional future. These projects are value-based, inventive in terms of their institutional design, and require the admittance of intellectual concepts and imaginary superstructures with a meta-legal and in fact transcendental character. Constitutional utopias are transcendental projects because they are invitations to believe in higher realities and in the possibility to change the future via constitutional imagination.

Hence, constitutional utopias are tools for shaping and moulding the constitutional future. Thus, they can also be conceived as visions of the constitutional future improved and perfected through recourse to symbolic-imaginary means rooted in an ideal and meta-legal reality. This is the particular value of constitutional semiotics, which is only able to signify properly border between the ideal and the real, the existing and the desired, the factual, the normative and the imaginary. Constitutional semiosis is necessary in order to mark, represent and signify the counterpoint between the constitutional past, but especially the constitutional present and the constitutional future, which inevitably lies at the root of constitutional utopias. In that regard, constitutional utopias are both signifiers and signifieds: they are signifiers of meta-legal imaginaries with a transcendental character constructing a better constitutional order and thus the constitutional future; and they are signifieds which are represented through the semiotic means of textual, visual and performative constitutionalism and, to a limited extent, also via music.

A multitude of various constitutional utopias have been proposed in theory. Most of them had a predominant symbolic-imaginary dimension and thus were prone to semiotic signification and representation via text, art, architecture, music and performance. Many of them were transformed and implemented in constitutions and constitutional law, and tested in constitutional practice. Hence, constitutional modernity is based on rationalism as its intellectual pillar, but it was also largely dependent on forms of symbolic-imaginary constitutionalism in general and constitutional utopias in particular. That is why it was also searching for tools for the generation and expression of symbolic, imaginary and emotional content which can serve as a bridge between collective reason, the collective imagination and collective emotions. Constitutional utopias included all these components of modern constitutional enchantment and were signified through the means of constitutional semiotics.

Thus, politics has always been full of utopias and utopian thought, and constitutional politics has also been penetrated by constitutional utopias. Constitutional utopias proliferated especially in times of crisis and transition, when the opportunity for believing in a radical shift towards a bright new constitutional future is much greater. Such beliefs have been stabilised as normative beliefs and have been entrenched in the collective constitutional subconscious and unconscious with the help of a range of constitutional imaginaries. These imaginaries have largely been a result of a process of constitutional semiosis.

Typical examples of this are the political utopias of early modernity, which had the task of paving the way towards constitutional modernity and thus have been of huge constitutional relevance, and the constitutional utopias of the interwar period that promoted a range of authoritarian and totalitarian regimes. Constitutional utopias have been embedded in the socio-cultural context and were part of a general cultural movement aiming at the establishment of a new stage in civilisational development or even of a new constitutional civilisation. They have been signified in constitutional text and texture through the means of textual constitutionalism. Furthermore, they have also been signified in visual and performative constitutionalism, in art, architecture, literature and music. This extra-textual and extra-constitutional signification of constitutional utopias clearly demonstrates the huge dependence of constitutionalism on culture, anthropology and the overall structure of the collective constitutional imaginaries and collective constitutional archetypes.

Political utopias have existed in philosophy and political theory since premodern times. The emergence of modern constitutional civilisation has been paralleled by the rising level of interest in the perfect constitutional order framing a better state and society. Hence, from the eighteenth century onwards there has been a mushrooming of constitutional or constitutionally relevant utopias.

Many of them have remained theoretical, provoking only theoretical concerns, interest and debate, but others have been put into practice. They have been formally or substantially, implicitly or explicitly implemented as part of concrete constitutional models. Thus, they have impacted collective constitutional imaginaries and have been signified through a range of semiotic signifiers – textual, visual, performative or musical.

The most powerful utopias which have massively influenced modern constitutionalism can be organised into several groups. This typology of the utopias is based on their ideological distinction.[15] This shows that constitutional utopias are closely related to and dependent on another form of symbolic-imaginary constitutionalism: normative ideologies. Actually, constitutional utopias have an ideological character and underpinning. They can be conceived as an extreme variant of normative constitutional ideologies claiming the achievement of a perfect and thus hardly achievable constitutional future in practice.

The first group are the authoritarian and totalitarian constitutional utopias. The most important constitutional utopias have been practised in the context of different forms of authoritarianism. The most powerful and systematically implemented examples have been Nazism and the communist regime that has been constitutionally framed as Soviet-type democracy. Austrian and Italian fascism and different forms of military authoritarianism have also been based on powerful myths, mythologies and normative ideologies, some of which have gained the form, intensity and direction of utopias, and have to a certain extent been provided by the constitutions. Hence, many of them have not just impacted the socio-political order, but have also gained a constitutional dimension. Thus, they have been upgraded to constitutional utopias and have been signified through the means of textual constitutionalism.

Utopian elements have also been used for staging the constitutional foundations of theological and autocratic monarchies in the field of modern constitutionalism conceived as a game of imaginaries and a game of semiotic codes, as explained earlier in this book. They have been built upon the beliefs in the supernatural and divine origin of the monarch and have aimed at the establishment of a divine society following rules that have a religious origin. This has been the case with some European monarchies in the early modern era in the context of the transition to constitutionalism. A monarch with divine right existing at the centre of clear social hierarchy has also been part of utopias practiced in Asia (eg, in China and Japan). Religious utopias also underlie the Sharia-based regimes in some Muslim states.

Authoritarian and totalitarian utopias are usually based on concepts of hierarchy, authority and order, and presuppose a degree of transcendental predestination of the political and constitutional order. The main forms of their constitutional geometry entrenched in structured constitutional imaginaries and signified via

[15] Mannheim ((n 3) 192–264) differentiates between socialist-communist, conservative, liberal-humanitarian and Anabaptist utopias.

geometric metaphors are the hierarchy and the pyramid.[16] The concrete manifestations of these utopias are divergent and even contradictory, ranging from the belief in extraordinary leadership and public authority organised around some kind of Nietzschean superhero, to the trust in society based on predominance of classes and estates or, vice versa, the class-free society, and to the hope placed in the superpower of the community to impose its common will for the sake of the common good.

The second group is formed around a range of liberal utopias. Hence, the promotion of utopias and the ascription of constitutional shape and dimension to them is reserved not only to totalitarian or authoritarian orders. Liberal and democratic utopias have been abundant throughout the course of modern political and constitutional history.

Most recently, three powerful liberal utopias have been launched. Although not entirely and exclusively constitutional, they have had huge relevance for the conceptualisation and development of contemporary constitutionalism. These are Francis Fukuyama's belief in the liberal end of history,[17] Friedrich Hayek's trust in the self-ordering power of the free market,[18] and John Rawls' concept of the social contract based on free and just negotiation of the rules of the game under what he defines as the 'veil of ignorance'.[19]

The most powerful liberal constitutional utopias are organised on the basis of the assumption of the social contract. In fact, the social contract, the ability for the self-ordering of society and the magical role of free will, freedom and rationality have been the pillars of the symbolic-imaginary world of liberal orders, some of which have gained utopian character and forms.[20] This shows how rational constitutionalism can be transformed into imaginary exaggeration through utopian elements. The shapes of such irrational hyper-rationality are also detectable in formal-procedural legal positivist utopias.

The third group contains the democratic utopias. These are utopias aiming at the establishment of an egalitarian, politically active and inclusive society based on all-encompassing participation. A typical feature of democratic utopias is the ascription of a quasi-magical role to the majoritarian will. In fact, the community and its majority have a transcendental character and frequently perform the role

[16] On the concept and forms of constitutional geometry, see Part V of this book.

[17] See F Fukuyama, *The End of History and the Last Man* (London, Penguin, 1993) 1–448.

[18] See F Hayek, *Law, Legislation and Liberty, Volume 1: Rules and Order* (Chicago, University of Chicago Press, 1978) 1–191; F Hayek, *Law, Legislation and Liberty, Volume 2: The Mirage of Social Justice* (Chicago, University of Chicago Press, 1978) 1–210; and F Hayek, *Law, Legislation and Liberty, Volume 3: The Political Order of a Free People* (Chicago, University of Chicago Press, 1981) 1–258.

[19] See J Rawls, *A Theory of Justice* (Cambridge, MA, Belknap Press, 1999) 1–560; and L Imbeau and S Jacob, 'Is the "Veil of Ignorance" in Constitutional Choice a Myth? An Empirical Exploration Informed by a Theory of Power' in Marciano (n 13) 53–71.

[20] All these social and constitutional values are also bound to the image of the rational and reasonable person, human and citizen. On the mythological-imaginary character of these figures, see S Stern, 'The Legal Imagination in Historical Perspective' in A Amaya and M Del Mar (eds), *Virtue, Emotion and Imagination in Law and Legal Reasoning* (Oxford, Hart Publishing, 2020) 222–31.

of constitutional demiurge, while the people taken as a metaphysical entity function as a secular god. These characteristics of mass democracy have been widely discussed in the theory on the subject.

Democratic utopias are wide-ranging. They include radical democratic, direct democratic, participatory and revolutionary but also liberal-democratic and representative democratic utopias. They all aim at signifying the place, role and function of the people and the elites in the constitutional order. Thus, they use a range of signifiers relating to leaders, classes and masses. Democratic utopias have emerged in the constituent phase of the constitutional civilisation. A clear example is the theory of Jean-Jacques Rousseau and later also the Jacobin utopias. Nevertheless, the typical age of spread and implementation of democratic utopias has been the era of the emergence and development of mass democracy in the late nineteenth and twentieth centuries.

The fourth group are the constitutional utopias based on the suggestion for the political neutrality of the legal order and the possibility for the emancipation of law from the political will. Most of the theories of legal positivism belong to this group. Naturally, the most visible and clear example is the Kelsenian pure theory of law.

The fifth group includes the technocratic constitutional utopias.[21] These offer legitimation of expert-based governance justified through self-sufficient efficiency. In fact, technocratic utopias are extreme versions of rationalism. They are based on hyper-rationalism stretched between magic and deceit.[22] They provide further proof that excessive rationalism is in fact an irrational phenomenon where accountability, democratic control, checks and balances, freedom and self-determination are replaced by belief, trust and efficiency expectations. Technocratic utopias transform science and scientific-based technocracy into quasi-religious and ideological phenomena. Moreover, even technocracies can fail and they usually also have troublesome periods of inefficiency. Thus, they are also in need of justification through recourse to constitutional magic, which is usually delivered via utopian signifiers.

Technocratic utopias are gaining momentum due to three main reasons. The first reason is the constitutionalisation of international law and the spread of 'constitutionalism beyond statehood'.[23] These produce democratic detachment in international and supranational regimes, which requires ideological bridging of the democratic legitimacy gap that can also be accomplished through recourse to technocratic constitutional utopias. The second reason is the unfolding of the IT revolution and the upcoming medical revolution and biorevolution.

[21] A recently published book in this field is J Steffek, *International Organization as Technocratic Utopia* (Oxford, Oxford University Press, 2021) 1–256.

[22] See G Frankenberg, *Comparative Constitutional Studies: Between Magic and Deceit* (Cheltenham, Edward Elgar, 2018) 1–360.

[23] See P Dobner and M Loughlin (eds), *Twilight of Constitutionalism?* (Oxford, Oxford University Press, 2010); and N Walker, 'Taking Constitutionalism beyond the State' (2008) 56(3)*Political Studies* 519.

Transhumanism and post-humanism[24] are key examples of such biotechnological utopias that are prone to technocracy. The third reason is the constitutional polycrisis. Financial, migration, health and possibly also other forms of crisis and subsequent emergency regimes promote shifts in power from the people and democratically elected political institutions (eg, parliaments and governments) to expert bodies. Such a rise of 'emergency and crisis management technocracy' is a powerful trigger of constitutional utopias that will start to challenge and compete with traditional schemes for the legitimation of representative constitutional democracy.

All these forms of constitutional utopia are signified via a multitude of semiotic signifiers. They have developed their own style affecting all spheres where constitutional and constitutionally relevant meaning can be expressed, represented and signified. Indeed, the authoritarian and totalitarian utopias have been more consistent in the pursuit of the establishment of a holistic semiotic world with visual, performative, art and architecture, music and textual signification. The other variants of constitutional utopias have been persistent in that sense as well, although without such consistency and pathos. Starting with the uniforms of soldiers, state officials and magistrates,[25] going through official state symbols and finishing with the imposition of performative patterns of behaviour, they have striven to achieve the overall enchantment of the public and the imposition of durable collective constitutional imaginaries.

[24] See M Belov (ed), *The IT Revolution and its Impact on State, Constitutionalism and Public Law* (Oxford, Hart Publishing, 2021) 15–41; N Lee (ed), *The Transhumanism Handbook* (Dordrecht, Springer, 2019) 1–882; B Ross, *The Philosophy of Transhumanism: A Critical Analysis* (Bingley, Emerald Publishing, 2020), 1–200; and L Ferry, *La Revolution Transhumaniste* (Paris, Edition Plon, 2016) 1–216.

[25] See S Isani, 'Visual Semiotics of Court Dress in England and Wales: Failed or Successful Vector of Professional Identity' in A Wagner and W Pencak (eds), *Images in Law* (Farnham, Ashgate, 2006) 51–71.

PART IV

Visual Constitutionalism

1

Visual Constitutionalism as a Post-modern Semiotic Concept

The concept of visual constitutionalism requires special attention and thorough elaboration. The reason for this is that the mainstream legal theories that are traditionally predominant as explanatory paradigms in constitutional law, namely legal positivism and legal institutionalism, would question or even deny the possibility of the existence of such a phenomenon. Visual models of the public power institutions, visual metaphors of constitutional principles, values, ideas and design, visual signification of constitutional and constitutionally relevant signifieds through signifiers belonging to the realms of heraldry,[1] the visual arts[2] and architecture are clearly outside of the scope of institutionalism and positivism. Actually, they are beyond the scope of all traditional analytical paradigms in constitutionalism and constitutional law, with the exception of some novel branches and trends in socio-legal studies relating to the 'law-and-arts' movement.

Indeed, if we limit constitutionalism to valid law, equalizing constitutionalism with constitutional law, no matter whether constitutional law is defined in terms of norms, the broader realm of legal regulators (eg, including legal principles)[3] or is conceived as organised in institutions and if we focus entirely on rational and textual constitutionalism, then, of course, visual constitutionalism seems rather like a meta-legal, extra-legal and non-legal phenomenon. Stretched between rational and textual constitutionalism, visual constitutionalism appears as *tertium non datur*.

Hence, entirely normative-institutional and textual approaches to constitutionalism should make it impossible to engage with visual constitutionalism. This is the case if textual constitutionalism is conceptualised in its narrower version limiting constitutional texture to constitutional text. This issue and the relationship between constitutional text and constitutional texture have already been explored in detail in Part II of this book.

[1] See P Goodrich, *Legal Emblems and the Art of Law: Obiter Depicta as the Vision of Governance* (Cambridge, Cambridge University Press, 2013) 1–313.

[2] On the signification of legal signifieds through visual signifiers and the resulting emergence of visual law, see J Bainbridge, 'Visual Law: The Changing Signifiers of Law in Popular Visual Culture' in A Wagner and J Broekman (eds), *Prospects of Legal Semiotics* (Dordrecht, Springer, 2010) 193–95.

[3] See R Dworkin, *Taking Rights Seriously* (Cambridge, MA, Harvard University Press, 1978) 14–131; R Dworkin, *A Matter of Principle* (Cambridge, MA, Harvard University Press, 1985) 33–104; and R Alexy, *Theorie der Grundrechte* (Frankfurt am Main, Suhrkamp, 1994) 71–159.

Also from the viewpoint of rational constitutionalism, one can question visual constitutionalism and disqualify it as a misleading and rather perplexed concept that is fuzzy, imprecise and even dangerous. This is because it is not well-ordered or at least not composed in terms of systematic rationality based on an intelligible and reasonable plan structured around unambiguous concepts. Visual constitutionalism, being less systematic and at times even non-systematic and anti-systematic, which is not organised through precise ordering blocks such as norms, principles and institutions, should be deprived of any legitimate claim to be defined in terms of the constitution, constitutional law and constitutionalism.

In that regard, visual constitutionalism appears as a post-modern, fragmented, highly speculative and multidiscursive concept. It is dependent on a range of visual narratives. It is prone to interpretation that may be dubious, diverse and may expand to a range of visual narrators. It is centred on the signification of constitutionally relevant phenomena, but this signification can occur through a range of expressive means.[4] From the viewpoint of rational and normative-institutional constitutionalism, these varied visual signifiers are of questionable constitutional relevance. Most of them either do not have explicit constitutional standing or are considered as marginal constitutional phenomena from the viewpoint of the predominant institutionalist approach to constitutional law. This is the case, for example, for state symbols –coats of arms, flags etc.

To sum up, visual constitutionalism, if approached from the viewpoint of rational constitutionalism in its clearest theoretical forms (normativism, positivism and institutionalism), seems like pure fiction and even non-scientific invention disturbing the well-ordered concept of legal and constitutional order, and bringing fuzziness and delusion with it. The accumulation of a post-modern perspective with a semiotic approach and visual expressive forms can make the positivist or institutionalist lawyer and legal scholar rather suspicious of visual constitutionalism. Seen from such a perplexed and novel perspective, visual constitutionalism may seem to be almost delusional, obscuring, vague, speculative, imprecise and, last but not least, disturbing the logical equilibrium of the precise mixture of positivism, institutionalism and textualism[5] that have been balanced in such a cautious but systematic way in the course of the unfolding of Western legal modernity.

Delusional constitutionalism is impossible and wrong. Constitutionalism must be clear, rational and ordered. It is possible only if it is institutionalised, systematised and ordered, and if it is expressed in textual form. Constitutional semiosis

[4] See, eg, K Nikielska-Sekula and A Sesille (eds), *Visual Methodology in Migration Studies: New Possibilities, Theoretical Implications, and Ethical Questions* (Dordrecht, Springer, 2021) 1–368.

[5] The term 'textualism' is used in various senses in scientific literature. For some of its uses, see, eg, R Rorty, 'Nineteenth-Century Idealism and Twentieth-Century Textualism' (1981) 64(2) *The Monist* 155, https://doi.org/10.5840/monist198164211; W Eskridge, 'The New Textualism' (1989–90) 37 *UCLA Law Review* 621; T Leigh Grove, 'Which Textualism?' (2020) 134 *Harvard Law Review* 265; J Molot, 'The Rise and Fall of Textualism', *GWU Law School, Public Law Research Paper*, No 134, available at: https://ssrn.com/abstract=696681; and J Manning, 'Textualism and Legislative Intent' (2005) 91 *Virginia Law Review* 419, http://dx.doi.org/10.2139/ssrn.2853690. Nevertheless, I use 'textualism' differently from the meaning implied in the US theory examples given above.

is possible only through the medium of constitutional text and through an exclusive recourse to textual constitutionalism. These are the postulates of rational and textual constitutionalism in its traditional positivist and institutionalist manifestations. But is this really the case? Is it not true that constitutionalism – as a socio-legal phenomenon, as 'law in action' and 'law as imagination'[6] – rests on reason, but also on emotion, symbols, magic and deceit?[7] The latter seems to be true since people are not only rational but also emotional creatures, and the visual signification of reality triggers powerful emotions with huge socio-political implications. These emotions possess the potential to sustain and support or, conversely, to undermine and distort the practical perception and performance of the constitution and constitutional law.[8]

The construction of the socio-political world has always been based on the interplay between political engineering and constitutional tradition. The result of this process is typically a mixture of rationally created and imposed external models of 'better constitutional order' and inherited forms of constitutionalism, constitutional axiology and constitutional design. In order to be legitimate and well accepted, such a constitutional model needs to gain convincing power that is based on collective imaginaries. Moreover, it frequently results in semiotic content that expresses and represents these imaginaries to the public. This is even more valid for the organisation and comprehension of constitutional order that is based on constitutional imaginaries, some of which have visual manifestations. In that regard, visual constitutionalism and visual constitutional semiotics may or actually should be perceived as a precondition for the due performance and the emotionally convincing understanding of constitutional 'law in books' in the socio-legal reality and its supportive collective imaginaries.

Visual constitutionalism is yet another projection of constitutional magic and deceit[9] in the sphere of official visual signifiers of statehood and in the visual arts and architecture. It is part of the art of visual-emotional enchantment of the constitutionally framed socio-legal community through the visual signification of constitutional phenomena.

At the same time, visual constitutionalism is not purely magical, deceptive and imaginary; it is also rational to a great extent. Sometimes it unfolds on the basis of rational plans, strategies and agendas for the visual enchantment of the constitutional public and players. It contains a rational core represented and signified through visual symbols. This is particularly true of official visual constitutionalism,

[6] On the concept of visual imagination and the consequences it has for constitutionalism and constitutional law, see Z Oklopcic, *Beyond the People: Social Imaginary and Constituent Imagination* (Oxford, Oxford University Press, 2018) 19–22.

[7] In that regard, I rather agree with Gunter Frankenberg, who wrote a prominent book on the role of magic and deceit in constitution, constitutionalism and constitutional law. See G Frankenberg, *Comparative Constitutional Studies: Between Magic and Deceit* (Cheltenham, Edward Elgar, 2018) 1–360.

[8] For more on the psychological reasons and triggers of deceit, see K Lynch, 'An Agentive Non-intentionalist Theory of Self-Deception' (2017) 47(6) *Canadian Journal of Philosophy* 779.

[9] Frankenberg (n 7) 1–360.

but is also applicable to semiotic strategies implied in and implemented through forms of unofficial visual constitutionalism.

Visual constitutionalism is also rational because it frames the process of the semiotic signification of constitutional phenomena via symbolic-imaginary visual signifiers. Thus, visual constitutionalism exists at the point of intersection between rational, emotional, normative-institutional and symbolic-imaginary constitutional discourses. Nevertheless, it remains an autonomous form of constitutionalism.

Textual constitutionalism seems to be much more incompatible with visual constitutionalism than rational constitutionalism. In a sense, textual and visual constitutionalism may appear to be semiotic alternatives, being different means or plains for the unfolding of constitutional semiosis. Constitutional law is either limited to 'textual law' – law that is confined within the text and is expressed only through words or spreads beyond it. If constitutional law – even in the form of practised law and not in the positivist account of law as a normative model – can also be found beyond legal text, then we are coping with a different conceptual paradigm that goes beyond the textual dimension and textual entrenchment of the constitution, constitutional law and constitutionalism.

In fact, this dilemma also concerns the problem of the scope of constitutional semiotics. It results in different and competing understandings of the nature, scope and expressive means of constitutional semiotics. If textual constitutionalism is the only form of expression of constitutional meaning and if words are the only tools for the semiotic signification of constitutional signifieds, then visual constitutionalism is deprived of any raison d'etre. On the contrary, if constitutional meaning is also contained and represented beyond words, and thus beyond constitutional text and textual constitutionalism, then visual constitutionalism is an important phenomenon offering a valuable toolkit for the semiotic signification with huge constitutional relevance. In the latter case, textual and visual constitutionalism are the two most important instruments for the shaping of symbolic-imaginary and emotional constitutionalism. In that regard, they appear to be the two arms of constitutional semiotics and the main sets of instruments for the constitutional signification of meaning. Visual and textual constitutionalism may thus be perceived as the two main containers of semiotic signifiers of constitutional and constitutionally relevant meaning.[10]

The main claim of modern constitutional law is that it is systematically ordered. Systematic ordering traditionally seems to be possible only in and through written text. The systematic constitution and constitutional law require textuality. They are based on the development of textual constitutionalism. Modern systematic constitutional law is confined within a codified constitution that can eventually

[10] On the role of visual semiology in understanding meaning, its representation and its role in constructing imaginaries, see G Rose, *Visual Methodologies: An Introduction to Researching with Visual Materials* (New York, SAGE Publications, 2016) 106–47.

be expanded and further developed by other sources of constitutional law. These sources of law must again be systematically written and textually entrenched.

In such a context, visual constitutionalism appears as a challenge to the rational, systematic and written nature of the modern constitution and constitutional law. From the perspective of Western legal modernity, law in general and constitutional law in particular seem to be rational and systematically well-ordered only when they are written and safeguarded by the implicit rationality of text and scripture. According to one of the fundamental beliefs of modernity, written law can be unreasonable, non-systematic and badly ordered. However, there is a much higher chance of rationality, reasonableness and order if it is in written form. Visual law may be a nice metaphor, but it is a delusion that impedes rationality. Nevertheless, the impossibility of visual law does not preclude the existence of visual dimensions and aspects of law.[11]

In more radical terms, textual and visual constitutionalism may even seem to be competitive and antipode concepts. Textual and visual means for expression of meaning can be alternatives that may even be mutually exclusive. Textuality and visual reality produced by fine arts, sculpture, architecture and even pop art may be conceived as different, competitive and antipode fields for the representation and signification of constitutionally relevant meaning.[12] They may be understood as alternative realities allowing for the unfolding of constitutional semiosis and for the development of constitutional semiotic processes.[13]

Actually, textual and visual constitutionalism are alternative semiotic realities or, more precisely, competitive plains for constitutional semiosis only if one admits the existence of constitutionalism beyond constitutional text and texture. If constitutionalism is perceived as a multilayered and multidiscursive phenomenon that has not only normative but also socio-legal and imaginary aspects, then we can proceed with the conceptualisation not only of visual but also of symbolic-imaginary, performative and emotional constitutionalism. However, it will be shown that there are cases where visual constitutionalism is expressed in and through textual constitutionalism. These are the forms of official visual constitutionalism framed by the constitutional and legislative provisions on visual state symbols such as coats of arms, flags and, more rarely, the uniforms of the magistrates and administrators.

[11] See R Khorakiwala, *From the Colonial to the Contemporary: Images, Iconography, Memories, and Performances of Law in India's High Courts* (Oxford, Hart Publishing, 2020) 1–296.

[12] On the signification of legal meaning through animation and comic signifiers, see T Giddens, 'Lex Comica: On Comics and Legal Theory' and G Ferris and C Lunt, 'Devil's Advocate: Representation in Heroic Fiction, *Daredevil* and the Law' in T Giddens (ed), *Graphic Justice: Intersections of Comics and Law* (Abingdon, Routledge, 2015) 8–17; in T Giddens, *Graphic Justice: Intersections of Comics and Law* (Abingdon, Routledge, 2015) 8–16 and 36–54 respectively.

[13] For interesting and original ideas on law, graffiti and street art, see T Cresswell, 'The Crucial "Where" of Graffiti: A Geographical Analysis of Reactions to Graffiti in New York' (1992) 10(30 *Environment and Planning D: Society and Space* 329; T Flessas and L Mulcahy, 'Limiting Law: Art in the Street and Street in the Art' (2018) 14(2) *Law, Culture and the Humanities* 219; and A Young, *Street Art, Public City: Law, Crime and the Urban Imagination* (Abingdon, Routledge, 2013) 1–200.

This broader understanding of constitutionalism underlies the whole analysis offered in this book. The fundamental belief that serves as a pillar of this book is that constitutionalism is a much wider and complex phenomenon that expands and unfolds beyond the written constitution and written constitutional law. From that perspective, visual constitutionalism is not only possible, but de facto exists. And it is not just barely present, but its existence is clear and requires proper explanation. Such explanation is necessary not only for conceptual clarity or for the sake of better and clearer theory; it is also required by the evolving socio-legal reality in which the visual forms proliferate and have increasing importance.[14]

Constitution and constitutional law are rarely read by the people. Textual and rational constitutionalism is becoming more and more complex and technical. Thus, it is increasingly a matter for legal and political experts.

However, the constitution, constitutionalism and constitutional law are experienced, performed, expressed, visualised and felt, and not just read, implemented and obeyed. The people understand constitutional phenomena while they practise them on the ground in the empirical forms of performative constitutionalism. They feel them through their individual and collective emotions that together produce emotional constitutionalism and impact symbolic-imaginary constitutionalism. They imagine them in the collective imaginaries that jointly produce symbolic-imaginary constitutionalism. Last but not least, they express them, see them and communicate them in and through the forms of visual constitutionalism.

In that regard, visual constitutionalism is constitutional discourse that gains momentum especially in the contemporary world that is dominated by visual perceptions. The culture of visuality is promoted by the new media.[15] It is enhanced by the rising importance of visual media and visual arts. To an extent, modern (and especially post-modern) society is a visual society and contemporary people are increasingly relying on visual symbols signifying constitutional phenomena and the socio-political reality. In such a context, visual constitutionalism also has to be understood as part of contemporary visual culture[16] – dynamic, fragmented, post-modern, asymmetric and direct.[17]

Visual constitutionalism at the beginning of the twenty-first century is predetermined by the post-modern fragmentation of identities, concepts and socio-legal perceptions. It is defined by the increasing pluralism of visual and intellectual shapes and forms. It is also triggered by the emergence of pluralism of realities perceived, felt and performed by the constitutional players – a phenomenon that

[14] In that regard, see also R Sherwin, *Visualizing Law in the Age of the Digital Baroque: Arabesques and Entanglements* (New York, Routledge, 2011) 1–256.

[15] See J Helfland, *Screen: Essays on Graphic Design, New Media, and Visual Culture* (Princeton, Princeton Architectural Press, 2001) 1–208.

[16] See L Mulcahy, 'Sociology of Legal Images' in J Přibáň (ed), *Research Handbook on the Sociology of Law* (Cheltenham, Edward Elgar, 2020).

[17] For more on visual imagination and the role of images in law, see Sherwin (n 14) 1–256; and R Sherwin, 'Introduction to Picturing Justice: Images of Law and Lawyers in the Visual Media' (1995–96) 30(4) *University of San Francisco Law Review* 891.

is compared by some authors to the 'digital baroque'.[18] The processes of fragmentation and pluralisation mostly affect the socio-legal or empirical dimension of visual constitutionalism, its unofficial variants and forms expressed through the visual arts and architecture. They are not applicable – or at least not to a great extent – to official visual constitutionalism relating to formal visual significations of constitutional phenomena through legally provided and determined signifiers.

The fragmentation of constitutional perception is typical in post-modern societies, but has also spread globally due to the export of constitutional civilisation, objective factors and the overall zeitgeist. The fragmentation of constitutional reality is not necessarily legal in the sense of the decomposition of the system of valid law.[19] It does not automatically relate to the normative-institutional order and thus to normative-institutional constitutionalism, which may itself remain holistic. In fact, it is the way in which it is perceived, practised and visualised that is becoming fragmented and pluralistic.

The shapes and forms through which constitutional phenomena are signified in the performative and visual discourse, and thus define their imprint on collective constitutionally relevant emotions and on collective constitutional imaginaries proliferate. The decompression of traditional and established imaginary, symbolic and visual constitutional realities is visible. It is stimulated by the same factors that produce the post-modern insecurity of the human, the citizen and society. Moreover, our constitutional orders are exposed to unprecedented pressure in terms of visual representation and visual signification of meaning in increasingly pluralistic and diverse ways through a range of conventional and unconventional shapes and forms. This trend for visual representation and signification is not necessarily bound by common or unifying visual logic, but rather includes a range of semiotic forms for the representation and signification of meaning.

Indeed, the main signifieds in constitutional semiotics remain the ideas and concepts of hierarchy, authority, power, freedom and justice.[20] They are signified directly or through their manifestations in the fields of human rights and constitutional institutions. Territory, institutional orders and normative structures are among the main signified objects that are symbolically represented in supra-textual and meta-textual discourses, including in visual constitutionalism.

However, the range of signifiers used for the visual signification of constitutional and constitutionally relevant meaning as well as the standpoints for visual symbolic-imaginary representation increasingly vary. Signifiers may be legally provided or derived from the law in action. They may enjoy legal normativity or factual convincingness and persuasive power. Standpoints vary according to the range of actors in the semiotic process of the visual signification of meaning. Visual representation may stem from official players or may be the consequence

[18] ibid.

[19] On fragmentation in international law, see M Koskenniemi, 'Constitutionalism as Mindset: Reflections on Kantian Themes about International Law and Globalization' (2006) 8(1) *Theoretical Inquiries in Law* 13 et seq.

[20] On the signification of hierarchy in law, see Goodrich (n 1) 89–124.

of informal visual semiosis, resulting in constitutionally relevant visual depictions produced by visual art and architecture.[21]

In that regard, a brief clarification on the plurality of semiotic players in the different constitutional discourses is needed, which will demonstrate the overall resemblance between the visual and emotional, performative, and textual forms of constitutionalism as well as their conceptual difference compared to normative-institutional constitutionalism. The plurality of semiotic players and especially the existence of unofficial and not explicitly institutionalised semiotics of visual and emotional, performative, and textual constitutionalism have important consequences that expand constitutional semiotics beyond the realm of state-centred constitutionalism in the sphere of societal constitutionalism.[22]

Normative-institutional constitutionalism can be only official. This is because it is contained in legal provisions and is reduced to the valid law. This does not mean that normative-institutional constitutionalism is reducible to written law. Constitutional norms and institutions also exist beyond textual constitutionalism, but they are still official. In contrast, visual, emotional, performative, symbolic-imaginary and textual constitutionalism may contain both official and unofficial parts.

Emotional constitutionalism is based on common feelings spread through the constitutionally framed socio-political community and relating to constitutional phenomena. Thus, emotional constitutionalism may be unofficial, societal and dispersed. However, there is also an official element to emotional constitutionalism. Official constitutionally relevant emotions may be expressed, for example, through official days of remembrance and mourning or official days of celebration of great national events, victories etc. The date of 4 July in the US and 14 July in France are good examples of this. These events may have explicit constitutional standing. They may also be generally provided by the constitution or may have legislative standing provided by other sources of constitutional law.

Constitutionally relevant emotions are expressed and thus institutionalised in many constitutions. This means that many constitutions contain explicit or much more frequently implicit attitude towards fear, hate, love, admiration,[23] homage, rejection, frustration and other feelings that ought to be collectively experienced by the constitutionally framed socio-political community. The research of constitutional emotions is of huge importance for constitutional semiotics. It has to be accomplished in the context of emotional constitutionalism as a framing analytical paradigm. Due to space constraints, such analysis cannot be undertaken here.

[21] See K Walton, *Mimesis as Make-Believe: On the Foundations of Representational Arts* (Cambridge, MA, Harvard University Press, 1993) 1–480.

[22] See G Teubner, *Constitutional Fragments: Societal Constitutionalism and Globalization* (Oxford, Oxford University Press, 2012) 38–42; and J Přibáň, *Constitutional Imaginaries: A Theory of European Societal Constitutionalism* (Abingdon, Routledge, 2020) 1–251.

[23] See A Amaya, 'Admiration, Exemplarity and Judicial Virtue' in A Amaya and M Del Mar (eds), *Virtue, Emotion and Imagination in Law and Legal Reasoning* (Oxford, Hart Publishing, 2020) 25–45.

Performative constitutionalism rests on the signification of constitutional law in books through public performance shaping the law in action. Such performance may be official if it is related to the official rituals of the state provided in the constitution or other sources of law.

The official parades, manifestations and ceremonies are also forms of the joint accomplishment of both emotional and performative constitutionalism. Some of these ceremonies may be purely declarative, political and symbolic. In such cases, they are focused on their task of symbolically representing statehood, society and their mutuality and reciprocity. However, there may also be acts of performative constitutional semiotics that have not only symbolic but also constitutive effect. Clear examples of this are the official taking of oaths of heads of state, MPs, ministers, magistrates etc that are features of the procedures of taking office. The same is true for coronation ceremonies in monarchies or for official openings of parliamentary sessions.

The performative constitutional signification of meaning and thus performative constitutional semiotics may also be unofficial. In such a case, it should be based on the daily performance of the constitutional players that has semiotic relevance in signifying constitutional signifiers through behavioural acts and thus via performative signifiers. Hence, the official state and public protocol, ceremonial and procedures form part of the official performative constitutionalism, while the other performative acts of the constitutional players are elements of its informal part.

Textual constitutionalism includes both official parts and unofficial parts. Official textual constitutionalism is contained in the legal texts framed as sources of constitutional law. The unofficial parts are the texts that are produced by the authoritative narrators of the community beyond the state institutions.

Similarly, there are official visual signifiers of the state, constitutionalism and constitutional law, but there are also a wide range of unofficial visual signifiers of constitutionally relevant phenomena which result in the expansion of visual constitutionalism. Hence, visual constitutionalism can be either official or unofficial. It can rest upon official, legally defined forms of semiotic signification of meaning, but it may also include unofficial visual semiotic processes grounded in signifiers and produced by semiotic players that are beyond the realm of valid law.

In that regard, what has been said in relation to the increasing plurality of the authoritative speakers of the community regarding textual constitutionalism[24] is even more applicable to the sources of visual representation and the key players of visual constitutionalism. In contrast to textual constitutionalism, where there is a traditional claim for the limitation of authoritative narrators and for the justification of the inclusion of additional speakers and writers in the 'club of authoritative speakers', the range of visual narrators and producers of visual signification of constitutionally relevant meaning is almost unlimited. This is due to the unlimited

[24] See Part II of this book.

scope of the unofficial visual semiotics of constitutionalism and constitutional law. It is bound by a single condition – to signify constitutionally relevant phenomena and constitutional content that relates to the object of constitutional law, namely constitutional axiology, constitutional design relating to human rights and institutions, and also constitutional ontology and teleology.

The unlimited nature and scope of visual creators – the visual narrators of constitutional semiotic stories and designers of visual constitutional signifiers – is applicable to unofficial visual constitutionalism. These creators can be visual artists and architects, but also other producers of visual content with constitutional relevance. Thus, the visual semiotic constitutional community – both in terms of the producers and addressees of visual signifiers – is almost unlimited in its size. This makes visual constitutionalism both elitist and democratic. It is elitist in terms of official visual constitutionalism and the visual design of official building and symbols of the state (eg, governmental buildings and official depictions of constitutional phenomena). However, it is also democratic, since it includes all visualisers of constitutional content that have a practical influence on the constitutional perception and imagination of the constitutionally framed socio-legal community. In that regard, conceptually, the boundaries of the visual community targeted by visual constitutionalism are almost unlimited.

2

Official Visual Constitutional Semiotics

The Constitutional Embeddedness and Constitutional Relevance of Official Public Visuals

Official visual constitutionalism includes visual content defined in the constitution and the other sources of constitutional law. Due to the explicit legal framing of official visual constitutionalism and the symbols that it includes in valid constitutional law, its signifiers are produced only by official constitutional narrators: the constitutional and the ordinary legislators. Thus, official visual constitutionalism is produced, framed and described in textual constitutionalism.

Official visual constitutionalism includes the official visual signifiers. The range of official visual signifiers includes flags and coats of arms of international and supranational organisations, states, units of federations and confederations and other subnational units of regional and local self-government. Their ontology and teleology make them elements of constitutionalism – in this case, of both visual and textual constitutionalism. In other words, they can be defined as phenomena with constitutional relevance because they are regulated by the constitution and other sources of constitutional law, and thus have constitutional standing. Another reason is that they are the official symbols of the state symbolising its constitutional independence, autonomy, standing and other aspects of public power.

The official visual signifiers that jointly form the official part of visual constitutionalism are the official flags and coats of arms. Other official visual signifiers are the uniforms of soldiers, magistrates, state administrators etc. These possess more indirect constitutional relevance since they are not explicitly provided in the constitution and other sources of constitutional law. However, they play an important role in the symbolic representation of key state functions, constitutional institutions and their socio-political constitutionally framed role. These formal visuals, which visually express the constitutional role of different legal and administrative professions or of other holders of state and public power, are organised according to specific and common semiotic logic. Together, they represent the idea of statehood while separately they stand for different constitutional ideas that are signified visually: justice, authority, hierarchy, compulsion, power etc.

Thus, the flag, its composition and colours are also a very important part of official visual constitutionalism.[1] Flag, together with coats of arms, are important semiotic phenomena. They are instruments for the visual expression of the semiotic signification of meaning, most of which has huge constitutional relevance.[2] They may signify proximity, similarity and belongingness or difference and divergence.[3]

The visual details included in state symbols are bearers of explicit and implicit, official and overt, but also encoded and hidden meaning. This is quite clear in the case of state heraldry where different elements of coats of arms and other state symbols serve as signifiers of constitutionally relevant codes, myths, mythologies and signs of belongingness. State heraldry will not be explored in detail here.[4] However, it should be noted that lions, eagles, stars, pyramids, pentagrams, the sun, the moon and many other visual forms are powerful signifiers of meaning. They draw lines of state continuity (eg, in the case of the two-headed eagle visible in the coat of arms of Russia and also of Montenegro and Albania, and showing an imaginary line of inheritance with the Byzantine civilisation) and of lines of belongingness (eg, the case of the cross on the Scandinavian flags or the crescent on the flags of some Muslim countries). It should be mentioned that sometimes the resemblance is coincidental – for example, this is the case for lions in the coats of arms of the UK and Bulgaria.

State symbols – especially flags and coats of arms – are metaphors for power and belongingness.[5] They are not only visual depictions of statehood, but also bearers of deep semantic and epistemic content. In fact, they are semiotic power centres with strategic importance in terms of drawing demarcation lines of cultural and civilisational belongingness.[6] In that sense, they are both inclusive and exclusive. In any case, they are nodes in the process of signification of ideas that not only determine constitutionalism in civilisational terms, but also serve as bridges between constitutional cultures and civilisations, and between ages and epochs in the constitutional development.[7] They are points of intersection between secular

[1] See A Wagner and S Marusek (eds), *Flags, Color, and the Legal Narrative: Public Memory, Identity, and Critique* (Dordrecht, Springer, 2021) 1–745; and T Zhang and Y Shi, 'Color Preference and Color Meaning in the Context of Flags' (2020) 48 *Social Behavior and Personality: an International Journal* 1–9.

[2] See J Becker, C Butz, D Sibley et al, 'What Do National Flags Stand for? An Exploration of Associations across 11 Countries' (2017) 48(3) *Journal of Cross-cultural Psychology*, https://doi.org/10.1177/0022022116687851.

[3] See T Eriksen and R Jenkins, *Flag, Nation and Symbolism in Europe and America* (Abingdon, Routledge, 2007) 1–208; K Cerulo, 'Symbols and the World System: National Anthems and Flags' (1993) 8(2) *Sociological Forum* 243, https://doi.org/10.1007/BF01115492.

[4] For interesting research on emblems and their role as semiotic signifiers of legal ideas, see P Goodrich, *Legal Emblems and the Art of Law: Obiter Depicta as the Vision of Governance* (Cambridge, Cambridge University Press, 2013) 1–313.

[5] See S Callahan and A Ledgerwood, 'On the Psychological Function of Flags and Logos: Group Identity Symbols Increase Perceived Entitativity' (2016) 110(4) *Journal of Personality and Social Psychology* 528.

[6] For colour as an identity signifier, see F Janssens, *Identity Colour Codes: How Colours Unite Us All* (Amsterdam, BIS Publishers, 2014) 1–304.

[7] See Eriksen and Jenkins (n 3) 1–208; Cerulo (n 3).

and religious, overt and hidden visual ideologies.[8] Visual ideologies are the ideologies that determine the conceptual core of visual constitutionalism. They also serve as a bridge between symbolic-imaginary and visual constitutionalism.

For example, the cross and the crescent are signs of belongingness to Christian or Muslim civilisations and traditions. The same is true for the Star of David, which is used on the flag of the state of Israel and shows continuity with Jewish traditions. All three religious signs are transformed into constitutional visuals by virtue of their inclusion in visual constitutionalism. Thus, they go beyond their religious connotations and overall signify cultural belongingness with its axiological core and constitutional implications.

The star is a powerful symbol used in both national and supranational visual constitutionalism. It is used in all types of constitutional regimes – liberal-republican (the US), liberal-democratic (Italy), authoritarian-populist (Venezuela) and communist (the USSR, the former communist states, Cuba etc). The star is also used in constitutional regimes beyond statehood that have supranational constitutionalism, such as the EU.[9]

Key elements of Soviet-type or communist visual semiotics and visual constitutionalism are the cogwheel, the hammer, the reaping hook, the compass and other working toolkit elements form a common semiotic framework of Soviet-type constitutional regimes in Europe, but also beyond the 'old continent'. Sometimes these symbols of Soviet-type constitutionalism are combined with local visuals with constitutional semiotic importance depicted on official state symbols such as flags. Examples are the machete depicted on the national flag of Angola or the hoe and weapon included on the national flag of Mozambique.

Furthermore, several national coats of arms include symbols from national historical, political and constitutional mythology. Such coats of arms are common in Latin America (Mexico, Bolivia, and Ecuador), Africa (Angola and Mozambique) and Asia (India, Cambodia and Kyrgyzstan), but are also represented in other parts of the world such as Canada and Lebanon.

The colours of the flag are also important signifiers of meaning that has overall relevance for constitutionalism.[10] Such importance relates not only to the emotional appeal of the flag, but also to the demonstration of belongingness to groups of states and to constitutional families and civilisations. Thus, the colours of the flag and their organisation and composition also have civilisational appeal and importance.[11]

The colours of the flag are bearers of meaning taken alone or in conjunction with their organisation as part of the overall colour scheme of the flag (as well as

[8] See Zhang and Shi (n 1).

[9] See P Dobner and M Loughlin (eds), *Twilight of Constitutionalism?* (Oxford, Oxford University Press, 2010); and N Walker, 'Taking Constitutionalism beyond the State' (2008) 56(3) *Political Studies* 519.

[10] See Wagner and Marusek (n 1) 1–745.

[11] Zhang and Shi (n 1). See also Callahan and Ledgerwood (n 5); and Janssens (n 6) 1–304.

the coat of arms).[12] There are actually families of flags that can be grouped together on the basis of colour and colour structure. The tricolour flag has had important semiotic meaning at least since the French Revolution and has influenced a great number of flags throughout the world. It has huge importance for modern visual constitutionalism and visual constitutional semiotics. For example, the Italian national flag, which was inspired by the French tricolour flag, has itself served as a source of inspiration for a range of other flags such as the Hungarian and Bulgarian flags.

The four-colour flag, including red, green, black and white, has been used with a range of variations in the Arab world. Thus, these colours may be considered as a semiotic marker of the Arab civilisation and its visual semiotics. Similarly, use of blue, red and white is widespread on flags in the Slavic world, Thus, this group of colours can be viewed as a symbol of the Slavic visual constitutionalism, although there are four visible exceptions to these pan-Slavic colours: Bulgaria, North Macedonia, Montenegro and Poland.

The meaning of colours is important. A clear example of this point is given by the flag of Bulgaria. Officially Bulgaria is supposed to be a Slavic state, so the colours of its flag have to be blue, red and white. However, blue has been replaced with green due to the huge influence of the masonic movement and especially of Giuseppe Garibaldi on the Bulgarian revolutionary elite and, more precisely, on its key ideologists and strategic leaders – Georgi Rakovski and Vasil Levski. In that regard, green was an important colour in the Bulgarian revolutionary movement in the nineteenth century.

The colours of liberalism – blue and yellow – have been used on the flags of some states that emerged in the Western Balkans after the fall of Yugoslavia, such as Bosnia and Herzegovina and Kosovo.

The flag of Kosovo also resembles the flag of Cyprus, since both of them contain a depiction of the state territory. Thus, the idea of territorial integrity is also signified through constitutional semiotics in official visual constitutionalism.

[12] See Wagner and Marusek (n 1) 1–745; and H Amavilah, 'Flags, Constitutions, and the Well-Being of Nations' (2008) 11368 *MPRA Paper* 1.

3

Visual Constitutionalism and Digital Constitutional Semiotics

'Iconisation', 'Emojification' and 'Memefication' as Forms of the Signification of Constitutionally Relevant Meaning

The pressure for the visual representation and visual signification of meaning results from the increasing adherence of people to visual forms of communication in general and of political and constitutional communication in particular. New media and especially Facebook are clear proof of the striving towards visual representation of meaning and the efficiency of the visual signification of constitutional and constitutionally relevant content.

In the current context, when the IT revolution is gaining momentum, it would not be an exaggeration to say that if something is not visually represented and visually communicated, then it has almost no effect on public opinion. 'Show it or leave it' – this seems to be a motto of the new generation that has been raised and educated worldwide (but especially in the technologically developed countries) in the context of a radically new visual reality. Even the expression of emotions is accomplished through formalised visual signifiers of meanings such as emoticons.

In addition, the activity of state and public power institutions is becoming increasingly digital. Remote sittings, including remote debates and remote voting, have also recently been promoted by the COVID-19 pandemic and the impossibility of holding regular sittings. Thus, the new visual reality of the digital age has also been largely embraced by parliaments, governments and courts. The raising of digital hands, digital applause and other forms of digital expression of emotions through formal digital visual signifiers of meaning have greatly enriched the traditional semiotics and the semiotic toolkit of the visual constitutionalism related to public power institutions. The visual world of collective deliberation and decision-making included in the sphere of constitutionalism and public policy-making has been deeply penetrated by platforms for distant and thus digital discussion and voting. In a sense, the emerging digital constitutionalism has been 'overzoomed' and thus submerged by the visual logic of electronic platforms with their systems for the signification of meaning. Thus, the expressive, emotional and performative world of practical policy-making has been framed by the realm of new digital visual reality with its semiotic signifiers and specific visual logic.[1]

This new visual reality with huge semiotic importance has been produced by the IT revolution that has meanwhile interfered with pressures for digitalisation stemming from emergency and pandemic constitutionalism.[2] It has led to the emergence of digital constitutionalism addressing the context of an algorithmic society.[3] Digital constitutionalism is a new strand of constitutionalism that emerged in the late twentieth century, but became increasingly important at the beginning of the twenty-first century and has gained momentum during the COVID-19 lockdown policies that resulted in a massive push for digitalisation of the world and the constitutional system in particular. Digital constitutionalism includes not only algorithmic constitutionalism, but also all other aspects of the impact of the IT revolution on the state, constitutionalism and constitutional law.[4] Digital constitutionalism has its own visual reality of semiotic signifiers representing constitutional and constitutionally relevant meaning.

In other words, digital constitutionalism has its own visual world and its own particular visual constitutionalism with a distinct visual ideology[5] and logic of the semiotic signification and representation of meaning. Digital visual constitutionalism is part of visual constitutionalism, with certain specifics imposed by the imperatives of digital semiotics. It includes semiotic signifiers of concrete constitutionally relevant artefacts and visual representations of the digital dimension of state and public power institutions, instruments for civic engagement and human rights. For example, there is a whole visual world of symbolic and visual depiction of state institutions, public institutions and human rights on the digital realm and in the digital reality. In other words, the digital imprint of constitutional institutions is not limited to the direct representation of their overall physical outlook and design in the non-digital world, such as the retranslation of sittings of institutions or public events, the showing of architectural depictions of institutions etc; it also includes the specific digital representations of these constitutional institutions expressed through the means of digital art and digital design. Such official digital

[1] See N Feigenson, 'Digital Visual and Multimedia Software and the Reshaping of Legal Knowledge' in A Wagner and W Pencak (eds), *Images in Law* (Farnham, Ashgate, 2006) 89–117.

[2] See R Albert and Y Roznai (eds), *Constitutionalism under Extreme Conditions: Law, Emergency, Exception* (Dordrecht, Springer, 2020) 1–461; and M Belov, *Courts and Judicial Activism under Crisis Conditions: Policy Making in a Time of Illiberalism and Emergency Constitutionalism* (Abingdon, Routledge, 2021) 1–236.

[3] M Delli Carpini (ed), *Digital Media and Democratic Futures* (Philadelphia, University of Pennsylvania Press, 2019) 1–352; J Cannataci, V Falce and O Pollicino (eds), *New Legal Challenges of Big Data* (Cheltenham, Edward Elgar, 2020) 1–328; and E Celeste, 'Digital Constitutionalism: A New Systematic Theorisation' (2019) 33(1) *International Review of Law, Computers & Technology* 76, doi:10.1080/13600869.2019.1562604.

[4] See M Belov (ed), *The IT Revolution and its Impact on State, Constitutionalism and Public Law* (Oxford, Hart Publishing, 2021) 15-41.

[5] See M Raheja, *Reservation Reelism: Redfacing, Visual Sovereignty, and Representations of Native Americans in Film* (Lincoln, NE, University of Nebraska Press, 2011) 1–360.

representations may also include highly compressed and symbolic forms of the visual signification of meaning.

Thus, all constitutional phenomena now have a digital identity that is signified and represented as a visual digital identity. This digital identity exists in parallel to the physical, socio-political and textual identity of constitutional phenomena and constitutional institutions. It should be noted that digital identity is typical of both citizens and their organisations, and the institutions of public power. Consequently, this digital identity has to be represented visually through a range of semiotic shapes and forms that expand the traditional scope of visual constitutionalism.

In fact, digital identity has become not only an upgrade and additional layer of the previous biological, psychological, social, cultural, national and political identities of human beings; it has also started merging and fusing with them. It is gaining momentum and requires adequate tools and forms for the signification and representation of meaning. These can be visual forms, some of which are part of the physical reality represented through digital means, while other have a purely digital ontology, provenance and essence.

The same is true of the digital identity of state and public power institutions and their semiotic signification in the field of visual constitutionalism. Logos and other visual depictions of European institutions are known around the world and especially in Europe. National and subnational institutions are also enhancing their visual identity, which was previously expressed mainly through coats of arms and flags, through forms of digital identity and visual forms of the signification of identity – this is the case for NATO, the UN, the Council of Europe and many other international organisations.

Digital aesthetics increasingly influences the semiotic process that leads to the construction of the shapes and forms of visual constitutionalism. Digital aesthetics itself is largely shaped by pop art. New technologies have produced novel forms of the signification and communication of meaning through visual content, pictures and depictions, memes, figures and even visual icons.[6] Thus, constitutional law and constitutionalism are also dependent on the increasing pressure for formalised, symbolic, visual communication and for the compressed and iconic representation of meaning. This all leads to a kind of 'iconisation' and 'memefication' of constitutional meaning signified through visual constitutionalism.[7]

[6] On the iconography of law in a non-digital context, see R Khorakiwala, *From the Colonial to the Contemporary: Images, Iconography, Memories, and Performances of Law in India's High Courts* (Oxford, Hart Publishing, 2020) 1–296; V Paumen, 'The Exhibition The Art on Law: Three Centuries of Justice Depicted' and M Korpiola, 'Medieval Iconography of Justice in a European Periphery: The Case of Sweden, ca 125–1550' in S Huygebaert, G Martyn, V Paumen, E Bousmar and X Rouseaux (eds), *The Art of Law: Artistic Representations and Iconography of Law and Justice in Context, from the Middle Ages to the First World War* (Dordrecht, Springer, 2018) 25–43 and 89–111 respectively; and M Loughlin, *Sword and Scales: An Examination of the Relationship between Law and Politics* (Oxford, Hart Publishing, 2000) 55–65.

[7] On the difference between the three aspects of signs (icons, indexes and symbols), see A Berger, *Media Analysis Techniques* (New York, SAGE Publications, 2018) 4.

The processes of 'iconisation' and 'memefication' of constitutional meaning are also forms of constitutional semiosis.[8] They co-exist with but also challenge traditional forms of visual constitutionalism such as fine arts, sculpture and architecture. The 'iconisation' and 'memefication' of constitutional meaning are part of unofficial visual constitutionalism, unless provided by law and entrenched as part of the official visual identity of state and public power institutions. Examples of such official visual identity have been given above.

Nevertheless, the 'iconisation' and 'memefication' of constitutional meaning are increasingly important elements of constitutional discourse on the ground and especially in the information channels of digital constitutionalism. These semiotic tools allow for the emotionally appealing representation of constitutional and constitutionally relevant content that also produces constitutional enchantment. They result from digital performative acts that aim at the signification of constitutional content, actors and phenomena through visual signifiers.

The 'iconisation' and 'memefication' of constitutional meaning are proof of the increasing search and striving for symbiotically represented and semiotically compressed constitutional and constitutionally relevant content. The general public – the addressees of constitutional rules and the broader and diffuse participants in constitutional games – are getting used to communicating and exchanging information and opinion in visually represented symbolic forms through memes, sketches, visual jokes etc. It is used to expressing opinion via clicks on symbols, icons, visualisations of emotions and emotional reactions. Thus, political participation through synthetic visual forms – emoticons, memes and buttons – can be defined as the 'iconisation', 'emojification' and 'memefication' of visual constitutionalism.[9] These are processes which are intimately and genuinely semiotic. Hence, the 'iconisation', 'emojification' and 'memefication' of digital constitutionalism demonstrate the rising and even crucial importance of visual constitutionalism and constitutional semiotics in the algorithmic zeitgeist and society.

Formally, and to an extent superficially, the 'iconisation', 'emojification' and 'memefication' of meaning in the unofficial visual constitutional discourse can be compared to digital constitutional pop art.[10] Substantially, it shows a deep transformation of the role of public deliberation, the meaning of public participation

[8] On the impact of memes on general semiotics, see B Wiggins, *The Discursive Power of Memes in Digital Culture: Ideology, Semiotics, and Intertextuality* (Abingdon, Routledge, 2019) 1–175.

[9] On the impact of the extensive use of new semiotic forms of digital political communication on deliberative and participatory democracy, see A Xiao Mina, *Memes to Movements: How the World's Most Viral Media is Changing Social Protest and Power* (Boston, Beacon Press, 2019) 1–248; R Milner, *The World Made Meme: Public Conversations and Participatory Media* (Cambridge, MA, MIT Press, 2016) 1–272; and S Jackson and M Bailey, *#HashtagActivism: Networks of Race and Gender Justice* (Cambridge, MA, MIT Press, 2020) 1–296.

[10] On the interplay between pop art signifiers and legal signifieds, see T Giddens, 'Lex Comica: On Comics and Legal Theory' and G Ferris and C Lunt, 'Devil's Advocate: Representation in Heroic Fiction, *Daredevil* and the Law' in T Giddens (ed). *Graphic Justice: Intersections of Comics and Law* (Abingdon, Routledge, 2015) 8–17 and 36–54 respectively.

indicating a transition towards more synthetic, compressed and visually represented constitutional discourse. In such a context, the role of visual constitutional semiotics is huge. It must be developed extensively as a scientific approach in order to cope with the tendencies briefly described above and to offer an appropriate analytical toolkit for the semiotic analysis of the visual discourse of digital constitutionalism in algorithmic society.[11]

Digital constitutional semiotics relates to both traditional and digital constitutionalism and is an expression of the general tendency for digitalisation in our lives. Yet, the structure and functions of digital constitutional semiotics remain similar to those of traditional visual constitutionalism and the pre-digital forms for the signification of constitutionally relevant meaning. Visual constitutionalism in general, including digital visual constitutionalism,[12] has to represent and signify constitutionally relevant meaning. It demonstrates normative ideas and ideologies, constitutional myths and mythologies, constitutional codes, and the emotional and symbolic-imaginary appeals, claims and messages of constitutional institutions.

[11] On the impact of new technologies (eg, computer games) on socio-political practices and socially relevant performance leading to the establishment of new plains and modes of social imagination, see G Kirkpatrick, *Computer Games and the Social Imaginary* (Cambridge, Polity Press, 2013) 1–248.

[12] See N Feigenson, 'Digital Visual and Multimedia Software and the Reshaping of Legal Knowledge' in A Wagner and W Pencak (eds), *Images in Law* (Farnham, Ashgate, 2006) 89–117.

4

Visual Constitutionalism as a Proper Form of Constitutionalism Embedded in Semiotic and Socio-legal Approaches

The considerations in the previous three chapters demonstrate that visual constitutionalism is an important part of the ways in which the constitutional order and constitutionally relevant content is shown to the public,[1] demonstrated to present and future generations, and used as an additional device for constitutional communication and as a channel for the transmission of constitutional content in condensed, symbolic and visual form that is rationally feasible, emotionally appealing and capable of engaging the individual and collective constitutional imaginaries. This is true for both traditional and digital visual constitutionalism.

However, the question of whether visual constitutionalism can still be qualified as a form of constitutionalism or whether it is constitutionalism only in a very wide and metaphorical sense still deserves attention. Obviously, visual constitutionalism, in contrast to some other concepts covered in this book, is not a meta-theory. It is a form of constitutionalism delimited on the basis of the methods for the expression of constitutional and constitutionally relevant content. Visual constitutionalism has methodological relevance since it confronts the conceptual question of where constitutionalism is contained and whether it can be expressed through non-textual means. This problem concerns the interrelation between constitutional text and constitutional texture which was discussed in detail in Part II, Chapter 4 of this book. Clearly, visual constitutionalism is a phenomenon with huge importance for constitutional semiotics, since it offers powerful tools for the signification of constitutional and constitutionally relevant meaning. Hence, it can be defined as a variant of constitutionalism outlined on the basis of its content, substance and teleology, based on the socio-legal approach to constitutional law and deeply rooted in constitutional semiotics.

The definitional issues of visual constitutionalism require additional explanation and further consideration. They should deepen our understanding of

[1] For some quite telling examples of how the idea of justice is demonstrated and represented through art and, more precisely, via theatre and literature, see F-W Korsten, *Art as an Interface of Law and Justice: Affirmation, Disturbance, Disruption* (Oxford, Hart Publishing, 2021) 1–212.

the nature of visual constitutionalism, its relevance for constitutional law and its importance for constitutional semiotics. The problem can be reduced to the following key questions: what is the legal and constitutional relevance and the added constitutional value of visual art and architecture, whether digital or traditional? Is it possible to consider visual depictions of constitutional phenomena and constitutionally relevant context as part of constitutionalism, which is at the end of the day structured around the constitution itself being a legal act and thus part of valid law, entrenched in systematic rationality, institutionalism, positivism and textualism?

The answer to these questions is in the affirmative: visual constitutionalism can be defined as constitutionalism in a proper sense subject to three conditions. These conditions are separate and independent, but together contribute to the recognition of visual constitutionalism as a legitimate aspect of constitutionalism *stricto sensu*.

The first condition is to consider constitutionalism as a wide-ranging phenomenon that is not limited to positive law and legal institutions. Constitutionalism must be conceived as a socio-legal and intellectual phenomenon with a range of implications that have visual, performative, symbolic-imaginary and emotional manifestations. Thus, constitutionalism should not be perceived as equal to the constitution and valid constitutional law. Constitutionalism also includes the practice of constitutional law, the application of the constitution in legal, political and performative acts, the understanding of the constitution and constitutional law in theory, and its symbolic imprints in individual and collective imaginaries and in different forms of art, including visual art and architecture.

In that regard, visual art and architecture are means for the expression of constitutionalism in action and tools that give objective shape and standing to 'constitutionalism-as-imagination'. They are tools for the signification of constitutional phenomena derived from constitutional texture and expressing constitutional axiology or constitutional design. They are projections of constitutional phenomena and constitutionally relevant meaning in physical or digital reality expressed in symbolic and metaphorical forms. This visual expression of meaning may lead to the production of visuals containing compressed meaning or to the proliferation of visual representations of meaning. In any case, visual constitutionalism can also be expressed, organised and understood as a result of semiosis and through the analytical apparatus of constitutional semiotics. In that regard, constitutional semiotics is the key for the encoding and decoding of meaning in visual form and thus also serves as an epistemic device of constitutional theory.

Second, visual forms must be related to the expression of content stemming from or related to the constitution and constitutional law. Thus, visual constitutionalism necessarily relates to normative-institutional constitutionalism and so is not detached from either textual or rational constitutionalism. Visual constitutionalism is not an end in itself; it is a conceptual paradigm that allows for a better understanding of the constitution and constitutional law as social phenomena reflected through the medium of art and exposed through the expressive means of art and architecture.

In that regard, visual constitutionalism can also be considered as part of a broader intellectual and philosophical movement. These are several late modern and post-modern trends of thought that have jointly impacted social and political sciences (and, to a lesser extent, constitutional and legal theory) during the last few decades. These are the critical studies, including critical legal studies and studies of arts and social sciences. More precisely, visual constitutionalism is embedded in the intellectual power field created by law and arts theories and studies, post-modern deconstructivism and critical legal studies.[2] It is part of the so-called 'visual turn' in the social sciences and in law.[3]

In other words, visual constitutionalism may be useful as a tool for understanding the way in which people imagine constitutional phenomena through their depiction via different art forms, including architecture considered as a peculiar form of the visual arts. Naturally, such art forms are elitist products. They are produced and designed by highly qualified and skilled specialists (artists, architects etc). Some of them consider themselves to be authoritative visualisers, understand their work as part of a social and even political mission, and use it deliberately as an instrument for the expression of constitutional ideas, social and constitutional change or the justification of the existing constitutional order. Others produce such visual art forms that belong to visual constitutionalism incidentally or as a result of creative inspiration that does not explicitly aim at producing a social impact or having clear constitutional implications. In any case, visual constitutionalism is rarely the result of folk art. This is even the case for pop art, which is individualistic, deliberate and thus an elitist and professional product.

However, in both cases and notwithstanding the fact that artists may deliberately create constitutionally relevant art and architecture or incidentally and indirectly visualise constitutionally relevant content, visual artists and architects contribute to the emergence and development of visual constitutionalism. Thus, visual constitutionalism is part of the overall constitutional civilisation and constitutional culture. In that regard, visual constitutionalism is both a factor in the emergence of a particular constitutional civilisation and constitutional culture and a result of them. It must be taken into account that visual constitutionalism may be a part or a reflection of a particular constitutional culture that is nation-specific

[2] For a new and interesting debate on race, gender and algorithmic constitutionalism, which also involves a critical assessment of the tools for the semiotic representation of meaning via digital technologies, see, eg, M Bailey, *#HashtagActivism: Networks of Race and Gender Justice* (Cambridge, MA, MIT Press, 2020) 1–296; SU Noble, *Algorithms of Oppression: How Search Engines Reinforce Racism* (New York, NYU Press, 2018) 1–256; R Benjamin, *Race after Technology: Abolitionist Tools for the New Jim Code* (Cambridge, Polity Press, 2019) 1–172; A Brock Jr, *Distributed Blackness: African American Cybercultures* (New York, NYU Press, 2020) 1–288; and C Mcllwain, *Black Software: The Internet and Racial Justice, from the AfroNet to Black Lives Matter* (Oxford, Oxford University Press, 2019) 1–312.

[3] See L Mulcahy, 'Eyes of the Law: A Visual Turn in Socio-legal Studies?' (2017) 44(1) *Journal of Law and Society* 111; and L Mulcahy, 'Sociology of Legal Images' in J Přibáň (ed), *Research Handbook on the Sociology of Law*, (Cheltenham, Edward Elgar, 2020) 203–15.

or region-specific, or may adhere to a global or universal constitutional culture and civilisation.

Actually, the creation of a typology of visual constitutionalism is a separate but important problem which is beyond the scope of this book due to space constraints. Here it is sufficient to say that such a typology can be based on a range of criteria stemming from both constitutionalism and constitutional law and from the specifics of the art forms that are used for their depiction. A typology of visual constitutionalism must offer comprehensive classifications of types and subtypes, thus 'slicing down' the phenomenon, while also taking its holistic nature and general characteristics into account.

Third, visual constitutionalism can be meaningfully grasped and comprehensively conceptualised mainly through the lens of constitutional semiotics. Indeed, visual constitutionalism is entrenched in both visual arts (including architecture) and constitutionalism (including constitution and constitutional law). But the real bond between them is visual constitutionalism's task, role and function to signify meaning and to represent constitutional content in a visual way.

Thus, visual constitutionalism is a genuinely semiotic phenomenon. It is a concept that frames the overall process of constitutional semiosis or the constitutional semiotic signification of meaning. Through visual signifiers, it signifies different signifieds that are derived from normative-institutional and textual constitutionalism. It generates meaning that is relevant to symbolic-imaginary and emotional constitutionalism. Thus, the normative ideologies and ideas, myths and mythologies, codes and constitutional architecture and design extracted from normative-institutional and textual constitutionalism are signified through the visual arts and architecture. The results of this signification are embedded in symbolic-imaginary constitutionalism. Nevertheless, they also have important emotional implications, inspiring individual and collective emotions through visual imaginaries and the visual representation of constitutional ideals, ideas, codes, myths, mythologies and allegories in an emotionally appealing way. Thus, visual constitutionalism and its forms have a profound impact and are also deeply interrelated with emotional constitutionalism.

Seen from this perspective, visual constitutionalism does not appear irrational. It is a tool for the representation of key ideas and structures belonging to rational constitutionalism, expressed in textual constitutionalism and organised through normative-institutional constitutionalism. In such a context, visual constitutionalism can be conceptualised as an additional expressive mode of constitutionalism in parallel with textual constitutionalism. In other words, textual and visual constitutionalism seem to be mutually supportive containers of signifiers and thus of constitutional texture that promote the organisation of constitutional meaning. They can be both tools for the expression of elements of symbolic-imaginary constitutionalism, and for framing and stimulating emotional and performative constitutionalism.[4]

[4] For an alternative approach to perceptual experience going beyond the representation of meaning, see D Papineau, *The Metaphysics of Sensory Experience* (Oxford, Oxford University Press, 2021) 1–176.

Nevertheless, textual and visual constitutionalism are not always and not necessarily coordinated. They may offer synchronic, but also diachronic and counter-punctual representations of constitutional and constitutionally relevant signifiers. This is a result of the underestimation of visual constitutionalism by the predominant constitutional theory, the traditional understanding of visual representations of constitutional law and constitutional meaning as meta-legal phenomena and the underdevelopment of constitutional semiotics. In that regard, one of the tasks of constitutional semiotics may be to serve as a common platform for the coordination of the various forms of signification of constitutional and constitutionally relevant meaning, including textual, visual and performative constitutionalism. This task deserves special attention and will be further developed in subsequent publications, but cannot be explored in detail here due to space constraints.

In a broader sense, textual constitutionalism is a form of literature, albeit a specific and very specialised one. Hence, both textual and visual constitutionalism can be perceived as forms of art. This art approach to the constitution and constitutional law is prone to promoting the constitutional imagination and enchanting constitutionally derived, constitutionally formative or constitutionally promotional performance and emotions. It pushes the imaginary sight of constitutionalism and constitutional law to the fore, offering a chance for a novel approach to 'constitutionalism-as-imagination', constitutional symbolism and even 'constitutionalism-as-art-and-architecture'.

The forms of visual constitutionalism include a multitude of signifiers representing a wide variety of signifieds. These range from representations of ideas, myths, mythologies and codes in and on the official buildings of public power institutions or in forms of visual arts (paintings, sculptures, art installations etc) through to forms of visual constitutionalism and the visual assets of the official visual identity, such as coats of arms, flags, uniforms and the visual organisation of ceremonies.[5] Thus, visual constitutionalism seems to be a bulky concept both in terms of the signifiers and the signifieds. This also leads to multiple modes of signification of meaning, thus proliferating the semiotic means for the expression of constitutional content in visual form.

[5] On the visual legal semiotic codes provided in art, see, eg, R Lippens, 'Law, Code and Late Modern Governance in Prophetic Painting: Notes on Jackson Pollock, Mark Rothko and Gilles Deleuze' in A Wagner and J Broekman (eds), *Prospects of Legal Semiotics* (Dordrecht, Springer, 2010) 171–92.

5

Visual Constitutionalism in Pop Culture and Pop Art

This chapter is devoted to the role of pop culture and pop art in shaping and promoting visual constitutionalism.[1] At first glance, such an approach may seem rather unusual and provocative. Indeed, constitutionalism is something serious – a phenomenon that is related to the state and statehood, rights and liberties. It is a phenomenon entrenched in textuality and rationalism that is focused on axiology and institutional design. On the other hand, pop art and pop culture are visual-emotional phenomena devoted to pleasure, fun and entertainment. How do they combine with constitutionalism as a legal and thus rational and emotionally and visually austere phenomenon? Why should we concern ourselves with pop culture and pop art depictions of constitutional phenomena? Are they relevant for constitutional law directly or at least indirectly?[2]

There are several reasons why art and culture do matter for law.[3] There are even more specific reasons why pop culture and pop art are relevant for constitutionalism as a socio-legal phenomenon and especially for constitutional semiotics.[4] Culture and art are the most important social mediums for influencing the minds and the hearts of the people. They contain imprints of the collective constitutional imaginaries of the people and significations of key elements of rational and normative-institutional constitutionalism. In that sense, culture, art and constitutionalism are joint factors for constitutional semiosis on a mass scale, impacting a large number of people and leading to the production of art signifiers of huge constitutional importance.

[1] On the impact of pop culture on law, see S Redhead, *Unpopular Cultures: The Birth of Law and Popular Culture* (Manchester, Manchester University Press, 1995); A Chase, 'Popular Culture/Popular Justice' in J Denvir (ed), *Legal Reelism: Movies as Legal Texts* (Chicago, University of Illinois Press, 1996) 133–54; J Bainbridge, 'Lawyers, Justice and the State: The Sliding Signifier of Law in Popular Culture' (2006) 15(1) *Griffith Law Review* 153; and A Sarat (ed), *Imagining Legality: Where Law Meets Popular Culture* (Alabama, University of Alabama Press, 2011) 65–99.

[2] For a provocative answer to this dilemma, see S Burgess, *The Founding Fathers, Pop Culture, and Constitutional Law: Who's Your Daddy?* (Abingdon, Routledge, 2016) 1–154.

[3] See M Asimow and J Silbey, *Law and Popular Culture: A Course Book* (Lake Mary, Vandeplas Publishing, 2020) 1–22; and S Mader and M Asimow, *Law and Popular Culture: A Course Book* (New York, Peter Lang, 2013) 3–23.

[4] For range of arguments, see, eg, J Bainbridge, 'Visual Law: The Changing Signifiers of Law in Popular Visual Culture' in A Wagner and J Broekman (eds), *Prospects of Legal Semiotics* (Dordrecht, Springer, 2010) 193–215.

Pop culture is the form of culture that has the broadest impact on the widest possible range of people. Pop art as a form of pop culture is a specific phenomenon with huge semiotic potential. This potential derives from the spread of pop art signifiers via a multitude of objects that are both practical (thus generating huge demand for acquisition, possession and consumption) and visually appealing. Pop art is the form of art that is closest to advertisements. It can advertise sport or cultural symbols, trademarks, consumerist practices and attitudes etc. Simultaneously, with the same success, it can also promote political symbols and constitutional and constitutionally relevant phenomena. The selling and purchasing of constitutional symbols and depictions of collective constitutional imaginaries are of huge relevance for the forming of the constitutional and political culture of the people on a wide but basic and profound level.

Hence, pop art is a framework concept that includes a range of objects which can be imprinted, engraved and shaped with visually and emotionally appealing signifiers of constitutional and constitutionally relevant meaning. It has huge potential for the semiotic signification of constitutional signifiers on a daily basis and in a practical manner. If offers a range of objects that are capable of bearing condensed, symbolically structured, and enchanting and captivating constitutional meaning. Briefly, pop art can signify and sell ideas on the market, both literally and metaphorically.

Here I use the terms 'pop art' and 'pop culture' in a rather broad sense. They are meant to include all forms of art with pragmatic and consumer-oriented functions that are capable of being used as physical bearers of semiotic – or, more precisely, constitutional semiotic – content. This includes art forms per se (eg, posters, pictures, photography, sculptures and small pieces of art), but also a range of material objects that can be used for the representation of constitutionally relevant meaning (clothes, souvenirs etc). Hence, pop culture is not limited to pop art and pop art is not used in a limitative sense as restrained to the manifestations of concrete art style. Rather, it comprises denominating pragmatic art forms with symbolic importance and semiotic functionality that are capable of objectivising and spreading constitutional semiotic signifiers, and thus actually engaging in a process of constitutional semiosis.[5]

Since the second half of the twentieth century, components of symbolic-imaginary constitutionalism – especially ideas, symbols and myths, but also key elements of constitutional axiology and signifiers of constitutional design – are becoming increasingly signified in pop culture and pop art. This is a result of multiple phenomena which are not necessarily interconnected. The rise of simpler and more popular forms of art, and the mixture of art and consumerism in the context of the welfare state and consumer society are among the factors for the use of pop art as a tool for the representation of constitutionally relevant meaning.

[5] For an interesting study of the role of pop culture in jurisprudence that is also relevant for constitutional semiotics, see W MacNeil, *Lex Populi: The Jurisprudence of Popular Culture* (Stanford, Stanford University Press, 2007) 1–260.

Art forms became increasingly profane in parallel to the democratisation of politics and the rise of direct forms of constitutional communication and deliberation. Thus, there was a widespread need for more direct, more understandable, popular and even profane forms of the signification of constitutional and constitutionally relevant meaning.

Furthermore, there was an increasing demand for visual proxies for constitutional and constitutionally relevant ideas. Constitutional messages had to be delivered in a visually appealing, condensed and popular symbolic form that can be immediately accepted by all members of the constitutionally framed socio-political community.[6] People are not supposed to be constitutionalists, but constitutionalism as practice is largely dependent on their constitutional imagination and the shared beliefs relating to constitutional axiology and constitutional design. In that regard, pop art was an excellent medium for constitutional acculturation through the symbolic representation of constitutional and constitutionally relevant meaning. a range of practical signifiers stamped on clothes, engraved on tea and coffee mugs, printed on posters etc that played a huge role in the production and reproduction of constitutional symbols and in promoting constitutional ideas, myths and codes.

Let me give some examples that demonstrate the role of pop art and pop culture in the promotion of symbolic-imaginary visuals of constitutional semiotic importance. The depictions of Che Guevara on t-shirts serves as a device for the promotion of constitutionally relevant ideas that are related to this revolutionary leader or, conversely, for their simplification and transformation into casual pop culture,[7] pacifying revolution and turning it into an element of fashion.[8] The visual depiction of presidents, monarchs and religious leaders on clothes or souvenirs is also an instrument for the advertisement of the ideas that come with these iconic figures. These images serve as proxies for deeper and much more complex normative ideologies, ideas, myths, mythologies and codes. Winston Churchill showing the V-sign for victory, the pope blessing the community of believers, a smiling monarch or US president depicted on a t-shirt in the style of Andy Warhol – these are all symbols of different ideas of power, authority and legitimacy. The same is true of Soviet visuals styled according to the imperatives of the mass culture of the proletariat – for example, Lenin showing the path to the future or Stalin smiling at the masses are powerful constitutional metaphors.

Generally, there are constitutional semiotic wars for the hearts and minds of the people. They are conducted on the battlefield of pop culture through the weaponry

[6] On the representation of social ideas through representational arts, see the seminal account in K Walton, *Mimesis as Make-Believe: On the Foundations of Representational Arts* (Cambridge, MA, Harvard University Press, 1993) 1–480.

[7] See T Ziff, *Che Guevara: Revolutionary and Icon* (New York, Abrams Image, 2006) 1–128; L Shaw and S Dennison, *Pop Culture Latin America! Media, Arts, and Lifestyle* (Santa Barbara, ABC-CLIO, 2005) 179–207.

[8] For an interesting investigation of the impact of superheroes and their mythologies on law, see J Bainbridge, '"This is the Authority. This Planet is under Our Protection": An Exegesis of Superheroes' Interrogations of Law' (2007) 3 *Law, Culture and the Humanities* 455.

of pop art. Symbols of the West collided with symbols of the East, liberal dreams were sold as an antidote to communist utopias, consumerist values with strategic constitutional importance were counterweighted by post-modern ecological goals that originated in the Global North or the Global South. Five-pointed stars on all sides of the semiotic wars were painted with different colours, thus being loaded with different constitutional substance, rational, emotional and symbolic-imaginary content. Signs of unrestricted liberty and the eternal pursuit of happiness (such as the Statue of Liberty) were confronted with revolutionary fists and raised hammers and reaping hooks. Symbols of globalisation had to meet the semiotic claims of local, national or regional tradition and pride. Last but not least, signs of tradition and continuity were challenged by symbols of radical change and the deconstruction of secure identities.

Depiction of state symbols such as coats of arms and flags is another important strategy for the spreading of political and constitutionally relevant messages via visual pop culture framed in terms of constitutional semiotics. T-shirts with the US, UK or Canadian flags sold in shopping malls are an excellent example. Nationalist t-shirts featuring symbols of national pride are popular in many parts of the world. The depiction of Soviet or revolutionary symbols are semiotic instruments for the promotion of counter-culture or for their vulgarisation and consumerisation.

These examples are important in two ways. First, they spread political and geopolitical messages throughout the world in a semiotic form through the means of unofficial constitutional semiotics. Second, this is done in the 'cathedral of the consumerist society' – the shopping centre and the shopping mall[9] – which is the crossroads of the free exchange of capitalist production, the striving for material prosperity and the demonstration of belongingness to the middle class as pillar of the Western way of life and of democracy. Indeed, shopping centres have also spread globally, but initially they were symbols of Western (and especially American) consumerist dreams which were then exported as part of the capitalist way of life. Recently, a similar process is visible in the context of online shopping as an advancing form of digital society.

The clothes with flags are definitely bearers of semiotic signifiers. State symbols printed on clothes are one of the clearest examples of the consumerist promotion of political symbols and are thus instruments of visual political semiotics demonstrated via pop art. Nevertheless, state symbols also have their own specific constitutional standing. They are provided by the constitutional law of most states and are strategic semiotic signifiers of statehood and state authority. Thus, pop art depictions of state symbols on clothes, souvenirs and other commercial products are also bearers not only of political but also constitutionally relevant content expressed through semiotics – the semiotics of unofficial visual pop art constitutionalism.

[9] See also D Brion, 'The Shopping Mall: Signs of Power' in R Kevelson (ed), *Law and Semiotics*, vol 1 (New York, Plenum Press, 1987) 65–109.

This example shows the embeddedness of contemporary constitutionalism in the everyday life of people, its deep dependence on culture and subculture, and its entrenchment in the overall civilisation and culture. Thus, constitutionalism should definitely be conceived and explored not only as a normative but also as an empirical and societal phenomenon and as a form of culture.[10] Semiotics in general and constitutional semiotics in particular are the most appropriate devices for such an approach to constitutionalism-as-culture. It also requires the admittance of pop art forms and symbols as elements of unofficial visual and symbolic-imaginary constitutionalism.

Hence, pop art and pop culture are very important mass devices of the semiotic and visual influence, advertisement and promotion of concepts, myths and mythologies in the market of intellectual ideas. They are powerful instruments for the signification and conveying of political and constitutionally relevant meaning. They are semiotic proxies for 'constitutional truth' that is advertised at and promoted to the people as members of constitutionally framed mass society. Such pop art semiotic strategies and devices may be used in the context of liberal-democratic, consumerist or authoritarian society and order. In any case, the depictions of the state, the party or other symbols or of symbolic figures, political and religious icons or key constitutional and political signs in visual pop culture and art are part of a genuinely semiotic process. These pop culture and pop art devices of signification are the toolkit for the semiotic representation of different elements of symbolic-imaginary constitutionalism having widespread popular support. Such semiotic instruments are easy to comprehend. They are appealing and may spread the message in question widely amongst the population. They deliver condensed symbolic meaning in an understandable and rather pleasant way that is easy to swallow.

In that regard, pop art visuals are an important medium between symbolic-imaginary constitutionalism, visual constitutionalism and emotional constitutionalism. They are triggers, transmitters and results of collective political and constitutional imaginaries produced, engraved or imposed in the collective fantasies regarding the best, the ideal and the perfect political and constitutional order exemplified through codes, mythological figures from the past (leaders, heroes, saints etc) and other forms of constitutional dreaming and remembrance.[11] They are advertisement tools for dreamy constitutional and political order. They are instruments for the visualisation of constitutional codes. Thus, pop art forms devoted to elements of symbolic-imaginary constitutionalism are the perfect means and tools for the signification of constitutionally relevant signified objects

[10] See J Přibáň, 'Constitutional Imaginaries and Legitimation: On Potentia, Potestas, and Auctoritas in Societal Constitutionalism' (2018) 45(1) *Journal of Law and Society* 30; and J Přibáň, *Constitutional Imaginaries: A Theory of European Societal Constitutionalism* (Abingdon, Routledge, 2020) 1–251.

[11] M Belov, 'Constitutional Memories: How Do Constitutions Cope with Constitutional Past' in M Belov and A Abat i Ninet (eds), *Revolution, Transition, Memory, and Oblivion: Reflections on Constitutional Change* (Cheltenham, Edward Elgar, 2020) 107–26.

derived from rational or symbolic-imaginary constitutionalism through the signifiers of visual constitutionalism.

In addition, these signifiers are usually very emotionally appealing. They are triggers of socio-political imagination promoting feelings of belongingness, compassion,[12] appreciation, admiration[13] and adoration. Pop art visuals are used because they are modern, fancy, provocative and intriguing. Wearing the flag, strolling around symbolically 'embraced' by political pop art icons such as Che Guevara, Churchill, Obama or champions for human rights and personal emancipation seems a highly symbolic way of expressing the emotional sublimation of political feelings and constitutional affiliations. It is a path for emotional engagement in constitutionalism as a form of art through the medium of visuals expressed through constitutional semiotics and the forms of unofficial visual constitutionalism. Having the US or UK flag on one's clothes signifies belongingness to Western civilisation while wearing clothes with Soviet visuals means its rejection. Thus, pop art visuals can also be used as signifiers of alienation, provocation, negation and exclusion. Hence, these visuals are used as means for the expression of positive or negative emotions. No matter what these emotions are, they are part of emotional constitutionalism and signify elements of symbolic-imaginary constitutionalism in unofficial visual constitutionalism through the means of constitutional semiotics.

Pop art can also be used to signify constitutional codes. Symbols of different political and constitutional ideologies are frequently used as elements of pop art. This is true not only for democratic but also for totalitarian and authoritarian codes, despite the fact that some of them may be explicitly or implicitly forbidden. Such symbolic encoding of constitutional codes has huge emotional importance, but also serves for acculturation and education, for political socialisation and for the establishment of feelings of unconscious recognition and belongingness to a specific semiotic community.

Indeed, not all codes used in pop art are explicitly constitutional, since not all of them belong to the official visual constitutionalism or have clear constitutional meaning. Nevertheless, even the semiotic codes that are not clearly and immediately recognisable as part of the symbolic pantheon of constitutionalism have implicit and deep but feasible constitutional importance. This is due to the fact that they are signifiers of phenomena that go beneath the surface of official constitutionalism and 'fly under the radar' of official visual semiotics, but are still heavily influencing constitutional culture and constitutional civilisation on emotional and symbolic-imaginary levels.

[12] B Zipursky, 'Austerity, Compassion and the Rule of Law' in A Amaya and M Del Mar (eds), *Virtue, Emotion and Imagination in Law and Legal Reasoning* (Oxford, Hart Publishing, 2020) 59–76.

[13] A Amaya, 'Admiration, Exemplarity and Judicial Virtue' in Amaya and Del Mar (n 13) 25–45.

6

Visual Constitutionalism in Architecture

Architecture is a strategic device for the expression of constitutional ideas in semiotic shapes through signifiers of meaning, resulting in forms of unofficial or quasi-official visual constitutionalism. It is a strategic field for the accomplishment of semiosis. It is visible and expressive. It is capable of representing constitutional and constitutionally relevant meaning in condensed, symbolically and emotionally appealing forms that enchant the human mind and is capable of mastering the collective constitutional imaginaries. It is the perfect plain for the demonstration, visualisation and signification of signifiers belonging to the expressive toolkit of symbolic-imaginary constitutionalism: allegories, codes, normative ideas, constitutional myths and mythologies. This is due to the fact that architecture is public and permanently available for observation and adoration. In its capacity as an art form, it is a perfect tool for the expression of constitutional visions with normative, retrospective or even utopian functions and characteristics. Architecture is stretched between the pragmatic imperatives of efficiency triggered by the functional predestination of the building and the aspirations of the constitutional imagination carving out the visual models of collective constitutional imaginaries.

The pragmatic-functional features of the architecture of official buildings consist in the fact that they serve a practical purpose. However, not all forms of parliamentary, governmental and court building architecture purely and entirely follow the imperatives of pragmatism.[1] They also take into account the imperatives of symbolism and the signification of constitutionally relevant meaning. In fact, this mixture and entanglement of pragmatic-rational and symbolic functions of the architecture of state and public power institutions lies at the centre of their role and importance for symbolic-imaginary and visual constitutionalism.

In that sense, the architecture of official buildings is an excellent example of the combination between the imperatives of the rational, ideal and emotional in the field of visual constitutionalism. The architecture of buildings of constitutional

[1] See T Arthur Brown et al, *Building for Government: The Architecture of State Buildings, OPW, Ireland 1900–2000* (Dublin, Town House and Country House in association with the Office of Public Works, 1999) 1–269; and L Mulcahy and E Rowden, *The Democratic Courthouse: A Modern History of Design, Due Process and Dignity* (Abingdon, Routledge, 2020) 1–370.

institutions serves the role of a drawing board for constitutional semiotics and a plain for the signification of a range of constitutional and constitutionally relevant signifieds via architectural signifiers. In that sense, it is a form of constitutional conversation framed as a variant of constitutional semiosis and accomplished through the language of the visual arts. The architecture of official buildings – the buildings of international, supranational, national and subnational institutions of public and state power – offers excellent opportunities for the signification of fundamental constitutional ideas, ideologies, myths, mythologies and codes. Thus, it is the perfect 'drawing board' for the depiction and exposure of elements of visual constitutionalism. This is particularly true for parliament and court buildings, but other governmental buildings can be used for the visual semiotic expression of collective imaginaries and for the signification of symbolic-imaginary phenomena of constitutionalism as well.

Actually, the more important the institution and the more loaded it is with normative ideas and ideologies, the more appropriate it is for visual representation and for architectural-constitutional semiosis. For example, court buildings are often used to express the ideas of justice,[2] liberty and rights, while parliament buildings are tools for the visual demonstration of the concepts of democracy, democratic equality, deliberation, parliamentarism and reason, and governmental buildings express authority and power. In that sense, the least appealing in semiotic terms is the architecture of technocratic institutions belonging to the lower levels of public administration.

It has been noted previously that architecture is prone to both unofficial and quasi-official visual constitutionalism. This results in unofficial visual constitutionalism when it is related to the visual outlook of private buildings, such as private mansions and houses, but also corporate and law firms, and lawyers guild buildings, solicitors and barristers' buildings (such as the architecture of the Inns of Court in London) etc. This type of architecture has no direct link to the constitution, constitutional law or the legal framing of public power. Nevertheless, it still serves a as tool for the expression of collective imaginaries relating to constitutional semiotics. Such unofficial visual constitutionalism signified through the private architecture of buildings that due to their functions are of importance for the practice of law may evoke collective memories, dreams or aspirations, or trigger thoughts that focus on the external shapes and modes for expression of architectural signifiers with elements of symbolic-imaginary constitutionalism.

[2] See M Loughlin, *Sword and Scales: An Examination of the Relationship between Law and Politics* (Oxford, Hart Publishing, 2000) 55–65; V Paumen, 'The Exhibition The Art on Law: Three Centuries of Justice Depicted', M Korpiola, 'Medieval Iconography of Justice in a European Periphery: The Case of Sweden, ca 125–1550', G Delmarcel, 'Justitia, Examples and Allegories of Justice, and Courts in Flemish Tapestry, 1450–1550: Artistic Representations and Iconography of Law and Justice in Context, from the Middle Ages to the First World War' and V Hayaert, 'The Paradoxes of Lady Justice's Blindfold' in S Huygebaert, G Martyn, V Paumen, E Bousmar and X Rouseaux (eds), *The Art of Law: Artistic Representations and Iconography of Law and Justice in Context, from the Middle Ages to the First World War* (Dordrecht, Springer, 2018) 25–43, 89–111, 111–23 and 201–23 respectively.

Although the unofficial visual constitutionalism of private buildings has no legal normativity, it may possess a degree of factual normativity.[3] What is meant by factual normativity here is the convincing force, compelling character and psychologically binding nature of elements of visual constitutionalism as reflected in emotional and symbolic-imaginary constitutionalism. Such normativity is based on the convincing force of semiotic architectural signifiers that may be architectural elements, shapes and forms, signs, and the overall design of the structure of buildings. The more emotionally and sensually captivating the visual semiotic signifier using elements of architectural design as a tool for the representation of ideas, the greater its chances of shaping and forming symbolic-imaginary constitutionalism by expressing through visually appealing codes and semiotic proxies elements that relate to rational constitutionalism.

Thus, to an extent paradoxically, visual constitutionalism shaped as a range or a system of constitutional semiotic signifiers expressed via unofficial (or official) architecture also determines the social acceptance of some of the fundamental ideas of rational constitutionalism. Large columns in the Dorian, Ionian or Corinthian style express solidity, wisdom, nobility and classicism. Together with capitals, sealing and domes as forms of representation of visual messages with distinct architectural but also power and authority identity, they serve as a visual expression of might, power, hierarchy and authority. Allegories of justice, freedom and equality are abundant in both unofficial and quasi-official architecture relating to visual constitutionalism. They are signifiers of the most important semiotic systems entrenched in the constitution, provided by constitutional law and determining the pragmatics of symbolic-imaginary and emotional constitutionalism.

A famous example of this factual normativity of architecturally expressed constitutional semiotics enchanting the public and launching rational reformist ideas through semiotic visuals is the architecture revolution with huge sociopolitical importance that has been triggered by the Elgin Marbles.[4] These are architectural and sculpture artefacts of Greek antiquity that Lord Elgin imported from the Ottoman Empire, especially from the region of Athens.

The Elgin's Marbles, in conjunction with other important cultural and political events, produced a wave of interest in ancient Greek art and architecture. The result was the huge symbolic and in fact semiotic imprint on Regency architecture in the British Empire. It was a semiotic revolution that triggered a range of collective constitutional imaginaries. These imaginaries, which have been signified and thus materialised in architectural form, promoted novel ideas of constitutionalism which had otherwise and in parallel been entrenched in rational and textual constitutionalism.

The constitutional and political aspect of this architectural style was the establishment of civilisation bridges between the British society of the time and the ancient Greco-Roman world and traditions. These bridges introduced humanism

[3] J Stalev, *The Normative Power of the Factual* (Sofia, Feneya, 2007) 1–280 (in Bulgarian).
[4] See W St Clair, *Lord Elgin and the Marbles* (Oxford, Oxford University Press, 1998) 1–456.

and rationalism as key ideologies of the Enlightenment and, later on, as normative ideologies of modern constitutionalism and constitutional law.[5] This intellectual heritage, which is in fact a good example of an 'invented tradition'[6] and imagined cultural and civilisation belongingness, has been signified in general or in some of its most important elements (codes, myths and ideas) through architectural signifiers. These signifiers had a central role to play in the promotion of modern Western constitutionalism in relation to public opinion. They were of pivotal importance for the visual and imaginary representation of the normative ideas of Western modernity masquerading as 'invented tradition' and as creative borrowings from the ancient world in the realms of visual, emotional and symbolic-imaginary constitutionalism. This all demonstrates the huge importance of constitutional semiotics for the establishment of the factual (sociological and psychological) normativity of legal and constitutional ideas and for the understanding of the functioning of constitutionalism as a phenomenon that is deeply embedded in civilisation and culture and as dependent on collective imaginaries.

Architecture signifies quasi-official visual constitutionalism when it relates to the buildings of official state and public power institutions. Visual constitutionalism expressed in this way is not really official because the architectural outlook of parliamentary, governmental, courts and municipal council buildings is neither provided in constitutional law nor defined in any official legal or political act. However, it is quasi-official because it is the architecture of public institutions that shapes, forms and represents the predominant or at least the imposed collective constitutional imaginaries (ideas, myths, mythologies and codes) that relate to the formative and legitimation concepts of justice, power, authority etc.

The elements of symbolic-imaginary constitutionalism (eg, normative ideas and ideologies, constitutional myths and mythologies) create legitimate expectations in citizens for their visual representation in the architecture of official buildings. They long for visual satisfaction through adequate architectural expressive forms. This is why quasi-official visual constitutionalism must represent and stand for these collective imaginaries and signify them through visual encoding in the form, size, structure, visual elements and codes provided by the architecture of public buildings.

The citizens expect court buildings to signify justice and the might and power of the state in conjunction with the authority of the judiciary. Hence, Themis, the Goddess of Justice, has to stand on solid ground surrounded by powerful visual representations of the above-mentioned normative ideas.[7] This symbolic-imaginary

[5] For the invention of individualism as an ideology deeply interrelated with humanism and rationalism, all of which were typical of Western modernity, see L Siedentop, *Inventing the Individual: The Origins of Western Liberalism* (Cambridge, MA, Belknap Press, 2017) 1–448.

[6] E Hobsbawm and T Ranger (eds), *The Invention of Tradition* (Cambridge, Cambridge University Press, 2012) 1–324.

[7] For illustrative and telling analysis of different representations of the idea of justice, see R Weisberg, 'The Art of Memory and the Allegorical Personification of Justice' (2012) 24(1) *Yale Journal of Law & the Humanities* 259.

anticipation results in either the imposing, dominant and imperial architecture of the court buildings designed between the end of the eighteenth and the middle of the twentieth centuries, or in the austere and restrained official architecture of the second half of the twentieth century, or in the functional and transparent architecture of court buildings that has gained momentum in the last few decades.[8] Indeed, court house architecture was initially influenced by the predominant styles of the eighteenth, nineteenth and early twentieth centuries. Hence, the ideas of justice, power and authority have been represented via the expression tools of classicism, neo-classicism and neo-Baroque, but there have also been influences from other styles such as neo-Gothic and Brick Gothic, Art Nouveau and Art Deco.[9] Actually, classicism and neo-classicism are the perfect styles for the expression of collective imaginaries relating to the judiciary and justice, such as order, rationality, sequential-procedural character, and clarity and transparency of forms. Baroque and neo-Baroque, on the other hand, offered a great variety of tools for the visual manifestation of constitutional codes and allegories due to the multilayered, visually prolific character of these styles.[10]

Excellent and magnificent examples of court houses of this age belonging to these modes of visual signification of constitutionally relevant ideas are the US Supreme Court in Washington DC, the Palaces of Justice in Paris, Brussels and Rome, the German Supreme Administrative Court building in Leipzig (the former Reichsgericht building) and the Supreme Court building in London.[11] Imposing and impressive latecomers such as the Palace of Justice in Sofia, Bulgaria, which had been the largest building in the country before the Second World War, could also be included in this list.

Later on, functional architecture, Cubism, Le Corbusier and Brutalism have been quite influential in relation to the design of official buildings of public power and especially of buildings of judicial institutions. The straight lines and the cubic and squared architecture they sustain allowed for the visual representation of functionalism, impartiality and order. The neutral, mechanic-automatic character of judicial activity perceived as a task for the administration of justice in a scientific and procedural way and for the imposition of state authority was well signified by the rather imposing but also bureaucratic and restrained architectural visuals offered by the leading styles of the second half of the twentieth century mentioned above.

The best examples of this architectural period are the German Federal Constitutional Court building in Karlsruhe, the Buffalo City Court Building

[8] See Loughlin (n 2) 55–65. An interesting study of the early modern signification of meaning through the architecture of premises devoted to the delivery of justice and its perception and art representation in the post-revolutionary age is offered in J Feyaerts, 'Joseph-Jonas Dumont's Prison Gatehouses: *Architecture Parlante* in Neo-Tudor Style' in Huygebaert et al (n 2) 371–78.

[9] See Paumen (n 2); Korpiola (n 2); Delmarcel (n 2); and Hayaert (n 2).

[10] See R Sherwin, *Visualizing Law in the Age of the Digital Baroque: Arabesques and Entanglements* (New York, Routledge, 2011) 1–256.

[11] For excellent research on the architecture of court buildings, see J Wallsgrove, *The Architecture of Law Courts* (Trowbridge, Paragon Publishing, 2019) 1–230.

and the Australia High Court building. The Superior Court of Justice building in Brasilia is even part of a monumental effort to establish a new visual line, style and reality for government buildings that has been undertaken by the Brazilian government in the post-Second World War context since the 1950-s. An excellent example of Brutalist courthouse architecture – imposing, authoritative and powerful – is the Supreme Court building of Pakistan designed by the Japanese architect Kenzo Tange.

Recently, the above-mentioned functional architecture of courts has been upgraded with visuals that also signify the transparency and post-modern fragmentation of the holistic picture of the world. Glass and aluminium replaced or supplemented cement and concrete as visual signifiers of justice. Authority, power and might were supplemented by an increasing striving towards transparency. Glass has been asserted as the perfect material for the semiotic expression of transparency. Moreover, the harmonious and symmetric architecture of the previous generations of court buildings has been partially replaced by asymmetries, deliberate deviations from straight lines and forms in order to express the post-modern legal pluralism, the fragmentation of the legal discourse, and the increasing diversity of authoritative constitutional and legal narrators. Good examples of court buildings exemplifying post-modern quasi-official visual constitutionalism are the Palace of Justice in Antwerp (Belgium) and also the Paris Courthouse in France, which still pays homage to Le Corbusier, but with a clear emphasis on transparency.

A central place in visual constitutionalism is devoted to constitutional geometry. Indeed, constitutional geometry is a phenomenon that mainly relates to symbolic-imaginary constitutionalism. However, imaginative constitutional geometry also might have important visual projections. Such projections are visible in art, but are of special importance in architecture. It will be shown below that the architecture of parliament, government and especially court buildings is largely influenced by symbolic-imaginary constitutionalism and thus by constitutional geometry. It is a tool for the visualisation of elements of symbolic-imaginary constitutionalism through the means of architecture.

Hence, constitutional geometry may also be part of visual constitutionalism because it can be expressed through visual means. This includes art forms of both visual and performative arts. It can also be expressed in architecture. Such an expression of constitutional geometric imaginaries is very common in painting and sculpture.

In fact, art rarely expresses constitutional ideas only in geometric forms. It usually serves as a device for the depiction of semiotic codes, ideas, myths and mythologies relating to law in general or constitutionalism and constitutional law in particular, some of which may be demonstrated, represented and signified trough geometric metaphors. Hence, visual constitutional geometry should be perceived as an independent phenomenon of both symbolic-imaginary and visual constitutionalism. It is an instrument for the visual expression and the semiotic signification of elements of symbolic-imaginary constitutionalism, such as constitutional myths and mythologies, allegories and codes.

Architecture provides visual constitutional geometry with an excellent toolkit that is contained and signified via geometric metaphors. Architecture is geometric per se. It can even be perceived as the most geometric art form. It combines practical and symbolic functions which are both of huge importance for constitutional geometry. More precisely, it is the symbolic and practical functions of the architecture of buildings that house state institutions that are relevant for constitutional geometry and serve as forms of the signification of constitutional meaning. This is particularly true for the architecture of parliaments and court buildings, but is also detectable in the visual models of government buildings and the buildings of institutions for local and regional self-government.

The symbolic features and functions of official buildings of public power institutions are broadly visible everywhere. All buildings of state and public power institutions are designed to demonstrate power, authority, might, domination and will for governance. The more recently built buildings of state and public power institutions also try to express transparency and openness.

Apart from these broader and general features of the architecture of public power institutions and their symbolic appeal, there are more specific and clearer examples of visual constitutional semiotics expressed in architectural geometric forms. Three of the most important capital cities in the world – London, Washington DC and Paris – were planned and constructed following semiotic geometric metaphors. The public power institutions are entrenched in these architecture plans and have specific place and role therein.

A further example that could be given is Vienna. Its Parliament building and City Hall are deliberately constructed so as to express the ideas of democracy and self-government. They are represented through their symbolic resemblance to ancient Greek architecture in the case of the Parliament building and Hanseatic architecture – the architecture of the German Hansa – in the case of City Hall. In fact, the architects of these two buildings believed that democracy was most developed in ancient Greece and particularly in the city-state of Athens and the municipal self-government in the Hansa, so they have constructed these buildings as visual and symbolic-imaginary bridges to these imaginary destinations in Western political history. These buildings incorporate ideas that are of fundamental importance for constitutionalism and constitutional law. Thus, they stand for ideals and are visual-architectural signifiers of constitutional signifieds. This also makes them pillars of constitutional semiotics. Moreover, they are elements of visual and symbolic-imaginary constitutionalism which also have relevance for imaginative constitutional geometry.[12]

[12] On the imaginary capacities and features of geometry, geometry as an imaginary property and 'the geometry of imagining', see E Brann, *The World of the Imagination: Sum and Substance* (Lanham, MD, Rowman & Littlefield, 2017) 603–37.

Imaginative constitutional geometry plays an important role in this pursuit of mixing of functionality with symbolism. The structure of court buildings and parliamentary buildings and the architecture of court rooms[13] are the clearest examples of the imaginative constitutional geometry of visual constitutionalism. They are also expressions of the collective imaginaries relating to constitutional axiology and constitutional architecture. In a sense, real architecture functionally serves the role of a tool of expression of constitutional architecture and is also a device for the demonstration to the public of its own collective imaginaries and particularly of imaginative constitutional geometry. Normative ideas of justice, freedom and authority, founding constitutional myths relating to unity and the constituent role of people or leaders, of the structure of the state and the role of government are frequently expressed through visual means in architecture.

It also has to be taken into account that constitutional geometry in general and imaginative constitutional geometry in particular are not always at the centre of architecture and the visual arts. Sometimes they express other semiotic phenomena or simply serve pragmatic and functional purposes. Nevertheless, the role of art and architecture as tools for the expression of visual constitutionalism, constitutional semiotic codes, ideas and metaphors and, last but not least, imaginative constitutional geometry must be admitted and properly explained. And, indeed, there are already several theoretical efforts aiming at such scientific analysis of the role of visual forms for expressing legal and constitutional concepts.[14] However, they are not conceptualised either in terms of constitutional semiotics or of constitutional geometry as a semiotic device. This book is an attempt at both the continuation of the efforts of the academic community in that regard and filling in the above-mentioned gap by offering reflections on constitutional geometry in general and imaginative constitutional geometry and its implications in visual constitutionalism in particular.

The idea of hierarchy is expressed via the raising of judges on the podium, thus standing above the parties in proceedings. Thus, there is a vertical power relation expressed through the medium of the difference in the height allocated to the judge and the rest of the participants in the process. The allocation of the places

[13] See L Mulcahy, *Legal Architecture: Justice, Due Process and the Place of Law* (Abingdon, Routledge, 2011) 1–244; Wallsgrove (n 11) 1–230.

[14] See Huygebaert et al (n 2) 1–481; M Asimow and J Silbey, *Law and Popular Culture: A Course Book* (Lake Mary, Vandeplas Publishing, 2020) 1–221 S Mader and M Asimow, *Law and Popular Culture: A Course Book* (New York, Peter Lang, 2013) 3–23; R Lippens, 'Law, Code and Late Modern Governance in Prophetic Painting: Notes on Jackson Pollock, Mark Rothko and Gilles Deleuze' and J Bainbridge, 'Visual Law: The Changing Signifiers of Law in Popular Visual Culture' in A Wagner and J Broekman (eds), *Prospects of Legal Semiotics* (Dordrecht, Springer, 2010) 171–192and 193–215 respectively; S Redhead, *Unpopular Cultures: The Birth of Law and Popular Culture* (Manchester, Manchester University Press, 1995); A Chase, 'Popular Culture/Popular Justice' in J Denvir (ed), *Legal Reelism: Movies as Legal Texts* (Chicago, University of Illinois Press, 1996) 133–54; J Bainbridge, 'Lawyers, Justice and the State: The Sliding Signifier of Law in Popular Culture' (2006) 15(1) *Griffith Law Review* 153; Mulcahy (n 13) 1–244.

of the judge(s), the plaintiff (or the state prosecutor) and the defendant creates a triangular space that frames the power relations of the process. Thus, the triangle[15] as a powerful semiotic tool of visual and symbolic-imaginary constitutionalism is employed in the process of the semiotic signification of constitutional and constitutionally relevant meaning. There is also usually a clear visual distinction between the parties in the process and the public, which is determined by a demarcation line. This line (expressed through different architectural means) is an important instrument for showing distinction and division. In a sense, this is the division between the authority of the state and the pluralism and diversity of the civil society that are both connected and divided by the line.

Imaginative constitutional geometry is also visible in the process of copying the geometric civilisation of classical antiquity. The whole of Western modernity is to an extent an 'invented tradition'.[16] It is a product of the deliberate and creative transplantation and reception of ideas, values and concepts from Greco-Roman civilisation. The political and spiritual elites of Western modernity have carefully constructed intellectual bridges between late medieval Europe (later on also including the New World in North and South America) and the political and conceptual world of ancient Greece and Rome. Part of this process of massive intellectual borrowing and transplantation was the attempt to create a visual world that corresponds to the values of rationalism and humanism as normative ideologies borrowed or re-invented from the realm of wisdom of the ancient world and transformed into political and intellectual pillars of Western modernity. These normative ideologies had also an impact on constitutionalism.

The impact of visual borrowings from ancient Greek and Roman civilisation on imaginative constitutional geometry and visual constitutionalism is very clear. It has also been discussed with regard to other manifestations of visual constitutionalism relating, for example, to constitutional mythologies and normative ideologies. However, the ideas of hierarchy are visible in the architecture of parliaments, governments and courts. These hierarchical visualisations are present on the façades, but also in the buildings themselves. The plenary halls of parliaments are usually constructed along the lines of Greco-Roman amphitheatres. It is well known that the amphitheatrically organised plenary halls represent pluralism, the scaled variety of political parties ranging from the left to the right. The allocation of the seats of the parties on the basis of the distinction between left and right also has biblical connotations. It is grounded in the allocation of saints and sinners on both sides of Jesus Christ on Judgement Day and on the distinction between God's sheep and goats.

It is not a coincidence that some parliaments deliberately avoid the amphitheatre style and construct the plenary hall as a square or rectangle. An example of

[15] For an interesting interpretation of the triangle and the clash between different geometric forms of representation defined as 'image wars', see Z Oklopcic, *Beyond the People: Social Imaginary and Constituent Imagination* (Oxford, Oxford University Press, 2018) 343–47.

[16] Hobsbawm and Ranger (n 6) 1–324.

this can be found in the Bulgarian Parliament building. The amphitheatric allocation of seats was replaced with a square-rectangle allocation after the abolition of political parties and the introduction of a non-party regime in 1934.

The architectural representation of constitutionally relevant ideas is also visible in the design of the roofs of some parliaments. Evident example is the glass roof of the Bundestag, which represents the idea of transparency. Transparency is constitutive for representative democracy in general and parliamentary democracy in particular, and tops it the same way as the Bundestag's glass spiral roof, which was designed by Sir Norman Foster. Moreover, this concrete architectural marvel topping the German Parliament also geometrically expresses the striving towards perfection, the improvement of knowledge and development. These ideas are geometrically signified by the spiral staircase built in the glass dome of the Bundestag. Thus, the rooftop of the Bundestag and, more precisely, its dome signify two important constitutional ideas: transparency and gradual improvement. They are all elements of visual constitutionalism expressing imaginative constitutional geometry. The German example has been partially copied in the geometry of the new building of the Bulgarian Parliament. Its roof is also constructed from glass, thus expressing transparency, but has no in-built spiral demonstrating the striving towards knowledge and perfection.

Moreover, many parliamentary, government and court buildings are constructed on the basis of the interplay between squares and circles. It is well known in the history of art and architecture that both the square and the circle are powerful semiotic forms.[17] When combined, they express the interplay and the fragile equilibrium between heavenly and earthly features, between the corporal and the spiritual etc. These forms are also used in churches, but have particular constitutional signification in terms of the interaction between concepts and powers when used for parliaments or courts.

Finally, the role of constitutional allegories for visual constitutionalism should briefly be mentioned. Constitutional allegories are present in all forms of art. Hence, they are not limited to architecture. However, it has already been noted that this book cannot explore the manifestations of visual constitutionalism in all forms of art due to its methodological focus and space constraints.

Allegories are key elements of constitutional mythology. They are instruments for the signification and representation of constitutional myths and mythologies, but also of normative ideologies and normative ideas. Allegories are exactly that part of constitutional imaginaries which are prone to symbolic representation through the means of visual constitutionalism. In fact, constitutional allegories and constitutional myths are those elements of symbolic-imaginary constitutionalism which are most successfully and easily signified through visual signifiers. Hence, they are central objects of constitutional semiotics that appear at the point of intersection between symbolic-imaginary and visual constitutionalism.

[17] For the role of different geometric forms of representation of meaning in the context of 'image wars', see Oklopcic (n 15) 343–47.

Allegories depicted in paintings or sculptures are typical devices for the semiotic expression of constitutional imaginaries.[18] Ideas of justice,[19] liberty and equality, but also of authority, power, hierarchy, sovereignty,[20] domination and order are frequent objects of representation in art in all of its forms, but mostly through sculptures and large wall paintings. They are signified through different visual signifiers, some of which are based on geometric metaphors, although most of them are based on different types of allegories.

Constitutional allegories are key instruments of constitutional semiotics with projections in both symbolic-imaginary and visual constitutionalism. They are semiotic codes that are also containers of civilisational meaning. They may serve as nodes in the web of visualised symbolic meaning stretching throughout history, defining intellectual borders between constitutional cultures and setting bridges between constitutional civilisations. In that regard, constitutional allegories are also signifiers of intellectual continuity, succession in the line of formative visual imaginaries, normative ideas and founding constitutional myths. They are signifiers of proximity and distance, the approximation of constitutional visuals and imaginaries or, conversely, of ruptures and difference. They are semiotic proxies to deeper knowledge and meaning, bridging the gaps between rational, emotional and symbolic-imaginary constitutionalism.

Constitutional allegories are present everywhere in the world of constitutionally relevant art and architecture. Sculptural, architectural and art depictions of allegories signifying constitutional imaginaries and elements of symbolic-imaginary constitutionalism such as normative ideologies, ideas, myths, mythologies and codes are visual signifiers that are often found in the design of courts, parliamentary and governmental buildings, buildings of law faculties or any other institutions that are directly or indirectly related to constitutionalism. Hence, they are also visible in paintings, sculptures, monuments and park architecture. Constitutional allegories are most widespread in cities in which architecture plans are deliberately oriented towards the expressive and explicit demonstration of symbolic-imaginary and visual constitutionalism, such as Paris, London and Washington DC, but they are also clearly present elsewhere. This is especially true of global cities,[21] but is also visible in capital cities and other major cities.

It is interesting to note that constitutional allegories are not limited to one particular type of constitutionalism defined on the basis of its underlying and leading ideology. They also existed in the pre-constitutional ages of antiquity and the Middle Ages, where constitutionalism was limited to the factual constitution.

[18] See Delmarcel (n 2).

[19] See Paumen (n 2); Korpiola (n 2); Delmarcel (n 2); and Hayaert (n 2).

[20] On the concept of visual sovereignty, see M Raheja, *Reservation Reelism: Redfacing, Visual Sovereignty, and Representations of Native Americans in Film* (Lincoln, NE, University of Nebraska Press, 2011) 1–360.

[21] S Sassen, *The Global City: New York, London, Tokyo* (Princeton, Princeton University Press, 2001) 1–480.

However, they have blossomed during modernity and especially in the constitutive age of modern constitutionalism – the 'long nineteenth century'.[22]

The pressure for the visual representation of constitutional allegories was quite tangible during the formative epoch of modern constitutionalism, but it was also present at other points in the time-space continuum. An example is the powerful, impressive and imperial constitutional allegories that have been created in Soviet art and took the form of Soviet visuals or, more precisely, communist visual semiotics. Architecturally, Soviet-type visual constitutionalism was a mixture of neoclassicism and Brutalism. Semiotically, with a view to the range of Soviet visuals, it used both a secular and a mystical range of signifiers related to the symbolic-imaginary and visual world of Gnosticism. Allegories serving as proxies to tradition that at times took the shape of 'invented tradition'[23] are also visible in non-Western contexts.

[22] E Hobsbawm, *The Age of Revolution: 1789–1848* (New York, Vintage, 1996) 1–368.
[23] Hobsbawm and Ranger (n 6) 1–324.

PART V

Constitutional Geometry and Constitutional Algebra as Semiotic Paradigms for Ordering and Explaining the Constitution, Constitutionalism and Constitutional Law

1

Ordering and Explaining Constitutional Order through Mathematic Metaphors

An Introduction to the Semiotic Theory of Constitutional Geometry and Constitutional Algebra

This part of the book is devoted to two semiotic and epistemic conceptual devices for the organisation and understanding of the constitutional order: constitutional geometry and constitutional algebra. The here emphasis here will be on constitutional geometry due to its greater potential for grasping and framing the constitutional phenomena in a semiotic way. However, attention also will be paid to constitutional algebra since it shows on its own and especially in conjunction with constitutional geometry the potential for mathematic metaphors to explain the constitutional reality in a semiotic manner.[1]

Hence, both constitutional geometry and constitutional algebra are phenomena with combined and enhanced semiotic and epistemic importance and potential. This is due to the fact that they are able to condense, compress, represent and signify meaning related to the macro-structuring and the conceptual shaping and signifying of the normative-institutional, socio-legal, visual, textual and symbolic-imaginary discourses of constitutionalism. In that regard, they perform a range of functions at the crossroads between the above-mentioned dimensions of constitutionalism.

In this part of the book, I will explore constitutional algebra and constitutional geometry as semiotic forms that conceptually belong mainly to symbolic-imaginary constitutionalism.[2] This concerns both their epistemic and ordering

[1] An important contribution to the application of mathematical metaphors in constitutional theory can be found in L Tribe and M Dorf, *On Reading the Constitution* (Cambridge, MA, Harvard University Press, 1993) 81–97. On mathematics as a source of inspiration for constitutional theory and constitutional analysis, see M Termini, 'Proving the Point: Connections between Legal and Mathematical Reasoning' (2019) 5 *Suffolk University Law Review* 5.

[2] On the imaginary capacities and features of geometry, geometry as an imaginary property and 'the geometry of imagining', see E Brann, *The World of the Imagination. Sum and Substance*, (Lanham, MD, Rowman & Littlefield, 2017) 603–37.

dimensions. However, symbolic-imaginary constitutionalism is not a solipsistic and self-enclosed concept. It exists because it contains a representations of concepts, ideas and phenomena that belong to the other constitutional discourses. It is actually a container of imaginaries created through the different processes of the representation of constitutional phenomena. A large part of this process of imprinting of symbols, structures and ideas on the meta-level of the constitutional order shaped in the form of constitutional imaginaries is accomplished through the semiotic process of the signification of meaning. In the process of constitutional semiosis, the semiotic signification of meaning via metaphors[3] derived from natural sciences in general and mathematics in particular plays an important role.

Thus, constitutional geometry and constitutional algebra are of great importance for the organisation of symbolic-imaginary constitutionalism. Nevertheless, they derive some of their key ideas from and thus are also of relevance for other constitutional discourses. Bearing this in mind, I will analyse the relationship between constitutional geometry and constitutional algebra, and the forms of constitutionalism in which they are partially grounded and on which they have an important epistemic impact, resulting in semiotic knowledge. These discourses are especially textual, normative-institutional, visual, and performative constitutionalism. The relationship of constitutional geometry to visual constitutionalism and, more precisely, to architecture has been explained in detail in Part IV, Chapter 6 of this book. However, the assessment here will also take into account the huge emotional capacity of constitutional geometry. Constitutional geometry and, to a lesser extent, constitutional algebra have the ability to enchant the collective imagination of the constitutionally framed socio-legal community. Hence, these concepts are meaningful and even essential for emotional constitutionalism.[4]

This part will start with chapters that define the concepts of constitutional algebra and constitutional geometry. These are conceptual novelties that I propose should be included as part of the toolkit of constitutionalism in general and of constitutional semiotics in particular. They are instruments for semiotic constitutional analysis aiming at achieving a better understanding of the intellectual structures with symbolic and constructive potential that are explicitly or implicitly provided in constitutionalism, constitutional law and the constitution. Thus, constitutional algebra and constitutional geometry belong to the realm of constitutional semiotics in general and symbolic-imaginary constitutionalism in particular.

The very idea of order is based on assumptions of structure, while disorder is associated with broken structure, lack of structure, distorted frame, fluidity of

[3] On the role of metaphors in imaginary discourses of law, see M Del Mar, *Artefacts of Legal Inquiry: The Value of Imagination in Adjudication* (Oxford, Hart Publishing, 2020) 278–330.

[4] On the role of numbers in the social imagination, see E Cassierer, *The Philosophy of Symbolic Forms, Vol 2: Mythical Thought* (New Haven, Yale University Press, 1965) 166–87, who explores what he defines as 'mythical number' and a 'system of sacred numbers'.

content and fuzziness of rules.[5] Nevertheless, ordering may also have a different meaning. It may relate to the creation of an uncontroversial system of legal rules (norms or norms plus principles and other normative regulators). It may focus on the establishment of an institutional system that eventually contains subsystems. Ordering may apply to the consistency of constitutional axiology and normative ideologies, and ideas shaping the philosophy of the constitutional order.

Thus, the order may have structural but also logical, axiological and imaginary aspects and implications. Ordering may consist in structuring and organising through institutional framing, but also in coordinating principles and values, and in adjusting symbols, myths, imaginaries and ideas. In that regard, constitutional geometry and constitutional algebra are appropriate devices for both the structural and non-structural 'ordering of the constitutional order'.[6] They are appropriate intellectual devices for the organisation of both rational and symbolic-imaginary discourses on the macro-shapes and forms of the constitutional order. Consequently, they are instruments for the rationalisation, imagination and symbolic-imaginary signification of the meaning of order with various applications in constitutionalism and constitutional law.

The constitutional order and the constitutional system need to be both ordered and imagined in order to produce feasible regulative results. The constitutional imagination relating to the ordering of the constitutional order and the implementation of imaginary constructed constitutional ordering schemes are intrinsically interrelated in logical, conceptual and pragmatic ways. The constitutional order and the constitutional system are imagined by the authoritative constitutional narrators, visualisers and performers, but also by the members of the constitutionally framed socio-legal community. The addressees of constitutional provisions conceptualise the constitutional order in general and its particular substructures, components, institutional subsystems and the constitutional phenomena through their constitutional imagination. The constitutional imagination is based on a mixture of rational perceptions, but also on emotions and imaginary concepts, which are related to the conscious, subconscious and unconscious parts of constitutional psychology. Some of these imaginary reflections of constitutionally relevant phenomena serve as visual proxies for constitutional truth, understanding and meaning.

In other words, the addressees of the constitutional provisions understand the meaning implied by the authoritative narrators, visualisers and performers – the authoritative sources of constitutional semiotic signification – not only through direct rational reconstruction, but also via semiotic signifiers. These signifiers have

[5] For an alternative, 'liquid authority', see N Krisch, 'Liquid Authority in Global Governance' (2017) 9(2) *International Theory* 237; and M Zürn, 'From Constitutional Rule to Loosely Coupled Spheres of Liquid Authority: A Reflexive Approach' (2019) 9(2) *International Theory* 237.

[6] For the 'ordering of constitutional orders', see E Tanchev, 'The Contemporary Supranational Constitutional Pluralism or the Ordering of Constitutional Orders' in P Kirov (ed), *Constitutional Studies 2012–2013* (Sofia, 'St Kliment Ohridski' University Press, 2014) 171–98 (in Bulgarian).

explicit or implicit semiotic importance and are bearers of meaning represented through signification based on the use of visual-semiotic ordering schemes. Such schemes are the result of the construction, deconstruction and reconstruction of meaning, its symbolic representation and its conceptual compression. In that regard, constitutional imaginaries also require decompression, which is itself an invitation for discursive interpretation of meaning, having huge epistemic and semiotic potential.

The framing of the constitutional order through symbols and metaphors derived from natural sciences is an excellent method for achieving the semiotic signification of constitutionally relevant meaning. Thus, natural sciences serve as an important source of inspiration for the organisation and explanation of the constitutional order through the semiotic representation of meaning. They are containers of constitutional images, symbols and allegories that fuel constitutional semiotics in general and symbolic-imaginary constitutionalism in particular.

Thus, natural sciences have huge imaginary potential and play an important methodological role in the constitutional signification of meaning. Naturally, the influence of natural sciences on constitutionalism and constitutional semiotics must be matched by a critical attitude that should enable the use of semiotic metaphors derived from them, but not their expansion into ultimate and universal tools of constitutional science and constitutional epistemology. The example, signifier and metaphor, inspired by the natural sciences, must remain restricted to their role as additional analytical tools. They should be used cautiously and should not expand into universal instruments for exploring the constitutional order. Thus, the constitutional order as the core of constitutionalism should remain organised and understood as a humanitarian phenomenon and the result of the socio-legal process of the creation of constitutional meaning.

There are a range of constitutional imaginaries based on metaphors derived from the natural sciences. A good example of this is the idea of 'constitutional sedimentation'[7] used for the symbolic-visual depiction of the emergence of EU citizenship in a gradualist way on the basis of the case law of the Court of Justice of the European Union. The sedimentation metaphor has been borrowed from geology. Constitutional sedimentation is a powerful tool for the symbolic representation of legal processes with constitutional relevance.[8] It reveals the power of the symbolic signification of meaning that makes emotional reference to continuity, gradualness, approbation and a layered structure. It reduces the complexity of the phenomenon, condenses constitutionally relevant meaning and serves as a bridge between a rational understanding of the process of the emergence and

[7] On the concept of constitutional sedimentation, see D Curtin, 'The Sedimentary European Constitution: The Future of "Constitutionalisation" without a Constitution' in I Pernice and E Tanchev (eds), *Ceci n'est pas une Constitution: Constitutionalisation without a Constitution?* (Baden-Baden, Nomos, 2009) 76–86.

[8] On the sedimentation of imaginaries, see C Castoriadis, *The Imaginary Institution of Society* (Cambridge, Polity Press, 1987) 131.

development of EU citizenship in jurisprudential way, the visual signification of the emerging rational meaning, and the appeal to emotions and imaginaries relating to the sedimentation and gradual augmentation and changing of reality.

Another example is the exploring of the constitutional dimension of statehood through comparisons with squares and 'territorial containers'.[9] In this case, the metaphors have both geographical and mathematical origins. The 'squared' and 'container-like' territoriality is entrenched in the semiotic interplay between territory and territoriality conceived as a signifier of meaning in both the normative-institutional reality of valid law and in the intellectual discourses of constitutional theory and symbolic-imaginary constitutionalism.[10]

Ordering constitutionalism through recourse to geometry and the use of geometric forms in order to reduce the complexity of constitutional order, its imagining and visualising, and their application as ordering matrixes of the institutional design (mainly of the state institutions and, to a lesser extent, of human status and human rights) is rather underestimated by traditional approaches to constitutionalism and constitutional law. On the other hand, mathematics has had an intellectual imprint on constitutionalism and constitutional law. This is true of both algebra and geometry. An important example here is Bernhardt Windscheidt's 'Begriffsjurisprudenz', which defined law as humanitarian mathematics and tried to reduce the legal process to counting with legal concepts.

The following chapters will demonstrate that constitutional algebra and constitutional geometry have the epistemic and semiotic potential to grasp structural qualities of the constitutional order and represent them in visually and symbolically appealing ways, thus adding a layer of imaginary flair and visual persuasiveness to the rational austerity of the normative and institutional design. Although clearly semiotic devices – and thus forming important part of the realm of constitutional semiotics – constitutional algebra and constitutional geometry also have explanatory power. In that regard, they serve as epistemic devices to both explain and order the constitutional order on the basis of visuals and imaginaries constructed as mathematic metaphors.

After elaborating and presenting coherent and comprehensive concepts of constitutional geometry and constitutional algebra, I will explore them in the context in which they are embedded. This part of the book will provide explanations of the relationship between these two phenomena, which conceptually mainly belong to symbolic-imaginary constitutionalism, and other forms of constitutionalism. More precisely, different aspects of constitutional geometry

[9] On the state as territorial container, see PJ Taylor, 'The State as Container: Territoriality in the Modern World-System' (1994) 18 *Progress in Human Geography* 2; PJ Taylor, 'Beyond Containers: Internationality, Interstateness, Interterritoriality' (1995) 19 *Progress in Human Geography* 1; and N Brenner, 'Beyond State-Centrism? Space, Territoriality and Geographical Scale in Globalization Studies' (1999) 28(10 *Theory and Society* 39.

[10] M. Belov, 'Territory, Territoriality and Territorial Politics as Public Law Concepts' in M Belov (ed), *Territorial Politics and Secession: Constitutional and International Law Dimensions* (London, Palgrave Macmillan, 2021) 15–43.

will be outlined with a view to its presence and appearance in the textual, visual, normative-institutional and socio-legal dimensions of constitutionalism.

In that regard, five main types of constitutional geometry have to be outlined, showing the multilayered and multidiscursive nature of this semiotic concept: first, 'official', normative-institutional and textually embedded constitutional geometry; second, performative constitutional geometry, which is related to the socio-legal discourse of constitutionalism; third, theoretical constitutional geometry outlined in the constitutional literature; and, fourth, imaginative constitutional geometry, which is part of constitutional and political anthropology and of the conscious, subconscious and unconscious constitutional imaginaries. Visual constitutionalism provides the fifth aspect of constitutional geometry; this has already been analysed in Part IV of this book.

It will be shown that all these types of constitutional geometry have semiotic relevance, since they represent and stand for phenomena at the crossroads between different constitutional discourses using symbolic-imaginary and metaphorical constructions derived from mathematics for the purpose of constitutional signification. It will also be demonstrated that all manifestations of constitutional geometry can be subsumed under constitutional geometry as an overarching semiotic concept belonging to symbolic-imaginary constitutionalism.

Furthermore, the concrete shapes and forms of constitutional geometry will be explored. The focus will be on hierarchies, pyramids, circles and networks.[11] The reason for this is that these are the most frequently used and most important forms of constitutional geometry. However, other geometric forms used for the signification and representation of constitutionally relevant meaning will also be outlined and critically compared and assessed. The specific aspects and manifestations of constitutional algebra will also be presented. The conceptual analysis of the shapes and forms of constitutional geometry will be delivered in Part V, Chapter 4, which is devoted to structured constitutional imaginaries, whereas their historical evolution and concrete manifestations will be explored as part of the presentation on the constitutional geometry of Westphalian, post-Westphalian and neo-Westphalian constitutionalism.

Last but not least, the most important functions of constitutional algebra and constitutional geometry will be systematised. They will demonstrate the practical role of these semiotic concepts and epistemic forms based on constitutional knowledge in general, and understanding the organisation of the macro-structures of constitutionalism and the constitutional order in particular. The functional

[11] See also M Belov, 'The Challenges to Westphalian Constitutional Geometry in the Age of Supranational Constitutionalism, Global Governance and Information Revolution' in M Belov (ed), *Global Constitutionalism and its Challenges to Westphalian Constitutional Law* (Oxford, Hart Publishing, 2018) 13–55. The use of squares, circles and triangles as significatory tools and explanatory metaphors of constitutional and constitutionally relevant phenomena is also discussed in Z Oklopcic, *Beyond the People: Social Imaginary and Constituent Imagination* (Oxford, Oxford University Press, 2018) 343–47; and D Roth-Isigkeit, *The Plurality Trilemma: A Geometry of Global Legal Thought* (London, Palgrave Macmillan, 2018) 1–310.

approach exposes the usefulness and the added value of constitutional algebra and constitutional geometry in terms of organising, structuring, exploring and understanding the constitutional order and its institutional design.

Constitutional geometry and constitutional algebra are devices for the organisation of our understanding of the constitutional order and for 'ordering of constitutional orders'.[12] This is done by using mathematic metaphors that are related to shapes and forms of geometry, but also connected to sequences and regularities derived from algebra. Constitutional geometry and constitutional algebra provide symbolic soundness to socio-political and constitutional phenomena shaped on the basis of analogies grounded in geometry and algebra. In that regard, what is important for constitutional geometry and constitutional algebra is the signification of meaning through recourse to geometric comparisons and eventually to mathematical-numerical operations.

This process of symbolising, signifying and standing for constitutionally relevant phenomena leading to an increase in epistemic clarity and to the semiotic representation of meaning is based on the use of the formal and symbolic-imaginary features of the derived mathematic metaphors. It is rarely paralleled by the substantial use of the corresponding forms, algorithms or regularities.

Hence, constitutional geometry and constitutional algebra employ the shapes and forms, the formal structure and the general conceptual design of mathematics. They 'distil' the overall symbolic appeal of mathematic metaphors. However, they usually detach the symbolic geometric structure or the algebraic sequence or phenomenon from its internal quality, which is typical for the epistemic context – the realm of mathematics – in which it is traditionally embedded. Such detachment of the shape and the symbolic parameters of the structure from the content and context are typical for the process of the semiotic signification of meaning through metaphors. It is also applicable in the context of constitutional semiosis.

Hence, it is not the inner quality, the content and the substantial meaning which is important for constitutional algebra or constitutional geometry, but rather the epistemic and semiotic potential, the emotional appeal and the capability for the visual representation of constitutional phenomena in symbolic-imaginary constitutionalism in general and in constitutional theory in particular. It is the symbolic capacity of the mathematical metaphors that renders them able to also signify meaning through visual signifiers in visual constitutionalism as well as of engaging emotional persuasiveness that makes them relevant for emotional constitutionalism. All this qualifies constitutional algebra and constitutional geometry not as mathematic but as semiotic concepts and tools. This makes them important elements of constitutional semiotics and symbolic-imaginary constitutionalism.

Constitutional geometry and constitutional algebra are also tools of constitutional theory for the structuring and organising of the process of signification of meaning derived from textual, normative-institutional or performative

[12] On the 'ordering of constitutional orders', see E Tanchev, 'The Contemporary Supranational Constitutional Pluralism or the Ordering of Constitutional Orders' in Kirov (n 6) 171–98.

constitutionalism in the fields of constitutional theory. They are also instruments for of mastering of the constitutional anthropology of the authoritative speakers and indirectly for shaping the collective constitutional imaginaries of the constitutionally framed socio-political community.

Thus, while the signified objects may have a textual, normative, institutional or factual (empirical) nature, the signifiers are imaginary geometric (or less frequently algebraic) constructs that are part of symbolic-imaginary constitutionalism and have projections in theory, valid law, practice and the collective imagination. Some of the signifiers are also part of visual constitutionalism. Moreover, the signifiers based on mathematic metaphors that are organised as forms of constitutional geometry also have important projections in the fields of emotional and visual constitutionalism. In that regard, they are bridges between ranges of constitutional discourses constructed through a multidiscursive constitutional semiotic process. This process is semiotic because it leads to the symbolic-imaginary production of meaning on the basis of the signification of constitutional signifieds through signifiers derived from mathematics. The semiotic process is constitutional and not mathematical. This is due to the fact that semiotic signification concerns constitutional phenomena and the represented meaning is constitutional and not mathematical. Mathematics is used here only as a source of symbolic comparison and as a repository of metaphors used in the course of constitutional semiosis.

2

Inspiration, Imagination and Signification through Rationalisation

The Concept of Constitutional Algebra

Constitutional algebra is a phenomenon of constitutional semiotics. It is a concept that includes semiotic metaphors, which can be used for the signification of constitutional meaning in the process of constitutional semiosis. It includes signifiers arranged around the symbolic-imaginary repertoire derived from mathematics and, more precisely, from algebra. Constitutional algebraic signifiers are capable of signifying meaning stemming from normative-institutional and textual constitutionalism. Thus, it is a semiotic resource showing the intellectual imprints of algebraic phenomena entrenched in constitutional text and texture, and derived from valid law in the realm of the constitutional imagination. Hence, constitutional algebra is a phenomenon with epistemic value and semiotic capacity that may provide additional knowledge of constitutionalism as a symbolic-imaginary phenomenon.

Constitutional algebra is present in different ways in constitutionalism and in constitutional law. It is the main formal ordering scheme for the organisation of the text of normative acts, including the normative acts as sources of constitutional law and the constitution itself. Acts of Parliament and acts of government, frequently even the decisions of the apex courts, are organised on the basis of mathematical – or, rather, algebraic – sequences. They are structured in articles, paragraphs, points and other numerical series. Furthermore, the text of most constitutions is organised into numerical sequences. An exception is the Hungarian Fundamental Law of 2011, which is organised into both letters and ciphers. However, the sequential character of ordering constitutional texture is also present in this Hungarian constitution. Typically their different parts (chapters, articles, paragraphs and subparagraphs) follow different numbering systems.

Thus, algebraic sequences lie at the core of the structure of textual constitutionalism. They predetermine the organisation of the constitutional text and subsequently also the structuring of the constitutional normative regulators (principles, values and norms). Hence, algebraic sequences are the main instrument for the arrangement of the official outlook of valid constitutional law and, subsequently, of its textual and normative-institutional dimensions. They are of pivotal importance in nomotechnics. Therefore, the algebraic structure of constitutional text also has a symbolic role in terms of signifying and underlying its rational, logical and consequential character. Constitutional algebra is a signifier of reason, logic and order, and of the sequential character of constitutional relations.

Constitutional algebra performs an organising function for the logical sequencing of constitutional texture. It aids the overall efforts of the constitutional legislator to offer systematic, ordered and consequential text that is based on explicit rationality. This rationality is also visible in this case of constitutional algebra. At first glance, constitutional algebra seems to have a rather technical character, serving as an instrument for ordering the main 'building blocks' of constitutional law – norms, principles and institutions. In fact, and to an extent paradoxically, it is exactly the technical nature of this aspect of constitutional algebra in its capacity as an ordering scheme of the constitutional text that shows its potential for signification. The abstract-technical essence of constitutional algebra allows it to signify the sequential character of constitutional texture and to represent the striving of modern rational constitutionalism for the logical and quasi-mathematical perfection of the constitutional law. In a sense, the more formal constitutional algebra is, the more visible is its potential for the symbolic detachment of constitutional content from constitutional form and the greater its semiotic potential.

Thus, in parallel to the ordering role of constitutional algebra, its numeric-ordering aspect is also of huge symbolic importance. It demonstrates the belongingness of the constitution as a textual phenomenon to the general legal effort for mastering the complexity of the world in a reductionist, rationalist and prescriptive manner. It signifies the overall rationalist attempt at the rational organisation of the socio-political world, following the example of the natural sciences and its concrete implications for structuring valid law in relation to text and texture as both written and ordered reason. 'Having the state in your pocket' in the form of a written text that is organised following the mathematical sequential logic of constitutional algebra has been the dream of many political philosophers and reformers of constitutional modernity and the Enlightenment.

Thus, in parallel to its function to order and structure the constitutional texture in mathematic sequences, the numerical aspect of constitutional algebra has also a civilisation function in terms of modernising, rationalising, systematising and reducing the immense complexity of socio-political relations, their imaginary projections in the collective imaginaries and in the constitutional and political anthropology,[1] and their framing within the system of valid law. In that regard, as already mentioned above, the numerical-sequential aspect of constitutional algebra is also of semiotic importance. It is a form of signification via simplification, the construction of sequential logic and systematisation following very basic mathematical logic. Rationalising means ordering, while ordering means sequential systematising. Furthermore, sequential systematising leads to the need to make recourse to constitutional algebra for both structural-organisational and

[1] See E Cassierer, *The Philosophy of Symbolic Forms, Vol 2: Mythical Thought* (New Haven, Yale University Press, 1965) 166–87.

symbolic reasons. It is exactly these symbolic reasons that highlight the semiotic relevance and capacity of constitutional algebra.

Indeed, this numerical-sequential aspect of constitutional algebra is mostly related to the formal structure and instrumental organisation of textual constitutionalism. It has relatively limited appeal to the constitutional imagination, since it is considered as a traditional organising scheme of the constitution that is usually present in all constitutions and constitutional orders. Moreover, it is the overall idea of human reason being able to order the constitutional world through text and the constitutional text through numerical sequences that is emotionally appealing and captures the constitutional imagination. However, this ordering capacity of collective constitutional reason has been taken for granted since the nineteenth century.

There are also other manifestations of constitutional algebra which are more visible and influential, but less emotionally appealing. They are phenomena entrenched in rational constitutionalism without inspiring and enchanting the collective constitutional imagination of the constitutionally framed socio-political community. In fact, these are expert models and tools for organising or explaining constitutional law which have huge epistemic value, but play a rather limited semiotic role. Examples of this are the mathematical models for the functioning of state institutions and for the qualification of different constitutional forms of civic engagement in the political process. The procedural hurdles in the way of access to state institutions – for example, the electoral threshold for being represented in Parliament and other institutions, or the number of signatures required before a state institution can be presented with a petition or civic initiative or for triggering a referendum – are examples of constitutional algebra. The same is true of the quorums and majorities for the functioning of state institutions or for adopting different decisions via direct or representative democracy.

Constitutional algebra is also used with regard to constitutional timing. Constitutional procedure is organised around many terms and temporal sequences that are capable of mathematical organisation and representation in textual and normative-institutional constitutionalism. This is particularly true of the judicial process, the parliamentary process (including the legislative, budgetary and controlling processes and procedures) and electoral and other direct democratic processes. Here constitutional algebra is reduced to the counting of terms, periods and deadlines, and thus is intrinsically related to rational constitutionalism.

Consequently, at first glance, both the formal-procedural and the temporal aspects of constitutional algebra are purely rational. They seem to be deeply entrenched in rational and normative-institutional constitutionalism, as well as having projections in textual constitutionalism, and look as if they have nothing to do with symbolic-imaginary, visual or emotional constitutionalism. This is partly but not completely true. It is true that constitutional algebra and its formal-procedural and the temporal aspects claim to have extensive rationality. This is the reason why they are so important for the different variants of rationalism in constitutional law. This is especially true of rational choice, public choice and veto players' theories,[2] which rely heavily on the rationality of the constitutional process and are clear examples of an overemphasis on rational constitutionalism.

Hence, constitutional algebra also has relevance beyond valid law. It is used in theory and in political management for measuring the power of different veto players in the constitutional field. It is also put into practice in qualitative scientific approaches constructing coordinate schemes, maps and continuums for exploring the allocation and behaviour of political players such as constitutional institutions, political parties and citizens.

Thus, constitutional timing seems to be a central element of rational constitutionalism perceived as a composite construct, including theoretical and normative-institutional dimensions. More precisely, it has multiple manifestations in the institutional design of constitutional procedures. It is an additional dimension of the separation of powers – the temporal separation of powers[3] – and the specific discourse of constitutionalism and constitutional law.

Nevertheless, the organisation of time in constitutional law also has implicit symbolic meaning. Time may be conceived as a political resource distributed among constitutional players and related to key procedures that together have a huge hidden impact on symbolism and the constitutional imagination. The distribution of time for the different decision-making processes, the allocation of time for different topics, and the temporal separation of powers are indicators of power. Time is both power and an indicator of power;[4] it is a political resource with constitutional forms and dimensions.

Time is also inspirational. It is an indicator of strength, of substantial and political importance, and also a source of constitutionally relevant imagination. It may be an element of constitutional imaginaries, constitutional mythology and normative ideologies. The imagination of time is part of imaginary constitutionalism. And time – although framed in terms of constitutional pragmatism and described using tools of constitutional algebra – is also embedded in symbolism and imagination. This is particularly true of the way in which constitutions conceptualise and imagine the past and the future. The symbolic-imaginary potential of time is especially visible with regard to constitutional memories.

In summary, the semiotic strength of constitutional algebra seems to be hidden in its apparent symbolic weakness. Constitutional algebra is entrenched in rationality. Its ontology, teleology and axiology seem entirely rational. The mathematical – or, more precisely, algebraic – ordering of the constitutional

[2] See, eg, G Tsebelis, *Veto Players: How Political Institutions Work* (Princeton, Princeton University Press, 2002) 1–344; and T Konig, G Tsebelis and M Debus (eds), *Reform Processes and Policy Change: Veto Players and Decision-Making in Modern Democracies* (Dordrecht, Springer, 2010) 1–298.

[3] On the temporal separation of powers, see M Belov, 'Separation of Powers Reconsidered: A Proposal for a New Theoretical Model at the Beginning of the 21st Century' in A Geisler, M Hein and S Hummel (eds), *Law, Politics and the Constitution: New Perspectives from Legal and Political Theory* (Frankfurt am Main, Peter Lang, 2014) 47–60.

[4] On the constitutional relevance of time, see, eg, S Ranchordas and Y Roznai, *Time, Law and Change* (Oxford, Hart Publishing, 2020) 1–408.

order appears to be at the same time a product and a safeguard of rational and normative-institutional constitutionalism explicated through their textual dimensions. However, it is precisely the capacity of constitutional algebra to appear formal, rational and logical that entails its great power to represent and signify. Constitutional algebra is a signifier of rational constitutionalism taken as a holistic phenomenon and in its particular manifestations and dimensions. It is a device for the conveying of the hidden symbolism of rationality entrenched in the sequential character of constitutional texture and in the different mathematical schemes for organising constitutional processes and procedures. This is quite evident when it comes to the signification of time as a fundamental constitutional resource and phenomenon that enables the organisation and exploration of the constitutional past, present and future. Thus, constitutional algebra is a semiotic device for signification through rationalisation and for the triggering and representation of rationalist imaginaries.

3

The Concept of Constitutional Geometry

Imagining, Signifying, Understanding and Ordering the Constitutional Order through Geometric Metaphors

Constitutional geometry is a concept that makes it possible to structure the constitutional order using geometric metaphors. It is a theory for understanding the ordering and intellectual representation of constitutional order through the lens of constitutional semiotics. It is also a meta-theory of constitutional law – a theory on how to structure and understand theory or, more precisely, how to cope with geometric metaphors used in constitutional theory.[1]

Constitutional geometry is a central object in the research and exploration of constitutional semiotics. Simultaneously, it is also a methodological approach to constitutionalism and constitutional law from a semiotic perspective. Constitutional geometry as an ideal, normative, institutional, textual, visual and factual phenomenon is an object of theoretical framing and exploring through an analysis of geometric signifiers used for the signification of constitutional and constitutionally relevant meaning. Thus, it promotes a thematic focus on constitutional semiotics as a holistic and autonomous scientific method and theory. At the same time, constitutional geometry as a result of theory is also one of its key devices for the production and representation of semiotic meaning. Its elements trigger semiotic representation, which has repercussions in normative-institutional and socio-legal reality explicitly or implicitly expressed through the means of the semiotic signification of textual, visual and performative constitutionalism. Hence, constitutional geometry may even be conceived as an intellectual game for the signification of constitutionally relevant meaning through geometric metaphors that transversally penetrates the range of fields or dimensions of constitutionalism.

[1] Geometric metaphors are widely used in order to explain constitutional principles, institutions and phenomena, and to order constitutional theories. See Z Oklopcic, *Beyond the People: Social Imaginary and Constituent Imagination* (Oxford, Oxford University Press, 2018) 343–47; T Beukers and M van der Sluisand, 'The Variable Geometry of the Euro-Crisis: A Look at the Non-Euro Area Member States' (2015) 33 *EUI Working Papers, Law* 1; D Roth-Isigkeit, *The Plurality Trilemma: A Geometry of Global Legal Thought* (London, Palgrave Macmillan, 2018) 1–310.

Constitutional geometry is a theory that lies at the crossroads between constitutional semiotics and constitutional epistemology. It is a phenomenon of symbolic-imaginary constitutionalism with huge relevance for other constitutional discourses. It offers a semiotic lens for the observation of the constitution, constitutional law and constitutionalism in general. It is key in the decoding of geometric codes via the semiotic deconstruction of textual, normative-institutional, visual and performative constitutionalism. It is also a device for the signification of meaning via its encoding in the above-mentioned constitutional discourses. Constitutional geometry and its forms are explained, expressed and conceptualised mainly by the authoritative narrators, performers and visualisers of the constitutional community, although it is generally based on the structured constitutional imaginaries which have a diffuse but palpable presence in a phenomenon that I define as cloud constitutionalism (this is explained in Part V, Chapter 7 of this book).

Constitutional geometry is a semiotic concept because it focuses on the process of the expression of meaning relating to the organisation of institutional design through its signification via geometric metaphors of symbolic importance. Hence, the signifieds are phenomena belonging to the institutional and normative discourse of constitutionalism, but also to its socio-legal, empirical discourse. In addition, the signifiers may vary. They may appertain to both the symbolic-imaginary realm of theory and shared constitutional imaginaries in the constitutional anthropology of the socio-legal community or to the institutional-normative discourse of valid law. These theoretical proposals require further explanation. In other words, the rather complex, multilayered and multidiscursive process of constitutional semiosis through geometric metaphors must be explained in more detail.

Constitutional phenomena with semiotic importance that can be represented using metaphors derived from geometry exist in both the empirical reality of the socio-political relations between the constitutional players and in the normative reality of valid law where constitutional architecture organises constitutional norms and constitutional institutions according to specific institutional logic. This logic stems from, follows and itself produces durable patterns of institutional behaviour that can be visually represented through recourse to constitutional geometry. It has been explained in Part IV that constitutional geometry as a signification tool and a strategy of constitutional semiotics is also used in visual constitutionalism. Thus, it also has a visual dimension that is different from the performative-institutional aspects of constitutional geometry discussed here.

Phenomena that play the role of signified objects in the process of constitutional semiosis may also be produced in performative constitutionalism where the constitutional players implement constitutional architecture on the ground. An example of this are the institutional triangles, squares, circles, networks or hierarchies shaped through the durable patterns of behaviour of office holders. They delineate inter-institutional relations through recourse to geometric metaphors.[2]

[2] See Oklopcic (n 1) 343–47.

Such inter-institutional performative constitutional geometry signifies the relationship within the horizontal and vertical structure of the state in national as well as in supranational and subnational constitutionalism. The general shapes of such inter-institutional performative constitutional geometry are broadly preconditioned and partially entrenched in constitutional texture, which can describe or prescribe institutional patterns of behaviour. Nevertheless, these patterns are also drawn in an invisible and gradual way through performance. Hence, both texture and performance contribute to the establishment of the durable semiotic patterns of constitutional architecture. Thus, constitutional geometric signifieds can also be found in textual constitutionalism and in the institutional design of the constitutional order.

In fact, it is the interplay between the constitutional discourses – textual, normative-institutional, performative, visual and symbolic-imaginary – and, more precisely, the figurative phenomena and results they produce which triggers the need for an overarching explanatory and ordering paradigm and a meta-theory of the signification of the structural characteristics of the constitutional order. Such a function can be most suitably performed by constitutional geometry as an element of the theory of constitutional semiotics, a component of symbolic-imaginary and visual constitutionalism, and a meta-theory of constitutional law.

In that context, textual constitutionalism (and, to a lesser extent, visual constitutionalism) and the normative-institutional constitutional discourses are engaged in the process of constitutional geometric semiosis in two ways: they are both signifiers and signifieds. This means that elements of the constitutional design represent factual phenomena, while themselves being represented in theory and in constitutional imagination. When such a multilayered process of representation of meaning is accomplished through recourse to geometric metaphors, this is also a process of constitutional semiosis. Constitutional geometric semiosis is based on the signification of meaning via geometric shapes and forms, and its translation from performative in textual and institutional constitutionalism, and then from this to symbolic-imaginary constitutionalism (including both constitutional anthropology and constitutional theory).

Constitutional semiosis based on geometric metaphors is even more dubious. Phenomena of the empirical socio-political world are represented in the constitution and constitutional law through institutional design following a structural approach that sometimes results in geometric forms of constructivist signification of meaning. In this case, the signifieds are elements of factual reality and the pragmatic and performative dimensions of power relations. These may be inter-institutional relations, relations between the spheres and levels of power, schemes for organising the relationship between the state, the society and the individual etc.[3] The signifiers belong to the realm of normative-institutional and textual constitutionalism. They are institutions that are validated through expression in

[3] For a critical assessment of the 'level' metaphor used in multilevel constitutionalism theories, see G della Cananea, 'Is European Constitutionalism Really "Multilevel"?' (2010) 70 *ZaöRV* 301.

norms and are framed and represented via textually constructed metaphors. Such textual and normative-institutional signification of empirically derived or empirically oriented meaning usually leads to the establishment of macro-shapes and forms of constitutional architecture.[4]

For example, the natural tendency towards the hierarchical and pyramid-like organisation of power relations in executive power is signified through institutional pyramids and hierarchies provided by constitutional law, entrenched in normative and institutional hierarches, and expressed through textual constitutionalism. The concentration of power in authoritarian orders is represented in schemes of political supremacy of the institution, leader, party etc. in the text and the normative order of the constitution, and again results in institutional hierarchies. They regulate, symbolise and incite pro-authoritarian constitutional imagination at the same time.

These hierarchies have pragmatic, epistemic, ideological and semiotic dimensions. It is precisely the interplay between hierarchy as an empirical model of power relations, a pragmatic scheme for their normative provision and institutional organisation, and an ideological matrix for shaping the socio-political constitutionally relevant behaviour that justifies the need for a semiotic approach to constitutional power relations structured in geometric forms. Winning over minds and shaping constitutional anthropology to follow the general or specific structures of the constitutional order cannot be achieved in an entirely rational manner through rational, textual or normative-institutional constitutionalism. It requires the engagement of constitutional imagination stemming from significations in constitutional texture, resulting in institutional ideal models and institutional imaginaries, but going beyond them in the realm of the collective imaginaries of the members of the constitutionally framed socio-political community and even in the domain of the collective unconscious and the constitutional archetypes.[5]

To express this metaphorically: Kelsen is not sufficient for having legitimate, emotionally expressive and imaginary impressive and enchanting constitutional order. Freud and Jung are also welcome as an aid in excavating the deeper constitutional meaning. And there is also the need to engage with Peirce and de Saussure as translators of the constitutionally embedded meaning in the symbolic language of semiotics. In the case of constitutional law, this intellectual enterprise can result in attempts at grasping the constitutionally relevant meaning of the way in which the constitutional order in general and the constitutional architecture, design and

[4] Architecture is used as a metaphor for the structure of law, its institutional design and organisation in B McCall, *The Architecture of Law: Rebuilding Law in the Classical Tradition* (Notre Dame, IN, University of Notre Dame Press, 2018) 1–560. Thus, architecture is used as a signifier of the structure of law.

[5] On the concept of constitutional archetypes, see D Law, 'Constitutional Archetypes' (2016) 95 *Texas Law Review* 153; and G Frankenberg, 'Comparing Constitutions: Ideas, Ideals, and Ideology – Toward a Layered Narrative' (2006) 4(3) *International Journal of Constitutional Law* 439, https://doi.org/10.1093/icon/mol012.

inter-institutional relations are structured in particular by using the theory of constitutional geometry.

Nevertheless, the process of semiotic representation usually follows a reverse logic and is constructed in a reverse manner. In other words, the constitutional architecture and the constitutional geometry entrenched in textuality and texture, and organised in normative and institutional constructions may serve as an object of signification – the signified – which is then reconstructed and represented through signifiers belonging to visual and performative constitutionalism. In fact, this is the more frequent and typical sequence of semiotic representation. It is due to the predominance of the prescriptive over the descriptive nature of the constitution. The constitution prescribes the shapes and forms through which the constitutional order is demonstrated, performed, visualised and thus perceived by the members of the constitutionally framed socio-political community. Hence, the constitution is much more the authoritative ideal model of the constitutional order than a direct reflection of the political order. Consequently, it is the socio-political performance of the constitutional actors that signifies the meaning implied in textual constitutionalism and expresses it through performative and visual signifiers. In that regard, the practical expression of constitutional law by the political players via symbolic behaviour in visual and performative constitutionalism is comparable to its reflection in constitutional theory and in the collective constitutional imaginaries.

The normative-institutional constitutional geometry of valid law expressed in textual constitutionalism may be signified not only via constitutionally relevant visuals and performance, but especially through constitutional imaginaries. Thus, the most important semiotic process relating to constitutional geometry concerns the representation of the constitutional order via geometric metaphors in constitutional theory and in symbolic-imaginary constitutionalism in the form of cloud constitutionalism.[6] In this process, the institutions and the shapes and forms of normative and institutional order provided by valid constitutional law, underlying its constitutional architecture and expressed in constitutional texture, are the signifieds, while the structured constitutional imaginaries are the signifiers.

Constitutional geometry is also an epistemological concept. This is due to the fact that it offers alternative insights in terms of understanding the structure and organisation of the constitutional order. These alternatives differ from more traditional institutional schemes, such as the separation of powers, the principle of competence, institutional patterns of behaviour regulated as constitutional procedures and the general institutional design enshrined in the constitutional institutions. Thus, constitutional geometry goes beyond different forms and variants of institutionalism and positivism. Yet, it reveals implicit methods for shaping constitutional design based on constitutional semiotics as a general theory for approaching the constitutional order from the viewpoint of symbolic-imaginary,

[6] On the concept of cloud constitutionalism see Part V, Chapter 7 of this book.

visual and performative constitutionalism. Constitutional analysis based on constitutional geometry allows for the detection of additional shapes and forms that implicitly organise constitutional relations. It is a structural cognitive approach for explaining the geometric patterns of organisation of the constitutional order through recourse to constitutionally entrenched or practised geometric and thus structured imaginaries.

Constitutional geometry is also a meta-theory due to the fact that it is a theory that explains how to reorganise constitutional theory according to the postulates of constitutional semiotics. In addition, it is a meta-theory because it theorises how the theory of constitutional law conceptualises constitutional imaginaries framing constitutional phenomena, constitutional institutions, constitutional schemes and the constitutional order via geometric metaphors. Constitutional geometry as a meta-theory should be understood as a contribution to constitutional methodology offering a structural approach to constitutional law based on a mixture of constitutional semiotics and constitutional epistemology.

Constitutional geometry is a paradigm which aims at both organising and understanding the constitutional order. Thus, it is both an important instrument of constitutional epistemology and of constitutional constructivism at the pragmatic, institutional, theoretical and meta-theoretical levels. Constitutional constructivism here means mainly the intellectual constructivism relating to constitutional theory and constitutional imagination, while legal constructivism mostly relates institutional design. In that regard, constitutional geometry has huge epistemic potential. It reveals meaning that is not immediately available when using traditional legal positivist, legal philosophic, legal realist or socio-legal methods. It is also a device for the uncovering of organising models of the constitutional design related but not limited to the official constitutional architecture based on institutionalism.

Constitutional geometry is both a semiotic and an epistemological paradigm. Its epistemic nature consists in its capacity to serve as an instrument for the achievement of meaning that is different from the traditional legal positivist, legal realist, socio-legal and philosophical approaches. This is also what situates it in the realm of semiotics. Constitutional geometry is an explanatory, and thus an epistemic, paradigm, which relies on symbolic forms for the representation of meaning. Thus, the epistemological and semiotic features of constitutional geometry are mutually reinforcing and mutually interdependent.

Constitutional geometry allows for a different approach to the constitutional order viewed through the semiotic lens. Thus, the meaning achieved through recourse to constitutional geometry is bound to the symbolic-imaginary discourse of constitutionalism. The epistemic value of constitutional geometry is implied in its ability to convey hidden meaning symbolised and represented through the means of constitutional semiotics. On the other hand, it is conceptually vague and pragmatically meaningless from an epistemological perspective if it is not combined with semiotic approaches, interpreted and appreciated in the context of the semiotic signification process and rooted in symbolic imaginary constitutionalism.

Constitutional geometry is an intellectual and conceptual bridge between textual, visual, performative and symbolic-imaginary constitutionalism. Like all constitutional phenomena, it has a textual dimension. It is a textually related concept because the conclusions related to its specific manifestations should be done with a view to the valid law which reveals itself in the forms of textual constitutionalism. Thus, the textual character of constitutional geometry is a result of the central role of textual constitutionalism in shaping constitutionalism as a multilayered phenomenon. The constitutional text is a core container of epistemic content for constitutional geometry. And, conversely, constitutional geometry is used by the constitutional and ordinary legislators as a framing and ordering concept that has its implications for textual constitutionalism and imprint for valid constitutional law based on constitutional texture.

However, constitutional geometry is a phenomenon that stretches far beyond constitutional text, constitutional texture and textual constitutionalism. It is a central device for organising the explanatory models constructed and represented as part of visual and symbolic imaginary constitutionalism based on processes of semiotic organisation and the conveying of meaning. It is an instrument for the representation of meaning contained in constitutional texture and performed in durable patterns of behaviour of the constitutional players in the field of the collective imaginary. It is a device for both the rational construction of explanatory shapes and forms of the constitutional order, and for conveying their symbolic-imaginary and affectual influence on the process of understanding the constitutional phenomena and the constitutional system.

Constitutional geometry in its broadest sense, which does not coincide with the meaning I am implying here, may be used to denominate different phenomena and divergent processes for the explication, construction and representation of meaning. First, it may be a tool that can be used to organise theories – for example, this approach has been used by David Roth-Isigkeit.[7] Second, it can be a set of descriptive tools for the visual illustration of inter-institutional relations.[8] This approach has been borrowed from political science and sociology and is used, for example, by Laurence Tribe and Michael Dorf,[9] and has been conceptually promoted in the form of 'mapping of legal institutions' and the development of the 'institutional imagination' by Roberto Mangabeira Unger.[10] Third, the institutionalist approach also is implicitly and intuitively inspired by geometry in order to arrange or explain the structure of complex institutions as well as inter-institutional relations. Last but not least, Hans Kelsen has offered very important

[7] See Roth-Isigkeit (n 1) 1–310.

[8] On the role of geometric representations of social meaning in social studies, see M Bauer and P Johnson-Laird, 'How Diagrams Can Improve Reasoning' (1993) 4(6) *Psychological Science* 372; and M Lynch, 'Pictures of Nothing? Visual Construals in Social Theory' (1991) 9(1) *Sociological Theory* 1.

[9] See L Tribe and M Dorf, *On Reading the Constitution* (Cambridge, MA, Harvard University Press, 1993).

[10] According to Unger, 'the focus of mapping is the attempt to construct a picture of our institutions'. See RM Unger, 'Legal Analysis as Institutional Imagination' (1996) 59(10 *Modern Law Review* 22.

insights for the development of a theory of constitutional geometry. In that regard, special attention should be paid to his theory of the hierarchical and pyramid-like structure of the legal order based on the ontological assumption of the existence of the basic norm (the 'Grundnorm').

However, none of the above-mentioned approaches has framed its intellectual endeavour as constitutional geometry. And none of them has used it as a tool for constitutional semiotics. Thus, the theory of constitutional geometry that I am proposing here is an original conceptualisation of the structured constitutional imaginaries based on a creative mixture of epistemological and semiotic approaches. In this regard, I am offering an approach in which constitutional geometry is used as an explanatory and ordering scheme and as an epistemic and semiotic tool belonging mainly to symbolic-imaginary constitutionalism, but also having important repercussions for textual, normative-institutional, visual and performative constitutionalism.

4

The Semiotic Role of Structured Constitutional Imaginaries

Constitutional imagination can take different shapes, forms and instantiations that emerge in a range of fields of constitutionalism.[1] Constitutional imagination and its embodiments in constitutionalism are produced by a multitude of processes for the collective deconstruction, construction and reconstruction of meaning expressed in imaginary, symbolic, metaphorical and allegoric forms. Some of them have also performative and visual dimensions and manifestations.

Many attempts have been made in the social sciences and the humanities to analyse how imaginaries emerge, develop, take different shapes and forms, and stabilise in collective consciousness, but also in the collective unconscious. Freud, Karl Jung, Lacan[2] and Lévi-Strauss are just some of the most obvious names in that great, complex and polyphonic scientific endeavour. Psychoanalysis,[3] the study of the collective unconscious, exploration of archetypes, structural and post-structural studies, critical, post-modern and deconstructivist approaches, social, political and cultural anthropology co-existed and have been practised as intellectual competitors or have been merged and used with a degree of synergy or in an asymmetric and counter-punctual manner as patchwork devices for the achievement of epistemological progress in research on the symbolic, the imaginary and the real.[4]

However, no persistent and sufficiently systematic attempts have been made to explore the role of collective imaginaries in the sphere of law and, more precisely, in constitutional law. In particular, legal science in general and constitutional science

[1] According to Přibáň, 'constitutional imaginaries as polysemous and polyvalent societal forces which are internally constituted by the systems of positive law and politics yet have the paradoxical capacity of communicating the common good and values in functionally differentiated modern society'. See J Přibáň, *Constitutional Imaginaries: A Theory of European Societal Constitutionalism* (Abingdon, Routledge, 2020) viii.

[2] On the importance of Lacan for legal semiotics, see J Broekman and L Cata Backer, *Lawyers Making Meaning: The Semiotics of Law in Legal Education II* (Dordrecht, Springer, 2013) 67–83.

[3] For an interesting mixture of psychoanalytical and semiotic approaches to law and signs, see P Goodrich, 'Psychoanalysis in Legal Education: Notes on the Violence of the Sign' in R Kevelson (ed), *Law and Semiotics*, Vol. 1 (New York, Plenum Press, 1987) 193–215.

[4] See J Lacan, *Écrits* (New York, WW Norton & Company, 2007) 1–896; J Lacan, *The Language of the Self* (Baltimore, Johns Hopkins University Press, 1956) 29–53; C Castoriadis, *The Imaginary Institution of Society* (Cambridge, Polity Press, 1987) 160–65; and B Olivier, 'Lacan's Subject: The Imaginary, Language, the Real and Philosophy' (2005) 23(1) *South African Journal of Philosophy* 1.

practised intellectual self-restraint, refraining from engaging with collective legal and constitutional imaginaries. They were rather indifferent and insensitive to the problems of the symbolic and the imaginary, while being preoccupied with the real. The real has been defined differently – as valid law, as case law, as 'law-in-action' or as the sum of these methodological and conceptual discourses.

This has been the situation until recently, when a range of studies devoted to emotions, imaginaries and visuals in law have developed in the scientific discourse. All these studies have jointly contributed in one way or another to the emergent 'linguistic turn',[5] 'visual turn'[6] and 'emotional turn'[7] in law in general and in constitutional law in particular. Nevertheless, most of them did not approach these phenomena and issues from a semiotic perspective, and they were largely insensitive to structural constitutional imaginaries.

The predominant legal and constitutional discourses are stuck in constructivist and rationalist ontologies and teleological approaches to law. They are obsessed with power, authority, compulsion, legitimacy and reason as key factors for making, unmaking, understanding and justifying law. Indeed, these are valid concerns and objects of scientific exploration, since the above-mentioned power phenomena are the organising centres of law and the legal order. However, such a preoccupation is somewhat one-sided. It underestimates the fact that people construct, obey and apply not only constitutional law, but also their performative choices as subjects of constitutional law are not restricted to constitutional creativity, constitutional obedience and constitutional disobedience. Their constitutionally relevant acts are not limited to textual, visual and performative constitutionalism, and thus to 'constitutional doing'. The people also imagine constitutional law and dream about the constitutional past, present and future. They sublimate constitutional experience in conscious, subconscious and unconscious, individual and shared, collective ways. Consequently, 'constitutional doing' is paralleled and to an extent predetermined by 'constitutional dreaming', 'constitutional imagining', 'constitutional emotion sharing' and 'constitutional showing'.

The process of constitutional imagination can take different forms and directions. It may be moulded, casted and contained in concrete forms having a textual, visual or performative explication and nature, but it can be also unrestrained by

[5] See R Rorty (ed), *The Linguistic Turn: Essays in Philosophical Method* (Chicago, University of Chicago Press, 1992) 1–416; K Hirschkop, *Linguistic Turns, 1890–1950: Writing on Language as Social Theory* (Oxford, Oxford University Press 2019) 1–337; and B Alderman, *Symptom, Symbol, and the Other of Language: A Jungian Interpretation of the Linguistic Turn* (Abingdon, Routledge, 2015) 1–161.

[6] See L Mulcahy, 'Eyes of the Law: A Visual Turn in Socio-legal Studies?' (2017) 44(1) *Journal of Law and Society* 111; and M Jay, 'Cultural Relativism and the Visual Turn' (2002) 1(3) *Journal of Visual Culture* 267.

[7] See K Abrams and H Keren, 'Who's Afraid of Law and the Emotions?' (2010) 94(6) *Minnesota Law Review* 1997, available at: https://ssrn.com/abstract=2434251; A Sajo, 'Emotions in Constitutional Institutions' (2016) 8(1) *Emotion Review*) 44; A Sajo, 'Emotions in Constitutional Design' (2010) 8(3) *ICON* 354; S Bandes, J Madeira, K Temple and E Kidd White (eds), *Research Handbook on Law and Emotion* (Cheltenham, Edward Elgar, 2021) 1–640; and A Amaya and M Del Mar (eds), *Virtue, Emotion and Imagination in Law and Legal Reasoning* (Oxford, Hart Publishing, 2020) 1–275.

forms. It can be dynamic, fluid and may well go beyond the capability of law to impose its rationality and to restrain it in durable, explainable and communicable 'shared containers of legal and constitutional meaning'.

Constitutional imagination can be a fuzzy, imprecise, intuitive and diffuse process of 'constitutional feeling'. It can be stuck in individual and the collective subconsciousness. Constitutional imaginaries may be bulky concepts that broadly frame the overall process of constitutional dreaming and the psychological engagement of the people with the rather hidden and implicit domains of constitutional subconsciousness. These kinds of constitutional imaginaries are difficult to stabilise and frame in concrete shapes and forms. They are instead emotional categories that evaporate when shared publicly.

Nevertheless, such an 'evaporation of constitutional imaginaries', their fluidity and fuzziness, and the impossibility of their objective sharing and structured public stabilisation do not preclude their role as important determinants of the collective constitutional consciousness and subconsciousness. Thus, even these non-stabilised, diffuse and unstructured imaginaries are key factors of constitutional anthropology and, subsequently, of the practical performance of the constitution and the constitutional order. Moreover, they also frame the socio-political community's attitudes towards the constitutional past and the parameters of their collective constitutional aspirations for the future, resulting in different forms of symbolic-imaginary constitutionalism.

This is the reason why the academic community must start exploring constitutional imaginaries more intensively. Hence, the promotion of new disciplines of scientific research such as constitutional semiotics, constitutional psychology and the comparative constitutional research of constitutional imaginaries can result in the achievement of better knowledge in that regard. It should be mentioned that academia has recently responded to the scientific challenges outlined above with an increase in literature devoted to imaginaries and their role in law,[8] to 'law-and-emotions' and particularly to emotional constitutionalism.[9] Nevertheless, the semiotic issues stemming from constitutional imaginaries and taking into account the differentiation between diffuse and unstructured constitutional imaginaries remain largely unexplored.

[8] See Přibáň (n 1) 1–251; J Přibáň, 'A Social Theory of Constitutional Imaginaries: Beyond the Unity of "Topos-Ethnos-Nomos" and its European Context' in U Belavusau and A Gliszczyńska-Grabias (eds), *Constitutionalism under Stress: Essays in Honour of Wojciech Sadurski* (Oxford, Oxford University Press, 2020) 175–90; J Komárek (ed), *European Constitutional Imaginaries: Between Ideology and Utopia* (Oxford, Oxford University Press, 2021); and J Komárek, 'Political Economy in the European Constitutional Imaginary – Moving beyond Fiesole', *Verfassungsblog*, 4 September 2020, https://verfassungsblog.de/political-economy-in-the-european-constitutional-imaginary-moving-beyond-fiesole. There are also several projects devoted especially to constitutional imaginaries. Probably one of the most visible ones is 'IMAGINE – European Constitutional Imaginaries – Utopias, Ideologies and the Other', https://imagine.sites.ku.dk. This is a project led by J Komárek and is devoted to the research of European constitutional imaginaries.

[9] Sajo (n 7); Bandes et al (n 7) 1–640; and Amaya and Del Mar (n 7) 1–275.

Due to space constraints and the specific focus of the analysis provided here, I will also limit my exploration of this kind of unstructured constitutional imagination. Indeed, I also explore its role and impact on constitutionalism elsewhere in the text when discussing the different features of symbolic-imaginary, but also of performative and visual constitutionalism. However, I will have to leave its proper and detailed exploration for the near future. Thus, here I will focus on the forms of structural constitutional imagination and the structured constitutional imaginaries it produces. These possess stronger semiotic potential, especially when used in the context of constitutional geometry as a meta-theory of constitutional law.

Structured constitutional imaginaries result from processes of shared psychological experience relating to the constitution, constitutional law and constitutionalism. Here constitutionalism is understood as a bulky concept that includes a range of constitutionally relevant phenomena, processes and performances 'on the ground', in the real life of the constitutionally framed socio-political community and in the forms of textual constitutionalism comprising valid law and scholarly or otherwise constitutionally influential literature.

The constitutional imaginaries are structured because they possess distinct forms in which – or, more precisely, through which – constitutional reality in all its complexity is perceived, remembered, imagined and psychologically (re-)created and reconstructed. Typically, structured constitutional imaginaries result in geometric forms. These become stabilised and objectivised in the shared imaginary experience imprinted in textual, visual and performative constitutionalism in the forms originally created in geometry, and subsequently metaphorically used as epistemic, semiotic and ordering devices in law and, more precisely, in constitutional law.

That is why the structured constitutional imaginaries are actually forms of constitutional geometry. In fact, constitutional geometry is based on the existence of structured constitutional imaginaries, which are its expressive tools for the representation and signification of meaning. Thus, constitutional geometry is the overall ordering paradigm that enables the theoretical conceptualisation of structured constitutional imaginaries. Conversely, the structured constitutional imaginaries constitute the semiotic means for the concretisation of the general intellectual messages and the conceptual appeal of constitutional geometry.

Both constitutional geometry and the structured constitutional imaginaries which are frequently being explicated in constitutional geometric shapes and forms make reference to valid law and thus to textual and normative-institutional constitutionalism. However, they are frequently not explicitly provided as such by valid law and are definitely not reducible to it. In fact, structured constitutional imaginaries are devices that serve semiotic, epistemic and ordering functions for all constitutional discourses and all forms of constitutionalism. Hence, they also perform a bridging function, serving as a semiotic juncture between textual, normative-institutional, rational, emotional, visual, performative and symbolic-imaginary constitutionalism.

In that regard, the overall role of structured constitutional imaginaries and thus also of constitutional geometry for explaining constitutional law in a metaphorical way through the constitutional imagination and subsequently via the constitutional signification of meaning is rather significant. Constitutional geometry and structured constitutional imaginaries allow for the stabilisation of symbolic meaning, expressed in geometric shapes and forms, for its signification and communication between the members of the constitutionally framed socio-political community. Thus, constitutional geometry promotes a partially objective approach and thus allows for a proper exploration of collective constitutional imaginaries. It offers proxies for the constitutional imagination organised as shapes and forms of constitutional geometry and representing important examples of structured constitutional imaginaries.

Consequently, constitutional geometry and structured constitutional imaginaries are key epistemic tools of symbolic-imaginary constitutionalism. They are independent of other forms of symbolic-imaginary constitutionalism. Nevertheless, they may also merge with them, thus producing normative ideologies, ideas, myths, mythologies, allegories and even utopias expressed in and thus signified through geometric forms.

Constitutional geometry is a semiotic approach for explaining the ordering of constitutional order on the basis of structured constitutional imaginaries. An important reason for this is the fact that it explores the macro-shapes and forms of constitutional design with the help of geometric metaphors that have huge semiotic and epistemic potential. Hence, constitutional geometry is an instrument for the revealing of hidden meaning entrenched in the constitutional order by the constitutional legislator or the other authoritative speakers of the community via different tools for expression of normativity – norms, principles, institutions and eventually also normative ideologies.

The structured imaginary meaning can be deliberately hidden due to political considerations or an elitist desire to construct multiple constitutional discourses, only some of which are revealed to the wider public. However, it may also be hidden due to other unpremeditated reasons. For example, it may not be overt due to the fact that the forms of constitutional geometry are gradually negotiated in the constitutional discourse, mainly by the authoritative constitutional narrators of textual constitutionalism or in the socio-legal interaction by the authoritative performers of performative and visual constitutionalism. This may also be the result of unintended but feasible trends of signification and construction of meaning structured in the shapes and forms of constitutional geometry that is gradually being entrenched in the constitutional imagination and symbolic-imaginary constitutionalism.

Last but not least, the meaning may be produced in the theoretical discourse. Thus, it is not exactly hidden – it is overtly elaborated in constitutional literature and in other authoritative constitutional texts – but its transposition to the relevant areas of valid law requires the semiotic reconstruction of meaning. This process of conceptual construction and reconstruction, resulting in the alignment of theoretical and normative meaning, produces creative tension between the theoretical and the normative-institutional discourses of constitutionalism. This is actually a semiotic process – a process of the semiotic alignment of symbolic-imaginary representations of meaning, since such representations are both textual and are expressed in the adjustment of symbolic content structured in geometric metaphors.

This is the reason why constitutional geometry results in structured constitutional imaginaries encapsulating meaning. Hence, the shapes and forms of constitutional geometry in their capacity as signifiers of meaning can be valuable containers of information not only for the durable attitudes of the authoritative constitutional narrators and performers, but also for the general realm of imaginaries produced by the community. Thus, they can also be defined as epistemic bubbles or capsules of condensed meaning. The range of these epistemic-semiotic capsules can be indicative of the overall characteristics of symbolic-imaginary constitutionalism. If properly studied and compared, they may constitute an additional device of comparative constitutional epistemology rooted in constitutional semiotics.

The concept of macro-shapes and forms of constitutional geometry is bulky. It is intentionally constructed so as not to be fully internally coherent, which would be impossible due to the incoherency of its object – the collective constitutional imaginaries and the way in which they are manifested and explicated in the realm of constitutionalism as a multidiscursive and multifaceted phenomenon. In contrast to the concepts of institutional design or constitutional architecture and even unlike the very concept of constitutional geometry, the macro-shapes and forms are and actually have to be kept somewhat undefined and fuzzy.

This is due to the fact that the constitutional geometric shapes and forms are post-modern concepts that approach the constitutional phenomena in a deconstructive, but also in a reconstructive way. They conceptualise constitutional order as a patchwork of imaginary 'bits and pieces' that are informative and telling, precisely because of their partial inconsistency and their focus on those segments of constitutional (dis)order that are emotionally, symbolically and imaginary appealing. The strengths of the constitutional order metaphorically deconstructed and reconstructed in geometric metaphors and based on 'bits and pieces' – the macro-shapes and forms as being geometrically signified – are in its engagement with symbolic representation of constitutional meaning and in its fragmented (and thus focused) multidiscursive character.

The macro-shapes and forms include all manifestations and instantiations of constitutional geometry that have relevance for the signification of constitutionally relevant meaning concerning the broader structures of constitutional phenomena and the constitutional order. They are reflections of the constitutional imagination and are instantiations of structured constitutional imaginaries. The constitutional geometric macro-shapes and forms may relate to institutions, institutional complexes (composite constructs of constitutional institutions), constitutional processes and procedures or any other phenomena that may be symbolically represented in geometric metaphors and thus may be durable, appealing to the collective imagination, and expressive, while representing structural characteristics of constitutional phenomena in an emotionally and visually persuasive way.

Let us briefly compare constitutional geometric shapes and forms with other structural and constructivist paradigms in constitutional law and constitutional order. These are mainly institutional design and the constitutional architecture.

Institutional design is a phenomenon that comprises the system of constitutional institutions ordered according to an overarching organisational logic. It is the deliberate design used by the constitutional legislator to 'order the constitutional order' through the methods of legal institutionalism. The broader concept of institutional design has its concrete manifestation in constitutional law as constitutional design. In that regard, these are mutually related concepts, the former being broader and including the latter.

Institutional design may result in macro-shapes and forms of the constitutional order, and thus in forms of constitutional geometry. Institutional design is frequently based on specific constructive logic that can metaphorically be expressed through geometric metaphors. Thus, it is prone to the semiotic signification of meaning via constitutional geometry. Nevertheless, it is based on explicit or implicit logic that predetermines its ontology, teleology, axiology and overall structure. In contrast, the macro-shapes and forms are more intuitive, discursive parts of the constitutional order conceptualised as a bulky concept that also includes symbolically appealing 'bits and pieces'. They stem from imaginary deconstructions and aim at the construction of symbols and signifiers of meaning that are appealing to the constitutional imagination. Hence, they are prone to semiotic representation and emotional-imaginary speculation through metaphorical geometric narratives.

The constitutional architecture is a somewhat more provocative, original and thus unclear concept.[10] Nevertheless, it is more open to the semiotic signification of constitutional phenomena through extra-legal metaphors than the concept of constitutional design. The concept of constitutional architecture is based on a comparison between the constitution, constitutionalism and especially the constitutional order with architectural and construction metaphors.[11] It is actually the construction metaphor that lies at the core of the concept of constitutional architecture that is the bearer of semiotic potential. It is capable of engaging constitutional imagination by triggering structural metaphors derived from the constructivist approach to architecture. In that regard, while resting on metaphors derived from the positivist natural sciences and aiming at constructing visuals and constitutional imaginaries that signify constitutional meaning relating to the organisation of the constitutional order, constitutional architecture is closer to the idea of constitutional geometry. Again, similarly to institutional design, the constitutional architecture is a semiotic figure having huge symbolic potential and based

[10] On the concept of constitutional architecture see G Frankenberg, *Comparative Constitutional Studies: Between Magic and Deceit* (Cheltenham, Edward Elgar, 2018) 27 et seq.

[11] On the use of architectural metaphors relating to constitutional timing, see R Izquierdo, 'The Architecture of Constitutional Time' (2014–15) 23(4) *William & Mary Bill of Rights Journal* 1089.

on holistic assumptions that follow internal logic. In contrast, the constitutional shapes and forms are not holistic, but are fractured significations of structural meaning and institutional constructive imaginaries which do not presuppose entirely consequential institutional logic.

In a sense, the macro-geometric shapes and forms relate to both constitutional design (the institutional design applied to constitutional law) and the constitutional architecture. This is due to the fact that they may eventually coincide with the design and architecture of constitutional institutions, and thus may also have regulatory and institutional organising force. Clear examples of this are bicameralism and multicameralism, and the hierarchical pyramid-like ordering of the executive and judicial power institutions. Architectural and construction metaphors may also be used in conjunction with constitutional geometry with regard to the territorial models of power provided by the constitution.

Nevertheless, the macro-shapes and forms as structured forms of constitutional imaginaries mainly relate to constitutional geometry because they are mostly devices for the signification of symbolic meaning. They are much more semiotic figures with epistemic importance for symbolic-imaginary constitutionalism and its relation to textual and normative-institutional constitutionalism than instruments for the ordering of the constitutional order in a systematic and internally coherent way.

It must also be clarified that the macro-shapes and forms are different geometric metaphors with symbolic meaning that are practised as explanatory and, to a lesser extent, ordering devices of constitutional phenomena by the authoritative narrators, visualisers and performers of the community. As already explained above, they do not necessarily coincide with the institutional or normative design. This is due to the fact that they are mostly a product of the constitutional imagination and of the constitutional signification of meaning produced by the authoritative narrators and performers of the community.

Thus, while institutional and normative design has legal normativity, being part of the system of valid law, the structures of constitutional geometry may possess it or not. They do have such normativity if they are explicitly provided by the constitution and the other sources of constitutional law as an element of the constitutional architecture and institutional design, examples of which have been given above. However, frequently they possess only factual normativity stemming from the inspirational power of the constitutional imagination (sometimes exposed and further developed by constitutional theory) that is triggered and provoked by them.

This inspirational power is a rather fuzzy concept from a legal positivist viewpoint. However, it may vary in practice, depending on the convincing potential of the constitutional geometric form and its capacity to sustain stable imaginary structures with a durable imprint on theory, constitutional anthropology and the collective constitutional imagination of the constitutionally framed socio-legal community.

The inspirational power and the convincing potential of constitutional geometry are generated in the process of constitutional semiosis which flows through the different constitutional discourses (textual, performative, normative-institutional and symbolic-imaginary). Thus, it is dependent on both normative and factual phenomena, and is only partially institutionalised and legally traceable. It requires multidiscursive research via creative and critical semiotic deconstruction using the joint research power of positivist legal studies, constitutional anthropology, constitutional semiotics and constitutional epistemology.

Consequently, the macro-shapes and forms are the result not only of constitutional and ordinary legislation leading to valid law; they are also the product of constitutional deliberation and thus stem from the activity of authoritative constitutional narrators, performers and visualisers. These are constitutional actors capable of producing constitutionally relevant meaning via deliberative and performative acts accomplished in the empirical (socio-legal) discourse and having imprints in visual and performative constitutionalism due to their legal or factual recognition as sources of symbolic normative meaning. Moreover, constitutional geometry and its shapes and forms are signifiers of explicit or, more frequently, hidden meaning. This meaning is entrenched in textual constitutionalism and is also shaped and moulded in performative constitutional discourses, sometimes expressed in constitutionally relevant visuals, but appealing to normative constitutional imaginaries.

The concrete shapes and forms of constitutional geometry will be explored in Part V, Chapter 8 of this book. They will be analysed in a socio-legal context in conjunction with the shifts from Westphalian to post-Westphalian and neo-Westphalian constitutionalism[12] – concepts that will also be explained in that chapter.

This approach will make it possible to demonstrate that the transition from one constitutional civilisation to another is not only paralleled by changes, shifts and abruptions in institutional design and constitutional axiology; it also massively affects symbolic-imaginary constitutionalism and produces novel structured constitutional imaginaries. Hence, the constitutional transition also has semiotic relevance. Conversely, this means that each constitutional civilisation has its own constitutional imaginaries, including specific constitutional geometry. Subsequently, the theory that I am going to prove is that constitutional transitions may be approached and also explained through the analytical lens of constitutional semiotics. The variations of constitutional geometry as a framing model of structured constitutional imaginaries and of the constitutional semiotics underlying not only the constitutional model and constitutional order but also the entire constitutional civilisation will demonstrate the ability of constitutional semiotics to serve as a tool of comparative constitutional law in general and comparative constitutional transitions in particular.

[12] On the concept of Westphalian and post-Westphalian political orders, see also R Falk, 'Revisiting Westphalia, Discovering Post-Westphalia' (2002) 6 *Journal of Ethics* 311.

5

Constitutional Geometry as an Explanatory and Ordering Paradigm of Constitutionalism

Rational constitutionalism is preconditioned upon processes of shaping, structuring, ordering, organising and systematising. Ordering is produced by systematisation stemming from the rational and systematic use of reason and, vice versa, systematisation is naturally connected to a process of giving durable shape and form to the ordered constitutional content. Thus, the process of ordering, structuring and systematising is indispensable for a positivist and institutionalist approach to constitutionalism. The establishment of order, the maintenance of a holistic, coherent and entirely uncontroversial constitutional system, the imposition of structures that are institutionalised, normatively provided and textually entrenched is the main impetus and raison d'etre of modern rational constitutionalism. Rational and normative-institutional constitutionalism are heavily dependent on ordering and systematising, which themselves are embedded and entrenched in rationality as a normative ideology, an axiological axis, a pragmatic imperative, legal and intellectual method, and an overall conceptual paradigm of modern constitutionalism.

Thus, using shapes and forms presented as institutions, institutional design and institutional relations is an indispensable feature of institutionalism as the predominant theory of rational constitutionalism. Giving concrete shape to and investing order in the socio-political disorder is the core teleological concern of all forms of rational constitutionalism and legal positivism. Legal realism and socio-legal studies of constitutionalism and constitutional law may also be organised and explained through various shapes and forms. Thus, they also work with and rely on structured imaginaries as a form of semiotic reflection of the shapes and forms of the constitutional order.

The constitutional imagination relies on shapes and forms as well. It has been clarified that shapes and forms are manifestations of the structured constitutional imagination. They exist at the crossroads between rational and symbolic-imaginary constitutionalism and are a result of both reason and imagination. In fact, they demonstrate the deep and inseparable connection between the intellect and intuition,[1] the rationality and capacity of the individual, and the collective imagining and symbolising of constitutionally relevant meaning.

The constitutional imagination underlies the process of constitutional semiosis. It results in forms of the structured constitutional imagination. These serve as epistemic bubbles and bearers of symbolically signified knowledge, metaphorical signs of meaning and proxies of constitutional knowledge and wisdom that are represented through geometric comparisons, allegories and metaphors. In that regard, structured constitutional imaginaries not only have the function of triggering imagination and promoting the symbolic signification of meaning; they also have the epistemic function of the promotion of information, knowledge and wisdom implied in symbolic and semiotic forms. Last but not least, they are ordering devices of the constitutional order – building blocks of a semiotic ordering of constitutional meaning.

The specific character of this mode of ordering of constitutional meaning is that it is neither holistic nor entirely systematic. Constitutional geometry does not pretend to be a universal device for explaining the essential characteristics of the constitutional order. It is also not a holistic model for ordering the constitutional order in an uncontroversial and fully logical way. There is no holistic truth behind the signification system of constitutional geometry and no ultimate and universal ordering logic. In this sense, constitutional geometry orders symbolic-imaginary constitutionalism through structured constitutional imaginaries in an asymmetric way – as an 'order of bits and pieces'. Hence, constitutional geometry proves to be a post-modern device for the achievement of a necessary degree of adjustment of rational, textual and normative-institutional constitutionalism into symbolic-imaginary constitutionalism. This is done in a discursive way using semiotic methods for the representation of meaning.

Imaginary constitutional constructions rely extensively on the production of ordering symbols, symbolic shapes and forms, and the creation of forms of the structured constitutional imagination. They perform a dual role, having two main functions – reductionist and signification functions.

First, imaginary constitutional constructions have a reductionist function. They reduce the complexity of the legal order with its range of issues spread throughout its normative, institutional and socio-legal fields into recognisable symbolic forms. Reductionism is produced by the symbolic signification of meaning through recourse to a range of symbols derived from geometry. In that sense, constitutional semiosis results in the geometric reductionism of constitutional meaning. The reduction of constitutional content and constitutional meaning to geometric shapes and forms is a method of signification of condensed meaning that is highly appealing due to its further intellectual representation and reconstruction

[1] See H Bergson, *The Creative Mind: An Introduction to Metaphysics* (New York, Dover Publications, 2010) 1–240; and G Deleuze, *Bergsonism* (Princeton, Zone Books, 1990) 13–37.

using constitutional semiotics as a tool for the encoding and decoding of structured constitutional imaginaries. Hence, imaginary and conceptual reduction is paralleled by a process of signification of meaning. This is done through geometric signifiers of signifieds contained in the constitutional order. Hence, the process is predominantly semiotic.

In that regard, the second function of imaginary constitutional constructions is to signify and reproduce meaning. Thus, the shapes and forms that are produced by the constitutional imagination and form part of symbolic-imaginary constitutionalism are necessarily bound by a process of constitutional semiosis. They are the result of the semiotic production of imaginary reality and are elements of semiotic processes of representation and signification of meaning in the symbolic-imaginary discourse based on phenomena that are initially part of the textual, performative, socio-legal and normative-institutional constitutional discourses.

If the general intellectual paradigm of ordering is translated into legal reality, having a legal system means ordering the bricks of legal texture according to universally recognisable rules that are valid for all, giving compulsory shape to the fluid content of facts, and structuring durable patterns of behaviour united by concepts, paradigms and institutions that are interrelated in a logical and uncontroversial way. The general motto of legal modernity is 'making order out of disorder'. Although order is achieved differently by legal institutionalism, legal positivism, legal normativism and legal realism, it is achieved on the basis of general, universally applicable and durable epistemic rules. Some of them also have semiotic importance. For example, this is the case when constitutional meaning is represented through geometric visuals and is signified via recourse to geometric metaphors that serve as explanatory and ordering matrices of structured constitutional imaginaries.

It is exactly at the point of intersection between constitutional epistemology and constitutional semiotics where the theory of constitutional geometry steps in. To order the constitutional order, constitutional and ordinary legislators need building bricks that have epistemic content and possess legal normativity. Textually, the legislator builds up normativity via textual provisions, thus also producing textual signification of meaning. Contextually, we can also detect and outline forms of constitutional texture, many of which have semiotic relevance. On the basis of constitutional texture, the constitutional and ordinary legislator constructs different epistemic nodes of normative order – values, aims, principles, norms and norms with principle character.[2] They are arranged according to broader conceptual paradigms containing an overall logic that governs the shaping of the constitutional order.

According to the predominant institutional discourse, these are the constitutional institutions. Following institutionalist logic, the institutions are the universal

[2] See also R Alexy, *Theorie der Grundrechte* (Frankfurt am Main, Suhrkamp, 1994).

forms of constitutional law: the ultimate formal signifiers of substantial unity and functional coherence. They are internally consistent and based on coherent logic. They are instruments for the achievement of constitutionally permissible interests that are defined in advance as being legitimate according to the general axiology and teleology of the constitutional model. Institutions interact in a predictable way, leading to the establishment of typical patterns of inter-institutional behaviour. Thus, they are sufficient for the construction of the constitutional system in terms of its organisation and structuring.

Moreover, institutions are the main epistemic containers of the constitutional order, demonstrating its overall logic, functionality and structural design. In other words, for legal institutionalism, the creation of a coherent institutional system is the ultimate goal of the constitutional and ordinary legislator. It is the perfect and exhaustive device for the ordering of the constitutional order and for the mutual adjustment of multilayered constitutional orders.

However, this is only partially true. Institutions are the skeleton of constitutionalism. They are based on presumptions of rationality, the predictability of institutional performance, and the existence of durable patterns of behaviour and of typical roles that must be fulfilled and performed by rationally inspired and minded players. All these assumptions are to an extent valid. However, if applied exclusively as the only ordering and explanatory matrix, they may skew our understanding of the constitutional world and constitutionally relevant socio-legal behaviour. An exclusively applied institutional approach does not take the social context as well as the symbolic, imaginary, emotional and empirical dimensions of constitutionalism seriously. It is overburdened with rationalist assumptions and perceives the world in an entirely holistic and thus distorted way. It relies on excessive rationalism overshadowing the symbolic-imaginary aspect of constitutional performance.

Nevertheless, institutionalism as theory and normative practice contains a very powerful idea: that we need to order constitutional relations in a durable way through rationally constructed shapes and forms. Actually, institutionalism does not use the concept of shapes and forms, but that of institutions. The institutions themselves are not necessarily moulded into clear forms. There are exceptions (eg, the bicameral structure of some parliaments, the hierarchy in the executive power and the pyramid-like organisation of the judiciary, the territorial structure of state and public power on the basis of geometric interrelations of vertical subordination); however, these confirm the rule that institutionalism focuses on institutions and not on macro-shapes and forms for their visual representation. Moreover, institutionalism does not engage with problems of representation and signification of meaning via semiotic figures. Thus, it is generally insensitive to structured constitutional imaginaries.

However, structured constitutional imaginaries are of key importance for understanding the semiotic structure of the constitutional order. The macro-shapes and forms for the signification of symbolically relevant meaning and for the conceptual imaginary representation of the constitutional order in general or its most important containers of structured meaning in particular are bridges between rational, textual, normative-institutional and symbolic-imaginary constitutionalism. They have both epistemic and prescriptive value, serving the function of explaining and ordering the constitutional order. The human mind perceives the constitutional reality not only in a systematic and rational way, but also in a reductionist and symbolic-imaginary way. It reduces the complexity of the constitutional order and its socio-legal and intellectual implications by using proxies of reality.

The institutions are to an extent such reductionist proxies. They reduce the complexity of constitutionalism through the imposition of frameworks of political behaviour and patterns of permissible institutional behaviour. Thus, they contribute to the systematisation of the normativity of power relations.

Institutions are even conceptual centres of powerful mythology based on normative ideologies and ideas. Institutional mythology enchants people with the magic of the typical functions, traditional roles and powerful path-dependency of institutional behaviour and design. Clear examples of this are the normative ideologies of parliamentarism, the concept of the head of state as a 'neutral power',[3] the doctrines of political neutrality of courts etc. Some structural principles of constitutional law such as sovereignty,[4] the separation of powers and political pluralism are deeply embedded in normative ideologies and are dependent on structural myths and mythologies that are further developed and concretised on the basis of institutionalism.

Thus, the institutionalist approach is also entrenched in symbolic-imaginary representations of reality which have to make the otherwise rational design of the constitutional institution fit the collective imaginaries of the constitutionally framed socio-political community. Hence, institutions are themselves signifiers of constitutional meaning which is rational, but also symbolically and emotionally loaded. They are proxies of both legal and socio-political reality and are embedded in the social context with its symbolic-imaginary dimension.

Nevertheless, institutions also need to be explained, ordered and signified. They are phenomena of normative-institutional constitutionalism, but they also have important implications in textual and rational constitutionalism. Their standing in valid law must be signified in textual, visual, performative and symbolic-imaginary constitutionalism. This is done through constitutional semiosis and forms of constitutional semiotics. The most appropriate tools for the semiotic signification of institutional meaning are the forms of constitutional geometry. The macro-shapes and forms of constitutional geometry are of particular importance here. They serves as semiotic representations of institutional design and impact the moulding of structured constitutional imaginaries. Hence, the

[3] B Constant, *Principes de politiques applicables à tous les gouvernements représentatifs* (HACH. LIVRE-BNF, 2016) 1–333.

[4] See Z Oklopcic, *Beyond the People: Social Imaginary and Constituent Imagination* (Oxford, Oxford University Press, 2018) 1–416.

semiotic representation of institutions through constitutional geometry occurs via the reduction of institutional complexity to general shapes and forms.

Thus, constructing geometric metaphors for the elements of constitutional order and for the constitutional order itself is an important method for achieving epistemic simplicity, semiotic enchantment, the combined rational-emotional-imaginary persuasiveness of the institutional design and the constitutional architecture, and for intellectually grasping the overall logic of the constitutional order. This epistemic-semiotic reductionism is paralleled by the signification of constitutional meaning through geometric metaphors producing structured constitutional imaginaries. The shapes and forms used for mastering the institutional and normative complexity of constitutional law promote the creation of new meaning. They are themselves sources and containers of meaning. They are intellectual bridges between the institutional-normative and the symbolic-imaginary dimensions of constitutionalism.

Hence, the compression and creative restructuring of meaning through the mechanism of conceptual reduction to forms of constitutional geometry is also a source of new constitutional and constitutionally relevant meaning. It is an element of constitutional semiosis revolving around constitutional geometry in a permanent process of signification, the representation of meaning, and the evolution-production of meaning and its shaping through structured collective imaginaries. The elements of constitutional geometry condense ideas that allow for the deconstruction and reconstruction of normative worlds, and serve as triggers of the constitutional imagination.

In this context, it should again be noted that constitutional geometry is a bridging concept. It lies at the crossroads of constitutional discourses, while at the same time packs them in its striving to convey hidden meaning and its ambition at organising them according to the normativity and the logic of symbolic-imaginary and visual constitutionalism. Through its shapes and forms, constitutional geometry represents structured constitutional imaginaries and signifies the normative-institutional reality of valid law. Thus, it creates and offers visually representable messages of textual and rational constitutionalism in the field of symbolic-imaginary constitutionalism.

In terms of constitutional semiotics, geometric metaphors are signifiers of the organising schemes institutionalised by the constitution and constitutional law, based on rational constitutionalism and explicated via textual, performative and visual constitutionalism. These organising schemes of normative-institutional constitutionalism are the signifieds – the objects represented through geometric metaphors in the process of constitutional semiosis. The result of this process of signification of constitutional meaning entrenched in textuality and institutional normativity is its representation in the form of geometric metaphors that serve as constitutional imaginaries. These imaginaries are then used as containers of symbolic and thus reductionist and condensed meaning, and are put in practice as analytical devices in constitutional theory. They serve as building blocks of symbolic-imaginary constitutionalism and belong to the toolkit of constitutional semiotics.

In that regard, the semiotic process for the construction of constitutional geometric metaphors includes a range of intellectual activities. It starts with the deconstruction of meaning implied in textual and rational constitutionalism, mainly through norms and institutions as well as via constitutional axiology. Sometimes the reconstruction of constitutional geometry and the establishment of its signifiers (the macro-shapes and forms of the constitutional order) is achieved through the deconstruction of factual phenomena exposing geometric orderings of institutions and institutionalised patterns of behaviour in performative and visual constitutionalism. This meaning gained through the intellectual deconstruction of facts and norms is then compressed, condensed and reduced into geometric metaphors. This is the proper process of the semiotic reconstruction of meaning. Finally, the geometric shapes and forms – being capsules or containers of the semiotic representation of meaning – are used as triggers of epistemic processes of knowledge of the broader shapes and forms of the constitutional order and of the construction of their imprints in symbolic-imaginary constitutionalism.

The above process of constitutional geometric semiosis demonstrates that constitutional geometry is an important analytical device with epistemic, symbolic and ordering functions. It is an instrument for the shaping and ordering of the symbolic-imaginary constitutionalism in the course of the semiotic representation of meaning derived from various signified phenomena provided by textual and normative-institutional constitutionalism. It shows that constitutionalism can be presented not only as an institutional chessboard and 'game of codes', as demonstrated elsewhere in the book, but also as a 'game of shapes and forms' and a 'game of structured collective constitutional imaginaries'. In that regard, constitutionalism is not just valid law and a normative framework ordering the constitutional order in a holistic, deductive, imposed and thus one-sided way; it is also an intellectual enterprise and challenge to the objective stabilisation of the realms of facts and norms triggered by the constitutional imagination. Hence, constitutional geometry is the result and demonstration of the imaginary anxieties and intellectual perplexities of the post-modern world explicated in semiotic terms and resulting from processes of signification of meaning and thus of constitutional semiosis.

The constitutional order and the constitutional system need to be shaped and formed. Law requires structure, but constitutional law in particular is preoccupied with structures. Public law in general and constitutional law in particular are highly dependent on a range of structural approaches (the most visible of which is institutionalism) and is thus prone to exploration via structural metaphors. This opens up space and gives legitimacy for constitutional geometry as both a structural and a semiotic approach to the constitutional order. In fact, this is the only semiotic approach that is applicable to constitutional structures.

The structures of the constitutional order – its geometric parameters – are shaped by the constitutional and ordinary legislators and by the apex courts (the supreme and constitutional courts).[5] Hence, there are valid procedures for carving the 'official' and textually entrenched shapes and forms of the constitutional order and its institutional subsystems. The structure of bicameral and multicameral parliaments, the structure of the court system, the structure of constitutional and supreme courts with more complex organisation, the structure of the government, the territorial structure of the state, and the structure of the sources of law are some of the most visible cases of 'official' constitutional geometry provided by valid constitutional law and signified through signifiers belonging to textual constitutionalism.

Consequently, constitutional geometry in its normative-institutional aspect is part of rational and textual constitutionalism. Thus, it is an intellectual product of the activity of the official and authoritative narrators provided in the official narratives and written in the authoritative texts of the constitutional community. The 'official' constitutional geometry is textually entrenched and needs intellectual and epistemic reconstruction via the deconstruction of the textual means through which it is expressed. This reconstruction is based on interpretation, a large part of which is and should be semiotic interpretation. Normative-institutional constitutional geometry is expressed via textual metaphors requiring textual approaches to constitutional semiotics.

It has been mentioned that constitutional geometry is traditionally overshadowed by institutional design. While the institutional schemes of public power and the institutional aspects of the constitutional design constitute the 'official' and visible aspects of structural constitutionalism, constitutional geometry is its implicit, 'unofficial' and hidden aspect. Hence, constitutional geometry needs to be discovered and (re)constructed. It has to be 'excavated' via constitutional interpretation. It needs to be exposed through the semiotic interpretation of the constitutional text. The constitutional text and texture must be considered as containers of signified objects that have to be 'decoded' and deconstructed in an interpretative process of constitutional semiosis producing the signifiers – the shapes and forms of constitutional geometry.

Semiotic interpretation means the cognition of symbolic structures concealed by or partially overlapping with the overall normative-institutional design of constitutional texture. It is actually an imaginative recognition and reconstruction of the shapes and forms of constitutional geometry on the basis of discovery of the logic of symbolism that underlies the construction, maintenance and functioning of the constitutional architecture and constitutional design. This logic of symbolism has its rational dimension that serves the constructive purposes that are implied and latent in the legal order. However, it is not unilaterally directed

[5] On the concept of apex courts, see S Schlegel, 'Activism as Defence: The Role of Courts in Shaping the Relationship between Constitutions and International Law. A Comparison of the Apex Courts of Switzerland, Germany, and Austria' in M Belov (ed), *Courts and Judicial Activism under Crisis Conditions: Policy Making in a Time of Illiberalism and Emergency Constitutionalism* (Abingdon, Routledge, 2021) 43–61.

towards the rational construction of institutional design, but also aims at fostering the processes of the signification and representation of constitutional meaning.

Constitutional law reflects the reality. Simultaneously, it creates a partially invented and artificial reality. This normative-institutional and 'invented' reality is imposed on the empirical reality. Thus, constitutional law engages with two plains of the socio-political order – the normative-institutional and the socio-legal – both of which are in fact invented and imagined by the constitutional players and especially by the authoritative narrators, performers and visualisers of the community. Hence, the constitutional mastering of empirical reality – both directly and through its normative model that is textually imprinted and authoritatively superimposed on the realm of facts – requires engagement with the constitutional imagination. The deconstruction, reconstruction and construction of reality with all its constitutionally relevant manifestations is heavily preconditioned on semiotic procedures, including those of the visualisation of implied meaning which takes constitutional geometric shapes. Again, some of these shapes are explicitly or implicitly provided in the constitution and other sources of constitutional law. Thus, they are part of constitutional semiosis at the crossroads between textual, performative, visual and symbolic-imaginary constitutionalism.

There are also shapes and forms of constitutional geometry created in the course of the empirical social and political behaviour of the subjects of constitutional law. These shape the durable patterns of behaviour, showing the ways in which constitutional law is practised by those on the ground. These forms of constitutional geometry are the structured collective constitutional imaginaries relating to 'constitutional law in action'. They are reflections of the durable patterns of socio-legal behaviour in the field of symbolic-imaginary constitutionalism. Hence, this 'constitutional geometry in action' bridges the gap between the performative and the symbolic-imaginary discourses of constitutionalism, showing the dependence between 'law in books' ('or law as text'), 'law in action' (or 'law as performance') and 'law as imagination'. The production of such geometric imaginaries resulting from socio-legal constitutionally relevant behaviour is entrenched in and largely dependent on the process of constitutional semiosis.

The inter-institutional relations organised in the form of institutional lines, triangles, squares, circles, networks and even more complex geometric forms may be the result of the application of constitutional law. Thus, they can stem from textual and normative-institutional constitutionalism and constitute a replication of textually embedded normative-institutional constitutional geometry. However, they may also deviate from it. In both cases, this performative-institutional geometry possesses the characteristics of constitutional geometry. This is due to the fact that it describes typical patterns of institutional behaviour and inter-institutional relations, and thus provides schemes of constitutional architecture and constitutional geometry in action.

Hence, in this latter aspect, constitutional geometry produced in performative constitutionalism as part of the socio-legal constitutional discourse is carved out through acts of authoritative constitutional performers with semiotic importance that signify structured constitutional imaginaries. This performative constitutional geometry is typically based on 'official', textual constitutional geometry, but may also deviate from it on the basis of institutional and personal preferences and interests of the players, and due to perception-representation-transaction costs or deviations from the model. They are produced by the interference between textual constitutional geometry, which is authoritative due to its inclusion in valid law, and imaginary constitutional geometry stemming from the symbolic-imaginary and theoretical realms of constitutionalism. From the perspective of constitutional semiotics, performative constitutional geometry is the result of the interplay between textual, normative-institutional and symbolic-imaginary constitutional geometry. It is shaped on the basis of multiple processes of transformation of meaning. More precisely, it is the result of the deconstruction, compression and signification of durable and socially representative forms of the semiotic expression of structural meaning. These forms are both informative and formative for the constitutional geometry of the constitutional order; thus, they possess epistemic and semiotic aspects.

Besides the 'official' normative-institutional constitutional geometry that is textually embedded in valid constitutional law and the performative constitutional geometry that relates to the socio-legal and visual discourses of constitutionalism, there is also a further dimension of constitutional geometry: theoretical constitutional geometry. It is contained in the constitutional literature and its main purpose is to offer theoretical conceptualisation of the shapes and forms of the constitutional order in constitutional doctrine and literature.[6]

[6] For the difference between constitutional imaginaries and the imagination offered by theory, see also J Přibáň, *Constitutional Imaginaries: A Theory of European Societal Constitutionalism* (Abingdon, Routledge, 2020) 10.

6

Theoretical Constitutional Geometry

Semiotics is rarely explicitly expressed and thoroughly elaborated in detail in constitutional theory. This is even more true of constitutional geometry as a specific form of constitutional semiotics. It is instead implicitly encoded, indirectly used and thus entangled in the overall structure of argumentation provided by a range of theories. Constitutional geometry plays a particular organising and signifying role as element of the overall theory in which it is embedded. This does not make the overarching theory (usually a form of legal positivism and legal institutionalism or, more rarely, legal realism or socio-legal theory) an overtly or explicitly semiotic one. Despite this hidden semiotic essence and teleology, the theories that use geometric metaphors to structure the legal or constitutional order are still dependent on the predominant institutionalist or positivist discourses, while their semiotic appeal remains largely oblique and hidden.

There are several examples of structural theories that implicitly use geometric semiotic metaphors and are important for the development of the conceptualisation and understanding of the constitutional order from a semiotic and, more precisely, a constitutional geometric viewpoint. The semiotic contributions of these theories in terms of content and, more specifically, the excavation of forms of structured constitutional imaginaries have to be accomplished through recourse to deconstruction as a method of scientific and intellectual cognition. Hence, the presentation of these theories traditionally belonging to the realm of legal positivism and legal realism in the light and context of the semiotic approach to constitutionalism and constitutional law is largely dependent on the use of appropriate methodology. In that sense, the development of constitutional geometry as a meta-theory of constitutionalism and constitutional law in conjunction with the deconstructivist approach is the means for the achievement of semiotic knowledge and meaning derived from theories that otherwise do not belong to the fields of knowledge of general semiotics, legal semiotics or constitutional semiotics.

Examples of such implicit semiotic approaches entrenched in and hidden by institutionalism and positivism are the theories of 'Begriffsjurisprudenz' (with Bernhardt Windscheid as its intellectual leader) and the Vienna legal positivist school (Hans Kelsen, Alfred Verdross, Adolf Merkel etc). In particular, Hans Kelsen's theory of legal normativism shows the implicit semiotic appeal of structural approaches to law and offers important insights for the overall theory of constitutional geometry. More precisely, the theory of the hierarchical pyramid-like structure of the legal order can also be conceived as an implicit and hidden suggestion for the geometric structuring of the constitutional order.

The network of concepts is also a powerful semiotic metaphor, although it is not promoted as a semiotic phenomenon per se by the 'Begriffsjurisprudenz' school. This school of thought has tried to organise the law as a web of concepts with vertical (inductive and deductive) and horizontal nodes. Windscheid and his followers perceived law and legal science as a form of legal mathematics.[1] Thus, according to them, law is reducible to an exercise resembling 'counting with concepts'. This is an intellectual enterprise which also requires the use of mathematic metaphors directly involving legal algebra and indirectly creating geometric structures, and thus also of relevance to constitutional geometry. Hence, Windscheid's 'Begriffsjurisprudenz' is implicitly a source of semiotic representation of meaning generated through recourse to mathematic metaphors. Obviously, law has never been so conceptually reduced to legal mathematics as in the case of this branch of legal positivism. And this reduction in fact results in legal semiosis producing the semiotic signification of legal meaning.

The theorists belonging to these powerful schools of thought have produced important schemes for ordering the legal order that are largely preconditioned on geometric metaphors such as the web or network of concepts, in the case of the 'Begriffsjurisprudenz' school, and the hierarchy and the pyramid, in the case of Kelsenian normativism. They are massively influenced by the positivist and constructivist spirit of the time and epoch in which they have been created. They are transmitters of the striving at legal perfection based on coping with the achievement of natural sciences that became quite visible at the end of the nineteenth and the beginning of the twentieth centuries. Thus, perhaps unconsciously, both groups of legal scholars produced important contributions to legal and constitutional semiotics using geometric metaphors.

Another example of the semiotic signification of meaning through geometric metaphors as an implicit intellectual byproduct of legal constructivism is offered by the institutionalist theories. These focus on the overall structure and pillars of the constitutional architecture of the state, thus being in dire need of visualising devices for their theoretical and practical efforts. Institutionalist structuring of the legislative, executive and judicial power – for example, focusing on the inner structure of the parliament, on the different aspects of the organisation of the courts and possibly other elements of judicial power, and on the institutional power grid within the government and within the overall framework of the executive power structure – show the importance of constitutional geometry for legal and constitutional institutionalism.

[1] See M Heidemann, *Bernhard Windscheid und die 'Begriffsjurisprudenz'. Die Pandektendogmatik im späten 19. Jahrhundert* (Munich, GRIN Publishing, 2015) 1–56.

The implicit use of geometric structures can also be detected in many other theories. For example, the line[2] and arrow as semiotic signifiers of the 'space-time continuum'[3] underline the theories of social contract. Indeed, representing the space-time continuum through semiotic signifiers of geometric origin is rather important for many political and constitutional theories. The geometric visualisation of time is a strategic epistemic strategy based on constitutional semiotics. The hierarchy and the pyramid are the explicit or concealed structures of the constitutional and power semiotics of sovereignty theories and of theories aspiring for the establishment of a strong and centralised order.

Many authors use mathematics (mathematical equations, concepts and metaphors) to explain legal phenomena. Such approaches are not reducible to a concrete school of thought. The mathematical approaches to law are especially visible in sociology of law, in legal realism as well as in rational choice and public choice legal theories. These theories use both geometric and algebraic metaphors as explanatory schemes. In fact, these approaches are quasi-mathematical because they remain largely humanitarian and use mathematics in a limited, selective and demonstrative way. Mathematics is used to give a limited number of examples or as a tool for the representation of inter-institutional dynamics that are reducible to mathematic regularities. Such reductionism embedded in the overall legal context and structure of scientific argumentation has huge semiotic potential. It is partially overshadowed by the claim for mathematical precision. But even when mathematics is used in its proper sense in order to quantify the scientific research and show quantitative inter-institutional relations, preferences and choices, it has an implicit semiotic appeal. It consists in the signification of the conceptual possibility for the quantification of constitutionalism, constitutional science and constitutional law.

The interim conclusion is that theoretical constitutional geometry is part of both the theory and meta-theory of constitutionalism and constitutional law. It is part of constitutional theory because it aims to explain constitutional structures provided by the constitution and constitutional law. The theoretical constitutional geometry is not limited to constitutional semiotics and to symbolic-imaginary theoretical discourses; it is also implicitly used by legal positivism and legal institutionalism, and, to a lesser extent, also by other schools of legal thought. This is due to the conceptual importance of legal structures and the structural approach of these theories that make recourse to structured constitutional imaginaries and geometric metaphors for organising and explaining the constitutional order without being semiotic theories themselves.

Theoretical constitutional geometry is contained, provided and shaped in the constitutional literature. It is the projection of normative-institutional, performative and symbolic-imaginary constitutional geometry in the realm of constitutional

[2] On the difference between 'temporal line' and 'spatial line', see C Castoriadis, *The Imaginary Institution of Society* (Cambridge, Polity Press, 1987) 193.

[3] On the 'spatialisation of time', see ibid 192.

theory. Constitutional theory and its textual dimension – constitutional literature – are the canvas on which the imaginaries generated on the basis of semiotic depictions of shapes and forms, and of performative or textually formed organising models of constitutionalism are stamped and represented in textual form. Thus, it is the point of intersection of other discourses of constitutional geometry transformed and reshaped by the scholarly community and resulting in a form of textual constitutionalism. This is a further demonstration that textual constitutionalism is a tool for the signification of constitutional semiotics. It also shows that constitutional theory is the 'melting pot' of constitutional imaginaries and the crossroads for the semiotic representation of meaning and of the semiotic signification of phenomena that originate in legal and socio-legal reality or in the collective constitutional imagination of the constitutionally framed socio-legal community. One of the implicit and hidden tasks of constitutional theory from a semiotic point of view is to transform unstructured constitutional imaginaries into structured ones. In that regard, constitutional geometry may serve as an important intellectual aid in its capacity as a meta-theory of constitutionalism.

Both normative-institutional and theoretical constitutional geometry possess textual dimension and are expressed in texts. However, there is also a difference between them – while textual constitutionalism relating to normative-institutional geometry is contained in authoritative texts, the textual dimension of legal theory is rarely authoritative. The main exception to this are normative theories containing normative ideologies and normative ideas. They also do not possess genuine legal normativity, being outside of the scope of sources of valid law; however, they are normative in the sense of being convincing and capable of the forming durable beliefs of constitutional players and authoritative speakers of the community.

The shaping of theoretical constitutional geometry occurs through the construction, deconstruction and reconstruction of meaning. This meaning stems from 'law in books' or 'law in action'. It is entrenched in constitutional archetypes which result from the constitutional and political imagination, which are both conscious and unconscious. In a sense, theoretical constitutional geometry is one of the most direct ways to approach and express structured constitutional imaginaries formed in conscious or unconscious ways by the socio-political community and narrated in a coherent way. Thus, constitutional theory is the medium for the expression of collective constitutional imaginaries. Naturally, this is done in a selective and consequently biased way reflecting the preferences of the constitutional theorists understood as authoritative constitutional narrators and as masters of the semiotic process for the establishment of normative ideologies and ideas and constitutional mythologies expressed through constitutional geometry.

The common denominator of all these processes for the production of meaning is constitutional semiosis based on the signification of normative, institutional and social signifieds with constitutional relevance through geometric signifiers. These signifiers are the result of a creative and selective semiotic process for the representation of meaning via geometric metaphors. In other words, the theoretical aspect of constitutional geometry comprises a semiotic process for the visual-imaginary representation of meaning through the 'stamping', framing and labelling of elements of the normative, institutional and empirical reality via geometric metaphors. This is done in a discursive way using the tools of textual constitutionalism as a means for the unfolding of the constitutional semiosis.

The signifieds may relate to institutional design (eg, the structure of different branches of power or constitutional institutions), human rights (eg, the situation of the players in the political process on the basis of political rights or the definition of political power relations) or the very concept of constituent power (eg, the explanatory models for the accomplishment of constituent power organised in geometric ways through lines, hierarchies or networks). These forms will be explained in more detail below.

Hence, theoretical constitutional geometry may signify elements of constitutional design and constitutional pragmatics relating to constitutional ontology, constitutional axiology or constitutional teleology. In other words, constitutional theories using constitutional geometry as an explanatory device may contain geometric signifiers of signifieds relating to the origin, organisation and functioning of the constitutional order. They may signify meaning concerning both constitutional statics (the organisation and structuring of the constitutional order) and constitutional dynamics (the emergence and functioning of the constitutional order, inter-institutional relations, path-dependency and different constitutional procedures).

This all shows that theoretical constitutional geometry is largely a semiotic phenomenon. It is a result of a process of the deconstruction and reconstruction of the legal and socio-legal reality via semiotic means. Constitutional theory may strive at properly and closely reflecting the legal and socio-legal reality. Depending on the methodology and scientific approach, constitutional theory may aim at a close description of the legal and constitutional order in parallel with an explanation of the legal relations as they are or ought to be. This is particularly true of the variants of legal positivism and legal realism.

However, constitutional geometry as a theory or a theoretical dimension of constitutional geometry differs considerably from the overall constitutional theory. It is based on procedures for intellectual and conceptual deconstruction, reconstruction, representation and signification. Theoretical constitutional geometry chooses phenomena that belong to the normative or institutional order, enshrined in textual constitutionalism or produced in performative constitutionalism in the socio-political context in different forms of 'law in action'. This choice is based on the semiotic capacity of the phenomenon; in other words, only phenomena that can be expressed through geometric comparisons and in geometric forms are capable of further processing through theoretical semiosis.

Once such phenomena are selected, they have to be deconstructed. Deconstruction is necessary in order to extract the semiotically signifiable core of the phenomenon and to reduce it to the essentials that are capable of being represented through geometric metaphors. Deconstruction is followed by reconstruction. In fact, the semiotic reconstruction of structural phenomena of the legal and socio-legal reality is a creative process of the selective representation of some of their features through semiotic means and in geometric forms. In that regard, deconstruction and reconstruction are mutually intertwined and interdependent. They are logically interrelated and have the same final purpose – to contribute to the signification of constitutionally relevant meaning and to jointly produce theoretical constructs that stand for constitutional phenomena, and to reorganise them at a theoretical and conceptual level in semiotic forms derived from geometry.

Constitutional semiotic deconstruction and reconstruction are cognitive procedures based on essentialism. Semiotic deconstruction and reconstruction are also based on structural and symbolic approaches to phenomena that have a rather different content. Semiotic deconstruction and semiotic reconstruction that produce theoretical constitutional geometry work with divergent phenomena. Some of them have a physical existence in performative, textual and visual constitutionalism, while others are purely intellectual constructs ranging from constitutional imaginaries to abstract institutional models negotiated by authoritative speakers and performers. In any case, they reshape intellectual models and intellectual imprints and are engaged in chains of signification of meaning. Deconstruction and reconstruction are always critical, selective and preconditioned upon an intuitive reliance on subconscious and unconscious imaginaries.

Thus, theoretical deconstruction and reconstruction is both objective and subjective. It is objective because it depends on the existence of structural features of the phenomenon which are capable of representation. This is the semiotic core of the phenomenon and its capability for semiotic representation via geometric metaphors. Semiotic deconstruction and reconstruction leading to theoretical constitutional geometry is possible only if the signified phenomenon exists, if it is capable of structured signification through geometric metaphors and if such representation is meaningful. It is meaningful when the semiotic process leads to enhanced epistemic value and brings new insights in terms of understanding normative-institutional, textual, visual or performative constitutional geometry or when it gives shape to undiscovered and implicit but important collective constitutional imaginaries.

Deconstruction and reconstruction as part of the semiotic process of production of theoretical constitutional geometry is subjective because it depends on the conscious, unconscious and subconscious preferences and the intellectual capabilities of the theoretical narrator. Great architects of constitutional geometric design – politicians, theorists, activist courts etc – impose their own imaginaries and imaginative-constructivist preferences on the understanding of the structure of the legal or constitutional order. They are themselves influenced by the zeitgeist – the spirit of the epoch and the civilisation in which they live. Thus, they serve as transmitters of normative ideologies, legal and constitutional mythologies, and semiotic preferences. These are preferences relating to the construction of the realm of constitutional geometry as a masterplan for semiotic representation in the field of legal and constitutional theory. The subjective element is present in all forms of the deconstruction, construction and reconstruction of meaning, regardless of whether it is expressed by authoritative narrators in authoritative texts or normative ideologies, or by other members of the constitutional discursive community.

Constitutional theory contains semiotic imprints of the shapes and forms of normative-institutional and performative constitutional geometry. These shapes and forms are signifiers of signifieds with a divergent nature (physical or imaginary) belonging to different realms, fields and coordination systems of constitutionalism. They signify the structuring of constitutional orderings entrenched in textual constitutionalism, produced by performative constitutionalism or resulting from formal or factual institutional patterns of behaviour. Theoretical constitutional geometry is also a realm for the signification of collective constitutional imaginaries that can be signified and represented through structural and, more precisely, geometric metaphors.

Thus, constitutional theory is a big drawing board on which signifieds of the legal or socio-legal reality can be detected, semiotically reshaped and symbolically represented. It is the grand arena in which the shapes and forms of constitutional geometry can be mastered. Last but not least, it is the source of shapes and forms of constitutional geometry which are then imposed on the institutional order and constitutional design, engraved in textual constitutionalism, implemented in performative constitutionalism, exposed and demonstrated in visual constitutionalism and collectively understood in emotional constitutionalism.

The geometric shapes and forms belonging to theoretical constitutional geometry are mastered through the imagination of normative theorists acting as de facto authoritative speakers, producing normative ideologies and normative ideas, and launching constitutional myths. Such imagination is never autonomous but is rather embedded in specific *Zeitgeist* and is influenced by the collective imaginaries determined by the particularities of space and time, epoch and civilisation.[4] Thus, theoretical constitutional geometry is context-dependent, while at the same time also having an impact on the socio-political context.

It is the interplay between geometric theoretical signifiers signifying signifieds from the empirical or normative-institutional reality capable of being represented through geometric shapes and forms that is of pivotal importance for constitutional semiosis grounded in constitutional geometry. And, vice versa, geometric metaphors launched in constitutional theory are signified to the constitutionally framed socio-political community through the performance, narratives and visualisations of the office holders and the people, but especially through the constitutionally relevant deeds of the authoritative narrators, performers and visualisers.

The embeddedness of authoritative narrators in a socio-legal context makes them intellectual detectors of the semiotic spirit of the time. They are signifying agents of semiotic content reflecting the collective imaginaries of the epoch, and the symbolic-imaginary and emotional visions of the community. Thus, they are

[4] See also R Kosellek, *Futures Past: On the Semantics of Historical Time* (New York, Columbia University Press, 2004) 1–313; and Castoriadis (n 2) 186–221.

generators of signifiers depicting power relations and transmitters of contextually predetermined semiotics.

This account of authoritative theoretical narrators is rather reductionist. It makes them look like simple resonators of the zeitgeist of the epoch. This is frequently but not always the case. That is why if we want to have a solid ground for explaining the functioning of theoretical constitutional semiotics and the role of constitutional theory for shaping and mastering constitutional geometry, we have to admit that the theorists may also be revolutionaries. They may be a source of counter-majoritarian constitutional semiotics that is different from the collective imaginaries in the socio-legal community. They may be intellectual adventurers discovering the shapes of new intellectual continents.

Such radical reformist endeavours for reshaping the world as we know it through new semiotic lenses and for framing it via novel geometric shapes and forms have been achieved on many occasions. This happened during the formative age of Western modernity, when novel theories for ordering the emergent constitutional order and for organising modern statehood, its territoriality and spatiality, its institutional design and constitutional architecture were proposed. Revolutionary semiotic projects were also launched during the last few decades in the context of the emergence and development of 'constitutionalism beyond statehood',[5] shaped mostly within the paradigms of multilevel constitutionalism[6] and constitutional pluralism.[7] Concrete examples of such revolutionary semiotic projects shaping Westphalian, post-Westphalian and neo-Westphalian constitutional geometry will be offered in Part V, Chapter 8 of this book.

[5] See P Dobner and M Loughlin (eds), *Twilight of Constitutionalism?* (Oxford, Oxford University Press, 2010); and N Walker, 'Taking Constitutionalism beyond the State' (2008) 56(30 *Political Studies* 519.

[6] See EU Petersmann, *Multilevel Constitutionalism for Multilevel Governance of Public Goods* (Oxford, Hart Publishing, 2017) 1–416; G della Cananea, 'Is European Constitutionalism Really "Multilevel"?' (2010) 70 *ZaöRV* 283; and I Pernice, 'Multilevel Constitutionalism and the Crisis of Democracy in Europe' (2015) 11(3) *European Constitutional Law Review* 541, doi:10.1017/S1574019615000279.

[7] M Poiares Maduro, 'Contrapunctual Law: Europe's Constitutional Pluralism in Action' in N Walker (ed) *Sovereignty in Transition* (Oxford, Hart Publishing, 2003) 501–38; and M Poiares Maduro, 'Three Claims of Constitutional Pluralism' in M Avbelj and J Komarek (eds), *Constitutional Pluralism in the European Union and Beyond* (Oxford, Hart Publishing, 2012) 67–84.

7

Imaginative Constitutional Geometry and the Concept of Cloud Constitutionalism

Imaginative constitutional geometry is a concept that serves as a tool for the establishment of the conceptual foundations of the anthropological dimension of structured collective constitutional imaginaries. It theoretically frames the intellectual projection of constitutionally relevant geometric metaphors in the individual and collective consciousness of people. Thus, imaginative constitutional geometry is a concept at the point of intersection between constitutional semiotics, constitutional epistemology and constitutional anthropology. It is a phenomenon that has psychological, sociological, political, semiotic and legal dimensions. Thus, it is relevant for constitutional semiotics and can be approached through the prism of socio-legal studies, while it is not relevant from a legal positivist, legal realist or even strictly institutionalist viewpoint.

Imaginative constitutional geometry is a concept that handles the process of constitutional semiosis in a twofold way. First, it denominates the process of the creation, production and sustaining of collective constitutional imaginaries. In that regard, it defines and explores the emergence of constitutional imaginaries and their materialisation in the realm of constitutionalism. In a sense, it is an underlying concept that binds together all dimensions of production of constitutional meaning, resulting in structured constitutional imaginaries. It is also a process of framing the collective constitutional consciousness in geometric metaphors. Moreover, the constitutional subconscious of the constitutionally framed socio-political community is also partially revealed through the manifestations of the structured constitutional imaginaries.

Second, imaginative constitutional geometry defines the theoretical reflection and normative shapes through which collective constitutional imaginaries persist as part of the constitutional anthropology of the constitutionally framed socio-political community. It exposes the semiotic map of structured constitutional imaginaries drawn by the authoritative speakers, writers, narrators, performers and visualisers of this community, which is permanently challenged, shifted, legitimised and delegitimised by the interplay between the societal and socio-psychological forces.

Imaginative constitutional geometry produces structured collective imaginaries mainly through the processes of psychological internalisation of meaning via the sedimentation or imposition of semiotic figures.[1] It determines the overall outlook of the constitutional anthropology of the constitutionally framed socio-legal community. It may stem from the interplay between the collective constitutional subconscious and unconscious, the collective constitutional imagination and the way in which they are explicated and signified via geometric metaphors. In any case, it must relate to constitutional phenomena and, more precisely, to the macro-shapes and forms of the constitutional order.

Constitutional sedimentation[2] occurs in an evolutionary way throughout the course of constitutional history. It is a result of the gradual entrenchment of structured constitutional imaginaries in the individual and collective constitutional consciousness of the people. Hence, the sedimentation of structured constitutional imaginaries is dependent on the constitutional history, resulting in constitutional tradition and constitutional culture.

In contrast, the imposition of imaginative constitutional geometry is a radical and revolutionary mode of creation of structured constitutional imaginaries. It stems from volitional acts that usually have an elitist origin for the establishment of official constitutional imaginaries via the transposition of structured images. Hence, the imposition of imaginative constitutional geometry is related to constitutional engineering[3] in the sphere of symbolic-imaginary constitutionalism.

Typically, imaginative constitutional geometry is a result of the combination of both methods for carving out structured constitutional imaginaries – the evolutionary, conservative and time-consuming approach of constitutional sedimentation and the revolutionary, authoritative, reformist and volitional approach of their imposition. No imposition of imaginaries can occur without at least some time for its internalisation in the collective imagination of the constitutionally framed socio-political community. And no sedimentation is possible without a 'triggering event' or a 'push for imagination' by the authoritative speakers, interpreters, narrators, performers and visualisers of the community.

Imaginative constitutional geometry lies at the core of the societal, socio-psychological and anthropological process of constitutional semiosis. It is a key determinant of the collective imaginaries. It is also the framing concept of structured constitutional imaginaries produced through the merger of the individual into the collective conscious and unconscious and expressed through visual, performative and emotional constitutionalism.

[1] On the concept of constitutional sedimentation, see D Curtin, 'The Sedimentary European Constitution: The Future of "Constitutionalisation" without a Constitution' in I Pernice and E Tanchev (eds), *Ceci n'est pas une Constitution: Constitutionalisation without a Constitution?* (Baden-Baden, Nomos, 2009) 76–86.

[2] Ibid.

[3] G Sartori, *Comparative Constitutional Engineering: An Inquiry into Structures, Incentives, and Outcomes* (New York, New York University Press, 1994) 1–229; and X Contiades (ed), *Engineering Constitutional Change: A Comparative Perspective on Europe, Canada and the USA* (Abingdon, Routledge, 2012) 1–490.

'Imaginative' does not mean 'purely imagined' because constitutional geometry is a result of the constitutional imagination focused on objective phenomena provided by textual, normative-institutional, performative or visual constitutionalism. Hence, imaginative constitutional geometry is partially objectively based on real phenomena that are provided by valid law through textual and normative-institutional constitutionalism or are available in 'law in action' shaped by performative, visual and emotional constitutionalism. In fact, the very concept of imaginative constitutional geometry is a daring claim that imagination has objective strands and features that are not only constitutionally relevant, but are also of formative importance for the construction and signification of constitutional and constitutionally relevant meaning.

The process of formation of imaginative constitutional geometry is comparable not only to sedimentation, but also to the evaporation of constitutional phenomena from the objective ground of their textual, normative or factual existence. The legal texts, the scientific texts and the realm of facts are the mountains, rocks and woods of meaning. The constitutional institutions in their twofold existence as legal phenomena of rational, textual and normative-institutional constitutionalism and as factual phenomena and elements of performative and visual constitutionalism form the forests of meaning. When the moist air of individual and collective imagination that stems from the ocean of the conscious, subconscious and unconscious reaches these mountains and forests of meaning, it creates huge clouds of meaning through the process of symbolic-imaginary evaporation.

This evaporation emerges at the boundary between the rational and the emotional, the imaginary and the real. It is a result of the process of individual and collective constitutional imagining. Its temporal frames concern the dreaming of the future, the remembering of the past and the symbolic-imaginary conceptualisation of the present. These clouds of meaning may contain different and even all elements of symbolic-imaginary constitutionalism. They are containers of dispersed meaning, collective imaginaries, dreams, hopes and fears. Together, they form the symbolic-imaginary landscapes of the constitutionally framed socio-political community. An important feature of these landscapes are the structured constitutional imaginaries and, more precisely, imaginative constitutional geometry.

Imaginative constitutional geometry is the result of the evaporation of the structural essence and the semiotic core of constitutional phenomena paralleled by two interrelated and mutually dependent phenomena. These are the distillation of constitutional meaning through semiotic representation and its spread via the dispersed sharing of structured constitutional imaginaries. The meaning is distilled and then spread in controlled and rational ways (eg, by the authoritative speakers, narrators, writers, performers and visualisers of the community), but also in scattered and diffuse ways by all of its members. Thus, it is grounded in both the individual and collective consciousness of the constitutionally framed community, having its roots and projections in the collective unconscious.

The evaporation and subsequent emergence of 'constitutional clouds of meaning', some of which have geometric forms and result in structured constitutional imaginaries, is a genuinely semiotic process and phenomenon. It is firmly entrenched in constitutional semiosis and is largely dependent on the semiotic approach to constitutionalism and constitutional law. Hence, the emergence and stabilisation of imaginative constitutional geometry seems reasonable and understandable through the analytical optics of semiotics adjusting the existing anthropological and socio-legal methods to the requirements and specifics of constitutional semiotics.

This triggers the need for conceptualisation of a new form of constitutionalism: cloud constitutionalism. Cloud constitutionalism rests on the assumption that the constitutional imagination and the constitutional imaginaries stemming from it are of fundamental constitutional relevance not only for constitutionalism as a socio-legal phenomenon, but also for constitutional law. It determines the ways in which constitutional law is perceived, psychologically accessed, comprehended and imagined by the constitutionally framed socio-political community. The interaction between the constitutional imagination, constitutional law and constitutional practice produces clouds of meaning. This is constitutional and constitutionally relevant meaning emerging out of constitutionalism as an intellectual enterprise and a societal process. The result is chiefly symbolic-imaginary constitutionalism and constitutional geometry, which is then stored and preserved in a dispersed way through cloud constitutionalism.

Hence, symbolic-imaginary constitutionalism, imaginative constitutional geometry and cloud constitutionalism are mutually interrelated and interdependent phenomena. Moreover, cloud constitutionalism itself rests on geometric assumptions. It is based on the idea of the dispersed containment, allocation and storage of meaning. In that regard, the 'clouds of meaning' are themselves semiotic figures, whereas cloud constitutionalism is a semiotic phenomenon and framing concept. It explains how structured constitutional imaginaries and other less organised forms of constitutional imagination are signified in the network of meaning, based on individual perceptions and entrenched in the collective constitutional conscious and unconscious.[4]

The clouds of constitutional meaning are allocated everywhere and nowhere, since they are part of the collective constitutional imagination and the constitutional anthropology of the people. They contain a range of semiotic signifiers of constitutionally relevant phenomena which form the signification objects: the signifieds. Some of them are diffuse imaginaries that are accessible only through intuition; they do not have concrete shape and form. In that regard, cloud

[4] Apart from the cloud and network metaphors I use here, there are also other approaches to the signification of the social imaginaries contained in the collective unconscious. One of the most important of these is the comparison with volcanic magma provided by Cornelius Castoriadis, who speaks of the 'imaginary-representative magma of the unconscious'. See C Castoriadis, *The Imaginary Institution of Society* (Cambridge, Polity Press, 1987) 276.

constitutionalism as a 'pool of meaning' also requires intuitive constitutionalism as the key to access it. It is accessible and comprehensible not just through the intellect but also via the use of intuition.[5] This is a difficult enterprise since constitutionalism is traditionally overburdened with structuralism[6] and rationalism, and tends to disapprove of intuitive approaches to constitutional law. Other constitutionally relevant phenomena included in constitutional clouds of meaning and thus in cloud constitutionalism are the structured imaginaries. These contain symbolically signified meaning shaped through the forms of imaginative constitutional geometry.

Cloud constitutionalism resembles cloud computing in the sense that both phenomena relate to the cloud storage of data. While cloud computing is based on the digital storage of data in external servers, cloud constitutionalism relies on the dispersed storage of imaginaries in the collective consciousness of the constitutionally framed community composed of the multitude of individual forms of consciousness of its members. Thus, the people constitute the overall storage capacity and facility of symbolic-imaginary constitutionalism in general and constitutional geometry in particular. The multitude of human minds are the physical infrastructure of cloud constitutionalism in general and symbolic-imaginary constitutionalism in particular. Moreover, cloud constitutionalism frames not only a simple process of data storage; it is also based on and contains collective constitutional memories, dreams, imaginaries, ideologies, ideas, myths and mythologies.

In this context, imaginative constitutional geometry is not only an object of the signification of meaning and its imaginative 'storage' in the collective psychological pool of cloud constitutionalism. It is not simply one of its elements. It is also an important tool for storing data and preserving symbolic-imaginary representations of the constitutional reality and the constitutional order. This occurs through the processes of framing, packing and organising constitutional information and its semiotic signification through geometric metaphors. Hence, imaginative constitutional geometry is a key instrument for the organisation of the collective constitutional imaginaries as part of cloud constitutionalism. In this process of the construction, representation and storage of meaning, the semiotic approach plays a decisive role. Hence, constitutional geometry in general and imaginative constitutional geometry in particular are key assets for the production and maintenance of structured constitutional imaginaries that are among the pillars of cloud constitutionalism.

[5] For the role of intuition see H Bergson, *The Creative Mind: An Introduction to Metaphysics* (New York, Dover Publications, 2010) 18–133.

[6] On the relationship between structuralism and semiotics beyond particular legal problems, see T Hawkes, *Structuralism and Semiotics* (Abingdon, Routledge, 2003) 1–192; and J Broekman and L Cata Backer, *Lawyers Making Meaning: The Semiotics of Law in Legal Education II* (Dordrecht, Springer, 2013) 181–95.

Imaginative constitutional geometry is the particular aspect of constitutional geometry which is extremely important but the least feasible, palpable and capable of scientific exploration. It is not a phenomenon which is immediately easy to understand through the interpretation, deconstruction or reconstruction of meaning. It is not a phenomenon that can easily be understood and ordered on the basis and through the means of rational and normative-institutional constitutionalism. It requires a move beyond traditional constitutional epistemology in the field of symbolic-imaginary constitutionalism conceived through the lens of constitutional semiotics. The semiotic importance of imaginative constitutional geometry requires the mobilisation of efforts and the use of both conventional and non-conventional methods of conquering this epistemic fortress. More precisely, it demands the use of intuition, imagination and the imaginative reconstruction of the legal and socio-legal reality on the basis of semiotic figures produced as a result of constitutional semiosis that takes into account the cloud character of imaginative constitutional geometry.

The existence of constitutional geometry as part of collective imaginaries can be discovered via a range of methods belonging to the spheres of social and political psychology, political and constitutional anthropology, and sociology. It may even be prone to quantitative research and statistic measurement (via interviews, sociological surveys etc). Thus, although it is a diffuse, volatile and abstract phenomenon, imaginative constitutional geometry exists in a dispersed but intelligible way in the collective consciousness of the community. Hence, it is scientifically provable and discoverable.

The importance of imaginative constitutional geometry stems from the fact that its theoretical conceptualisation and the recognition of the forms of constitutional semiotic through which it reveals itself is important for the proper understanding of constitutionalism as a phenomenon relating not just to valid law, but also to constitutional law as a practice and as imagination. Imaginative constitutional geometry predetermines the overall structure and concrete manifestations of structural constitutional anthropology and the structured collective imaginaries of the people. However, it requires an exploration with methods that go beyond traditional legal and constitutional science that is preoccupied with text and texture, valid law and thus 'law in books'. It demands a more daring and unconventional approach to constitutional law centred on 'law in action' and, more precisely, 'law as performance and imagination'. In that regard, it relates not only to symbolic-imaginary constitutionalism, which is its conceptual centre, but also to visual, emotional and performative constitutionalism.

Imaginative constitutional geometry cannot be distilled from valid law through constitutional interpretation. It is not immediately available in constitutional theory and is not directly recognisable as a theoretical construct. It has to be extracted from real-life imaginary experiences via empirical methods derived from sociology, psychology and anthropology. The complexity of such analysis and its methodological and conceptual specifics precludes its extensive and detailed examination as part of this book, not only due to space constraints but also because the general focus of the book is devoted to the conceptual outline of the main features of constitutional semiotics as a theory and a meta-theory of constitutionalism and constitutional law. In such a context, imaginative constitutional geometry is only part of the overall theoretical enterprise. Thus, in this chapter, I offer a concise theoretical analysis of imaginative constitutional geometry from the viewpoint of the general theory of constitutional semiotics. However, imaginative constitutional geometry deserves special attention, which I hope to be able to provide in subsequent publications on constitutional semiotics.

Imaginative constitutional geometry organises the collective constitutional imaginaries relating to constitutionalism and constitutional law in imaginary shapes and forms structured around geometric metaphors. This is done jointly with or separately from constitutional myths and mythologies, and normative ideologies and ideas. All of these belong to the realm of symbolic-imaginary constitutionalism and together contribute to the metaphorical and symbolic signification of constitutionally relevant signifieds. They jointly produce dreams, hopes, fears, expectations and remembrance engraved through imaginary cues, codes and triggers in collective memories,[7] collective dreams and collective imaginaries.

In that regard, imaginative constitutional geometry may be perceived as a twofold phenomenon. It is the result of the semiotic process of the psychological representation of constitutional phenomena and especially the macro-shapes and forms of the constitutional order. It is also a trigger of the processes of constitutional imagination and thus of constitutional semiosis. The shapes and forms of imaginative constitutional geometry are imaginary triggers starting semiotic processes that result in emotional, visual and performative constitutionalism. When they produce constitutional or legislative amendment or the adoption of case law that includes the geometric metaphorical depiction of constitutional phenomena, these shapes and forms also function as imaginary triggers of textual and normative-institutional constitutionalism.

Imaginative constitutional geometry is a phenomenon of constitutional psychology and anthropology. It covers the ways in which the public, the people and the citizen imagine the macro-shapes and forms of the constitutional order. It includes the geometric representations of the institutional and normative orders, the system of sources of law, inter-institutional relations, the structuring of the relationship between the state, civil society and the public sphere, the organisation of different institutions, and the relations between the agents and players of constitutional law on the constitutional chessboard.

[7] M Belov, 'Constitutional Memories: How Do Constitutions Cope with Constitutional Past' in M Belov and A Abat i Ninet (eds), *Revolution, Transition, Memory, and Oblivion: Reflections on Constitutional Change* (Cheltenham, Edward Elgar, 2020) 107–26.

Imaginative constitutional geometry is applicable to constitutionalism both within and beyond statehood.[8] This is due to the fact that people need signifiers of public order and psychological rationalisation through the reduction and simplification of the world. This reduction is paralleled by the signification of constitutional meaning and its visual representation via geometric forms. Such semiotic representations based on geometric metaphors are used with regard to the internal constitutional order, but also to the emergent constitutional (dis)order of global constitutional pluralism[9] and EU multilevel supranational constitutionalism.[10] The use of constitutional geometry as an explanatory and ordering scheme of constitutionalism beyond statehood[11] will be demonstrated in the next chapter, in which I will discuss the constitutional geometry of Westphalian, post-Westphalian and neo-Westphalian constitutionalism.

[8] See P Dobner and M Loughlin (eds), *Twilight of Constitutionalism?* (Oxford, Oxford University Press, 2010); and N Walker, 'Taking Constitutionalism beyond the State' (2008) 56(3) *Political Studies* 519.

[9] For a novel paradigm that aims at ordering the European societal constitutionalism and its underlying social imaginaries, see J Přibáň, *Constitutional Imaginaries: A Theory of European Societal Constitutionalism* (Abingdon, Routledge, 2020) 1–251. For an original theory of the images of Europe and the related collective European imaginaries in the age of populist constitutionalism, see P Blokker, *Imagining Europe: Transnational Contestation and Civic Populism* (London, Palgrave Macmillan, 2021) 1–364.

[10] See EU Petersmann, *Multilevel Constitutionalism for Multilevel Governance of Public Goods* (Oxford, Hart Publishing, 2017) 1–416; G della Cananea, 'Is European Constitutionalism Really "Multilevel"?' (2010) 70 *ZaöRV* 283; and I Pernice, 'Multilevel Constitutionalism and the Crisis of Democracy in Europe' (2015) 11(3) *European Constitutional Law Review* 541, doi:10.1017/S1574019615000279.

[11] See Dobner and Loughlin (n 8); and Walker (n 8).

8

Westphalian, Post-Westphalian and Neo-Westphalian Constitutional Geometry

Each constitutional epoch has its own constitutional geometry. Indeed, there is also a degree of continuity between the shapes and forms through which we organise, institutionalise and imagine the constitutional order. Such continuity may be based on a transgenerational and transtemporal consensus. It may consist in the reception and migration of geometric signifiers of constitutional and constitutionally relevant meaning through the space-time continuum. It may also be the result of the deliberate sticking to traditional forms of constitutional geometry or may be grounded in 'invented tradition'.[1] Sometimes constitutional geometry is context-dependent, but on many occasions it is a transgenerational and transtemporal project which may even be entrenched in constitutional archetypes and contained in cloud constitutionalism.[2]

Moreover, each constitutional geometric form has the potential to unfold in the time-space continuum. It has a distinct set of qualities, features and core messages to deliver. It has distinct signification strengths and a recognisable capacity to signify a range of constitutional signifieds. The realisation of the signification capacity of the constitutional geometric form is largely context-dependent. Thus, constitutional geometry projects differently in different contexts which shows that it is part of quantum constitutionalism.[3]

Nevertheless, there are also grand epochs of constitutional civilisation which distinctly diverge from each other. They differ with regard to their constitutional axiology, constitutional design and constitutional performance. In parallel to these differences in the 'law in books' and in the 'law in action', there is also usually deep divergence in terms of 'law as imagination', 'law as visualisation' and 'law as performance'. These are based on variations of symbolic-imaginary, visual, emotional and performative constitutionalism. In that regard, the constitutional epochs also differ in terms of their constitutional geometry in its capacity as both an epistemic and ordering semiotic matrix.

[1] On the concept of 'invented tradition', see E Hobsbawm and T Ranger (eds), *The Invention of Tradition* (Cambridge, Cambridge University Press, 2012) 1–324.

[2] On the concept of cloud constitutionalism, see Part V, Chapter 7 of this book.

[3] On the concept of quantum constitutionalism, see Part I, Chapter 2 of this book.

This chapter is devoted to the analysis of civilisation shifts from the perspective of constitutional semiotics. It explores transitions of constitutional geometry as markers of civilisation change of the explanatory and epistemic and ordering matrices of the constitutional order. Thus, it aims at clarifying how big constitutional civilisations try to make order out of disorder using structured constitutional imaginaries.

The analysis focuses on three constitutional civilisations which are actually three phases of the development of constitutional civilisation: Westphalian, post-Westphalian and neo-Westphalian constitutionalism. Thus, I will offer a comparative and historical semiotic perspective on the emergence and development of constitutional civilisation from its beginnings in early modernity, through to its unfolding during modernity and the current early post-modern age.

Westphalian constitutionalism is a phase in the development of a constitutional civilisation with a long existence, a profound impact on human societies and a well-established range of constitutional imaginaries and signifiers of constitutional and constitutionally relevant signifieds. Westphalian constitutional geometry is deeply entrenched in the constitutional anthropology of modern societies. It is part of the established visual, performative and emotional culture of constitutional and legal modernity, and has a multitude of textual projections in constitutional text and constitutional texture.

Conversely, post-Westphalian constitutionalism and its constitutional geometry have a relatively short history that exists in the period of the emergence and development of 'constitutionalism beyond statehood'. Post-Westphalian constitutional geometry already exists and we have some experience of it, although this is limited to a few decades. Nevertheless, it is much fuzzier and unclear in comparison to Westphalian constitutional geometry. This is annoying because it is grounded in the deconstruction of traditional constitutional geometry and the critical reassessment of semiotic signifiers that already belong to our constitutional heritage and have served us well as ordering and explanatory schemes during constitutional modernity. Thus, post-Westphalian constitutional geometry is novel, challenging and insecure. It is also post-modern in the sense of being fragmented, non-holistic and pluralist. Moreover, it is fragile since its chances of lasting as an established form and thus pass the 'tests of time' are unclear. The question is whether it can serve as a reliable scheme for the signification of constitutional and constitutionally relevant meaning in the context of global post-modernity and visual, performative, emotional and even normative-institutional pluralism. Nevertheless, it is necessary due to its promises to signify post-modern constitutional imaginaries – post-modern normative ideologies and ideas, constitutional myths and mythologies, constitutional codes etc.

Neo-Westphalian constitutional geometry is the newest, fuzziest and most unclear concept. It is partially based on old geometric schemes developed during Westphalian modernity. Thus, it has some solid intellectual – normative-institutional and textual, but also ideal, visual, emotional and performative – heritage on which it can build. Despite this fact, it is not a mere replica of old and established constitutional semiotic concepts and ordering schemes. Globalisation, the IT revolution, 'time-space compression',[4] the deconstruction of secure traditional identities and the emergence of new constitutional issues which have not been detected on the radar of modern constitutionalism foster the need for new explanatory and ordering matrices of global constitutional and legal disorder. Such an intellectual challenge may be framed within the semiotic design of post-Westphalian constitutionalism. However, especially in terms of the global political trends of the last decade, it seems that neo-Westphalian constitutional schemes for explaining, understanding, ordering and signifying the new world order shall prevail.

Here I will not focus either on general constitutional history or on the particularities of axiological or institutional design. My purpose here is to give a semiotic account of the shifts of structured constitutional imaginaries during the course of the emergence, establishment, dismantling and transition of different constitutional civilisations. Thus, I will mainly explore the forms of constitutional geometry, while the explanation of the key features of Westphalian, post-Westphalian and neo-Westphalian constitutionalism will play only a supportive role.

The analysis undertaken here will be accomplished in several steps. First, I will briefly outline the main elements and aspects of Westphalian, post-Westphalian and neo-Westphalian constitutionalism. Second, I will offer a concise summary of their constitutional geometry. The last and third step will consist in the comparative assessment of the trends in the evolution of constitutional geometry that undergoes transition over time from Westphalian to post-Westphalian and neo-Westphalian constitutionalism. Thus, I will also provide concrete examples of structured constitutional imaginaries and will offer a comparative typology of constitutional geometry with regard to its unfolding throughout the course of history, which will be both synchronic and diachronic. This will provide a solid foundation for my theory of constitutional geometry and structured constitutional imaginaries, and will show that comparative and comparative-historical constitutional semiotics are both possible and necessary.

Westphalian constitutionalism is the term I use as a partial synonym of modern constitutionalism. This is the phase of historical development whose intellectual roots – both philosophical and socio-political – were prepared in the seventeenth and eighteenth centuries. It became the dominant form of constitutional civilisation in the West (including Europe, North and South America, and also, to a lesser extent, other parts of the world) during the 'long nineteenth century'.[5] It was established as a predominant and even monopolistic version of constitutionalism during the 'short twentieth century'.[6] Thus, although it became a universal theory

[4] On the concept of 'time-space compression', its main proponents and thesis, see, eg, http://routledgesoc.com/category/profile-tags/time-space-compression.

[5] E Hobsbawm, *The Age of Revolution: 1789–1848* (New York, Vintage, 1996) 1–368.

[6] E Hobsbawm, *Age of Extremes: The Short Twentieth Century 1914–1991* (New York, Time Warner Books, 1995) 1–627.

and constitutional matrix for the whole world, it was still performed, represented and imagined differently in different socio-legal, cultural and anthropological contexts. In any case, Westphalian constitutionalism started to be challenged following the emergence and massive spread of international law in the course of the twentieth century. It became increasingly deconstructed, dismantled, and less and less compatible with the constitutionalisation of international law and the internalisation of constitutional law.[7]

Hence, the last decades of the twentieth century saw the gradual demise or at least the visible signs of challenge of Westphalian constitutionalism, which had been the only constitutionalism known to the world before the emergence of forms of international constitutional law and supranational constitutionalism. Key political decisions relating to the deconstruction of national and Westphalian and the promotion of global, supranational and post-Westphalian constitutionalism were taken in the course of modern history, but especially after the Second World War and in the 1970s. Nevertheless, the trend for the transition to constitutionalism beyond Westphalian constitutional law has become increasingly visible since the 1990s.

Initially, it seemed that Westphalian constitutionalism will most probably compete and may even be partially or fully replaced by post-Westphalian constitutionalism. Post-Westphalian constitutionalism was a paradigm that aimed at framing and explaining the constitutional orders in the era of globalisation. In a sense, post-Westphalian constitutionalism is an alternative conceptual framework applicable to 'constitutionalism beyond statehood'.[8] It is a paradigm for coping with global constitutionalism and global governance at the crossroads between national modernity and post-national and global post-modernity.

However, the recent trends since the outbreak of the global COVID-19 pandemic also point in another direction. They enable the return to Westphalian constitutionalism while also promoting post-Westphalian constitutionalism in a specific sense. Nevertheless, the return to Westphalian constitutionalism seems rather unlikely, despite the rise of neo-nationalism, the stagnation of EU integration and the crisis of global constitutionalism. These phenomena impede the unrestrained unfolding of neoliberal globalisation preventing the unproblematic rise of post-Westphalian constitutionalism. In fact, the growth of post-Westphalian constitutionalism seems to be impossible in the short term, or at least in the form which we have witnessed in the Global North and especially in Europe since the fall of the Berlin wall.

Thus, a new competitor to both Westphalian and post-Westphalian constitutionalism is emerging: neo-Westphalian constitutionalism. This builds upon the achievements of both of its predecessors, while at the same time appears

[7] See P Dobner and M Loughlin (eds), *Twilight of Constitutionalism?* (Oxford, Oxford University Press, 2010); and N Walker, 'Taking Constitutionalism beyond the State' (2008) 56(3) *Political Studies* 519.

[8] ibid.

as an alternative to both of Westphalian nationalism and neo-nationalism, and post-Westphalian globalism and neoliberalism. The rise of neo-Westphalian neo-regionalism seems to be a conceptual challenge to both constitutionalism 'within' and 'beyond' statehood. This challenge is axiological, institutional, conceptual and pragmatic, but also has symbolic-imaginary, emotional and visual dimensions.

Thus, the clash between nationalism, globalism and regionalism, and between Westphalian, post-Westphalian and neo-Westphalian constitutionalism also seems to be a 'clash, competition and battle of forms'. These are the macro-shapes and forms through which constitutional law orders and constitutional and international law theory explain the constitutional orders below, above or at the national level and thus 'within' and 'beyond' statehood. In that regard, the competition between these three forms of constitutionalism must also be explored from the perspective of constitutional semiotics and, more precisely, on the basis of my theory of constitutional geometry. A prerequisite for the proper analysis of these here is an outline of the main features of Westphalian, post-Westphalian and neo-Westphalian constitutionalism, which will be given below.

Westphalian constitutionalism is a concept which partially overlaps with modern constitutionalism. The term 'Westphalian' is preferred here to 'modern' for several reasons. Modern constitutionalism is a broader concept, while Westphalian constitutionalism puts the emphasis on the sovereigntist, hierarchical and territorial aspects of modern constitutionalism. These are precisely the aspects which are of special relevance for constitutional geometry because they are prone to the symbolic-imaginary and visual signification of meaning through the use of structured constitutional imaginaries and geometric metaphors.

Thus, Westphalian constitutionalism exposes the semiotic features of modern constitutionalism. It brings to the fore the hierarchy, the pyramid, the square and the polygon as key shapes for mastering the complexity of modern constitutional orders. The very concept of 'Westphalian constitutionalism' has deep semiotic importance and is a signifier of encoded meaning bound to the normative ideologies, mythologies and codes of constitutional modernity.

In other words, Westphalian constitutionalism is that part of modern constitutionalism which is mostly related to constitutional geometry as both an explanatory and an ordering matrix, and is thus capable of engaging in constitutional semiosis. This semiosis is accomplished through the deconstruction and reconstruction of the Westphalian features of constitutional modernity –sovereignty, the supremacy of the constitution, the hierarchy of sources of law and the system of state institutions, the territoriality of state and public power etc.

Moreover, Westphalian constitutionalism is also the proper term from the perspective of constitutional semiotics in relation to its counterparts. In other words, the concepts of post-Westphalian and neo-Westphalian constitutionalism are to be preferred to the concept of post-modern or neo-modern constitutionalism.

Postmodern constitutionalism places emphasis on issues which are different from post-Westphalian and neo-Westphalian constitutionalism. It puts the accent on the non-existence of absolutely objective truth, the pluralism of constitutional discourses, narratives and viewpoints, and the need to deconstruct constitutional phenomena relating to constitutional ontology, teleology, axiology, design and pragmatics which have axiomatic value for constitutional modernity. Postmodern constitutionalism conceptualises the constitution as the central object of constitutionalism in a way that differs significantly from modern constitutionalism both conceptually and in terms of content. It conceives the constitution as a range of narratives. Thus, the text of the constitution and the initial constitutional model launched by the sovereign through the constitutional legislator is simply an invitation for the interpretation and further development of the constitutional story, and not an objective truth or an eternal, fixed, static and retrospective originalist project.

On the other hand, post-Westphalian and neo-Westphalian constitutionalism have different focus, content and reformist intellectual message to deliver. They are not necessarily post-modern in the above-mentioned sense.

Neo-Westphalian constitutionalism in particular may be even neo-modern or anti-post-modern. This is due to the fact that neo-Westphalianism is based on the re-establishment of objective, eternal and absolute truths, albeit territorially and jurisdictionally restrained at a regional rather than a national level. From the little empirical information that is available at present, neo-Westphalianism aims at the establishment of holistic and quasi-objective truths and at the confinement of regionally based constitutionally framed communities through adherence to or even adoration of such imposed wisdom.

Neo-Westphalianism is post-modern since it is deconstructive. Neo-Westphalian constitutionalism is currently being built upon the deconstruction of modern truths and some of the pillars of constitutional modernity.

Nevertheless, neo-Westphalianism is also anti-post-modern or neo-modern because neo-Westphalian regionalism tries to gain legitimacy through the assertion of axiology, normative ideology and elements of symbolic-imaginary constitutionalism that are both quasi-objective and exclusive. It aims at stabilising meaning through the justification methods of modern constitutional epistemology and semiotics, especially in relation to symbolic-imaginary constitutionalism, while giving different content to traditional constructions, figures and forms. It is exclusive because it increasingly makes recourse to the traditional 'friend-enemy' distinction scheme that was launched during nationalist modernity and has been extensively theorised by authors such as Carl Schmitt.[9]

Hence, post-Westphalian and neo-Westphalian constitutionalism are also centred on the concepts of sovereignty, supremacy, hierarchy and territoriality, although negating or altering them substantially and formally. Post-Westphalian constitutionalism is post-sovereign, post-hierarchical, post-supremacist, post-national, post-territorial and aterritorial. It is also more horizontal and networked,

[9] See C Schmitt, *The Concept of the Political* (Chicago, University of Chicago Press, 2007) 19–80.

and in this sense is open to societal constitutionalism.[10] Neo-Westphalian constitutionalism is neo-supremacist, but only post-sovereigntist, post-hierarchical and post-national to an extent. It combines sovereigntist with post-sovereigntist features and hierarchical with post-hierarchical features, as well as elements of open and closed territoriality. In fact, neo-Westphalianism is a mixture of territorial, post-territorial and aterritorial forms and realms of power.

All these features of Westphalian, post-Westphalian and neo-Westphalian constitutionalism significantly affect the constitutional semiotic schemes and tools they use. More precisely, they contribute to the different designs of Westphalian, post-Westphalian and neo-Westphalian constitutional geometry. In other words, Westphalian, post-Westphalian and neo-Westphalian constitutionalism use different models of constitutional geometry applied as explanatory and ordering devices of the constitutional order. Sometimes these models show a degree of continuity and partially overlap, but in many cases, they are different and even hostile and antipodal.

Westphalian constitutionalism contains several main characteristics. This is national constitutionalism – constitutionalism that has emerged within the logic and the general scheme of the territorial nation state. Thus, it is bound to key elements of national constitutionalism which emerged in the late eighteenth century and was the exclusive form of constitutionalism until the 1990s. Hence, Westphalian constitutionalism actually coincides with modern and Western constitutionalism, which has been exported and transplanted during the course of the 'long nineteenth century' and the 'short twentieth century' to the whole world. Nevertheless, the concept of Westphalian constitutionalism has a different focus, putting the analytical accent and focusing on hierarchy and forms of closed territoriality, which differentiates it from the otherwise related concepts of modern and Western constitutionalism.

Westphalian constitutionalism contains all the typical features of 'constitutionalism within statehood'. It is grounded in the hierarchy and the square/polygon as central ordering and explanatory macro-shapes and forms of its constitutional geometry.

Hierarchy has been inherited from the history of political ideas dating back to antiquity but especially from the theory and practice of the late Middle Ages and has been further developed and adjusted to the requirements of modernity. It is the key ordering matrix of Westphalian constitutionalism.[11] It is used as a general ordering and explanatory scheme of constitutional modernity, and is thus

[10] See G Teubner, *Constitutional Fragments: Societal Constitutionalism and Globalization* (Oxford, Oxford University Press, 2012) 38–42; and J Přibáň, *Constitutional Imaginaries: A Theory of European Societal Constitutionalism* (Abingdon, Routledge, 2020) 1–251.

[11] See M Belov, 'The Challenges to Westphalian Constitutional Geometry in the Age of Supranational Constitutionalism, Global Governance and Information Revolution' in M Belov (ed), *Global Constitutionalism and Its Challenges to Westphalian Constitutional Law* (Oxford, Hart Publishing, 2018) 13–55.

a strategic device of constitutional epistemology, constitutional design and constitutional pragmatics. In Westphalian constitutionalism, it is used for the ordering of the general design of the constitutional order. It is also used for the structuring of systems of sources of law and different jurisdictions – the executive power institutions system, the court system, the of state prosecutor's office system etc. Moreover, it is the key matrix for ordering the institutional design of state institutions; in that regard, it is a determinant of bicameralism, the principles for the organisation of executive power and the government, the relationship between the government and the state and public administration etc.

Last but not least, hierarchy is the geometric ordering form of Westphalian territoriality. It is quite visible and indispensable for multilevel constitutional orders such as federations, confederations and unitary states with autonomous regions, regionalism and devolution. Nevertheless, it is also underlies the structure of unitary states with regard to its composite levels of regional and local government and self-governance.

The intermediate conclusion to be reached here is that hierarchy is the main signifier of inter-institutional relations in modern constitutionalism. It is used as a signifier of levels of power, jurisdictions and degrees of validity. Thus, Westphalian constitutionalism and the modern territorial state – regardless of whether it is a nation state or a multicultural state – is impossible and unthinkable without hierarches and pyramids as geometric signifiers of constitutional meaning.

Hierarchy and the pyramid are the most important signifiers in normative-institutional, symbolic-imaginary, visual and performative constitutionalism during Westphalian modernity. They signify institutions, institutional design, institutional relations and fundamental constitutional concepts relating to territoriality, validity, jurisdiction, the public–private divide and relations etc. Hierarchy is the perfect explanatory and ordering matrix in the context of the territorial state. It is clear and understandable, easily applicable and semi-natural, despite the fact that in early modernity, it had to compete with the network as a geometric semiotic form for the signification and ordering of the emerging state system.[12]

Moreover, hierarchy can also be emotionally appealing. It can be inspirational in terms of generating, promoting and signifying heroic imaginaries of supreme leadership, a clear line of command, and vested and personalised authority, as in the case of many totalitarian and authoritarian orders in either a monarchical or a republican form. Clear examples of this are absolute monarchies, different republican dictatorships and personal regimes, the forms of personalised constitutional populism and also some revolutionary regimes. Such constitutional orders have generated a huge range of constitutional imaginaries, some of which are

[12] See M Antonsich, 'On Territory, the Nation-State and the Crisis of the Hyphen' (2009) 33 *Dialogues in Human Geography* 6.

part of revolutionary constitutionalism,[13] whereas others are elements of illiberal constitutionalism[14] and authoritarian constitutionalism.[15]

Hierarchy is both a rational ordering scheme and an emotionally appealing signifier of authority and the distribution of power in a democratic context. It is the geometric signifier of the two most important signifieds of Westphalian modernity: the legal supremacy of the constitution and the political supremacy of the sovereign. Thus, both constitutional supremacy and political sovereignty in all of its forms (monarchical, national, popular or parliamentary sovereignty) are preconditioned on hierarchy as a strategic explanatory and ordering form of Westphalian constitutional geometry.

The intermediate conclusion is that the Westphalian constitutional order is a hierarchical constitutional order. Hierarchy matters for both the legal and the political dimensions of the constitutional order. It is provided by textual constitutionalism, entrenched in normative-institutional constitutionalism, and widely signified through the forms of symbolic-imaginary and visual constitutionalism. It predetermines the performative constitutionalism of authoritarian constitutional orders and is also important for democratic societies. Some of its forms are also emotionally appealing. This is particularly true of hierarchies based on heroism, populism, illiberalism, authoritarianism and identitarian constitutional orders. Nevertheless, hierarchy is also frequently experienced, performed, demonstrated and visualised in democratic orders. This is quite visible in institutional design, official protocols, the constitutionally relevant architecture expressing authority etc.

The square and the polygon have been inherited by the nation state from the territorial state that emerged with the absolute monarchy. It was the main form of constitutional geometry used for the constitutional conceptualisation of space and

[13] On the concept of revolutionary constitutionalism and its different aspects, see R Albert, *Revolutionary Constitutionalism: Law, Legitimacy, Power* (Oxford, Hart Publishing, 2020) 1–424; G Jacobsohn and Y Roznai, *Constitutional Revolution* (New Haven, Yale University Press, 2020) 1–384; B Ackerman, *Revolutionary Constitutions: Charismatic Leadership and the Rule of Law* (Cambridge, MA, Belknap Press, 2019) 1–472; and M Belov and A Abat i Ninet (eds), *Revolution, Transition, Memory, and Oblivion: Reflections on Constitutional Change* (Cheltenham, Edward Elgar, 2020) 1–244.

[14] On the concept of illiberal constitutionalism and its different aspects, see T Drinóczi and A Bień-Kacała (eds), *Illiberal Constitutionalism in Poland and Hungary: The Deterioration of Democracy, Misuse of Human Rights and Abuse of the Rule of Law* (Abingdon, Routledge, 2021) 1–224; T Drinóczi and A Bień-Kacała (eds), *Rule of Law, Common Values, and Illiberal Constitutionalism: Poland and Hungary within the European Union* (Abingdon, Routledge, 2020) 1–348; and M Belov (ed), *Courts and Judicial Activism under Crisis Conditions: Policy Making in a Time of Illiberalism and Emergency Constitutionalism* (Abingdon, Routledge, 2021) 1–236.

[15] See J Přibáň, 'The Promise of Authenticity: On Imaginaries of Constitutional Populism and European Communitas' in *'The End of Globalisation? Resurging Nationalism, Authoritarian Constitutionalism and Uncertain Futures of Democracy'*, Transnational Law Institute Research Paper Series, TLI Think!, 2020 (22), 38–67.

territory during Westphalian modernity.[16] In fact, the squared territoriality has won the conceptual competition with other forms of territoriality which existed in late Middle Ages or which have emerged in early modernity.[17] These are the undetermined and unfixed territorialities of the late medieval, composite, multicultural empires, the 'transversally bordered spaces' produced by global religions and the networked territoriality of the early modern trade empires.[18]

The proponents of the modern territorial state in early modernity created and promoted the semiotic shape of the 'container-like' self-enclosed state. The rectangular structure of territorial constitutional geometry was a great intellectual innovation. It replaced the diffuse, undetermined and non-self-contained territoriality of the medieval empires that was grounded in the patchwork of territories without a clear limit in terms of either territorial expansion or territorial implosion.

When territorial statehood was combined with political absolutism, a new geometric form was imposed on the emerging legal and existing socio-legal and political playground. This semiotic structure, which became a powerful ordering and explanatory tool of constitutional semiotics, was hierarchy. In fact, the theories of sovereignty may also be conceived as theories of political domination, the legitimation of authority and compulsion,[19] and the imposition of hierarchy as the main explanatory and ordering matrix of power relations and the constitutional order. The same is true of the principle of hierarchy of the system of sources of law. The hierarchical structure of the legal order, its subordination to supreme ordering principles such as Hans Kelsen's Grundnorm and the supremacy of the constitution are epistemic and structural schemes that are of huge semiotic importance.

Hence, hierarchy as a political and legal ordering matrix, the pyramid-like structures of the constitutional order in general and its sub-orders (eg, the territorial structure of public power, the system of executive power institutions, the system of courts, the system of sources of law etc.) and the container-like squared-polygonal organisation of the modern constitutional territoriality are the most important and visible products of Westphalian constitutional and

[16] See PJ Taylor, 'The State as Container: Territoriality in the Modern World-System' (1994) 18 *Progress in Human Geography* 2; PJ Taylor, 'Beyond Containers: Internationality, Interstateness, Interterritoriality' (1995) 1 *Progress in Human Geography* 1; and N Brenner, 'Beyond State-Centrism? Space, Territoriality and Geographical Scale in Globalization Studies' (1999) 28(1) *Theory and Society* 39.

[17] ibid.

[18] See S Sassen, *The Global City* (Princeton, Princeton University Press, 2001) 1–480; S Sassen, 'When Territory Deborders Territoriality' (2013) 1(1) *Territory, Politics, Governance* 23; and S Sassen, 'From National Borders to Embedded Borderings: One Angle into the Question of Territory and Space in a Global Age' in W de Been, P Arora and M Hildebrandt (eds), *Crossroads in New Media, Identity and Law* (London, Palgrave Macmillan, 2015) 17.

[19] M Weber, *Soziologie. Weltgeschichtliche Analysen. Politik* (Stuttgart, Kröner Verlag, 1968) 151 et seq.

political theory. They are the intellectual contributions of Westphalian theory and doctrine for the establishment of modern constitutional semiotics. These grand theoretical narratives shape the theoretical dimension of constitutional semiotics. At the same time, they also have a profound formative impact on the normative-institutional dimension of constitutional semiotics. The theories of sovereignty, constitutional supremacy, normative and institutional hierarchy, bicameralism, federalism etc shape and form the structured constitutional imagination of the constitutionally framed socio-political community. They form the intellectual context of the epoch and serve as a source of argumentation and inspiration for the authoritative narrators, speakers, performers and visualisers of the community.

Territoriality has been an important signifier of territory.[20] Westphalian territoriality has been based on several normative ideologies relating to territory and its constitutional and international law dimensions. Two of these normative ideologies have been of key strategic importance for the geometric signification of the modern national territorial state. The first of these is the 'three element' theory of Georg Jellinek,[21] where territoriality and nationality are key determinants of state power. This predetermined the territoriality of power with all its subsequent paradigmatic consequences – the concepts of territorial jurisdiction, the territorial validity of law, the territorial competence of state institutions, the relationship between territorial and personal jurisdiction etc.

The 'three element' theory is very compatible with the hierarchy, pyramid, square and polygon as forms of constitutional geometry. Thus, it fits excellently into the overall design of symbolic-imaginary, visual and normative-institutional Westphalian constitutionalism.

The second normative ideology builds upon the first one. It consists in the imposition of a specific type of territoriality as a semiotic signifier on the territory as fact, which is thus transformed into a legal – and, more precisely, constitutional – phenomenon. This is the normative ideology of the squared-polygonal territoriality that shapes the constitutional design of territory and the state as a 'territorial container'.[22]

The mixture of both normative ideologies conceptualises the state as a squared-polygonal territorial container of the people and the power. In most cases, the people are defined as a nation, although the same constitutional geometric construction is also applicable to multinational states. Nevertheless, multinational states frequently imply pluralism, which in the context of Westphalian constitutional geometry is framed and 'pacified' through hierarchy as an additional constitutional geometric form. In such a context, hierarchy and squared-polygonal

[20] M Belov, 'Territory, Territoriality and Territorial Politics as Public Law Concepts' in M Belov (ed), *Territorial Politics and Secession: Constitutional and International Law Dimensions* (London, Palgrave Macmillan, 2021) 15–45.

[21] G Jellinek, *Allgemeine Staatslehre* (Charleston, Nabu Press, 2010) 1–835.

[22] See Taylor, 'The State as Container' (n 16); Taylor, 'Beyond Containers' (n 16); and Brenner (n 16).

territoriality result in multilevel constitutionalism that is usually designed as a federation and much less frequently as a confederation.

Several phenomena have produced a long-lasting and deep impact on Westphalian statehood, constitutionalism and constitutional geometry. They have profoundly changed the constitutional geometry of the modern national territorial state. These phenomena are globalisation, the emergence and development of spaces of flows[23] (of information, migration, financial capital, pandemics etc), the IT revolution, and the emergence of post-territorial and aterritorial forms of public power. An important role is also played by the emergence and spread of 'constitutionalism beyond statehood', with subsequent challenges to constitutional supremacy and state sovereignty as the main manifestations of hierarchy as a key explanatory and ordering matrix of Westphalian constitutionalism. What is also interesting and to an extent paradoxical is that phenomena which were supposed to be initially post-Westphalian, such as constitutional identity and judicial dialogue, both profoundly challenge the hierarchical and pyramid structure of sources of law and power, but are also used for their reintroduction, reinforcement and installation.

Other factor in the crisis of hierarchy and 'container-like territoriality' (squared or polygonal) is open statehood. This provides an important challenge to Westphalian constitutional geometry both in terms of its legal dimension (mostly related to rules of recognition)[24] and its socio-political aspect, which concerns the 'dehermetization of the territorial container' and its penetration by 'spaces of flows'.[25]

The constitutional polycrisis in which we live also profoundly impacts Westphalian constitutional geometry in both of its dimensions – as an explanatory and as an ordering paradigm. Thus, constitutional systems are swiftly undergoing a profound process of restructuring in terms of their axiology, teleology and constitutional design. This change is not limited to normative-institutional, rational and textual constitutionalism; it also impacts symbolic-imaginary, visual, performative and emotional constitutionalism.

The constitutional polycrisis and the deep civilisation challenges it produces also have increasingly visible impacts on constitutional geometry, consisting of challenges to traditional forms of Westphalian constitutional geometry, to the hierarchy and the pyramid, and to closed, polygonal, squared and 'container-like' territoriality. Moreover, the constitutional polycrisis promotes new forms of constitutionalism both as holistic projects and as a range of partial manifestations and tendencies. These are the post-Westphalian and the neo-Westphalian constitutionalism.

The shaping of constitutional reality in the post-Westphalian age and in times of 'constitutionalism beyond statehood' is bound to another conceptual problem

[23] See M Castells, *The Rise of the Network Society* (Oxford, Wiley-Blackwell, 2009) 407–60.
[24] HLA Hart, *The Concept of Law* (Oxford, Oxford University Press, 1997).
[25] See Castells (n 23) 407–60.

of huge epistemic and semiotic importance. This is the problem of how to order multiple constitutional orders based on different forms of constructive logic, axiology and teleology, which are sometimes mutually contradictory in terms of their institutional design, axiological design and schemes for the framing of legal and socio-legal relations. Thus, although partially deconstructive, post-modern constitutionalism also needs conceptual frames that it can extract from or impose on the rising complexity of the constitutional order or to use for the reshaping and understanding of the word in times of constitutional disorder.

Constitutional post-modernity required ordering and explanatory schemes for the emerging 'constitutionalism beyond statehood'.[26] Thus, novel constitutional geometric forms have been proposed by constitutional theory. The most visible of these have been the circle, the network and the different semiotic approaches for explaining and geometrically containing phenomena relating to globalisation, deglobalisation, the crisis and re-emergence of territoriality, and the constitutionally relevant forms of post-territoriality.

In summary, great political transitions, triggered by events that profoundly change the political, economic and social structures and their constitutional infrastructure and superstructure, also require deep change in the explanatory and ordering structures of constitutional semiotics in general and of constitutional geometry in particular. In other words, the transitions from the late Middle Ages to modernity and from modernity to post-modernity have had important intellectual, conceptual, political and constitutional effects. Some of these effects have semiotic relevance which has been somewhat underestimated. This semiotic relevance relates to the shifts in the semiotic schemes for mastering the constitutional and political transition and for signifying the shapes of the new order through constitutional imaginaries, symbols and visuals using geometric metaphors. The transition from Westphalian to post-Westphalian and neo-Westphalian constitutional geometry that semiotically represents the civilisation shifts and the transition from nationalism and nation state to globalism, global constitutionalism and global governance or to constitutional regionalism is one of the most important examples of such a shift in the conceptual lenses through which we perceive, explain and conceptually arrange reality in textual and performative constitutionalism on the basis of semiotic theoretical constructs.

We are currently experiencing a crisis of both hierarchy and 'container-like' territoriality at the crossroads between Westphalian, post-Westphalian and neo-Westphalian constitutionalism. The crisis of hierarchy consists in challenges to the constitutional supremacy by the primacy of EU law and international law. Monism and dualism – which presuppose hierarchy – are challenged and partially replaced by pluralism. There are also internal reasons for the challenges to the supremacy of the constitution. The most important of these is the role of the courts in general and of the apex courts (especially the constitutional courts) in particular.[27]

[26] See Dobner and Loughlin (n 7); and Walker (n 7).
[27] Belov (n 14).

Hierarchy and the pyramid as signifiers of Westphalian constitutionalism are also challenged in their socio-political dimension relating to sovereignty. The clear lines of authority based on the normative ideologies of popular sovereignty, 'parliamentrocentrism' (the centrality of the parliament in the national constitutional order) and legicentrism (the centrality of the acts of parliament in the national system of sources of law) which are also implicitly based on hierarchy and linear forms of legitimacy stemming from the people–parliament–government–administration line of subordination have been gradually dismantled by the rise of technocracy, judicial policy-making and networked or circular forms of governance. These lines of authority have largely been dismantled by the transversal penetration of policies stemming from actors of supranational and global government and governance, and by the emerging powers of digital and algorithmic constitutionalism.

There are several key features of post-Westphalian constitutionalism. One of the most important is the fragmentation of sovereignty and the emergence of 'sector-specific' sovereignties (financial, humanitarian, military etc). Sovereignty is partially challenged, but also to an extent supported by constitutional identity based on judicial dialogue.

Furthermore, post-Westphalian constitutionalism is confronted with the rise of post-national and post-territorial forms of power, authority, government and governance based on open statehood, post-territoriality, transterritoriality, aterritoriality and the global fluidity of the demos. The internet and its power reality is to a great extent an example of a web-based, networked form of post-territorial and post-Westphalian constitutionalism. In the power reality of the internet, which also has a deep impact beyond the digital realm, hierarchies, pyramids and other forms of clearer and concentrated power co-exist with networks and circles where power nodes mark the new post-Westphalian polycentric design of the geometry of authority.

The territorial container of the nation state is penetrated by a multitude of flows – information, financial capital, migration, pandemic etc. These produce new forms of socio-political geometry – the spaces of flows[28] – which are largely incompatible with fundamental concepts of Westphalian constitutionalism such as territorial jurisdiction, the distinction between public and private, the hierarchical ordering of constitutional order and the constitutional confinement of public power within square or polygonal geometric forms of territoriality. Moreover, public space grounded in 'spaces of flows' is unstable, unpredictable and can hardly be framed within the forms of traditional, modern, Westphalian constitutional geometry.

Post-Westphalian constitutionalism is prone to more horizontal forms of constitutional geometry based on circles and networks. It is compatible with open statehood, societal constitutionalism, human rights beyond state control and novel

[28] See Castells (n 23) 407–60.

forms for 'ordering of constitutional orders',[29] such as constitutional identity, judicial dialogue, the toleration of legal orders and the migration of constitutional imaginaries, including normative ideologies and ideas, constitutional myths and mythologies, constitutional codes and even constitutional utopias.

The circle and the network are the main signifiers of post-Westphalian constitutional geometry. These semiotic forms were also competitors of hierarchy and the square/polygon in early modernity, but have become increasingly important for explaining and ordering constitutional and international legal orders in the age of globalisation, global governance and 'constitutionalism beyond statehood'.

Clear examples of circles and networks as ordering and explanatory paradigms can be found in the supranational constitutionalism of the EU. The very concept of 'l'Europe à plusieurs vitesses' is based on inner and outer circles of integration (eg, Schengen and the eurozone). In that regard, the EU looks like a 'Matryoshka' doll where the inner forms are included in the outer forms. A multitude of circles can be used to exemplify the partially overlapping but also partially diverging spheres of European integration.

The network is also an important signifier of EU constitutionalism. The relationship between the national parliaments in terms of Protocol No 1 on the Role of National Parliaments in the European Union and Protocol No 2 on the Application of the Principles of Subsidiarity and Proportionality is based on the network as an explanatory and ordering matrix. In other words, the control over the observation of the principles of subsidiarity and proportionality is vested in a network of national parliaments. However, the experience of the implementation of these protocols has demonstrated that such a networked institutional design is largely dysfunctional. The network is also applicable to the European Citizens' Initiative, the structuring of the European public sphere (eg, the European political parties) and the practising of political rights on a European scale. It has also produced barely any results. Thus, it seems that human societies are to a great extent incapable of efficiently using the network as a feasible and efficient explanatory and ordering paradigm; it seems much more applicable to scientific, lobbyist and business communities than to the official design of the constitutional architecture.

An important conclusion to draw from our current experience is that from the perspective of the early 2020s, both Westphalian and post-Westphalian constitutionalism are becoming increasingly dysfunctional. Westphalian constitutionalism seems to be an increasingly old-fashioned scheme for mastering the complexity of the global society. Its constitutional design and constitutional axiology, but especially its constitutional imaginaries (including constitutional geometry) have huge difficulties in terms of coping with the current reality. At the same time, post-Westphalian constitutionalism looks like a chimera and a utopia that has not

[29] On the 'ordering of constitutional orders', see E Tanchev, 'The Contemporary Supranational Constitutional Pluralism or the Ordering of Constitutional Orders' in P Kirov (ed), *Constitutional Studies 2012–2013* (Sofia, 'St Kliment Ohridski' University Press, 2014) 171–98 (in Bulgarian).

fulfilled its promises to modernise the world and create constitutional design and constitutional axiology, and to promote constitutional imaginaries and constitutional geometry that can empower the political elite and the people with reliable tools in order to adjust to new realities. It also did not provide science with a sound analytical toolkit that is adequate to meet the challenges of post-modernity and the non-Westphalian world.

Recent years have shown that a new form of constitutionalism is on the rise. Neo-Westphalian constitutionalism is swiftly spreading and is challenging both Westphalian and post-Westphalian constitutionalism. These challenges concern constitutional axiology, the constitutional design, the collective constitutional imaginaries and, last but not least, the constitutional geometry of both modern, national, territorially restrained, sovereigntist Westphalian constitutionalism and post-modern, post-national, partially post-territorial, aterritorial, open, supranational and global post-Westphalian constitutionalism.

In fact, neo-Westphalian constitutionalism can also be defined as regional supranational neo-Westphalianism. This is due to the fact that it borrows from Westphalian nationalism the ideas of the territorial confinement of power and the Schmittean 'friend–enemy' distinction. On the other hand, it dismantles traditional hierarchies relating to sovereignty, constitutional supremacy and jurisdiction. It deconstructs the squared-polygonal 'closed territoriality' of the nation state and continues the trend towards the supranationalisation of power. It challenges the constitutional imaginaries generated in the course of nationalist constitutional modernity, thus deconstructing Westphalian constitutional modernity, despite borrowing some inspiration from it. Simultaneously, it reverses the trends of neoliberal globalisation and provokes the deconstruction of or at least a stalemate in post-Westphalian globalisation. Thus, neo-Westphalian constitutionalism establishes constitutional regionalism which partially stands on the shoulders of Westphalian modernity and post-Westphalian post-modernity, but also challenges them conceptually, institutionally, axiologically, pragmatically and ideologically.

Neo-Westphalian constitutionalism draws a map of the world which is both traditional and novel. It reinstates superpowers that assume the form of states (national or multinational), such as the US, China and Russia. It also preserves the trend towards the supranationalisation of power in the form of regional unions with constitutionalism. The clearest example of this is the EU. To an extent paradoxically, it is a promoter of both neo-nationalism and neoliberalism. This is due to the fact that it brings neo-nationalist, illiberal and populist imaginaries and rhetoric to the fore, while at the same time contributing to the further development of the neoliberal institutional design of supranational and global constitutionalism. It does not prevent the trend towards the establishment of global governance as a phenomenon enhancing the political role of global technocracies in public and private forms (agencies, advisory bodies and think-tanks, but also global corporations).

Neo-Westphalian constitutionalism promotes the establishment of a legal infrastructure that is capable of maintaining multi-centric global legal (dis)order. However, this is not paralleled by a corresponding ideological infrastructure and a coherent set of constitutional imaginaries including constitutional geometry – or, at least, this is the situation so far.

Actually, neo-Westphalian constitutionalism fosters the establishment of principles for the global co-existence of power centres and actors with diverging axiology, institutional design and structures of authority and legitimacy. It leads to the establishment of coherent legal orders within the power entities without allowing for the sufficient coherence of the external relations capable of maintaining peaceful co-existence. Thus, in its current form, it is much more disorder than order. But history shows that order is always made out of disorder. And both order and disorder have a constitutional imaginary dimension, being shaped in the forms of constitutional geometry. From a semiotic perspective and especially looking through the prism of constitutional geometry as an explanatory and ordering paradigm, the situation very much resembles a Kandinski painting.[30]

Regretfully, neo-Westphalianism does not necessarily seem to be a variant of liberal-democratic constitutionalism. It is much more a modus vivendi of different, sometimes even radically different, constitutional orders. Thus, it is necessarily based on the concept of global constitutional pluralism. Neo-Westphalian constitutionalism may take the form of global administrative law (detached from claims for democracy), a global, regional or national technocracy, a post-democratic authoritarian formal constitutional order or a non-homogeneous mixture of constitutionalism, authoritarianism, and administrative and judicial technocratic governance.

In that regard, the constitutional geometry of neo-Westphalian constitutionalism is messy, controversial and still rather unclear. It partially uses hierarchy due to the fact that there is no sufficiently efficient alternative universal scheme for ordering and explaining the constitutional order. But it also preserves and promotes the 'decompression of the territorial container' of the state, as well as the supranationalisation, deterritorialisation and dispersion of power, which is a huge impediment to the use of hierarchy and the pyramid as universal devices of neo-Westphalian constitutional geometry. Moreover, it combines the square-polygonal structure of state territory with neo-imperial forms of territoriality that go beyond firm territorial constraints, being potentially permanently expansive and increasing forms of post-territoriality and aterritoriality. Hierarchies and pyramids are on the rise both nationally and regionally. At the same time, they are competing with circles, networks and asymmetric forms of counterpunctualism. Time will show us whether this is just a temporal transition to new constitutional shapes, forms

[30] I borrow this comparison from Martti Koskenniemi's speech delivered at the 2014 IACL World Congress in Oslo, Norway.

and regimes also having their projections in the spheres of symbolic-imaginary, textual, normative-institutional, visual, performative and emotional constitutionalism or whether we are experiencing the emergence of genuinely post-modern global constitutionalism that is capable of making order out of disorder. One thing is certain – we are in need of critical reflection on the tools for the generation and signification of meaning. This is the task of constitutional semiotics in its capacity as both a constitutional theory and a constitutional meta-theory, which has been proposed in this book.

BIBLIOGRAPHY

Abbott, A, 'Against Narrative: A Preface to Lyrical Sociology' (2007) 25 *Sociological Theory* 33

Abrams, K and H Keren, 'Who's Afraid of Law and the Emotions?' (1997–2004) 94(6) *Minnesota Law Review* 1997, available at: https://ssrn.com/abstract=2434251

Ackerman, B, 'Constitutional Politics/Constitutional Law' (1989) 99(3) *Yale Law Journal* 453

——. *We the People: Foundations* (Cambridge, MA, Harvard University Press, 1991)

——. *Revolutionary Constitutions: Charismatic Leadership and the Rule of Law* (Cambridge, MA, Belknap Press, 2019)

Adams, S (ed), *Ricoeur and Castoriadis in Discussion: On Human Creation, Historical Novelty, and the Social Imaginary* (Lanham, MD, Rowman & Littlefield, 2017)

Ahmed, S, *The Cultural Politics of Emotion* (Abingdon, Routledge, 2014)

Albert, R, *Revolutionary Constitutionalism: Law, Legitimacy, Power* (Oxford, Hart Publishing, 2020)

Albert, R and Y Roznai (eds), *Constitutionalism under Extreme Conditions: Law, Emergency, Exception* (Dordrecht, Springer, 2020)

Alderman, B, *Symptom, Symbol, and the Other of Language: A Jungian Interpretation of the Linguistic Turn* (Abingdon, Routledge, 2015)

Alexy, R, *Theorie der Grundrechte* (Frankfurt am Main, Suhrkamp, 1994)

Alvarez-Nakagawa, A, 'Law as Magic. Some Thoughts on Ghosts, Non-humans, and Shamans' (2017) 18(5) *German Law Journal* 1247

Amavilah, H, 'Flags, Constitutions, and the Well-Being of Nations' (2008) *MPRA Paper*, https://mpra.ub.uni-muenchen.de/11368/1/MPRA_paper_11368.pdf

Amaya, A, 'Admiration, Exemplarity and Judicial Virtue' in A Amaya and M Del Mar (eds), *Virtue, Emotion and Imagination in Law and Legal Reasoning* (Oxford, Hart Publishing, 2020)

Amaya, A and M Del Mar, 'New Horizons for the Study of the Legal Mind: Relating Virtue, Emotion and Imagination' in A Amaya and M Del Mar (eds), *Virtue, Emotion and Imagination in Law and Legal Reasoning* (Oxford, Hart Publishing, 2020)

——. (eds), *Virtue, Emotion and Imagination in Law and Legal Reasoning* (Oxford, Hart Publishing, 2020)

Anderson, B, *Imagined Communities: Reflections on the Origin and Spread of Nationalism* (New York, Verso, 2016)

Angeli, O 'Global Constitutionalism and Constitutional Imagination' (2017) 6(3) *Global Constitutionalism* 359

Antonsich, M, 'On Territory, the Nation-State and the Crisis of the Hyphen' (2009) 33(6) *Dialogues in Human Geography* 789

Arthur Brown, T et al, *Building for Government: The Architecture of State Buildings, OPW, Ireland 1900–2000* (Dublin, Town House and Country House in association with the Office of Public Works, 1999)

Asimow, M and J Silbey, *Law and Popular Culture: A Course Book* (Lake Mary, Vandeplas Publishing, 2020)

Bailey, M, *#HashtagActivism: Networks of Race and Gender Justice* (Cambridge, MA, MIT Press, 2020)

Bainbridge, J, 'Lawyers, Justice and the State: The Sliding Signifier of Law in Popular Culture' (2006) 15(1) *Griffith Law Review* 153

——. '"This is the Authority. This Planet is under Our Protection": An Exegesis of Superheroes' Interrogations of Law' (2007) 3 *Law, Culture and the Humanities* 455

——. 'Visual Law: The Changing Signifiers of Law in Popular Visual Culture' in A Wagner and J Broekman (eds), *Prospects of Legal Semiotics* (Dordrecht, Springer, 2010)
Balaguer, M, *Free Will* (Cambridge, MA, MIT Press, 2014)
Balibar, E, 'After Utopia, Imagination?' in S Chrostowska and J Ingram (eds), *Political Uses of Utopia: New Marxist, Anarchist, and Radical Democratic Perspectives* (New York, Columbia University Press, 2016)
Balkin, J, 'The Hohfeldian Approach to Law and Semiotics' (1990) 44 *University of Miami Law Review* 1119
——. 'The Promise of Legal Semiotics' (1990–91) 69 *University of Texas Law Review* 1779
——. 'Transcendental Deconstruction, Transcendental Justice' (1994) 92 *Michigan Law Review* 1131
——. *The Cycles of Constitutional Time* (Oxford, Oxford University Press, 2020)
Bandes, S, J Madeira, K Temple and E Kidd White (eds), *Research Handbook on Law and Emotion* (Cheltenham, Edward Elgar, 2021)
Barnett, R, 'Constitutional Legitimacy' (2003) 103 *Columbia Law Review* 111
Barthes, R, *Mythologies* (New York, Noonday Press, 1972)
——. *Elements of Semiology* (New York, Hill & Wang, 1977)
——. *Image-Music-Text* (New York, Hill & Wang, 1978)
Bates, M 'An Introduction to Metatheories, Theories, and Models' in KE Fisher, S Erdelez and L McKechnie (eds), *Theories of Information Behavior* (Medford, NJ, Information Today, 2005)
Bauer, M and P Johnson-Laird, 'How Diagrams Can Improve Reasoning' (1993) 4(6) *Psychological Science* 372
Baume, S, 'De l'usage des pouvoirs neutres' (2012) 143(4) *Pouvoirs* 17
Becker, U, *Das 'Menschenbild des Grundgesetzes' in der Rechtsprechung des Bundesverfassungsgerichts* (Berlin, Duncker & Humblot, 1996)
Becker, J, C Butz, D Sibley et al, 'What Do National Flags Stand for? An Exploration of Associations across 11 Countries' (2017) *Journal of Cross-cultural Psychology*, https://doi.org/10.1177/0022022116687851
Belsey, C, *Poststructuralism: A Very Short Introduction* (Oxford, Oxford University Press, 2002)
Belov, M, 'The Preamble of the Constitution in the European Constitutionalism' (2013) 20 *Revista General de Derecho Romano*, https://www.academia.edu/20001843/The_Preamble_of_the_Constitution_in_the_European_Constitutionalism
——. 'Separation of Powers Reconsidered: A Proposal for a New Theoretical Model at the Beginning of the 21st Century' in A Geisler, M Hein and S Hummel (eds), *Law, Politics and the Constitution. New Perspectives from Legal and Political Theory* (Frankfurt am Main, Peter Lang, 2014)
——. 'The Challenges to Westphalian Constitutional Geometry in the Age of Supranational Constitutionalism, Global Governance and Information Revolution' in M Belov (ed), *Global Constitutionalism and its Challenges to Westphalian Constitutional Law* (Oxford, Hart Publishing, 2018)
——. *The Role of Courts in Contemporary Legal Orders* (The Hague, Eleven, 2019)
——. 'Constitutional Memories: How Do Constitutions Cope with Constitutional Past' in M Belov and A Abat i Ninet (eds), *Revolution, Transition, Memory, and Oblivion: Reflections on Constitutional Change* (Cheltenham, Edward Elgar, 2020)
——. (ed), *The IT Revolution and its Impact on State, Constitutionalism and Public Law* (Oxford, Hart Publishing, 2021)
——. 'The Role of Fear Politics in Global Constitutional "Ernstfall": Images of Fear under COVID-19 Health Paternalism' in M Belov (ed), *Populist Constitutionalism and Illiberal Democracies: Between Constitutional Imagination, Normative Entrenchment and Political Reality* (Cambridge, Intersentia, 2021)
——. 'Territory, Territoriality and Territorial Politics as Public Law Concepts' in M Belov (ed), *Territorial Politics and Secession: Constitutional and International Law Dimensions* (London, Palgrave Macmillan, 2021)
——. (ed), *Courts and Judicial Activism under Crisis Conditions: Policy Making in a Time of Illiberalism and Emergency Constitutionalism* (Abingdon, Routledge, 2021)

——. (ed), *Global Constitutionalism and its Challenges to Westphalian Constitutional Law* (Oxford, Hart Publishing, 2018)

——. (ed), *Populist Constitutionalism and Illiberal Democracies: Between Constitutional Imagination, Normative Entrenchment and Political Reality* (Cambridge, Intersentia, 2021)

Belov, M and A Abat i Ninet (eds), *Revolution, Transition, Memory, and Oblivion: Reflections on Constitutional Change* (Cheltenham, Edward Elgar, 2020)

Benjamin, R, *Race after Technology: Abolitionist Tools for the New Jim Code* (Cambridge, Polity Press, 2019)

Bennett, R, *Constitutional Originalism: A Debate* (Ithaca, Cornell University Press, 2011)

Bergek, A and K Onufrey, 'Is One Path Enough? Multiple Paths and Path Interaction as an Extension of Path Dependency Theory' (2014) 23(5) *Industrial and Corporate Change* 1261, https://doi.org/10.1093/icc/dtt040

Berger, A, *Media Analysis Techniques* (New York, SAGE Publications, 2018)

Bergman, M *Peirce's Philosophy of Communication: The Rhetorical Underpinnings of the Theory of Signs* (London, Bloomsbury Publishing, 2011)

Bergson, H, *The Creative Mind: An Introduction to Metaphysics* (New York, Dover Publications, 2010)

Beukers, T and M van der Sluisand, 'The Variable Geometry of the Euro-Crisis: A Look at the Non-Euro Area Member States' (2015) 33 *EUI Working Papers, LAW*, https://cadmus.eui.eu/bitstream/handle/1814/36098/LAW_2015_33.pdf?sequence=1&isAllowed=y

Bianchi, A and A Saab, 'Fear and International Law-Making: An Exploratory Inquiry' (2019) 32 *Leiden Journal of International Law* 351, doi:10.1017/S0922156519000177

Black, E, *Our Constitution: The Myth That Binds Us* (Boulder, Westview Press, 1988)

Bleiker, R, *Visual Global Politics* (Abingdon, Routledge, 2018)

Blokker, P, 'Populist Constitutionalism' in C de la Torre (ed), *Routledge Handbook of Global Populism* (New York, Routledge, 2018)

——. 'Populism as a Constitutional Project' (2019) 17(2) *International Journal of Constitutional Law* 536

——. 'Populist Counter-constitutionalism, Conservatism, and Legal Fundamentalism' (2019) 15 *European Constitutional Law Review* 519

——. 'Varieties of Populist Constitutionalism: The Transnational Dimension' (2019) 20 *German Law Journal* 332

——. 'Imagining Europe: Transnational Contestation and Civic Populism (London, Palgrave Macmillan, 2021)

——. 'Political and Constitutional Imaginaries' in S Adams and J Smith (eds), *Social Imaginaries: Critical Interventions in a Paradigm-in-the-Making* (Lanham, MD, Rowman & Littlefield, 2021)

Blum, L, '"Black Lives Matter": Moral Frames for Understanding the Police Killings of Black Males' in A Amaya and M Del Mar (eds), *Virtue, Emotion and Imagination in Law and Legal Reasoning* (Oxford, Hart Publishing, 2020)

Boettke, P and A Fink, 'Agent Type, Social Contracts and Constitutional Mythologies' in A Marciano (ed), *Constitutional Mythologies: New Perspectives on Controlling the State* (Dordrecht, Springer, 2011)

Bolingbroke, H, *The Idea of a Patriot King: With Respect to the Constitution of Great Britain. By a Person of Quality* (Gale Ecco, 2018)

Bor, B and M Könczöl, 'Towards a Semiotic Theory of Style in Law: A Peircean Approach' (2019) 15(3) *International Journal of Law in Context* 263, doi:10.1017/S1744552319000272

Borowski, M and S Paulson (eds), *Die Natur des Rechts bei Gustav Radbruch* (Heidelberg, Mohr Siebeck, 2015)

Bottici, C, *Imaginal Politics: Images Beyond Imagination and the Imaginary* (New York, Columbia University Press, 2014)

——. *A Feminist Mythology* (Oxford, Hart Publishing, 2021)

Bouchard, G, *Social Myths and Collective Imaginaries* (Toronto, University of Toronto Press, 2015)

Boyd White, J, *The Legal Imagination* (Chicago, University of Chicago Press, 1985)
Brann, E *The World of the Imagination. Sum and Substance* (Lanham, MD, Rowman & Littlefield, 2017)
Brenner, N, 'Beyond State-Centrism? Space, Territoriality and Geographical Scale in Globalization Studies' (1999) 28(1) *Theory and Society* 39
Brion, D, 'The Shopping Mall: Signs of Power' in R Kevelson (ed), *Law and Semiotics*, vol 1 (New York, Plenum Press, 1987)
Brito Vieira, M and D Runciman, *Representation* (Cambridge, Polity Press, 2008)
Brkic, J and N Anderson, 'Drafting and Interpreting Legal Documents' in R Kevelson (ed), *Law and Semiotics*, vol 2 (New York, Plenum Press, 1988)
Brljak, V (ed), *Allegory Studies Contemporary Perspectives* (Abingdon, Routledge, 2021)
Brock Jr, A, *Distributed Blackness: African American Cybercultures* (New York, NYU Press, 2020)
Broekman, J and L Cata Backer, *Lawyers Making Meaning: The Semiotics of Law in Legal Education II* (Dordrecht, Springer, 2013)
Brooks, P, 'Narrative Transactions: Does the Law Need a Narratology?' (2006) 8(1) *Yale Journal of Law & the Humanities* 1
——. 'Legal Stories, the Reality Effect and Visual Narratives. A Response to Simon Stern' in M Hanne and R Weisberg (eds), *Narrative and Metaphor in the Law* (Cambridge, Cambridge University Press, 2018)
Burgess, S, *The Founding Fathers, Pop Culture, and Constitutional Law: Who's Your Daddy?* (Abingdon, Routledge, 2016)
Callahan, S and A Ledgerwood, 'On the Psychological Function of Flags and Logos: Group Identity Symbols Increase Perceived Entitativity' (2016) 110(4) *Journal of Personality and Social Psychology* 528
Cannataci, J, V Falce and O Pollicino (eds), *New Legal Challenges of Big Data* (Cheltenham, Edward Elgar, 2020)
Cassierer, E, *The Myth of the State* (New Haven, Yale University Press, 2009)
Castells, M, *The Rise of the Network Society* (Oxford, Wiley-Blackwell, 2009)
Castoriadis, C, *The Imaginary Institution of Society* (Cambridge, Polity Press, 1987)
Celeste, E, 'Digital Constitutionalism: A New Systematic Theorisation' (2019) 33(1) *International Review of Law, Computers & Technology* 76, doi: 10.1080/13600869.2019.1562604
Cerulo, K, 'Symbols and the World System: National Anthems and Flags' (1993) 8(2) *Sociological Forum* 243
Chase, A, 'Popular Culture/Popular Justice' in J Denvir (ed), *Legal Reelism: Movies as Legal Texts* (Chicago, University of Illinois Press, 1996)
Chandler, D, *Semiotics: The Basics* (Abingdon, Routledge, 2017)
Chrostowska. S and J Ingram (eds), *Political Uses of Utopia: New Marxist, Anarchist, and Radical Democratic Perspectives* (New York, Columbia University Press, 2016)
Cohen, A, *Symbolic Construction of Community* (Abingdon, Routledge, 1985)
Colón-Ríos, J, 'What is a Constitutional Transition?' (2018) 98 *Victoria University of Wellington Legal Research Papers* 43
Colmegna, M, 'Decoding the Code' in R Kevelson (ed), *Law and Semiotics*, vol 2 (New York, Plenum Press, 1988)
Constant, B, *Principes de politiques applicables à tous les gouvernements représentatifs* (HACH.LIVRE-BNF, 2016)
Contiades, X (ed), *Engineering Constitutional Change: A Comparative Perspective on Europe, Canada and the USA* (Abingdon, Routledge, 2012)
Cornell, D, 'The Problem of Normative Authority in Legal Interpretation' in R Kevelson (ed), *Law and Semiotics*, vol 1 (New York, Plenum Press, 1987)
Cresswell, T, 'The Crucial "Where" of Graffiti: A Geographical Analysis of Reactions to Graffiti in New York' (1992) 10(3) *Environment and Planning D: Society and Space* 329
Curtin, D, 'The Sedimentary European Constitution: The Future of 'Constitutionalisation' without a Constitution' in I Pernice and E Tanchev (eds), *Ceci n'est pas une Constitution – Constitutionalisation without a Constitution?* (Baden-Baden, Nomos, 2009)

Dale, E, 'Popular Sovereignty: A Case Study from the Antebellum Era' in A Marciano (ed), *Constitutional Mythologies: New Perspectives on Controlling the State* (Dordrecht, Springer, 2011)

De Saussure, F *Course in General Linguistics* (London, Forgotten Books, 2018)

De Sousa Santos, B, 'Three Metaphors for a New Conception of Law: The Frontier, the Baroque, and the South' (1995) 29(4) *Law and Society Review* 569

Deleuze, G, *Bergsonism* (Princeton, Zone Books, 1990)

Del Mar, M, *Artefacts of Legal Inquiry. The Value of Imagination in Adjudication* (Oxford, Hart Publishing, 2020)

——. 'The Legal Imagination: Individual, Interactive and Communal' in A Amaya and M Del Mar (eds), *Virtue, Emotion and Imagination in Law and Legal Reasoning* (Oxford, Hart Publishing, 2020)

Del Mar, M and W Twining (eds), *Legal Fictions in Theory and Practice* (Dordrecht, Springer, 2015)

Della Cananea, G, 'Is European Constitutionalism Really "Multilevel"?' (2010) 70 *ZaöRV* 283

Delli Carpini, M (ed), *Digital Media and Democratic Futures* (Philadelphia, University of Pennsylvania Press, 2019)

Delmarcel, G, 'Justitia, Examples and Allegories of Justice, and Courts in Flemish Tapestry, 1450–1550: Artistic Representations and Iconography of Law and Justice in Context, from the Middle Ages to the First World War' in S Huygebaert, G Martyn, V Paumen, E Bousmar and X Rousseaux (eds), *The Art of Law: Artistic Representations and Iconography of Law and Justice in Context, from the Middle Ages to the First World War* (Dordrecht, Springer, 2018)

Demertzis, N, *Emotions in Politics: The Affect Dimension in Political Tension* (Basingstoke, Palgrave Macmillan, 2013)

Denvir J (ed), *Legal Reelism: Movies as Legal Texts* (Chicago, University of Illinois Press, 1996)

Depaigne, V, *Legitimacy Gap: Secularism, Religion, and Culture in Comparative Constitutional Law* (Oxford, Oxford University Press, 2017)

Derrida, J, 'Force of Law: The "Mystical Foundation of Authority"' in D Cornell, M Rosenfield and D Carlson (eds), *Deconstruction and the Possibility of Justice* (Abingdon, Routledge, 1992)

——. *Of Grammatology* (Baltimore, Johns Hopkins University Press, 2016)

Dobner, P and M Loughlin (eds), *Twilight of Constitutionalism?* (Oxford, Oxford University Press, 2010)

Douzinas, C, 'The Legality of the Image' (2000) 63(6) *Modern Law Review* 813

Douzinas, C, P Goodrich and Y Hachamovitch (eds), *Politics, Postmodernity and Critical Legal Studies: The Legality of the Contingent* (Abingdon, Routledge, 1994)

Douzinas, C, S McVeigh and R Warrington, 'The Alta(e)rs of Law: The Judgement of Legal Aesthetics' (1992) 9(4) *Theory, Culture & Society* 93, doi:10.1177/02632769200900400

Douzinas, C and R Warrington, *Justice Miscarried: Ethics and Aesthetics in Law* (Edinburgh, Edinburgh University Press, 1997)

Drinóczi, T and A Bień-Kacała (eds), *Rule of Law, Common Values, and Illiberal Constitutionalism: Poland and Hungary within the European Union* (Abingdon, Routledge, 2020)

——. *Illiberal Constitutionalism in Poland and Hungary: The Deterioration of Democracy, Misuse of Human Rights and Abuse of the Rule of Law* (Abingdon, Routledge, 2021)

Drozdowicz, Z, *Faces of the Enlightenment Philosophical Sketches* (Berlin, Peter Lang, 2020)

Duverger, M, *Échec au roi* (Paris, A Michel, 1977)

Dworkin, R, *Taking Rights Seriously* (Cambridge, MA, Harvard University Press, 1978)

——. *A Matter of Principle* (Cambridge, MA, Harvard University Press, 1985)

Eco, U, *A Theory of Semiotics* (Bloomington, Indiana University Press, 1978)

——. *Semiotics and the Philosophy of Language* (Bloomington, Indiana University Press, 1986)

——. *Mouse or Rat: Translation as Negotiation* (New York, Orion, 2004)

Elkins, Z, 'Constitutional Transition' in R Congleton, B Grofman, and S Voigt (eds), *The Oxford Handbook of Public Choice*, vol 2 (Oxford, Oxford University Press, 2019)

Ellis, M, *Critical Global Semiotics: Understanding Sustainable Transformational Citizenship* (Abingdon, Routledge, 2021)

Eriksen, T and R Jenkins, *Flag, Nation and Symbolism in Europe and America* (Abingdon, Routledge, 2007)

Eskridge, W, 'The New Textualism' (1989–90) 37 *UCLA Law Review* 621

Falk, R, 'Revisiting Westphalia, Discovering Post-Westphalia' (2002) 6 *Journal of Ethics* 311

Farrell, D, 'Utility-Maximizing Intentions and the Theory of Rational Choice' (1993) 21(1) *Philosophical Topics*, https://www.law.upenn.edu/live/files/1338-farrellutility-maximization-intentions

Feibleman, J, *Justice, Law and Culture* (Dordrecht, Martinus Nijhoff, 1985)

Feigenson, N, 'Digital Visual and Multimedia Software and the Reshaping of Legal Knowledge' in A Wagner and W Pencak (eds), *Images in Law* (Farnham, Ashgate, 2006)

Ferris, G and C Lunt, 'Devil's Advocate: Representation in Heroic Fiction, *Daredevil* and the Law' in T Giddens, Graphic Justice. Intersections of Comics and Law (Abingdon, Routledge, 2015)

Ferry, L, *La Revolution Transhumaniste* (Paris, Edition Plon, 2016)

Fitzsimmons, M, *The Remaking of France: The National Assembly and the Constitution of 1791* (Cambridge, Cambridge University Press, 2002)

Flessas, T and L Mulcahy, 'Limiting Law: Art in the Street and Street in the Art' (2018) 14(2) *Law, Culture and the Humanities* 219

Florczak-Wator, M (ed), *Judicial Law-Making in European Constitutional Courts* (Abingdon, Routledge, 2020)

Foucault, M, *The Archaeology of Knowledge: and the Discourse on Language* (New York, Vintage, 1982)

——. *The Order of Things: An Archaeology of the Human Sciences* (New York, Vintage, 1994)

——. *Aesthetics, Method and Epistemology*, vol 2 (New York, The New Press, 1998)

——. *Ethics: Subjectivity and Truth* (New York, The New Press, 1998)

——. *Power* (New York, The New Press, 2001)

Frank, J, *Courts on Trial: Myth and Reality in American Justice* (Princeton, Princeton University Press, 1949)

Frankenberg, G, *Comparative Constitutional Studies: Between Magic and Deceit* (Cheltenham, Edward Elgar, 2018)

——. *Order from Transfer: Comparative Constitutional Design and Legal Culture* (Oxford, Edward Elgar, 2013)

Friedman, L, 'Lexitainment: Legal Process as Theatre' (2000) 50 *De Paul Law Review* 539

Fukuyama, F, *The End of History and the Last Man* (London, Penguin, 1993)

Fuller, L, *Legal Fictions* (Stanford, Stanford University Press, 1967)

Geuss, R, *Politics and the Imagination* (Princeton, Princeton University Press, 2010)

Giddens, T, *Graphic Justice: Intersections of Comics and Law* (Abingdon, Routledge, 2015)

——. 'Lex Comica: On Comics and Legal Theory' in *Graphic Justice: Intersections of Comics and Law* (Abingdon, Routledge, 2015)

Gilleard, C, 'From Collective Representations to Social Imaginaries: How Society Represents itself to itself' (2018) 5(3) *European Journal of Cultural and Political Sociology* 1

Goodrich, P, 'Psychoanalysis in Legal Education: Notes on the Violence of the Sign' in R Kevelson (ed), *Law and Semiotics*, vol 1 (New York, Plenum Press, 1987)

——. *Legal Emblems and the Art of Law: Obiter Depicta as the Vision of Governance* (Cambridge, Cambridge University Press, 2013)

Graham, C, *Ordering Law: The Architectural and Social History of the English Law Court to 1914* (Abingdon, Routledge, 2003)

Grant, J, 'On the Critique of Political Imaginaries' (2014) 13(4) *European Journal of Political Theory* 408

Grover, S, *Judicial Activism and the Democratic Rule of Law: Selected Case Studies* (Dordrecht, Springer, 2020)

Gutan, M, 'Romanian Tendential Constitutionalism and the Limits of European Constitutional Culture' in M Belov (ed), *Global Constitutionalism and its Challenges to Westphalian Constitutional Law* (Oxford, Hart Publishing, 2018)

Hallward, P, 'General Wish or General Will? Political Possibility and Collective Capacity from Rousseau through Marx' in S Chrostowska and J Ingram (eds), *Political Uses of Utopia: New Marxist, Anarchist, and Radical Democratic Perspectives* (New York, Columbia University Press, 2016)
Halmai, G, 'Populism, Authoritarianism and Constitutionalism' (2019) 20(3) *German Law Journal* 296, doi:10.1017/glj.2019.23
Halperin, J-L, *Five Legal Revolutions since the 17th Century: An Analysis of a Global Legal History* (Dordrecht, Springer, 2014)
Hamilton, S, 'A Genealogy of Metatheory in IR: How "Ontology" Emerged from the Inter-paradigm Debate' (2017) 9(1) *International Theory* 136, doi:10.1017/S1752971916000257
Hart, HLA, *The Concept of Law* (Oxford, Oxford University Press, 1997)
Haskell, F, *History and its Images: Art and the Interpretation of the Past* (New Haven, Yale University Press, 1993)
——. *Political Theology and International Law* (Leiden, Brill, 2018)
Hawkes, T, *Structuralism and Semiotics* (Abingdon, Routledge, 2003)
Hayaert, V, 'The Paradoxes of Lady Justice's Blindfold' in S Huygebaert, G Martyn, V Paumen, E Bousmar and X Rouseaux (eds), *The Art of Law: Artistic Representations and Iconography of Law and Justice in Context, from the Middle Ages to the First World War* (Dordrecht, Springer, 2018)
Hayek, F, *Law, Legislation and Liberty, Volume 1: Rules and Order* (Chicago, University of Chicago Press, 1978)
——. *Law, Legislation and Liberty, Volume 2: The Mirage of Social Justice* (Chicago, University of Chicago Press, 1978)
——. *Law, Legislation and Liberty, Volume 3: The Political Order of a Free People* (Chicago, University of Chicago Press, 1981)
Heidegger, M, *Being and Time* (New York, Harper Perennial, 2008)
Heidemann, M, *Bernhard Windscheid und die 'Begriffsjurisprudenz'. Die Pandektendogmatik im späten 19. Jahrhundert* (Munich, GRIN Publishing, 2015)
Hein, M, 'Entrenchment Clauses in the History of Modern Constitutionalism' (2018) 86(3–4) *Tijdschrift voor Rechtsgeschiedenis/Revue d'Histoire du Droit/Legal History Review* 434, https://doi.org/10.1163/15718190-08634P06
Helfland, J, *Screen: Essays on Graphic Design, New Media, and Visual Culture* (Princeton, Princeton Architectural Press, 2001)
Herman, S 'Constitutional Utopianism' (2016) 12 *UTOPIA500* 93, https://scholarlycommons.pacific.edu/utopia500/2016/events/12
Hirschkop, K, *Linguistic Turns, 1890–1950: Writing on Language as Social Theory* (Oxford, Oxford University Press, 2019)
Hobsbawm, E, *Age of Extremes: The Short Twentieth Century 1914–1991* (New York, Time Warner Books, 1995)
——. *The Age of Revolution: 1789–1848* (New York, Vintage, 1996)
Hobsbawm, E and T Ranger (eds), *The Invention of Tradition* (Cambridge, Cambridge University Press, 2012)
Holcombe, R, 'Consent or Coercion? A Critical Analysis of the Constitutional Contract' in A Marciano (ed), *Constitutional Mythologies: New Perspectives on Controlling the State* (Dordrecht, Springer, 2011)
Holdcroft, D *Saussure. Signs, System and Arbitrariness* (Cambridge, Cambridge University Press, 1991)
hooks, b, *Art on My Mind: Visual Politics* (New York, The New Press, 1995)
Howser, N and C Kloesel (eds), *The Essential Peirce, Volume 1: Selected Philosophical Writings (1867–1893)* (Bloomington, Indiana University Press, 1992)
Hubrich, K, Multilayered Functions of Early Modern Courtroom Equipment: Luneburg for Example' in S Huygebaert, G Martyn, V Paumen, E Bousmar and X Rouseaux (eds), *The Art of Law: Artistic Representations and Iconography of Law and Justice in Context, from the Middle Ages to the First World War* (Dordrecht, Springer, 2018)

Huxley, A, *Brave New World* (New York, Harper Perennial, 2006)
Hyvärinen, M, 'Prototypes, Genres, and Concepts: Travelling with Narratives' (2012) 2(10 *Psychology*, https://journals.lib.unb.ca/index.php/NW/article/view/19496/21111
Imbeau, L and S Jacob, 'Is the "Veil of Ignorance" in Constitutional Choice a Myth? An Empirical Exploration Informed by a Theory of Power' in A Marciano (ed), *Constitutional Mythologies: New Perspectives on Controlling the State* (Dordrecht, Springer, 2011)
Ioanide, P, *The Emotional Politics of Racism: How Feelings Trump Facts in an Era of Colorblindness* (Stanford, Stanford University Press, 2015)
Isani, S, 'Visual Semiotics of Court Dress in England and Wales: Failed or Successful Vector of Professional Identity' in A Wagner and W Pencak (eds), *Images in Law* (Farnham, Ashgate, 2006)
Izquierdo, R, 'The Architecture of Constitutional Time' (2014–15) 23(4) *William & Mary Bill of Rights Journal* 1
Jackson, B, *Semiotics and Legal Theory* (London, Kegan Paul, 1985)
——. *Making Sense in Law: Linguistic, Psychological, and Semiotic Perspectives* (Liverpool, Deborah Charles Publications, 1995)
——. 'Legal Semiotics and Semiotic Aspects of Jurisprudence' in A Wagner and J Broekman (eds), *Prospects of Legal Semiotics* (Dordrecht, Springer, 2010)
Jackson, S and M Bailey, *#HashtagActivism: Networks of Race and Gender Justice* (Cambridge, MA, MIT Press, 2020)
Jacobsohn, G and Y Roznai *Constitutional Revolution* (New Haven, Yale University Press, 2020)
Janssens, F, *Identity Colour Codes: How Colours Unite Us All* (Amsterdam, BIS Publishers, 2014)
Jay, M, 'Cultural Relativism and the Visual Turn' (2002) 1(3) *Journal of Visual Culture* 12
Jellinek, G, *Allgemeine Staatslehre* (Charleston, Nabu Press, 2010)
Jung, CG, *Man and His Symbols* (New York, Dell Publishing, 1968)
——. *Psychology of the Unconscious* (Eastford, Martino Fine Books, 2016)
Kaasik-Krogerus, S, L Čeginskas and N Sääskilahti, 'Politics of Memory and Oblivion: An Introduction to the Special Issue' (2020) 21(3) *European Politics and Society* 1
Kahn, P, 'Comparative Constitutionalism in a New Key' (2003) 101(8) *Michigan Law Review* 2677
Kane, R, *A Contemporary Introduction to Free Will* (Oxford, Oxford University Press, 2005)
Kant, I, *Critique of Pure Reason* (Cambridge, Cambridge University Press, 1999)
Kelber, W, 'In the Beginning were the Words: The Apotheosis and Narrative Displacement of the Logos' (1990) LVIII(1) *Journal of the American Academy of Religion* 69, https://doi.org/10.1093/jaarel/LVIII.1.69
Kenski, K and K Hall Jamieson (eds), *The Oxford Handbook of Political Communication* (Oxford, Oxford University Press, 2019)
Kevelson, R *Peirce, Science, Signs* (New York, Peter Lang, 1996),
——. *The Law as a System of Signs* (New York, Plenum Press, 1988)
——. (ed), *Law and Semiotics*, vols 1 and 2 (New York, Plenum Press, 1988)
Khorakiwala, R, *From the Colonial to the Contemporary: Images, Iconography, Memories, and Performances of Law in India's High Courts* (Oxford, Hart Publishing, 2020)
Kidd White, E, 'On Emotions and the Politics of Attention in Judicial Reasoning' in A Amaya and M Del Mar (eds), *Virtue, Emotion and Imagination in Law and Legal Reasoning* (Oxford, Hart Publishing, 2020)
Kirkpatrick, G, *Computer Games and the Social Imaginary* (Cambridge, Polity Press, 2013)
Klabbers, J, 'Towards a Culture of Formalism? Martti Koskenniemi and the Virtues' (2013) 27(2) *Temple International and Comparative Law Journal* 399
Klinck, D, *Word of the Law: Approaches to Legal Discourse* (Ottawa, Carleton University Press, 1992)
Koerner, E *Ferdinand de Saussure* (Berlin, Vieweg+Teubner Verlag, 1973)
Kølvraa, C, 'Past and Future in the Construction of Communal Identity: Collective Memory and Mythical Narratives' (2015) 6(3) *Scandinavian Studies in Language* 62
Komárek, J, 'Political Economy in the European Constitutional Imaginary: Moving Beyond Fiesole', *Verfassungsblog*, 4 September 2020, https://verfassungsblog.de/political-economy-in-the-european-constitutional-imaginary-moving-beyond-fiesole

——. (ed), *European Constitutional Imaginaries: Between Ideology and Itopia* (Oxford, Oxford University Press, 2021)
Koncewicz, T and L Strother, 'The Role of Citizen Emotions in Constitutional Backsliding: Mapping out Frontiers of New Research', *Verfassungsblog*, 21 March 2019, https://verfassungsblog.de/the-role-of-citizen-emotions-in-constitutional-backsliding-mapping-out-frontiers-of-new-research
Konig, T, G Tsebelis and M Debus (eds), *Reform Processes and Policy Change: Veto Players and Decision-Making in Modern Democracies* (Dordrecht, Springer, 2010)
Korpiola, M, 'Medieval Iconography of Justice in a European Periphery: The Case of Sweden, ca 125–1550' in S Huygebaert, G Martyn, V Paumen, E Bousmar and X Rouseaux (eds), *The Art of Law: Artistic Representations and Iconography of Law and Justice in Context, from the Middle Ages to the First World War* (Dordrecht, Springer, 2018)
Korsten, F-W, *Art as an Interface of Law and Justice: Affirmation, Disturbance, Disruption* (Oxford, Hart Publishing, 2021)
Kosellek, R, *Futures Past: On the Semantics of Historical Time* (New York, Columbia University Press, 2004)
Koskenniemi, M, *The Gentle Civilizer of Nations: The Rise and Fall of International Law 1870–1960* (Cambridge, Cambridge University Press, 2004)
——. *From Apology to Utopia: The Structure of International Legal Argument* (Cambridge, Cambridge University Press, 2006)
——. *To the Uttermost Parts of the Earth: Legal Imagination and International Power 1300–1870* (Cambridge, Cambridge University Press, 2021)
Kothari, U and R Wilkinson, 'Colonial Imaginaries and Postcolonial Transformations: Exiles, Bases, Beaches' (2010) 31(8) *Third World Quarterly* 1395
Kotiaho, P, 'A Return to Koskenniemi: Or the Disconcerting Co-optation of Rupture' (2012) 13(5) *German Law Journal* 483
Krisch, N, 'Liquid Authority in Global Governance' (2017) 9(2) *International Theory* 1
Lachs, J, 'Law and the Importance of Feelings' in R Kevelson (ed), *Law and Semiotics*, vol 2 (New York, Plenum Press, 1988)
Lacan, J, *The Language of the Self* (Baltimore, Johns Hopkins University Press, 1956)
——. *Écrits* (New York, WW Norton & Company, 2007)
Landqvist, M, 'Semiotic Spaces in Antidiscriminatory Political Discourse: Naming Practices as Indexes' (2019) 48 *Language in Society* 721, doi:10.1017/S0047404519000459
Law, D, *Constitutionalism in Context* (Cambridge, Cambridge University Press, 2021)
Lecky, W, *History of the Rise and Influence of the Spirit of Rationalism in Europe* (LEEAF.com Classics, 2013)
Lee, D, *Popular Sovereignty in Early Modern Constitutional Thought* (Oxford, Oxford University Press, 2016)
Lee, N (ed), *The Transhumanism Handbook* (Dordrecht, Springer, 2019)
Leigh Grove, T, 'Which Textualism?' (2020) 134 *Harvard Law Review* 265
Lerner, M, 'Constitution and Court as Symbols' (1937) 46(8) *Yale Law Journal* 1290
Lincoln, B, *Discourse and the Construction of Society: Comparative Studies of Myth, Ritual, and Classification* (Oxford, Oxford University Press, 1992)
Lind, H (ed), *Fictional Discourse and the Law* (Abingdon, Routledge, 2006)
Liotard, F, *The Postmodern Condition: A Report on Knowledge* (Minneapolis, University of Minnesota Press, 1984)
Lippens, R, 'Law, Code and Late Modern Governance in Prophetic Painting: Notes on Jackson Pollock, Mark Rothko and Gilles Deleuze' in A Wagner and J Broekman (eds), *Prospects of Legal Semiotics* (Dordrecht, Springer, 2010)
Liszka, J, *A General Introduction to the Semiotic of Charles Sanders Peirce* (Bloomington, Indiana University Press, 1996)
Long, G, 'The Written Story: Toward Understanding Text as Representation and Function' (1999) 49(2) *Vetus Testamentum* 165, doi:10.1163/156853399774228957

Loughlin, M, 'The Constitutional Imagination' (2015) 78(1) *Modern Law Review* 1
Loughlin, M, *Sword and Scales: An Examination of the Relationship between Law and Politics* (Oxford, Hart Publishing, 2000)
Lynch, K, 'An Agentive Non-intentionalist Theory of Self-Deception' (2017) 47(6) *Canadian Journal of Philosophy* 779
Lynch, M, 'Pictures of Nothing? Visual Construals in Social Theory' (1991) 9(1) *Sociological Theory* 1
Mader, S and M Asimow, *Law and Popular Culture: A Course Book* (New York, Peter Lang, 2013)
Manderson, D, 'The Metastases of Myth: Legal Images as Transitional Phenomena' (2015) 26(3) *Law and Critique* 207
——. *Songs without Music: Aesthetic Dimensions of Law and Justice* (Berkeley, University of California Press, 2000)
Mannheim, K, *Ideology and Utopia: An Introduction to the Sociology of Knowledge* (Eastford, Martino Fine Books, 2015)
Manning, J, 'Textualism and Legislative Intent' (2005) 91 *Virginia Law Review* 419
Marciano, A (ed), *Constitutional Mythologies: New Perspectives on Controlling the State* (Dordrecht, Springer, 2011)
Matravers, D, *Fiction and Narrative* (Oxford, Oxford University Press, 2017)
Maza, S, *The Myth of the French Bourgeoisie: An Essay on the Social Imaginary, 1750–1850* (Cambridge, MA, Harvard University Press, 2009)
McCall, B, *The Architecture of Law: Rebuilding Law in the Classical Tradition* (Notre Dame, IN, University of Notre Dame Press, 2018)
McDonagh, L, *Performing Copyright: Law, Theatre and Authorship* (Oxford, Hart Publishing, 2021)
McLagan, M and M McKee (eds), *Sensible Politics: The Visual Culture of Nongovernmental Activism* (Princeton, Zone Books, 2012)
McIlwain, C, *Black Software: The Internet & Racial Justice, from the AfroNet to Black Lives Matter* (Oxford, Oxford University Press, 2019)
Menezes de Carvalho, E, *Semiotics of International Law: Trade and Translation* (Dordrecht, Springer, 2011)
Miller, E, 'Metaphor and Political Knowledge' (1979) 73 *American Political Science Review* 155
Milligan, T, ' Speciesism as Variant of Anthropocentrism' in R Boddice (ed), *Anthropocentrism. Humans, Animals, Environments* (Leiden, Brill, 2011)
Milner, R, *The World Made Meme: Public Conversations and Participatory Media* (Cambridge, MA, MIT Press, 2016)
Mohamedou, M-M and T Sisk (eds), *Democratisation in the 21st Century: Reviving Transitology* (Abingdon, Routledge, 2016)
Molot, J, 'The Rise and Fall of Textualism', *GWU Law School, Public Law Research Paper*, No 134, available at: https://ssrn.com/abstract=696681
Mooney, A, 'The Drama of the Courtroom' in A Wagner and W Pencak (eds), *Images in Law* (Farnham, Ashgate, 2006)
Mulcahy, L, *Legal Architecture: Justice, Due Process and the Place of Law* (Abingdon, Routledge, 2011)
——. 'Eyes of the Law: A Visual Turn in Socio-legal Studies?' (2017) 44(1) *Journal of Law and Society* 111
——. 'Sociology of Legal Images' in J Přibáň (ed), *Research Handbook on the Sociology of Law* (Cheltenham, Edward Elgar, 2020)
Mulcahy, L and E Rowden, *The Democratic Courthouse: A Modern History of Design, Due Process and Dignity* (Abingdon, Routledge, 2020)
Mullender, R, M Nicolini, T Bennett and E Mickiewicz (eds), *Law and Imagination in Troubled Times: A Legal and Literary Discourse* (Abingdon, Routledge, 2020)
Murray, J, 'Nome Law: Deleuze & Guattari on the Emergence of Law' (2006) 2 *International Journal for the Semiotics of Law* 127
——. 'Deleuze & Guattari's Intensive & Pragmatic Semiotic of Emergent Law' (2007) 20 *International Journal for the Semiotics of Law* 7

Nead, L, 'Visual Cultures of the Courtroom: Reflections on History, Law and the Image' (2002) 3(2) *Visual Culture in Britain* 119

Neufeld, M, 'Who's Afraid of Meta-theory?' (1994) 23(2) *Millennium* 387, doi:10.1177/03058298940230020401

Nikielska-Sekula, K and A Sesille (eds), *Visual Methodology in Migration Studies: New Possibilities, Theoretical Implications, and Ethical Questions* (Dordrecht, Springer, 2021)

Noble, S U, *Algorithms of Oppression: How Search Engines Reinforce Racism* (New York, NYU Press, 2018)

Nozik, R, *Anarchy, State, and Utopia* (New York, Basic Books, 2013)

Noth, W *Handbook of Semiotics* (Bloomington, Indiana University Press, 1995)

Oakeshott, M *Rationalism in Politics and Other Essays* (Carmel, Liberty Fund, 1991)

Oklopcic, Z, *Beyond the People: Social Imaginary and Constituent Imagination* (Oxford, Oxford University Press, 2018)

Olivier, B, 'Lacan's Subject: The Imaginary, Language, the Real and Philosophy' (2005) 23(1) *South African Journal of Philosophy* 1

Olson, K, *Imagined Sovereignties: The Power of the People and Other Myths of the Modern Age* (Cambridge, Cambridge University Press, 2017)

Orwell, G, *Nineteen Eighty-Four* (New York, Signet Classics, 1961)

Panji Nugraha, T and S Na'afi, 'Legal Semiotics Approach: Understanding Asymmetrical Symbols behind Text of Positive Legal Norms' (2021) 1(1) *Indonesian Journal of Legal Thought* 67

Papineau, D, *The Metaphysics of Sensory Experience* (Oxford, Oxford University Press, 2021)

Paterson, B, L Thorne, C Canam and C Jillings, 'Meta-theory' in *Meta-study of Qualitative Health Research* (New York, SAGE Publications, 2001)

Patty, J and E Penn, *Social Choice and Legitimacy: The Possibilities of Impossibility* (Cambridge, Cambridge University Press, 2014)

Paul, J, 'The Politics of Legal Semiotics' (1990–91) 69 *Texas Law Review* 1779

Paumen, V, 'The Exhibition "The Art on Law": Three Centuries of Justice Depicted' in S Huygebaert, G Martyn, V Paumen, E Bousmar and X Rouseaux (eds), *The Art of Law: Artistic Representations and Iconography of Law and Justice in Context, from the Middle Ages to the First World War* (Dordrecht, Springer, 2018)

Peirce, C, *Collected Papers of Charles Sanders Peirce, Volumes I and II: Principles of Philosophy and Elements of Logic* (edited by Charles Hartshorne Paul Weiss) (Cambridge, MA, Belknap Press, 1932)

——. *Peirce on Signs: Writings on Semiotic* (edited by J Hoopes) (Chapel Hill, University of North Carolina Press, 1991)

Peirce Edition Project (ed), *The Essential Peirce, Volume 2: Selected Philosophical Writings, 1893–1913* (Bloomington, Indiana University Press, 1998)

Pernice, I, 'Multilevel Constitutionalism and the Crisis of Democracy in Europe' (2015) 11(3) *European Constitutional Law Review* 541, doi:10.1017/S1574019615000279

Perrone, N, *Investment Treaties and the Legal Imagination: How Foreign Investors Play by Their Own Rules* (Oxford, Oxford University Press, 2021)

Peters, A, 'Liberté, Égalité, Animalité: Human–Animal Comparisons in Law' (2015) 5(1) *Transnational Environmental Law* 1

Petersmann, EU, *Multilevel Constitutionalism for Multilevel Governance of Public Goods* (Oxford, Hart Publishing, 2017)

Poiares Maduro, M, 'Contrapunctual Law: Europe's Constitutional Pluralism in Action' in N Walker (ed), *Sovereignty in Transition* (Oxford, Hart Publishing, 2003)

——. 'Three Claims of Constitutional Pluralism' in M Avbelj and J Komarek (eds), *Constitutional Pluralism in the European Union and Beyond* (Oxford, Hart Publishing, 2012)

Pollicino, O, *Judicial Protection of Fundamental Rights on the Internet: A Road towards Digital Constitutionalism* (Oxford, Hart Publishing, 2021)

Ponzio, A, 'The European Constitution: A Semiotics Analysis of Ideology, Identity and Global Commun in Present-Day Europe' (2008) 21 *International Journal for the Semiotics of Law* 35, doi:10.1007/s11196-007-9055-z

Prakash, G and K Kruse (eds), *The Spaces of the Modern City: Imaginaries, Politics, and Everyday Life* (Princeton, Princeton University Press, 2008)

Přibáň, J, 'Constitutional Imaginaries and Legitimation: On Potentia, Potestas, and Auctoritas in Societal Constitutionalism' (2018) 45(1) *Journal of Law and Society* 30

——. *Constitutional Imaginaries: A Theory of European Societal Constitutionalism* (Abingdon, Routledge, 2020)

——. 'The Promise of Authenticity: On Imaginaries of Constitutional Populism and European Communitas' in *'The End of Globalization? – Resurging Nationalism, Authoritarian Constitutionalism and Uncertain Futures of Democracy'*, Transnational Law Institute Research Paper Series, TLI Think!, 2020 (22)

——. 'A Social Theory of Constitutional Imaginaries: Beyond the Unity of "Topos-Ethnos-Nomos" and its European Context' in U Belavusau and A Gliszczyńska-Grabias (eds), *Constitutionalism under Stress: Essays in Honour of Wojciech Sadurski* (Oxford, Oxford University Press, 2020)

Raheja, M, *Reservation Reelism: Redfacing, Visual Sovereignty, and Representations of Native Americans in Film* (Lincoln, NE, University of Nebraska Press, 2011)

Rajagopalan, S. and R Wagner, 'Constitutional Craftsmanship and the Rule of Law: Organizational Arrangement, Moral Imagination, and the Separation of Powers', *GMU Working Paper in Economics*, 2013 (13-08), available at: https://ssrn.com/abstract=2250935

Ranchordas, S and Y Roznai, *Time, Law and Change* (Oxford, Hart Publishing, 2020)

Rawls, J, *A Theory of Justice* (Cambridge, MA, Belknap Press, 1999)

Redhead, S, *Unpopular Cultures: The Birth of Law and Popular Culture* (Manchester, Manchester University Press, 1995)

Resnik, J and D Curtis, *Representing Justice: Invention, Controversy, and Rights in City-States and Democratic Courtrooms* (New Haven, Yale University Press, 2011)

Richardson, B, 'Recent Concepts of Narrative and the Narratives of Narrative Theory' (2000) 34(2) *Style* 168

Ricoeur, P, *La memoire, l'histoire, l'oubli* (Paris, Seuil, 2000)

Ritzer, G, 'Metatheory' in *The Blackwell Encyclopedia of Sociology* (Oxford, Blackwell, 2006)

Rolland, P, 'Comment préserver les institutions politiques? La théorie du pouvoir neutre chez B Constant' (2008) 27(1) *Revue Française d'Histoire des Idées Politiques* 43

Rorty, R, 'Nineteenth-Century Idealism and Twentieth-Century Textualism' (1981) 64(2) *The Monist* 155

——. (ed), *The Linguistic Turn: Essays in Philosophical Method* (Chicago, University of Chicago Press, 1992)

Rose, G, *Visual Methodologies: An Introduction to Researching with Visual Materials* (New York, SAGE Publications, 2016)

Rosen, L *Law as Culture: An Invitation* (Princeton, Princeton University Press, 2008)

Ross, B *The Philosophy of Transhumanism: A Critical Analysis* (Bingley, Emerald Publishing, 2020)

Rosselin, J-M, 'Making and Implementing the Rules of the Game: The Political Economy of Constitutional Myths and Rites' in A Marciano (ed), *Constitutional Mythologies: New Perspectives on Controlling the State* (Dordrecht, Springer, 2011)

Roth-Isigkeit, D, *The Plurality Trilemma: A Geometry of Global Legal Thought* (London, Palgrave Macmillan, 2018)

Rouhana, N and Nadera Shalhoub-Kevorkian, *When Politics are Sacralized: Comparative Perspectives on Religious Claims and Nationalism* (Cambridge, Cambridge University Press, 2021)

Ryder, R, *Animal Revolution: Changing Attitudes towards Speciesism* (Oxford, Berg, 2000)

Saage, R, 'Is the Classic Concept of Utopia Ready for the Future?' in S Chrostowska and J Ingram (eds), *Political Uses of Utopia: New Marxist, Anarchist, and Radical Democratic Perspectives* (New York, Columbia University Press, 2016)

Sacco, R, *Einfuhrung in die Rechtsvergleichung* (Baden-Baden, Nomos, 2001)

Sajó, A, 'Emotions in Constitutional Design' (2010) 8(3) *ICON* 354

——. *Constitutional Sentiments* (New Haven, Yale University Press, 2011)

——. 'Emotions in Constitutional Institutions' (2016) 8(1) *Emotion Review* 44
Salmon, P, 'How to Deconstruct the World', *Psyche*, https://psyche.co/guides/how-to-deconstruct-the-world-by-thinking-like-jacques-derrida?fbclid=IwAR1nVvSqfBr8VYxsDbQJdYct2k7B8QTgOwKmpB_zX2DhY-9rAvmNmRxgRA4
Saltman, M, 'Legal Realism in a Cross-cultural Context' in R Kevelson (ed), *Law and Semiotics*, vol 2 (New York, Plenum Press, 1988)
Sammons, J, 'The Law's Melody' (2010) 55 *Villanova Law Review* 1143
Sarat, A (ed), *Imagining Legality: Where Law Meets Popular Culture* (Alabama, University of Alabama Press, 2011)
Sartori, G, *Comparative Constitutional Engineering: An Inquiry into Structures, Incentives, and Outcomes* (New York, New York University Press, 1994)
Sassen, S, *The Global City* (New Princeton: Princeton University Press, 2001)
——. 'When Territory Deborders Territoriality' (2013) 1(1) *Territory, Politics, Governance* 21
——. 'From National Borders to Embedded Borderings: One Angle into the Question of Territory and Space in a Global Age' in W de Been, P Arora and M. Hildebrandt (eds), *Crossroads in New Media, Identity and Law* (London, Palgrave Macmillan, 2015)
Schinkel, W, *Imagined Societies: A Critique of Immigrant Integration in Western Europe* (Cambridge, Cambridge University Press, 2017)
Schlegel, S, 'Activism as Defence: The Role of Courts in Shaping the Relationship between Constitutions and International Law. A Comparison of the Apex Courts of Switzerland, Germany, and Austria' in M Belov (ed), *Courts and Judicial Activism under Crisis Conditions: Policy Making in a Time of Illiberalism and Emergency Constitutionalism* (Abingdon, Routledge, 2021)
Schmitt, C, *The Concept of the Political* (Chicago, University of Chicago Press, 2007)
——. *Politische Theologie: Vier Kapitel zur Lehre von der Souveränität* (Berlin, Duncker & Humblot, 2015)
Schmitter, P and T Karl, 'The Conceptual Travels of Transitologists and Consolidologists: How Far to the East Should They Attempt to Go?' (1994) 53(1) *Slavic Review* 173
Sebeok, T, *A Sign is Just a Sign* (Bloomington, Indiana University Press, 1991)
——. *Global Semiotics* (Bloomington, Indiana University Press, 2001)
——. *Signs: An Introduction to Semiotics* (Toronto, University of Toronto Press, 2001)
Segall, E, *Originalism as Faith* (Cambridge, Cambridge University Press, 2018)
Sherwin, R, 'Introduction to Picturing Justice: Images of Law and Lawyers in the Visual Media' (1995–96) 30(4) *University of San Francisco Law Review* 1023
——. *Visualizing Law in the Age of the Digital Baroque: Arabesques and Entanglements* (New York, Routledge, 2011)
Shaw, L and S Dennison, *Pop Culture Latin America! Media, Arts, and Lifestyle* (Santa Barbara, ABC-CLIO, 2005)
Shifman, L, *Memes in Digital Culture* (Cambridge, MA, MIT Press, 2013)
Siedentop, L, *Inventing the Individual: The Origins of Western Liberalism* (Cambridge, MA, Belknap Press, 2017)
Spiesel, C, R Sherwin and N Feigenson, 'Law in the Age of Images: The Challenge of Visual Literacy' in A Wagner, T Summerfield and F Benavides Vanegas (eds), *Contemporary Issues of Semiotics of Law* (Oxford, Hart Publishing, 2005)
St Clair, W, *Lord Elgin and the Marbles* (Oxford, Oxford University Press, 1998)
Stalev, J, *The Normative Power of the Factual* (Sofia, Feneya, 2007) (in Bulgarian)
Steffek, J, *International Organization as Technocratic Utopia* (Oxford, Oxford University Press, 2021)
Steger, M, *The Rise of the Global Imaginary: Political Ideologies from the French Revolution to the Global War on Terror* (Oxford, Oxford University Press, 2008)
Stern, S, 'Narrative in the Legal Text: Judicial Opinions and Their Narratives' in M Hanne and R Weisberg (eds), *Narrative and Metaphor in the Law* (Cambridge, Cambridge University Press, 2018)
——. 'The Legal Imagination in Historical Perspective' in A Amaya and M Del Mar (eds), *Virtue, Emotion and Imagination in Law and Legal Reasoning* (Oxford, Hart Publishing, 2020)

Tanchev, E, *Introduction in Constitutional Law* (Sofia, Sibi, 2003)
——. 'The Contemporary Supranational Constitutional Pluralism or the Ordering of Constitutional Orders' in P Kirov (ed), *Constitutional Studies 2012–2013* (Sofia, 'St Kliment Ohridski' University Press, 2014) (in Bulgarian)
Tanchev, E and M Belov, 'Constitutional Gradualism: Adapting to EU Membership and Improving the Judiciary in the Bulgarian Constitution' (2008) 14(1) *European Public Law* 3
Tans, O, 'The Imaginary Foundation of Legal Systems: A Mimetic Perspective' (2014) 26(2) *Law & Literature* 127, doi:10.1080/1535685X.2014.888204
——. 'Imagined Constitutionality: Rethinking Democratic Citizenship with the Aid of Fiction Theory' (2019) 5(2) *Law, Culture and the Humanities* 1
Taylor, C, *Modern Social Imaginaries* (Durham, NC, Duke University Press, 2003)
Taylor, PJ, 'The State as Container: Territoriality in the Modern World-System' (1994) 18(2) *Progress in Human Geography* 387
——. 'Beyond Containers: Internationality, Interstateness, Interterritoriality' (1995) 19(1) *Progress in Human Geography* 1
Termini, M, 'Proving the Point: Connections between Legal and Mathematical Reasoning' (2019) 52 *Suffolk University Law Review* 5
Teršek, A, 'Political Alternatives for Constitutional Democracy: Between Utopia, Pandemic and Dystopia' (2021) 4 *Open Political Science* 45
Teschner, G and F McCluskey, 'The Deconstruction of the First Amendment: Philosophical Reflections on the Foundation of the City in Speech' in R Kevelson (ed), *Law and Semiotics*, vol 2 (New York, Plenum Press, 1988)
Teubner, G, *Constitutional Fragments: Societal Constitutionalism and Globalization* (Oxford, Oxford University Press, 2012)
Thomas, J, 'Legal Culture and the Practice: A Postmodern Depiction of the Rule of Law' (2001) 48 *UCLA Law Review* 443
Tiefenbrun, S, *Decoding International Law: Semiotics and the Humanities* (Oxford, Oxford University Press, 2010)
Tribe, L and M Dorf, *On Reading the Constitution* (Cambridge, MA, Harvard University Press, 1993)
Trouvé, H et al, 'The Path Dependency Theory: Analytical Framework to Study Institutional Integration: The Case of France' (2010) 10 *International Journal of Integrated Care*, doi:10.5334/ijic.544
Tsebelis, G, *Veto Players: How Political Institutions Work* (Princeton/New York, Russell Sage Foundation/Princeton University Press, 2002)
Unger, RM, 'Legal Analysis as Institutional Imagination' (1996) 59(1) *Modern Law Review* 1
Valchev, D, *General Theory of Law*, vol 1 (Sofia, Ciela, 2016) (in Bulgarian)
Vesting, T, *Legal Theory and the Media of Law* (Cheltenham, Edward Elgar, 2018)
Vinding, M, *Speciesism: Why it is Wrong and the Implications of Rejecting it* (Independent Publishing Platform, 2015)
Vismann, C, 'Image and Law: A Troubled Relationship' (2008) 14(4) *Parallax*
Wagner, A, 'Images of Racial Discrimination in France' in A Wagner and W Pencak (eds), *Images in Law* (Farnham, Ashgate, 2006)
Wagner, A and V Bhatia (eds), *Diversity and Tolerance in Socio-legal Contexts* (Farnham, Ashgate, 2009)
Wagner, A and J Broekman (eds), *Prospects of Legal Semiotics* (Dordrecht, Springer, 2010)
Wagner, A and S Marusek (eds), *Flags, Color, and the Legal Narrative: Public Memory, Identity, and Critique* (Dordrecht, Springer, 2021)
Wagner, A and W Pencak. *Images in Law* (Abingdon, Routledge, 2006)
Wagner, A, T Summerfield and F Benavides Vanegas (eds), *Contemporary Issues of Semiotics of Law* (Oxford, Hart Publishing, 2005)
Wagner, A, T Summerfield and F Wanegas (eds), *Contemporary Issues of the Semiotics of Law* (Oxford, Hart Publishing, 2005)

Walker, N, 'Taking Constitutionalism beyond the State' (2008) 56(3) *Political Studies* 519
Wallsgrove, J, *The Architecture of Law Courts* (Trowbridge, Paragon Publishing, 2019)
Walton, K, *Mimesis as Make-Believe: On the Foundations of Representational Arts* (Cambridge, MA, Harvard University Press, 1993)
Wang, Z, *Memory Politics, Identity and Conflict: Historical Memory as a Variable* (London, Palgrave Macmillan, 2017)
Watson, A, *Legal Transplants: An Approach to Comparative Law* (Athens, GA, University of Georgia Press, 1993)
Weber, M, *Soziologie. Weltgeschichtliche Analysen. Politik* (Stuttgart, Kröner Verlag, 1968)
Weisberg, R, 'The Art of Memory and the Allegorical Personification of Justice' (2012) 24(1) *Yale Journal of Law & the Humanities* 259
Weithman, P, *Religion and the Obligations of Citizenship* (Cambridge, Cambridge University Press, 2004)
White, H, 'The Value of Narrativity in the Representation of Reality' (1980) 7 *Critical Inquiry* 5
Wiggins, B, *The Discursive Power of Memes in Digital Culture: Ideology, Semiotics, and Intertextuality* (Abingdon, Routledge, 2019)
Williamson, T, 'Ambiguous Rationality' (2017) 14(3) *Episteme* 263
Wintgens, L and A Daniel Oliver-Lalana, *The Rationality and Justification of Legislation: Essays in Legisprudence* (Dordrecht, Springer, 2013)
Wolf, M, *Building Imaginary Worlds: The Theory and History of Subcreation* (Abingdon, Routledge, 2012)
Wurman, I, *A Debt against the Living: An Introduction to Originalism* (Cambridge, Cambridge University Press, 2017)
Xiao Mina, A, *Memes to Movements: How the World's Most Viral Media is Changing Social Protest and Power* (Boston, Beacon Press, 2019)
Young, A *Judging the Image: Art, Value, Law* (London, Psychology Press, 2005)
——. *Street Art, Public City: Law, Crime and the Urban Imagination* (Abingdon, Routledge, 2013)
Zhang, T and Y Shi, 'Color Preference and Color Meaning in the Context of Flags' (2020) 48 *Social Behavior and Personality: An International Journal* 1
Ziff, T, *Che Guevara: Revolutionary and Icon* (New York, Abrams Image, 2006)
Zipursky, B, 'Austerity, Compassion and the Rule of Law' in A Amaya and M Del Mar (eds), *Virtue, Emotion and Imagination in Law and Legal Reasoning* (Oxford, Hart Publishing, 2020)
Zuckerman, N, 'Heidegger and the Essence of Dasein' (2015) 53(4) *Southern Journal of Philosophy* 493
Zürn, M, 'From Constitutional Rule to Loosely Coupled Spheres of Liquid Authority: A Reflexive Approach' (2017) 9(2) *International Theory* 261

INDEX

www.ingramcontent.com/pod-product-compliance
Lightning Source LLC
Chambersburg PA
CBHW071304180926
51613CB00001B/122
* 9 7 8 1 5 0 9 9 3 1 4 0 8 *